E

D. H. HILL –

Angel of Death!

"Lee's Fighting General" – Daniel Harvey Hill

THIS IS A 2ND EDITION OF THE BOOK "LEE'S FIGHTING GENERAL"

(WRITTEN FOR STUDY AT SECONDARY EDUCATION LEVEL)

- *a riveting narrative and serious historical study of the nineteenth century's most legendary {and obscurely studied} fighting General – D. H. Hill! This nonfiction biography provides an epic recount of his role in the* **two most litigious events** *of the American Civil War; Lee's* **Lost Dispatch** *and the* **Controversy at Chickamauga***!*

This 2nd edition of Lee's Fighting General draws from obscurity the personality of the Confederate Angel of Death – Lieutenant General Daniel Harvey Hill {CSA}; providing a gripping and original study of Lee's legendary "fighter from way back" while invoking vivid memories of our nation's bloody and fratricidal civil war.

This 2ND edition **"D. H. Hill – The Civil War's Angel of Death"** *has been edited to facilitate serious historical study of the Civil War era by* high school and undergraduate students *while the 1st edition* **"Lee's Fighting General"** *is geared for* post-graduate level research *and study.*

The sounds of clashing bayonets, thunderous cannonades and withering volleys of musketry echo thunderously through this brilliant motif, recounting with great specificity and historical accuracy the events of a bygone era - when legendary men as Robert E. Lee, ole "Pete" Longstreet and D. H. Hill, facing insurmountable odds, gallantly responded to the echo of a distant bugle and "charged" into history's desperate and bloody civil war battles.

"A must read for students of civil war & military history"

This captivating motif immerses the reader in a suspense-filled drama that rivals even the greatest Civil War literary novels of fiction, yet its compelling narrative is told with such historical precision and specificity that it stands noteworthy of higher level institutional study of war. Beautifully illustrated and comprehensively researched from the official archives of both armies, the events of a bygone era are validated with historical precision and accuracy as the Fighting General's namesake recounts his iconic life from cradle to grave.

So **fix bayonet**, **load your musket**, *move at the* **double quick** *and* **charge** *into history with Lieutenant General Daniel Harvey Hill – aka – "Lee's Fighting General"*

D. H. Hill – The Confederate

Angel of Death

"LEE'S FIGHTING GENERAL"

DANIEL HARVEY HILL

D. H. HILL

When General Hill was in command in North Carolina and had General Foster cooped up in the little town of Washington with his command entirely surrounded, and the river blockaded with cannon, Foster, who had allowed his troops to commit many depredations upon the homes and property of the citizens thereabout, sent a flag of truce to Hill to know upon what terms he could surrender. Hill replied at once:

"The officers and men under your command will be treated as prisoners of war, but you will be castrated."

[[General D. H. Hill]]

Q20

ISBN-13:
978-1481060486

ISBN-10:
1481060481

LIEUTENANT GENERAL DANIEL HARVEY HILL (CSA) –

The Confederate

Angel of Death

A Study in Bravery and Southern Valor

PROLOGUE

The story of Daniel Harvey Hill's conspicuous bravery on the Confederacy's many fields of battle has long since passed into the collective consciousness of our Southern culture. He has become the forgotten hero, a military icon whose unheralded bravery, courage and brilliant service to the Confederacy has been obscured by antipathy. Distinguished and well-known as a soldier, D. H. Hill the man was even greater. Truly he was an extraordinary Confederate General who rose to become a great Southern Gentlemen.

The most poignant insight into the life of Lieutenant General Daniel Harvey Hill may very well be drawn from the inscription upon his monument at the time of his death:

"He feared not the face of man but feared and trusted God with all his heart." 1

Lee's Fighting General emerged at a time of the Confederacy's greatest peril, within a sphere of supreme military accomplishments and unparalleled valor among so many of great courage. Yet his name would have risen far above his mostly obscure standing in history today were it not for the possibility or suggestion of two controversial topics: the Battle of Chickamauga and the Lost Dispatch. These two most arguable events of the Civil War stemmed neither from D. H. Hill's actions nor of historical facts. Rather they were put forward by historians greatly lacking in diversity and unprejudiced points of view. Fortunately Lieutenant General Hill was granted a long and fruitful life after the war, living to realize his complete exoneration from involvement in the former and total vindication for his correct actions in the latter. For too long these two events dominated a true historical accounting of his courageous life achievements; obscuring his greatness and denying him his proper place among the fighting legends in the history of modern warfare.

Indeed, we shall address these two events as we study the life of Daniel Harvey Hill. But it is my distinct purpose to wholly exhibit the total character of this man in all the critical traits which form the abiding test of his true greatness; rising above his unquestioned military heroism as the bravest of the Confederacy's brave while enhancing your understanding of D. H. Hill the Christian, Father, Educator, Author and my namesake; a man renown, not only for diligent military service to his beloved South, but for his contributions to the recovery of its shattered people – suffering from disastrous defeat - and the restoration of pride and honor in their heritage and culture. 2

It is however from his diligent military service that he emerged to become Lee's Fighting General. From the time of D. H. Hill's first Civil War fight; leading North Carolina soldiers with conspicuous courage into battle on Virginia's soil; until the day he led the last attacking column of Confederates to check General Sherman's advance at the Battle of Bentonville; upon conclusion of every battle General Hill's command was never to be found in the rear of any position, not once; notwithstanding the final result from any engagement, win – lose - or draw. 3   Hill family lore provides many tales of his exploits and claims that *"D. H. was responsible for killing more Yankees than dysentery!"* Such tales were inspirational in labeling "Lee's Fighting General" as the Confederacy's most prolific *"Angel of Death!"*

With reckless abandon he would courageously expose himself to all dangers of the fight, yet no officer in the Confederacy was more devoted to the health, happiness and safety of his soldiers. He firmly believed that spades were instruments of defense - bayonets were instruments of offense, but during desperate battles, they were both to be used with equal *"might and main."* 4

Lieutenant General Daniel Harvey Hill once proclaimed that *"Histories should be written by his generation's descendants."* 5 Renowned author Dr. Henry E. Shepherd was widely recognized as perhaps the most imminently qualified authority, among all historians of the Civil War era, most capable of producing an historical account and biography of the life of Confederate Lieutenant General Daniel Harvey Hill. He possessed a combination of God given literary talent and an intimate personal and professional knowledge of the General's life to do so. After all, he'd already written a magnificent account of the *"Life of Robert E. Lee as General in the Confederate Army."* 6 It came as no surprise when Dr. Shepherd accepted the task to produce the official, comprehensive biography for his friend, former teacher and personal hero D. H. Hill. But a combination of complex circumstances rendered his best efforts void. The greatest roadblock to his biographical efforts was a disruptive preoccupation, by purported historians of the day, to connect D. H. Hill with the Lost Dispatch; placing the main focus on Hill's military career while overlooking all other aspects of his life's accomplishments. 7 Historians lacking in diversity and unprejudiced points of view seemed hell bent on producing, either through incompetence or lack of understanding, superficial versions of history to suit an agenda and interests to their liking. 8

Understanding that, against these obstructions, his best efforts were doomed to certain failure, Dr. Shepherd withdrew his biographical literary efforts, choosing instead to publish his reflections of D. H. Hill in various publications that he deemed suitable and worthy of General Hill's remembrance. So, it came to pass that there was no creditable, comprehensive work of historical accounting of General Hill's biography, notwithstanding his prominent role and eminent place in the history of his time.

In early 1868, Confederate Lieutenant General Daniel Harvey Hill wrote an emotional article published in The Land We Love where he offered his view that histories should be written by his generation's descendants. The literary obstacles faced by Dr. Shepherd served to validate the General's claims to be absolute and painfully prophetic. D. H. Hill believed that, perhaps in a quarter of a century, when the passions and prejudices called to mind by the war had subsided; some calm, dignified, impartial man of learning, industry and ability, would gather together the materials furnished in the manner suggested, and from them produce a truthful history of the great rebellion. 9

I have felt from the very beginning of my adulthood that I was to become that man, the ancestor of whom General Hill spoke; the one that, in time, would provide a truthful accounting of his role in the great rebellion. I always considered it my destiny to fulfill this directive of my namesake. It is a challenge for which I have taken seriously, devoting over 41 years of my life to military service and many more years pursing higher education; as a precondition to fulfilling his order. So now, nearly a century and a half later, armed with a vast library of historical records and devotion of over 40 years of personal study; examining all available sources of relevant historical facts recorded in the annals of Official Records of the Union and Confederate Armies and beyond. I take with great privilege my charge from his direction: *"May God grant this humble author His grace and sufficient competencies to offer this generation's portrayal of Lieutenant General Daniel Harvey Hill."*

D. H. HILL

In response to an application for furlough submitted by a member of a brass band, D. H. Hill offered this classic quote:

". . . . shooters before tooters"

[[General D. H. Hill]]

[an iconic phrase within the Army of Northern Virginia]

Q5

CHAPTER I

THE EARLY LIFE OF D. H. HILL

It is the special purpose of this work to exhibit the life and achievements of Daniel Harvey Hill -- revealing those distinctive characteristics that define him as a Christian Man, Husband and Father. We shall also study his professional life as a General of the Confederacy, the whole examination of his brilliant and versatile story to be concluded by an outline of his career as a professor, an editor and as a college president. We will not contemplate a mechanical biography, full of details which have no essential relation to the main body of our narrative: Our study shall be of the courageous figure of Lee's Fighting General - the Confederacy's prolific Angel of Death, the embodiment of his moral grandeur, as well as his intellectual power and amazing personal courage, in itself deemed worthy to place Daniel Harvey Hill among the greatest men of another era: deserving a seat at the round table of King Arthur's Court. There was perfect balance of his characteristic features: an unwavering sense of duty that drove his determined courage accompanied by an unyielding sense of purpose; a deep sense of loyalty, honor and integrity; total resolve for truth and honesty with an accompanying disregard for deceit and cowardice. But above all he was a man of faith; the standard of Christian manhood who exhibited his faith in Almighty God in his daily walk -- ever in search of God's wisdom; always in peace but even in war: invoking the prayers of David before each battle: *"Deliver me from my enemies, O God; be my fortress against those who are attacking me."* Psalm 59:1 and wholly submissive to Him giving all praise for every outcome: *"Let them praise the name of the LORD, for his name alone is exalted; his splendor is above the earth and the heavens."* Psalm 21:13. 10

As we examine the character of Hill as a man, no one feature is more impressive than his total commitment to his convictions of honesty; for which he was sometimes judged as being sharp of tongue. But history can no longer allow the memory of this legendary fighter to be diminished by any scolding tones, offered so long ago from judgmental writers who possessed neither an understanding of the intellectual side of his nature nor considered the context of his remarks. Through this study, and the reader's analysis through critical thought, we will establish the truthful and historical account of the life of Daniel Harvey Hill - Lee's Fighting General. As we study this passionate man we will examine his life through times of both exceeding joy and great sadness, not failing to overlook any aspect of his nature; whether the circumstances may be positive or negative. There is no claim in this book that this great fighting General was without fault; no more so than it was ever a claim made by the General himself.

This study of the life of Lee's Fighting General begins not at the juncture of his birth but through examination of his Hill family lineage. During the years preceding the Revolutionary War, in the early 1700s, the Hill family was governed by William Hill, the grandfather of D. H. Hill. William was a young Scottish-Irish immigrant when his family, together with a large group of other immigrants, moved from Ireland to the English Colonies in North America prior to the American Revolution. William was known by constant display of his character to be a charismatic and a man of great courage. 11 The Hill family initially settled in Pennsylvania but soon moved farther south, becoming one of the earliest families to establish permanent residence in the area of northern South Carolina. This area, identified then as the York District, is today known as York County. William Hill settled in South Carolina in 1740 and by 1770 had become highly regarded, and his Hill family very influential, within the Piedmont borderlands of the Carolinas.

Prior to the Revolutionary War his family acquired nearly 5,000 acres through land grants in York District around Allison Creek, a small tributary of the Catawba River. The family continued to accumulate land until the estate eventually totaled 24,376 acres. Considering that the average land holding of that day was around 350 acres per settler's grant, the Hill estate was considered to be enormous. 12 William worked tirelessly establishing the Hill family estate; building their family home, a grain mill, saw mill and eventually establishing the Hill's Iron Works. Taking advantage of the huge quantities of iron ore deposits found in the area, he started the family's business; a commercial venture engaged in the production of farm tools, machinery and household utensils. Inventories of that era reflected good demand for a wide range of other uses for the iron ore: bake irons, flat irons, nails, spikes, plows, grates, hammers, hinges, swivels, pots, axes, etc. By 1780 William had acquired a business partner, Colonel Isaac Hayne, in order to expand the Iron Works operations. The two gentlemen added a huge complex of saw and grist mills to the iron furnace operation along the banks of Allison Creek. Their business eventually grew into a major operation that employed several hundred skilled slave and free workers. 13

From the very moment of his birth, Daniel Harvey Hill was destined to follow in the footsteps of previous members of his prominent family lineage; history records the name of no truer patriot than his paternal grandfather. The extremely successful businessman, William Hill, was also know as Colonel William *"Billy"* Hill of Revolutionary fame; a prominent friend of, and second in command to, the legendary General of the American Revolution - Major General Thomas Sumter. Legendary for his military exploits, General Sumter was one for whom Colonel Billy Hill could be held in comparison during that era. 14 Colonel Billy Hill was the elected leader of the Patriot resistance force around 1780 and became the leading and most vocal supporter of the Whig party of the Carolinas. It was at this juncture that he commenced his career of valor and patriotic service, always acting with characteristic resolve; often at great personal risk, to uphold his convictions to God, family and his fellow patriots. With great confidence, General Sumter trusted this great man of conscience to serve as his second in command; leading his small band of Patriots in Carolina during a critical era of our fledgling nation's history; a period of armed conflict when the British army, supported by their Tories, vigorously pursued the Whig Patriots upon every occasion.

During this extremely controversial period, known as the Exclusion Crisis, divisive political and religious views split the colonist into two groups; strongly holding to opposing points of view. Contention quickly escalated to armed conflict, both political and religious in nature. The Whigs were known as political and religious revisionist – political activist who were willing to risk unrest in their opposition to the English monarchy in order to modernize the systems of church and state. Conversely, the Tories were politically supportive of the existing rule of the throne by King George III and religiously supportive of the Anglican Church. [15]

Indicative of the crisis' religious environment, an unknown Hessian officer commented in 1778 of the war: *"Call this war by whatever name you may, only call it not an American Rebellion: it is nothing more or less than a Scotch-Irish Presbyterian Rebellion"*. [16]

The role of the Church held major significance to the Hill family due to their strong Presbyterian ethic and they passionately resisted the religious views placed upon them by the Crown's state supported directives of the Anglican Church. They held this imposition on their religious freedom to be despicable and responded with armed protest. Using their home, the Bethel Presbyterian Church and the Hill's Iron Works as rallying points, they responded with violent resistance as armed participants in the rebellion. However, their actions brought upon them the attention of the British army and their Tory allies; and eventually their wrath.

As commander of the local militia, Colonel Billy Hill held the responsibility of organizing local citizens whose followers were in great need of adequate food, clothing and ammunition. Colonel Hill shrewdly used his Hill's Iron Works to produce cannons, ammunition and other items needed to supply the Revolutionary militia and his small band of Patriots. [17] But on June 17th 1780, in retaliation for Colonel Hill's resistance, Captain Christian Huck, the British commander of the local Loyalist militia, accompanied by his dragoons, attacked the Whig encampment at Hill's Iron Works; killing and capturing several rebel militiamen, looting the plantation of jewelry and ninety slaves, then completely destroying the Hill's Iron Works and all dwellings upon the estate. [18]

In response to this attack, at sunrise on the morning of July 12th 1780, Colonel Hill led his volunteers in an assault upon a British Legion of dragoons and their loyal group of Tories along the Catawba River. The battle was over in about ten minutes as the Whigs totally routed and dispersed the whole force, killing the British commander Captain Huck and thirty four of his men while sustaining only one Patriot casualty. [19]

Later, on October 7th 1780, the Whigs again attacked the British upon the occasion of the Battle of Kings Mountain. Illustrating the religious tones of the Revolutionary War that were held, not only by the Patriots, but by the British and Tories as well, Major Patrick Ferguson boasted that upon leaving Kings Mountain he intended to: *"spend one night in Bethel Church, leave it in ashes by day-light... and be on the east side of the Catawba before nightfall."* After an intense battle approximately one hour in duration, filled with withering volleys of musketry and bayonet charges, the Patriots triumphed once again in routing the Loyalists. Ironically, Major Ferguson never made it off of the mountain, dying of wounds sustained during the battle. [20]

After their victory at King's Mountain, Colonel Billy Hill once again led his band of Patriots in an attack upon the post of Hanging Rock where his small, but skilled group of fighters, totally defeated the Prince of Wales's regiment and put to flight a large body of Tories. When Colonel Hill's men went into this battle not one of them had more than ten bullets. Towards the close of the fight, the arms and ammunition of the fallen British and Tories were used most resourcefully by Hill and his men to gain the victory. 21

By war's end, the name of Colonel William *"Billy"* Hill had become legendary among South Carolinians. He had distinguished himself with gallantry in the War of the Revolution, serving as second in command of General Sumter's legion.   In doing so, he consistently displayed great courage during his many engagements; even sustaining serious wounds during the Battle of Hanging Rock.   Despite these wounds he courageously rallied the scattered Patriots after their terrible defeat at Camden and was one of the architects in design of the strategy and plans for the Battle of King's Mountain. His gallant contributions on the field of battle had much influence in favorably turning the course of the war. 22 With his accomplishments Colonel Billy Hill rose to become the standard bearer for the Patriot's cause in the region and, by his courage and heroism, became widely known as one of the great heroes of the Revolutionary War.   His legendary accomplishments, associated with the Hill family name, would greatly influence his young grandson, Daniel Harvey Hill; who within his own right would grow to imitate his grandfather's heroism and even surpass his military achievements. 23

After the revolution, William attempted to restore the Hill family estate to its pre-war prominence. He sought and received additional public and private loans to rebuild the Hill's Iron Works, constructing a second furnace and acquiring fifty additional slaves.   24 But the business faltered as it became more difficult to get payment for products produced during the Revolutionary War and he was forced to sell his portion of the partnership to the family of Colonel Issac Hayne in 1796. William retained ownership, however, of his family plantation along Allison Creek. 25

William Hill wrote his memoirs in February 1815, long after the events that defined his own military exploits as an officer in the militia.   He straightforwardly stressed that a primary goal in writing his memoirs was to set straight the record among historians about the overlooked battles in South Carolina, most notably the Battle of Kings Mountain. He stubbornly and openly criticized historians for their the written records that mentioned only the South Carolina commander, Colonel James Williams, who was mortally wounded in the battle. It is noteworthy that Colonel Billy Hill reflected in his memoirs the revisionist tendencies of historians to overlook historical facts and the accomplishments of the battle's living veterans in favor of those who perished on the field of battle. Eerily, these same revisionist tendencies would revisit the battlefields of his grandson decades later. As a reflection of Colonel Hill's earnest character and the straightforward manner with which he addressed hard times, he sent his entire manuscript to General Sumter for his pre-publish viewing. Except for a few minor grammatical changes, General

Sumter did not alter the content of the manuscript, thus adding his own support of Colonel William Hill's accounting of events. 26

Colonel William Hill was a leader in peace as well as in war. He was a political activist, serving seven terms in the South Carolina State House of Representatives and nine years in the South Carolina State Senate in the late 1700s. History recognizes him today as one of the most distinguished South Carolinians of his era wherein his active service to his Presbyterian faith remains revered, even to this day, in the historical memories of the congregation of the Bethel Presbyterian Church; a faithful and dutiful service to Christ that remains inherent within the Hill family to this day. 27

Upon the death of the legendary Patriot Colonel William Hill in 1816, his third son, Solomon, inherited the family's estate, consisting of the entire plantation along Allison Creek. The estate was worth, in approximate value, $6,000.00; an extremely valuable property given the value of the dollar in the very early 1800s. 28 Solomon Hill married Nancy, the daughter of Thomas L. Cabeen; a family of proud Scottish descent with her father's birth in Scotland sometime during the year of 1752. During the Revolutionary War both the Hill and Cabeen families were sturdy patriots to the American army. Nancy's father served as a scout for General Thomas Sumter and, like Colonel Billy Hill, was widely admired throughout the South as a hero of the Revolution - remembered in reputation for extraordinary bravery. Known as the *"Fighting Gamecock"*, Thomas Cabeen was described by General Sumter as *"the bravest man in my command."* Thus, the marriage of Solomon to Nancy inserted yet another family's rich history of uncommon bravery into the young Harvey's pedigree; a family line from which he inherited a strong mind and an intense love of liberty. 29 Nancy Cabeen Hill was a noted beauty; a classical Southern Belle gifted with all the charm and wit deemed to be a common feature among the finest of South Carolina's Southern ladies. She was noted for her goodness, culture, common sense and devotion to God and family. 30 The marriage of Solomon Hill to Nancy Cabeen produced a family of great means and fashioned an honored lineage within the York community, worthy of carrying on the finest reputation and traditions of the Colonel William *"Billy"* Hill clan.

And, as his father before him, he served notably as an Elder in the Bethel Presbyterian Church. Solomon and Nancy bore eleven children, with the youngest being Daniel Harvey Hill. 31 He was born July 12th 1821 on the family farm in the hilly region of upper South Carolina, just south of the North Carolina line. Nancy was clearly the major influence of his life. Her deep religious faith, her efficiency in practical affairs, her iron rule of duty and her sweetness and humor were woven into the makeup of Harvey's character. Hill family lore tells of a young lad with light hair who grew to become a man of about 5 feet and 10 inches in height; pleasing in appearance with large deep-blue eyes and hair that darkened with age. 32

From an early age Harvey, as he was known, was used to hard work and a degree of hardship unknown to his older brothers and sisters; the point of defined hardship being associated with the timing of his father's death. Prior to Solomon's death, his older children were provided with the finest opportunities to become well educated. In fact, the oldest son's education included studies in Europe and law school where he became an accomplished attorney. Another son was equally educated and became a physician. The daughters, too, received the very best education obtainable. Life was good for the Solomon Hill family. But the family soon experienced a painful fall in family status; declining sharply from prominence of the glory days of *"Grandpa Billy's"* Revolutionary War exploits and the heyday of productivity at the Hill's Iron Works due to Solomon's financial woes and untimely death at the age of 49. 33

Young Harvey was just a child of 4 years when his father's death thrust his mother into the difficult position of managing the Hill Family estate. Late in his life, Solomon had acquired extreme financial obligations against the family estate, mostly in the capacity of collateral for friends. Immediately upon his death the family's fortunes rapidly dissipated, placing them in grim financial straits. Nancy was determined that no negative criticism should rest upon Solomon's memory and boldly took personal charge of the administration of the family estate; nearly cancelling all the obligations which had been assumed. But in her efforts to preserve Solomon's memory and good name, the family's wealth was exhausted as she was forced to sell their slaves and most of their land; retaining only the small home farm. This led to a sharp and immediate decline in wealth and family prestige for the Hill family within the community. With Solomon's debts being fully paid, Nancy then set about the task of raising and educating the younger members of their eleven children, including the youngest Daniel Harvey. Her love of education compelled Nancy to overcome all difficulties in order to provide a solid education for her children. 34

Harvey inherited his mother's deep, unquestioning Calvinistic faith and it served to mold his character and guide his actions throughout his entire life. Nancy was a stern but kindhearted disciplinarian who placed great merit on the need for biblical teaching and home education, often requiring the children to read bible verses aloud before going into the fields to plow the thin topsoil of the Piedmont. The family habitually gathered for prayer before breakfast and traveled to their church, the nearby Bethel Presbyterian Church, for Sunday service; wherein Nancy was famous for making the children remain awake and attentive during worship services. Harvey's somewhat wayward brother, John, often declared that during his boyhood he always *"took the blues on Thursday morning because Sunday was coming."* Some of Harvey's heartiest laughs were produced by the recollection of the childhood antics of his brother; clear and plain efforts to find and read the shortest verse in the bible, without regard to its fitness for the occasion. "Jesus wept." 35

From certain locations near his childhood home young Harvey could see the unmistakable shape of King's Mountain. Rising to great heights far in the distance, surely the mountain's view inspired memories of his grandfather's exciting military ventures; as the legendary patriot who served as General Sumter's second in command. 36 Along the tributaries of the Catawba River, the scenic land was covered in dense forests of giant oaks and hickory; which had long served to provide fuel for his grandfather's furnaces during the hey-day operations of the Hill's Iron Works. While furnaces further north were fueled with coal, Harvey's grandfather had depended on these beautiful giant hardwoods to provide the perfect fuel for his furnaces. Systematic clearing of the forest for firewood developed the land into a beautiful area of open fields; perfect for the family's farming activities and raising livestock. These open fields, combined with the thick forest and many creeks and streams along the flowing Catawba River, would seasonally fill with various wild flowers and birds native to the area. Growing up in the midst of all this beauty and grandeur had a most positive effect on young Harvey. It kindled his imagination and inspired deep within him an intense love for his beloved Carolina home and a deep sense of loyalty to his native Carolina. Importantly, it aroused in him an ambition to be of some great service to his country. 37

Certainly, Harvey's childhood was well occupied with structure and daily chores. His work ethic and character traits clearly reflect such a background. But it would be uncommon to think that Harvey didn't partake of the long list of usual activities for a young Carolina boy – fishing for bream and catfish along the muddy water of the Catawba River tributaries; hunting small game like rabbit, squirrel, and opossum; and of course, riding horses. As an adult, D. H. Hill was even cited as going *"possum hunting"* one night with his good friend and colleague C. D. Fishburne. So, it seems far-fetched that he would have acquired enjoyment in a common activity of that day as an adult, yet have been deprived of that same activity in his youth. 38

During the era of the middle 1800s, there were no good schools near young Harvey's home. But his mother insisted upon her children's educational development, schooling young Harvey in the home. Today, of course, the poorest boy in Carolina can easily find a better school right at his door than Harvey could have found in many a mile from his home at the Hill's Ironworks. Harvey seems to have minded his books well for his life's work offers wonderful reflections of a highly educated man; he gained a youthful passion for reading and writing. Later in life D. H. would speak of his mother in the fondest terms, most thankful for her efforts in raising a young lad without the presence of a husband and father for her children. Harvey's oldest brother was required, by the untimely death of Solomon, to serve as the male role model for this child who had lost his father at the early age of 4. Later in life, Harvey would speak most fondly of his eldest brother, expressing admiration and great respect for his brother's performance of such a vital role - helping his mother raise the family's younger children. 39 With all the personal achievements and professional accomplishments earned during his lifetime, D. H. Hill clearly acquired every cultural and personal trait reflective of a well rounded yet strong willed Southern gentleman. Later in life, Harvey commented to his wife, Isabella: *"I had always a strong perception of right and wrong - and when corrected from petulance or passion, I brooded over it, did not forget it, and I am afraid did not forgive it."* 40

The environment of Harvey's youth provided an excellent setting for character building. The religious atmosphere saturating his mother's home and the family's Church connections truly made a positive imprint on the young boy. Growing up with the experiences associated with his mother's strict devotion to *"taking the Christian path,"* as she so clearly displayed as a faithful wife in preserving Solomon's good name, account for many of his displayed character traits in all aspects of his adult life: as a man, teacher, soldier, author, professor, but most importantly as a husband and father. 41

As Harvey matured to the age of 16 years, Nancy faced the dilemma of providing her youngest child with a formal education. She was completely lacking in resources required to provide any form of future outside a life of farming; a common fate suffered my many young men living in York County in that era. As a consequence of estate matters, she did not have enough money to send her youngest child to college and was forced to look for a school offering free tuition. Given the family's financial circumstances, the family's legacy and tradition of military service greatly influenced her interest in gaining an appointment for Harvey with the United States Military Academy at West Point. In addition to Harvey's grandparents, his uncles William and Robert had also served with distinction in the United States Army during the War of 1812 and in numerous campaigns against the Native Americans. 42

Gaining acceptance at the prestigious United States Military Academy at West Point meant not only finding a supportive political sponsor, but also mandatory compliance with physical fitness requirements. Harvey's physical condition was problematic. At an early age, he'd developed some sort of spinal ailment and suffered from backaches throughout life. As he told fellow veteran Bradley Johnson in 1887, *"I had a spell of sickness in my boyhood which left me with a week and suffering spine."* 43 Fortunately, pre-civil war West Point did not have very strict health standards for admission, partly because the school often needed candidates to justify its existence among many politicians who believed the Academy was a breeding ground for the upper classes. Nancy's dilemma of Harvey's education was resolved, and her prayers were answered, when Harvey's application to the United States Military Academy was sponsored by South Carolina Congressman William Clowney; leading to his acceptance by Superintendent Major Richard Delafield into the Academy at West Point in 1838. Thus an inherited military lineage combined with a positive change in family fortunes defined his career path to be one of a soldier, otherwise It Is held within the Hill family lore that Daniel Harvey Hill most likely would have become a professional man – most likely a Presbyterian minister. 44'

CHAPTER II

THE WEST POINT YEARS

D. H. Hill began his formal military training on July 1st 1838, representing a major event in his life that placed him in direct contact with the highest caliber of American Soldier; exposing him to the assorted cultures of other young men from across the country. At the tender age of sixteen years and eleven months he found himself among a group of classmates, many destined to become rising stars and key participants in the impending War Between the States.

The West Point Class of 1842 included D. H. Hill's name with the names of *"Ole Pete"* Longstreet, A.P. Stewart, R.H. Anderson, Van Dorn, Rosecrans,

Pope, and Reynolds. Other notable classmates included Abner Doubleday and Lafayette McLaws, future Civil War Generals all. In the class next order to that of Hill were the names of U.S. Grant and George B. McClellan. Ironically, two of Hill's closest friendships acquired while a cadet at the Academy were Southerners who ended up fighting for the Union: George Sykes of Maryland and Theodore Laidley of Virginia. 45 While there were very few details on the young Cadet Hill during his four years at West Point, his youngest son Joseph recounted in numerous writings that his father did not particularly find the prescribed curriculum to be enjoyable or inspiring by any measure. 46

In stature, the new West Point plebe was about five feet and ten inches tall, and of slight frame. His health was never robust and only his inflexible will, simple habits and strict moderation from stimulating drinks, could have carried him through, not only his new life at the Academy but, through the many trials and hardships that he would face throughout his adult life. His manner was reserved and he did not easily make friends. Among his friends he was said to be a charming man, an original talker; and in his home circle no man was ever known to be gentler or more affectionate. His most striking characteristics were his intense religious faith, his steady sense of duty and his courage. With these were associated a perfect purity of life, unyielding steadfastness of purpose, and a vigorous mind. It is to be noted, however, that along with a fund of friendly humor he had a sarcastic vein which sometimes was reflected both in his speech and in his letters.   Although Hill could be quite sarcastic, never was he found to violate his principles or compromise his honor, honesty or integrity; and while he was sometimes short in tactfulness he was always known for his honesty – ever you knew exactly where you stood with D. H. Hill. Animosity, envy, and a disposition to indulge in criticism have led to many unjust reflections upon D. H. Hill, but the most unprincipled of his critics could never question his courage or integrity. 47

In his personal life, which the world did not see, there was sweetness, light and beauty; the real tenderness of his nature left an unfailing memory within generations of his beloved Hill family. 48 During Hill's tenure as a cadet West Point's infrastructure was in a state of disrepair. Money to adequately fund the Academy was contingent upon the Congressional, War Department and even Presidential support. Thus, severe funding conditions prevented much a needed enlargement and improvements of the cadet barracks. This forced the cadets to deal with cramped living conditions - lacking suitable buildings to deal with the region's humid summers and freezing winters.   Cadet study efforts were further reduced with the destruction by fire of the Academy's library in early 1838. Some portion of the library's contents was saved, mostly through the efforts of cadets and faculty quickly rushing books and scientific models out of the burning building.   Eventually, two stone buildings were constructed to house the library but the effect of the fire did negatively impact the academic pursuits of Hill's class. 49

In a class of fifty-six cadets, Hill ranked twenty-eighth in the general order of merit upon his June 1842 graduation where he attained the rank of Second Lieutenant.   In   engineering   he   stood   thirty-ninth;   in   infantry   tactics nineteenth; in artillery twenty-eighth; and in ethics nineteenth. Comparatively, A.P. Stewart was twelfth in the general order of merit, John Pope seventeenth and James Longstreet a distant fifty-fourth. During his graduating year D. H. Hill received 37 demerits, in comparison to 102 for Longstreet, 19 for Rosecrans and 78 for A.P. Stewart. By the end of his freshman year, Harvey ranked thirty-three out of eighty-five in his academic class. 50 This was a remarkable achievement for a young Southerner whose formal education consisted mainly of an elementary education provided in the home by his mother.   Hill excelled in French but scored near the bottom of his class in drawing; with performance at an average level in math and English. During his second year, he placed in the top half of his class overall where he excelled in philosophy and chemistry. His drawing skills however were noticeably lacking. Military classes in infantry and artillery were reserved for the senior class, along with ethics, mineralogy, geology, engineering and the science of war. His lowest mark as a cadet was earned in Professor Mahan's engineering class where he placed thirty-nine out of fifty-six. Although his academic standing upon graduation barred him from the exclusive corps of engineers, his performance did warrant and produce a billet in the artillery.

Later in life he would successfully apply his acquired skills in mathematics to his civilian teaching career. 51 Interestingly, although he received some of his lowest marks in mathematics, it's this academic discipline that he would later teach at Washington and Davidson Colleges. One of his quotes from 1860 revealed an acquired respect for what he considered to be the advantages and benefits of a military education in 1860: *"It is impossible to over-estimate the influence of military schools upon the welfare of society. Were it possible to train all our young men in them, lawlessness would be absolutely unknown and unheard of in the next generation."* 52

With respect to Hill's record of conduct while attending the Academy his freshman year, he finished number 154 out of the total student population of 231. His demerit sheet portrayed a somewhat rebellious attitude toward military discipline. In fact, he started off his cadet career by arriving late to dinner roll call on his first day of class. The very next day he was marked delinquent for *"inattention while marching from dinner."* He accumulated eighty three demerits during his freshman year, often for visiting other cadets during study time or after hours; twice he was cited for sitting down while on guard duty. However, over time as a cadet, Hill finally adjusted to military life, as reflected by his decrease in demerits received, both in frequency and severity of infraction. His typical offenses consisted mainly of minor uniform infractions such as an unbuttoned coat or a loose belt. Interestingly, the future artillery officer tended to incur most of these infractions during battery inspections. Near the end of his second class year, he was cited for being *"beyond limits"*—Academy language for being beyond the authorized distance a cadet was allowed to travel while on pass from post. This infraction gained him eight demerits and reflected the actions of a typical teenager enjoying his freedom away from home. 53 With his progression through the great United States Military Academy at West Point came graduation and the production of yet another warrior: Second Lieutenant Daniel Harvey Hill.

D. H. HILL

"Like Jackson he was, too, a born fighter – as aggressive, pugnacious and tenacious as s bull-dog, or as any soldier in the service, and he had a sort of monomania on the subject of personal courage."

[[General G. Moxley Sorrell]]

Q19

D. H. Hill had reached an important milestone with the realization of his formal education. He had achieved this lofty goal with its construct upon the foundational strength of Hill family guiding principles. Without question, the West Point Cadet had been positively influenced by many experiences of his youthful past. There were fond memories of shadows cast by a distant King's Mountain, looming against a setting Carolina sun. Surely a view of such magnitude would have brought back memories of the military exploits of both his grandfathers: the gallant Colonel William Hill and the Fighting Gamecock Cabeen – both men immortalized through Carolina and Hill family lore with many tales of their epic struggles against tyranny; desperate fights and pitched battles for the cause to preserve all things dear to their faith and family. These fond recollections would have certainly caused him to perceive glamour of the sword. 54 On the other hand, as a young cadet and student of the science of war, he would have developed a keen awareness of the direct and indirect effects that the Revolutionary War had upon the Hill family; specifically the destruction of Hill's Iron Works by the British and Tories. And he surely would have associated the second and third order effects that the revolution contributed to the Hill family's sharp decline in wealth and stature within the community; from the period of great prestige experienced by his older siblings to the family's assent into the genteel poverty from which he grew as a child. Finally, all influences, positive and negative, were subject to the primary Hill family devotion to their Presbyterian faith and doctrine. All things considered, the young boy was now a man – a Second Lieutenant in the United States Army. 55

It is understandable that, as an adult, D. H. Hill possessed a core belief and strong sense of duty to uphold and defend the integrity of his family's name. Understanding the impact that his youth had on the development of his faith and character provides great insight to many of his qualities and flaws later in life. It was surely a natural quality – a hidden trait deep within his soul – a defining piece of his character - that provides a glimmer of insight as to how his early development impacted his conduct and accounted for many of Lieutenant General Hill's actions.   He possessed extraordinary battlefield courage under fire; accounting for the inscription on his burial monument: he *"feared not the face of man but feared and trusted God with all his heart."* 56

D. H. Hill held the fiery temper of a Scottish-Irishman and often directed a lack of tolerance toward anyone failing to produce, achieve or sustain his measurement for acceptable standards of conduct. He would often address the shortcomings of subordinates and superiors alike – regardless of their rank and or position. This quality prompted some to complain that he was *"sharp of tongue."* But criticism of this nature no more diminished D. H. Hill's legendary valor on the field of battle than did similar criticisms when applied to another generation's great fighting general, George S. Patton. This is clearly understood by serious students of military history and veterans of war. But in truth, Daniel Harvey Hill was a Southerner Gentleman; a man who held the honor of his Hill family name, along with his Christian faith, to be untouchable and not subject to compromise. 57 Clearly, his family heritage sustained him throughout his entire adulthood and led him to achieve levels of greatness from which *"legends"* are truly made. Great insight can be gained into his stubborn defense to any allegation that would allow discredit and dishonor to fall upon his family name. After all, sprung from warlike and marital blood line, Hill might well have heard in his youthful period, charged with heroic spirit. *"Sumter's bugle blast re-echo from the haunted past."* 58

D. H. HILL

"In a portrayal of the character of Daniel Harvey Hill his all-prevailing moral courage first reveals itself with its correlated traits; absolute loyalty to truth, frankness, ingenuousness, an incapacity to play the hypocrite, effacement of self, and insensibility to fear. In this rarest of human virtues he was preeminent; his ethical creed might be concisely embodied in the language of a poet."

[[Colonel Henry Elliott Shepherd]]

Q29

CHAPTER III

THE MEXICAN WAR

"A FIGHTER FROM WAY BACK"

Daniel Harvey Hill spent six years in the United States Army, two of them during the Mexican War where he participated under the commands of Generals Scott and Taylor in nearly every important engagement; emerging from the conflict as one of America's authentic heroes. Being a most articulate officer, D. H. Hill kept abundant notes in his Mexican War Diary. Subsequently, D. H. Hill's war diary was published in a classical recounting of his Mexican War exploits in the book *"A Fighter from Way Back"* and provides a great read for further insight into the legendary fighter's personal observations of that war. 59 On June 18th 1842 the newly commissioned brevet Second lieutenant D. H. Hill was assigned to the 1st Artillery Regiment and ordered to an outpost at Fort Kent, Maine with orders to enforce the Webster-Ashburton Treaty of 1842; a product of the Aroostook War (1838-1839) between the United States and the United Kingdom that resolved the dispute over the international boundary between Canada and Maine.

The war involved no actual battles between military forces and negotiations between diplomats from the United Kingdom and the US Secretary of State Daniel Webster quickly settled the dispute. [60] After approximately one year Hill was transferred to the 3rd Artillery Regiment in Savannah, Georgia for a three month period and moved subsequently to Fort Moultrie, South Carolina in 1845. It was a complex time in American history that 2nd Lieutenant Hill began his military service in the United States Army. Major change was sweeping over the nation when James K. Polk became the United States President and the United States Congress approved the annexation of Texas. In the summer of 1845, anticipating the Texas government's at hand acceptance of statehood, President Polk directed the reinforcement of General Zachary Taylor's force with additional artillery units, re-designating the force as *"The Army of Occupation"* whereupon he ordered the newly re-designated Army to the Texas frontier. [61]

Brevet 2nd Lieutenant Hill's unit, Company Echo, 3rd Artillery, under the command of First Lieutenant Braxton Bragg, was included in the re-designation process and ordered to the Texas frontier, directed to take a position at the mouth of the Nueces River. [62] On October 13th 1845 Hill was promoted to the rank of full Second Lieutenant and subsequently reassigned back to Fort Monroe, Virginia to take a position in the 4th Artillery Regiment. Four of the Regiment's other companies were already in Texas and had participated in the first battles of the war at Palo Alto and Resaca de la Palma in May 1846 [63] 2nd Lieutenant Hill deployed with Company H, bound for the mouth of the Rio Grande, on June 8th 1846, landing with elements of the 4th Artillery at Point Isabel on July 7th 1846. [64] His unit stayed near the coast for approximately three weeks until ordered upriver in support of General Taylor's advance into the interior of Mexico, signifying the start of the Monterrey Campaign. This operation was planned by General-in-chief Winfield Scott as one of three simultaneous operations to send U.S. Army forces to occupy the northern Mexican states and force the Mexican government to give up all claims over Texas. [65] 2nd Lieutenant Hill's unit was assigned to the 1st Brigade of the 2nd Division, under the command of the legendary General William J. Worth, then subsequently ordered to lead the army's grand advance toward Cerralvo. The push toward Monterrey continued on September 14th 1846 and by September 19th 1846 General Taylor's army had advanced to within a few miles of the city. [66] Hill commented in his war diary that he heard hostile guns for the first time when the Mexicans fired shots at the American reconnoitering party. *"I hope to be in battle tomorrow, Sunday, the 20th,"* he wrote, adding, *"My worldly affairs are all right. I owe nothing and there is nothing due me."* Like many soldiers, D. H. Hill itched for his first fight and had certain expectations about what it would be like to *"see the elephant."* [67]

D. H. HILL

"Upon one occasion, his horse being shot under him, as he was in the act of writing an order, holding the paper in his hand, steed and rider sank to the earth and without the relaxation of a muscle or a movement of the head, he finished the order, handed it to a courier, as calm and unconcerned as if reviewing the battalion of cadets in the grounds of the Institute at Charlotte."

[[Colonel Henry Elliot Shepherd]]

Q13

W. WORTH   **Z. TAYLOR**   **W. SCOTT**   **D. E. TWIGGS**

PROMINENT GENERALS - MEXICAN WAR

J. SHIELDS   **SANTA ANNA**   **PEDRO de AMPUDIA**   **G. J. PILLOW**

The young lieutenant would not be disappointed as his opportunity soon arrived with the start of the Battle of Monterrey. Early in September 1846 the first division of General Taylor's army, under the command of General W. J. Worth, moved towards the strongly fortified capital of New Leon and strongly defended by Mexican General Pedro De Ampudia with a force of about 9,000 Mexican troops. On September 19th 1846 General Taylor soon joined General Worth, encamping within 3 miles of Monterrey with a U. S. force of about 7,000 men. On the morning of September 21st 1846 the U. S. soldiers attacked General Ampudia's stronghold. Joined by other divisions of the army, the assault became general on the 23d; the ensuing conflict in the streets was dreadful. 68 On September 21st 1846 Hill's company joined in the U. S. attack on Federation Hill. It was at this juncture of his military career that the young 2nd Lieutenant first displayed his gallant fighting style, definitively marking the beginning of his reputation as a fighter.

As U. S. forces advanced on Monterrey, the Mexicans delivered upon them a constant stream of musketry volleys from rooftops and windows of the strong storehouses, placing a withering fire upon the attacking American soldiers. The bloodshed was horrific. During the fight, Hill received his first true taste of round shot, canister grape, shells and musket balls as he courageously participated in the famous climb up Federation Hill; a most difficult assault with, at times, the climb being almost a 90 degree angle. Hill's men drove back the Mexican forces and pushed them from the field of battle, sending them running with great confusion in all directions. In their haste the Mexicans left one of their cannons, which Hill's artillerymen promptly put to good use as the rest of the charging American force pursued the fleeing Mexicans on foot. By 2 o'clock in the afternoon, Hill's unit had seized another gun and chased the defenders completely off Federation Hill. 69 On the fourth day of the siege, General Ampudia asked for a truce. General Taylor acknowledged his request but insisted upon an absolute surrender, granting the Mexican General an armistice for a period of eight weeks. During this siege the Americans lost over 500 men while the Mexican losses were double that number.

With the surrender of Monterrey 2nd Lieutenant Hill concluded his first actions in combat – he had surely *"seen the elephant."* Due to the heroic actions during the fight, his company was given the prestigious honor of leading the columns of Worth's Division as they marched triumphantly, to the tune of *"Hail Columbia,"* into the Citadel on September 25th 1846. Of the ensuing flag changing ceremony Hill wrote in his diary: *"I never felt so proud in my life,"* Of his hearing the martial music and witnessing the departure of the Mexican troops, he continued, *"We saluted the Mexican troops as they filed past and when they were beyond sight and hearing changed the flag against deafening cheers."* 70

D. H. HILL

"His absolute unconsciousness of danger was enough to thrill the ordinary brain with a sort of vertigo as it revealed itself in the most phenomenal situations or supreme crises."

[[Colonel Henry Elliott Shepherd]]

Q12

The next major engagements for Lieutenant Hill were the Battles of Contreras and Churubusco. 71 After the battle of Cerro Gordo, General Scott's American forces resumed their march to the north on Mexico City. Mexican General Antonio López de Santa Anna had dispatched his Army of the North, consisting of about 5,000 soldiers under the command of General Gabriel Valencia, in an effort to flank the Americans. 72 American General Twiggs encamped at St. Augustine, with the strong fortress of San Antonio before him.

Close upon his right were the heights of Churubusco and not far off was the strongly fortified camp of Contreras. In the rear of Contreras was Santa Anna with a reserve force of 12,000 men. 73 General Twiggs's Division was assigned the mission of attacking a fortified enemy position at the town of Padierna, located at the southwest corner of the Pedregal lava fields and along a major road leading to Mexico City. The other American divisions were directed to proceed north toward Churubusco. General Gideon Pillow assumed command of General Twiggs's forces and ordered Riley's brigade, including Hill's 4th Artillery unit, to move around the flank of the fort and cut off the garrison from reinforcements while he conducted a demonstration to their front. 74 During the afternoon of August 19th 1846 Generals Twiggs and Pillow, assisted by Generals P. F. Smith and Cadwallader, first engaged the camp of Contreras wherein a sharp conflict ensued. This action initiated an almost continual skirmishing throughout the entire encampment. 75

The main battle began at sunrise by General Smith's division. While Generals Shields and Pierce kept Santa Anna's reserve at bay, General Smith's troops marched toward the works in the darkness, gaining a position, unobserved, behind the crest of a hill near the Mexican works. Springing up suddenly from their hiding-place, the U. S. forces dashed pell-mell into the entrenchments and captured the batteries at the point of the bayonet, driving out the army of Mexican General Valencia and pursuing their fleeing remnants towards Mexico City. The contest, which had lasted only seventeen minutes, pitted the American force of 4,500 men against the much larger force of 7,000 Mexicans. The decisive action resulted in the capture of eighty Mexican officers, 3,000 Mexican troops and thirty three pieces of Mexican artillery. 76

Lieutenant Hill recorded in his war diary that the enemy was not surprised by the U. S. actions but their defenses were still incomplete, allowing the rapid storming of the hill by his 4th Artillery unit. *"Cannon now opened upon us, charged with grape and canister, but owing to the fright of the gunners did but little injury."* Nonetheless, artillery fire killed the color bearer and damaged the regimental colors; the unit suffered a total of thirty-seven casualties, fourteen of those casualties were from Hill's company. This bloody battle continued about six hours until nightfall put an end to the fighting, wherein the Americans took a brief break, expecting to renew the conflict the next morning. 77

Recording the day's events in his war diary, Lieutenant Hill wrote that nothing in the war to date had been *"so brilliant as the storming of the heights of Contreras."* He continued, *"Twas certainly a high honor for our Regiment to have led the attack and I shall always feel proud to have commanded the company which suffered most severely."* For his heroic actions, Lieutenant Hill received a brevet promotion to Captain by way of demonstrated bravery exhibited during the battle. 78

D. H. HILL

"never a more pluckier or determined fighter."

[[General James Longstreet]]

Q6

CHAPULTEPEC 1846

The next major engagement for the young Captain Hill was the Battle of Chalpultepec. General Scott, desiring to carry the strongly fortified post with as minimum loss of men practicable, was determined to batter the heavily fortified position with heavy cannon prior to their planed assault with infantry. Accordingly, on the night of September 11th 1846 four batteries of heavy cannons were erected on a hill between Tucabaya and Chapultepec. They were placed in position by the engineer officers Huger and R. E. Lee (the latter afterwards Commander-in-chief of the Confederate army). On the morning of September 12th 1846 these batteries opened fire with devastating effect, cannon balls crashing through the castle and shells tearing up the ramparts. The fire of the Mexican artillery was no less oppressive as the cannon duel continued throughout the day. Meanwhile, the U.S. main attack had effectively damaged Chapultepec but had failed to breach the thick, tall seemingly impenetrable walls. With the artillery proving ineffectual, General Scott decided to employ storming parties in advance of a general assault upon the fortress. General Worth's division, to whom Captain Hill was assigned, had not been designated to be part of the main battle.

Thus, the newly promoted brevet Captain Hill seemed destined to miss this, the most historic day of fighting in the entire Mexican war. But fate had other plans for the young fighter. General Worth's Division was asked to provide a force of thirteen officers and 250 men to complete the formation of General Scott's storming parties. It was to no one's surprise that Captain Hill promptly volunteered for the duty, along with thirty of his soldiers from the 4th Artillery. Soon, brevet Captain Hill would earn his reputation as the bravest man in the army. Hill and his men drew scaling ladders and pick axes then, after dark, moved into their designated positions, well within range of the Mexican fort's heavy cannonade. 79 The next morning, Captain Hill led his men forward with great courage to assail the works, attacking the enemy's defenses at their weakest point. The assault was executed in two columns; General Pillow led one column to assail the works on the west side while General Quitman made a demonstration on the easterly part. Each column was preceded by a strong storming party. While the troops advanced, American artillerist fired a continuous barrage over the heads of their friendly troops and upon the Mexican positions, with great effect, in an effort to prevent reinforcements from reaching the Mexicans. The men of Captain Hill's column bore the brunt of this battle and the fighting was fierce. Captain Hill, being one of the first Americans to breach the redoubt, led his troops in a ferocious storming of the enemy's fortification, driving them back from shelter to shelter. After a furious battle with the defenders to their front, the storming party reached the wall of the main work, engaging their scaling ladders and fascines. Leading the final assault, Captain Hill's men captured the position and unfurled the American flag over the ramparts, amid prolonged cheers of the storming parties. 80

Captain Hill described the chaos, and his storming party participation, in his war diary: *"The havoc among the Mexicans was now horrible in the extreme. Pent up between two fires they had but one way to escape and all crowded toward it like a flock of sheep. . . Our men were shouting 'give no quarter to the treacherous scoundrels' and as far as I could observe none was asked by the Mexicans. I collected my little party and for more than a mile was far in advance of all our troops in the chase of the enemy. They frequently formed across the road, but a few well directed shots from my little party put them promptly to flight again. 'Tis a sublime and exalted feeling that which we experienced whilst chasing some five thousand men with but little more than a dozen."* 81

In a simultaneous, coordinated assault, General Quitman's column advanced with great success, capturing two cannon batteries en route to linking up with General Pillow's men to participate in the final assault of Chapultepec. The Mexican defenders scattered before the attacking American in every direction. The assault on Chapultepec resulted in the castle's complete destruction. Captured within the fortification were 50 Mexican Generals and a huge number of Mexican soldiers of every rank and grade. There were also 100 cadets of the Mexican Military College, described by an American officer to be *"pretty little boys,"* from ten to sixteen years of age. Several of their little companions had been killed *"fighting like demons."* The fugitives fled to the city while decisively engaged in a fierce running fight with the pursuing forces of General Quitman. The divisions of Generals Twiggs and Pillow advanced westward, in fine fashion, along the causeway while General Worth's division rapidly advanced to storm the redoubt at the bridge. General Scott, at a mile's distance from Churubusco, was coordinating the overall movement of U. S. forces. After a fierce battle the redoubt at the bridge was finally carried, at the point of the bayonet, while simultaneously General Twiggs successfully assaulted the fortified church and hamlet; but only after a furious and extended battle. Mexican General Rincon, in command of three large gatherings of Santa Anna's forces, moved rapidly to decisively engage General Shields. The fearless combat veterans assigned to the command of General P. F. Smith's command, who had earlier displayed unheralded gallantry during the capture of Contreras, were conspicuous in this fearful contest as well. A most desperate defense at the church was made by forces of the American army, led by Thomas Riley. The alarmed Mexicans, on several occasions, hoisted white flags in token of surrender. But with the hoisting of each white flag the Americans, with halters about their necks, repeatedly tore them down. The battle raged with tremendous intensity for about three hours until the church and the other defenses of Churubusco finally surrendered. [82]

This was the fifth victory won on that memorable August 20th 1847: the Battles of Contreras, San Antonio, the redoubt at the bridge, the Church of San Pablo, and the engagement with Santa Anna's troops. In fact, the combined events of that day formed one great contest over a considerable expanse of territory and might aptly be known in history as the *"Battle of the Valley of Mexico."* On that day, during these five desperate battles, 9,000 American soldiers had defeated over 32,000 Mexicans.   [83] The result was the capture by the former of the entire exterior line of the Mexican defenses; opening the causeway to the city and leaving no other resources but the city of Mexico's fortified gates and the Castle of Chapultepec. Over 4,000 Mexicans had been killed or wounded that day; 3,000 were made prisoners; thirty-seven pieces of fine artillery had been captured along with a vast amount of munitions of war. The American losses, in killed and wounded, totaled about 1,100 men. [84]

Captain Hill recorded in his war diary that he was *"proud that he and his soldiers had led the charge down the causeway"* further noting they, *"though small in numbers, were more honorable than the thousands of retreating Mexicans."* Although horrific and sometimes blemished by the mistakes of commanders and volunteers, this was the glorious war in which Hill had hoped to participate. [85] Later, writing to D. H. Hill with regard to his participation in the battle, General Joseph E. Johnston asked of him: *"Do you know that in Mexico the young officers called you the bravest man in the army?"*

86 When the news of D. H. Hill's gallantry and valorous display of heroism on the fields of battle in Mexico reached South Carolina, both houses of his home State's legislature unanimously voted to award him one of three elaborate golden swords; proclaiming him to be one of the three bravest and most distinguished South Carolina veterans of the entire Mexican War. 87 Another recipient of his State's sword was Major Bernard Bee; a distinguished officer who would later gain fame as General Bee for his service to the Confederacy. This gallant officer, who would later fall mortally wounded at Manassas, is credited with bestowing upon Thomas J. Jackson his infamous nickname when he exclaimed: *"There stands Jackson like a stone wall."*

B. E. BEE

On October 26th 1856, in a letter to General Dunavant, addressing the accomplishments of D. H. Hill, Bee wrote: *"It gives me great pleasure to add my mite of praise to that which has already been given to Mr. Hill by his military superiors. I had the pleasure of knowing him intimately and serving with him in the storming party detailed from Twiggs' Division for the attack on Chapultepec. I can bear full testimony to his gallantry and to his ardent desire to do his duty well. In addition, I can testify to his State pride, evinced in his going up under a heavy fire to congratulate and praise a member of the Palmetto regiment who was behaving under fire most gallantly. For his services on that day he received honorable mention from his immediate commanders and also from Colonel Magruder, commanding a light battery, which battery Lieutenant Hill offered to support when it was menaced by a body of Mexican lancers. He received the brevet appointment of major, and was considered a loss to the service when he resigned. Your obedient servant,*

BERNARD BEE, Captain, U. S. Army. 88

Thus, history finally provided D. H. Hill with his fight; making possible his decisive participation in these honorable and historic victories. Indeed his combat service in the Mexican war defined him, not only as a great soldier, but by proclamation to be the *"bravest man in the army."* By God's grace and his personal demonstration of uncommon valor on the field of battle, on September 20th 1846, Captain Daniel Harvey Hill left that field victorious, having earned great distinction as *a fighter from way back.* [89]

For the next few months after the end of hostilities with the Mexican army, Major Hill often found himself in charge of his regiment; given bouts of illness and other duties that took his superior officers away. The security situation in Mexico remained shaky as guerrilla bands continued to roam the countryside and villages, sniping at American troops. At one point, the 4th Artillery regimental commander applied to take the unit back to Vera Cruz for safer duty but Major Hill and his comrades protested the move. *"I feel it to be a disgrace,"* he wrote in his war diary, referring to the prospect of a premature departure. [90] Major Hill spent his remaining months in Mexico commanding an artillery section assigned to the 9th Infantry, conducting counterinsurgency operations north of the capital. In early March 1848, he returned to Mexico City for the last time. Upon receiving news from home that his mother, Nancy, was sick he was granted leave and left Vera Cruz on March 24th 1848 for his return the United States. [91]

At this juncture, Major Hill's service in Mexico was complete. He reached Canton, Mississippi sometime around the beginning of April 1948 and, upon fulfillment of some administrative duties, departed for home due to the delicate state of Nancy's health. [92] Daniel Harvey Hill's valorous service and demonstrated heroism in the face of enemy fire during multiple bloody battles was nothing short of brilliant. He had distinguished himself with bravery in almost every battle of the Mexican campaign and, unquestionably, in every battle wherein he was a participant. The young officer was three times cited for valor in battle whereupon he was successively promoted for his gallantry in those actions to 1st Lieutenant, winning the brevet of Captain at the Battles of Contreras and Churubusco, and finally promoted to the brevet of Major at the Battle of Chapultepec; with merit based upon his exceptional display of heroism as one of the soldiers of the storming party that breached the ramparts. Hill shared this rare distinction only with Thomas J. *"Stonewall"* Jackson and perhaps four other officers of the American army of his era.

CHAPTER IV

CAMPUS LIFE FOR PROFESSOR D. H. HILL

Army life in peacetime offered very little appeal to the young Brevet Major, who had rapidly become a seasoned combat veteran and widely recognized for his demonstrated bravery and uncommon valor on the field of battle. Combat veterans from any era can offer their personal insights to describe the excitement and feelings of strong sense of purpose that comes while decisively engaged *"in the fight."* On the other hand, stark and contrasting descriptions can also be furnished to describe the boredom and lack of purpose associated with the everyday routine of garrison life. It is not uncommon for soldiers to consider a career change when, at any war's end, the guns fall silent. Such was the environment for Major Hill, providing him a most compelling reason for his resignation from the U.S. Army. 93 While on leave of absence from his unit during the Spring of 1848, Major Hill paid a visit to his sister, the wife of Dr. W. B. McLean, in Lincoln County, North Carolina. During this visit he made the acquaintance of the McLean family's neighbor and friend, Dr. Robert Hall Morrison. Dr. Morrison was a well-known and highly regarded Presbyterian Reverend who served as the first president of Davidson College; an institution of higher learning founded nearby in 1837.

Dr. Morrison had several daughters of whom the oldest, Isabella, caught the Major's eye. Isabella was known as a local belle, having been introduced to society in Raleigh. She was highly educated and the niece of the prominent North Carolina Governor, William A. Graham, later to become Secretary of the U.S. Navy and a distinguished Confederate Senator. 94

Upon his return from leave to Fort Monroe, Major Hill assumed command of Company M, 4th Artillery in September 1848. His command tenure was very brief for, within a few weeks, he was granted leave of absence to return home and marry Isabella. The marriage took place at the Morrison residence on November 2nd 1848 whereupon Major Hill submitted his letter of resignation. Effective February 28th 1849, he returned to civilian life and established residence for himself and his new bride in Lexington, Virginia. Interestingly, one of Hill's best men was John Gibbon, a fellow artillerist and graduate of the West Point Class of 1847. Originally from Pennsylvania, Gibbon was raised in Charlotte North Carolina but chose to remain with the U.S. Army during the Civil War while three of his brothers joined the Confederacy. Ironically, these two friends would face each other as foes at the Battle of South Mountain some fourteen years later; Major Hill as Commanding General of the Confederate's famed D. H. Hill's Division and Gibbon as the commander of the legendary Yankee's Iron Brigade. 95

During Major Hill's period of transition from soldier to civilian, he made applications for a position as a mathematics instructor at Washington College and the Virginia Military Institute, both institutions located in Lexington, Virginia. His applications were aided by his strong family association and ties with the distinguished John C. Calhoun, former Secretary of War and senator from South Carolina. Upon Calhoun's strong recommendation, where he cited both the young Hill's reputation as an Army officer and his grandfather's grand reputation as an ardent Whig, Major Hill was accepted and installed as Professor of Mathematics in Washington College; known today as Washington and Lee University. In this important position he was responsible for designing and teaching curriculums ranging from algebra to calculus. 96

Again, the influence of family played a profound role in Hill's obtaining and fulfilling his newfound career as an educator. In the finest Hill tradition, the newlywed couple's overarching focus immediately centered upon establishing a strong Christian family; rearing, training, educating their children while providing for them a happy family-centric home life. Harvey contributed wisdom and humor to the family whereas Isabella furnished tenderness and solicitude. Their youngest son, Joseph, recorded that his father was very proud of what he called Isabella's *"war record."* Until the beginning of the Civil War she had been provided with all the comforts of life. But marriage brought inherent challenges associated with caring for a large family with small children; replete with hardships, privations and dangers. She fulfilled her role admirably with fortitude during this most challenging period of her life, with willing hands and without fear. 97 D. H. Hill's personal and professional friendship with Stonewall Jackson, Hill's brother-in-law, was marked by warm regard and perfect confidence. From the earliest days of the war of secession, Hill predicted for Jackson a great career, while Jackson himself expressed a like assurance of Hill's high qualification as a soldier. 98

Professor Hill's students at Washington College held him in highest regard as a teacher. C. D. Fishburne, one of Hill's students and later a faculty colleague, said of Hill as an educator: *"He was regarded as strictly impartial and very generous in recognizing and encouraging any originality and unusual ability among his students."* Hill had a flair for instruction and possessed an instinctive talent for making topics interesting for his pupils; extremely artful at compelling them to use their gifts and abilities in a manner favorable to learning. He made constant use of the black-board and his methods of teaching compelled his pupils, not only to comprehend the subject under discussion but, to learn and expand on the topic with demonstrated understanding. He taught them to teach; many very successful teachers later credited him with their educational successes. He served to be a positive influence on his classes, inspiring confidence and trust with great give in return from the students. He was regarded as strictly impartial and very generous in recognizing and encouraging any originality and unusual ability among his students. 99

Major Hill combined with his native reserve and dignity a strong element of sharp wit, as well as a keen appreciation of the outrageous and the humorous. On one occasion a somewhat adverturous student wrote the word ASS in large chalk letters upon the back of a classmate who was engrossed in his demonstration at the blackboard. Major Hill's quick eye at once observed this and he remarked, *"Mr. _ _ _ _ _ somebody has been writing his name on your back."* The tension within the classroom was immediately subdued and serenity reigned supreme. On another occasion Major Hill said to a student who was pushing the outer limits of propriety: *"Mr _ _ _ _ _ if you do not conduct yourself properly I shall be obliged to put the door between us."* 100

Hill disciplined himself to learn the material and during instruction relied on his excellent communication skills to convey the material to his students. He artfully employed teaching methods acquired from personal experiences at the United States Military Academy to encourage his students to engage their intellect while upholding sound moral values and accepting personal responsibility in all their actions. Hill held these traits, for himself and his students, to be absolutely essential to achieve success in the classroom and in life. 101 Major Hill could masterfully determine the weaknesses and the strengths of every student and, as his classes never exceeded a rational number, he attempted to become personally acquainted with the mental and moral characteristics of the often crude and self-appreciative lads who were entrusted to his keeping. He possessed a natural ability to understand the intellects of his students, rapidly determining the level of learning needed to teach at their level of abilities, as needed to learn the topic. 102

Dr. Shepherd wrote of Hill's inclusion of religion into his teaching, saying: *"Above all, his far-ranging vitality of intellect was brought to bear upon the interpretation and elucidation of Holy Scripture. His daily comments upon the Psalms, the Gospels, or the Epistles, are wrought into my memory; despite the process of the suns, and the increasing years, I can, in part, recall them as clearly and vividly as if I had listened to them but yesterday."* 103

Hill resigned his position with Washington College in May 1854 to assume the Chair of Mathematics at Davidson College, a position for which he had been nominated the previous August. The move to Davidson enabled Hill and his wife to be closer to both of their families and in his words, *"to labor in a College, founded in the prayers, and by the liberality of Presbyterians,"* his life-long church. 104 It is unclear who was more pursuant of Hill's new position as Chair of Mathematics at Davidson College – Major Hill or Dr. Morrison. What can be said with assurance is that no one influenced Hill's life, after his service in the United States Army, as deeply as his father-in-law, Dr. R. H. Morrison; Davidson College's founder and first President. Dr. Morrison was a man of great learning and, for over 60 years, a pre-eminent minister of the Presbyterian Church. Hill's children spoke frequently of the affection, admiration and respect their father had for this stern old Calvinist. 105 The pursuit of Professor Hill to join the faculty of Davidson College was a direct effort to gain an educator who had the skills needed to reverse Davidson College's steep decline in academic standards and discipline. It seemed a logical move, from the perspective of both Dr. Morrison and Professor Hill, that he was the man for the job. Indeed, it was clearly a job that presented Hill with the very type of challenge for which he was best suited to handle. It also gave him a greater role in the day-to-day administration of a school and proved to be a perfect venue to test his ideas about reforming higher education. 106

With his obligations fulfilled at Washington College, Major Hill arrived on the Davidson Campus on May 28th 1854. Over the next five years at Davidson College the professor functioned with total drive and persistence in his pursuit to establish and implement policies and procedures that conformed to his philosophy for operating the College. His skills had been sought by the Davidson College Board of Trustees as they wanted him to take charge and subdue the violence that was threatening to destroy the college. According to Professor Fishburne, *"Major Hill was induced to accept the place by the urgent request of prominent friends of the College who were dissatisfied with its condition."* 107

Student behavior at Davidson College was dreadful and most of the 90 students were, by any measure, out of control. Practically every known vice deemed unacceptable by the staunch Christian Professor had become commonplace practice at the school. Drinking, gambling, carousing, even riots were common and widespread across the campus and surrounding small Southern town of Davidson, North Carolina. 108 He immediately began to implement major changes in the academic program; modeling the educational and disciplinary system at Davidson by prominently drawing from policies of the United States Military Academy. He also drew from functioning practices currently in use at other Colleges, including Washington College. He installed a grading system of merits and demerits which involved penalties for such acts as missing class, being drunk and dressing improperly in Chapel. The faculty was even given the authority to conduct unannounced inspections of students' rooms. Proclaiming that derelict students had been *"allowed to trample upon all laws, human and divine,"* Hill insisted that they were of *"undisciplined mind, and uncultivated heart, yet with exalted ideas of personal dignity, and a scowling contempt for lawful authority and wholesome restraint."* 109

There was notable push back, by the students, to the newly installed policies. Tensions increased between the student body and the faculty until they finally, predictably reached a flash point. Major Hill and his colleagues awoke in the middle of the night late in 1854 to find students in full riot mode. After much effort, and some physical clashes, the crowds were dispersed by faculty members. In the following days, after the faculty suspended a young man for starting the riot, over 50 percent of the student body walked out of class in protest. In January 1855, when classes at the College resumed, very few of the students had returned after Christmas break. Nonetheless, Hill's agenda prevailed and Davidson College soon settled into a routine of obedience to the new policies that marked a distinct, affirmative turning point in Davidson College's history. The purge of students resulting from the aforementioned events convinced a wealthy benefactor - Salisbury merchant Maxwell Chambers - to contribute $300,000.00 to the college; this represented an extraordinary dollar figure comparatively to Professor Hill's annual salary of just over $1,705.00 per year. At that time, Chamber's bequest was the largest ever to any Southern school and his charitable act served to further reinforce the Board of Trustees' support of Major Hill and his policies. 110 Hill was lauded throughout the entire region for *"acting decisively in breaking up the riot in a manner consistent with his personality and military training."* 111

Major Hill, as he was most often referred to with great admiration, devoted thirteen years of his life to combined service as a Professor of Mathematics in

Washington College, Davidson College and North Carolina Military Institute, successively. During this time he demonstrated himself to be a creative author, publishing numerous works of literature, including three books: *"Elements of Algebra – 1857"*; 112 *"A Consideration of the Sermon on the Mount - 1858,"* 113 and *"The Crucifixion of Christ – 1859."* 114

His first book, *"Elements of Algebra – 1857,"* became a textbook in several colleges and contained testimonials from three distinguished Professors of Mathematics attesting the book's value as a text. The textbook also contained a letter from a relatively unknown mathematician at the time of its publication – yet destined for great fame for his accomplishments in another field. His testimonial follows: *"From an examination of various portions of Major Hill's Algebra, in manuscript, I regard it as superior to any other work with which I am acquainted in the same branch of science – Thomas J. Jackson."* Jackson, latter to become the infamous Confederate General Stonewall Jackson, was then a professor in the Virginia Military Institute; a position for which he was hired upon the direct recommendation of Major Hill. 115 Hill's book *"Elements of Algebra,"* was designed for faculty use, complete with examples of problem sets designed as student assignments, and was favorably compared in its brilliant method and skill in demonstration to the work of Euler; a notable 18th century mathematician recognized, not only within the circles of other mathematicians, but widely known for his versatility of intellect. 116

Major Hill's other two other books, *"The Crucifixion of Christ,"* and *"The Sermon on the Mount"* remain relevant today as thorough and scholarly reviews of their subject; writings which grew out of his extensive study of the Bible during preparations for his Sunday school classes. *"The Crucifixion of Christ"* reflects his abiding faith in the narratives of the Four Apostles and is expressively written to convince others of their truth. In the analysis of these stories he applies the fundamental principles of evidence to interpret them. He brings through such interpretation, the Four Gospels into a mosaic. 117 *"The Sermon on the Mount"* reflects his religious belief and his comprehensive and scholarly analysis of each chapter and verse is indicative of his deep understanding of the Christian faith. He considered the stern and gloomy actions of professing Christians of that day to have caused great harm and reproach to Christ's religion. Hill said, *"The sour countenance of Pharisaic disciples has often made the young regard Christianity as the embodiment of all that is dismal and lugubrious; and thus a stone of stumbling has been thrown in the way of the youthful and lighthearted."* His writings on the Fatherhood of God, the Brotherhood of Man, and the Golden Rule, as he addressed them in this immortal sermon, brought forth a religion of cheerfulness, contentment and happiness; and that was the religion that he lived and taught his Bible classes for more than forty years. 118

With his invincible moral fearlessness there was in the nature of D. H. Hill no trace or suggestion of righteous pretension or any sense of superior holiness; either in his role as a fighter or within his sphere of professorial intellect, field of science or the realm of scholarship. [119] Within his moral fiber, D. H. Hill possessed the zeal of his Scottish- Irish ancestry, a moral temperament that was never invaded by the presence of doubt; a subtle judgment stimulated by his precise mathematical training; and a range of historical and literary acquirement, unequalled by any of the foremost soldiers in the armies of the North or South. More than this, his acquaintance with Scripture was detailed, exact and comprehensive. The Psalms were his chosen field above all; a circumstance which possibly finds its explanation in the ancient and now seemingly obsolete custom in Presbyterian house-holds, of requiring them to be committed to memory and recited by the children. As a child, this author benefited greatly from this family tradition and, to this day, I continue to hold my children and grandchildren to this time honored family practice of Psalms and other bible verse recitals. [120]

D. H. Hill was, in his own right, a great student and prolific reader. He possessed an acquired culture that few men held within so many fields of learning and displayed an ardent knowledge of human nature. Therefore, when you met him in the classroom or on the battlefield, in the councils of war or of peace, as an editor, writer, college professor or president, you quickly found that his quantitative attainments and qualitative experiences credited him with great wisdom with which to meet issues; whenever and wherever they arose, he had the courage to always carry out his convictions. [121]

D. H. Hill's youngest son Joseph, who rose within the legal profession to become a State Supreme Court Justice in Arkansas, wrote of possessing his father's large and comprehensive library; recalling therein the complete works of John Calvin and John C. Calhoun. Also included were works on Mathematics, Political Economy, Metaphysics, Greek and Roman Classics, Ancient and Modern History, English and American Literature and many biographies. Commenting that D. H. Hill's library was not a dust-covered library, Joseph Hill provided great insight to the depth and scope of this iconic figure's exposure to higher learning. [122]

D. H. Hill was an intense student of the Bible and of Greek so as to better understand the New Testament, as well as to enjoy the culture of the Greeks. He was also familiar with the Vulgate, a late 4th Century Latin version of the Bible. This knowledge was reflected in his two books - *"A Consideration of the Sermon on the Mount - 1858,"* and *"The Crucifixion of Christ – 1859"* and provides further insight to his intellect and in-depth knowledge of the Bible. [123] D. H. Hill was never a politician in the sense of wanting to hold elected office but after the start of the Civil War, when he saw that the leaders of the North had decided that no Southerner should be allowed to take his slaves to the territory wrested from Mexico by the blood and treasure of the South, as well as of the North, prophetically Hill believed that the conflict had then begun. He believed there would be no other recourse than to resolve the matter upon the bloody field of battle; and then only through a prolonged, fierce struggle. Fully c that the inevitable conflict was near at hand, he professed it to be his solemn duty to prepare the rising generation of his adopted State for war. In 1859 he relinquished his duties at Davidson College and sacrificed his pleasant lifestyle to become the Commandant of the Military Institute at Charlotte, North Carolina. [124]

CHAPTER V

SOCIAL CONDITIONS OF THE CIVIL WAR ERA

To fully grasp the complexities of the coming war and its effect, specifically upon D. H. Hill and generally upon most other Southerners, one must gain a learned comprehension of the prevailing social conditions that existed duing this controversial period of our nation's history. Although there are many, I respectfully invoke one such first hand account as offered by Ms. Delilah Tyler, an accomplished and published writer of the late 19th century. She began her exposition with this question: *"When the war was going on did not persons in the same community, some loyal and some secessionist, feel very bitter towards each other?"* 125

The cause, conduct and results of the Civil War have been recorded by numerous historians repeatedly but the social life of that period has seldom been sufficiently addressed. That there was some bitterness of feeling cannot be denied but Miss Tyler described much less of this than some writers would have us to believe, considering the intensity of those times. Communities seldom divided into cliques with secessionists on the one side and loyalists on the other. Friendly and kindred social ties were too strong for that occurrence. Many social pastimes, such as weddings and other forms of neighborly interaction, continued during the war with great frequency among people of different political inclinations, as much as the exigencies of the times would allow. During the war Miss Tyler resided in a town on the extreme Northern border of a Southern state. There were secessionists on both sides of the States' line, with a good number being from her family - fathers, sons and husbands – who joined the army of their individual choosing; Union or Confederate. Singular as it may seem, she recorded some instances where persons truly loyal to the Federal government assisted in equipping soldier friends for the Confederate army and, quite as often, secessionists lending aid to relatives and friends preparing to join the Union forces; each believing the other to be honest at heart but misguided. 126 Around July 1st 1862 a proclamation was issued by the officer in command of the Union forces, then in possession of her section of the State, announcing that a grand Fourth of July celebration would take place in a grove adjoining her town. Expectations of the day were that every one able would be present. The event called for active oratorations and a feast of good things to eat, so stated the written proclamation.

Excitement, accompanied with much dismay, grew to a fevor pitch as rumors spread that the Federal authorities intended to take that time and occasion to administer the oath of allegiance to the Union. This oath manifest an ironclad compact that, not only forbade citizens from taking up arms against the government, but prohibited any form of aid to any disloyal persons. 127 There was scarcely a man in her community, even the most loyal, who had no kindred or friends on the other side; associates whom one could never turn away in any hour of need. It was most feared that if anyone took this oath they might be subject to perjure themselves or act against their own nature and humanity. However, the escalating conflict induced the citizens to view this oath as being more pleasant due to the horrific bloodshed that was occuring upon so many battlefields.

On the morning of this memorable Fourth of July, an uncle of Miss Tylers declared to her: *"I will not go into town and subscribe to an oath which I think unjust and which I cannot keep."* Fearing that soldiers would be sent to scour the country in search of delinquents, unwilling to so pledge, her uncle proposed that she and the others of *genus homo* simply forgo the event, remaining unnoticed in their absence. Her uncle's scheme was agreeable to her for, while she never expected to commit any brazen acts against the government, they all had someone near and dear to them in the Southern army: *"if one of these had asked us for bread we could never have given him a stone."* 128

D. H. HILL

"....a capable, well read soldier, and positively about the bravest man ever seen. He seemed not to know peril and was utterly indifferent to bullets and shell...."

[[General G. Moxley Sorrell]]

Q18

The big celebration in town went off to the satisfaction of the originators and the oath was administered to hundreds; both loyal and disloyal. Noteworthy was the fact that two-thirds of the community's residents were against taking the oath of allegiance were natives of the free border State. Clearly the prevailing attitude of that day was that *"there never was a good war nor a bad peace."* She and her group were not missed and, for the time being, enjoyed immunity from the distaseful compact. However, as the conflict's horror presented a better understanding of the circumstances of the war, indifference turned to sympathy for many citizens and they were more inclined to willingly adhere to the government's oath and its mandates; considering the oath to be a pill not so bitter to swallow.

After July 4th 1862 the event was scarcely celebrated at all within most disputed regions of the country until the cruel war was finally over. Then, for the most part, kindred and friends reinstituted the celebrations; many hearts would ache, some tears would flow for missing ones who *"slept the sleep that knows no waking,"* but all seemed determined to be content if not cheerful. 129 Still, the condition of the existing social environment during the Civil War was in some respects peculiar. Yes, there was an existing gap between many people who held completely opposing points of view regarding specific aspects of both warring governments – and all considerations of war in general. To illustrate, one example was the the marriage of a young Northern lady to a Confederate soldier. The groom slipped through the Union lines for the occasion. The loyal guardian of the young bride provided a lavish wedding feast, to which he invited friends of both parties; Union and Confederate alike.

Another illustration of the better feeling that prevailed during the conflict was an affair most touching. A young man, indeed a mere boy, belonging to one of the best of families of the community, enlisted in the Confederate army. Tragically, he was killed soon after his enlistment. When his father learned of his death he procured a metallic coffin and traveled two hundred miles by wagon in order to bring home for burial the body of is son. He expected that his son's remains had merely been discarded into some ditch, with no covering but perhaps his army blanket; a stark reflection of the stern necessities often rendered necessary during war. He soon learned, however, that of the sixteen Confederate soldiers killed in the company, his son alone was burried in a coffin and his grave marked by a wooden slab bearing his name. 130 The father was deeply moved. Inquiring by whom this act of kindness was performed, he was told that a captain in command of the opposing Union forces had bought the coffin and had the young Confederate decently buried with his grave aptly marked. The father sought out the officer and thanked him warmly. At that time he ask why his dear boy had been selected, from the many who fell that dreadful day, for such a mark of human kindness?

"My wife wrote me," replied the captain, *"that during the severe weather of the past winter she was at one time entirely without fuel or money to buy it, and that a neighbor across the street, hearing of her condition, took a wagon and team, drove to the country, procured and brought her a load of wood. She said the man's name was M----; that he was a Confederate and had a son in General S-----'s command in the Confederate army. When this battle occurred the Confederates were defeated and driven from the field. I noticed in the reports of the slain who were left within our lines one named M----. Upon inquiry I found he was the son of the benefactor of my family. I was gratified that I was here to do what I could for your son."* 131

This conflict was so fierce in its nature. War was then, and today remains, such a dreadful thing. While it often furnishes opportunities and excuses for lawlessness and vicious acts it often summons forth the noblest of traits in humanity – unselfishness, forbearance and the greatest of all, charity. 132

History has recorded that D. H. Hill disagreed, sometimes intensely, with the views of many a Northerner; yet, he harbored no unkindness or personal animosity against them. He even demonstrated tolerance for the viewpoint of some radical but honest Yankees: but he did possess disdain for hypocrisy and despised dishonesty; leveling harsh ridicule upon guilty culprits. After the war he openly expressed the most sovereign contempt for that portion of Northerners who came to the South under the guise of driving a hard bargain with Southerners, all the while cheating them under false pretenses. He made no attempt to conceal his hatred and disgust for the men of the North who coveted the wealth of the Southern planters and were resolute to obtain such by dishonorable means. But prior to and during the war, his penchant for fighting was a reflection of his military experience and his principles of support for Confederate cause more than a personal inclination. 133

Even in this, the 21st Century, some traits of Southern pride and heritage remain embedded deep within the culture and conscience of many Carolinians. Upon the occasion of this author's ceremony for promotion to Colonel in the United States Army, and subsequent assumption of brigadier command, I was honored with my elderly mother's presence at the event. I shall not divulge her age at the time – for fear of violating a well-known tenant of Southern gentlemanly conduct - never divulge the true age of a Southern Belle. Shortly after the official ceremony, as I escorted mom among the many attendees of the event, she suddenly stopped, gained the attention of a distinguished looking Sergeant Major, whom she mistakenly took to be my Division's Commanding General, where she boldly commented: *"Thank you kindly young man for promoting my boy in your Yankee army."* To this day I am unsure if her comment was a spontaneous display of her familiar Southern wit and humor or if she was expressing some innermost feelings about my military service. Nonetheless, I had no inclination, then or now, to question, correct or apologize for my mother's comment and I later received reassurance from the Sergeant Major that her comment was of no offense and that, as a fellow Southerner, he was honored by her recognition and considered her comment to be a flattering portrayal of her Southern charm.

CHAPTER VI

EARLY DAYS OF THE WAR

The North Carolina Military Institute was founded in 1958 by a local Charlotte businessman by the name of Dr. Charles J. Fox under the patronage of a North Carolina General Statute that appointed a Board of Trustees: Charles J. Fox, James H. Carson, H. Alexander, T. H. Brem, S. M. Blair, David Parks, James H. Davis, Moses Heart, John A. Young, J. M. Davidson, J. H. Wayne, and D.H. Hill's brother-in-law James P. Irwin. 134 Under Dr. Fox's leadership, the Board of Directors pushed aggressively forward with the project with great zeal and secured a grant of $10,000 from the City of Charlotte, which was combined with another $15,000 that was raised by selling stock to individuals in order to finance the project. The Board purchased a tract of land approximately one-half mile south of Charlotte, in the vicinity of the Charlotte and South Carolina Railroad and contracted Sydney Reading to oversee the construction of Steward's Hall; a massive castle-like structure, measuring 270 feet in length, with a three and four-story brick structure based on the architectural designs of the buildings at West Point. 135 The cornerstone for Steward's Hall was laid during festivities on July 31 1858 where Governor William A. Graham spoke to a *"large assemblage of ladies and gentlemen."* 136

On September 28th 1858 it was announced in a local paper that Daniel Harvey Hill would become the Institute's Superintendent. *"The mere mention of this fact we think will insure confidence in the success of the undertaking."* 137 The Institute's first classes commenced on October 1st 1859, offering two departments: a Primary Department for boys ages 12 to 15; and a Scientific Department for young men ages 15 to 21. Student body enrollment grew from an initial 60 cadets in the Institute's first year of operation to approximately 150 by April 1861, at which time North Carolina's Governor Ellis ordered the cadets to Raleigh for service as drill masters. The Charlotte Observer, a paper of that time which is still in operation today, provided articles in 1889 that noted *"it was very popular"* and provided insight into the Institute's operations: *"As at first organized, the session lasted, without intermission throughout the year, the months of August and September being spent campaigning in the mountains of North Carolina. At the end of the second year cadets received a furlough of months. There were a scientific and a primary department. In the former the West Point curriculum was closely followed, and the students were required to board in the buildings and to be under military discipline. There was a primary department, which aimed to prepare students for any college. Such of these students as boarded in the buildings were likewise under military discipline. The institute provided board, lodging, fuel, lights, washing, arms, equipment, medical attendance, uniforms and all clothing except underclothes, for $200 per annum. No extra charges."* 138

As a note of historical significance, the Charlotte Observer cited in a 1915 article that: *"the first Confederate flag raised in the city (Charleston SC) was hosted there when Fort Sumter fell, by the students of the North Carolina Military Institute."* The school closed during the war and, at times, the buildings located at East Morehead Street and South Boulevard provided service as a Confederate hospital. When the war came every student volunteered and practically all became officers in the Confederate Army. 139 D. H. Hill's influence on the educational philosophy of the new military institute was profound as he carried over and installed many of the same rigorous policies that had served him successfully during his tenure at Davidson College. As the Institute's first Superintendent he succinctly framed the school mission: *"The organization of this Institution and the principles upon which it is based entitle it to the patronage of the State. The instruction imparted is peculiarly suited to our Southern agricultural population; the discipline is of the kind most popular with Southern youth; the prohibition of pocket- money and the dressing of all alike in one common uniform prevent extravagance and the indulgence in crime, and cut off the pride and ostentation engendered by fine clothes; the exercise required in drilling, parading and in guard duty, preserves the health, and occupies that time which might otherwise be spent in vice."* 140

During his tenure, Major Hill ensured that Christianity was held as a foundational tenant for the instructional program; requiring each Cadet to attend sermons and bible studies twice daily and, of course, participation in Sunday services was mandatory. Hill assumed the role of the institution's mathematics and artillery instructor. Hill's chair, and of the professors of engineering, drawing and architecture, were all top posts at the school while all others were filled by lieutenants. Charles Lee, fourth in his West Point Class of 1856, became the new commandant and instructor of chemistry, mineralogy, geology, and infantry tactics. Other subjects taught included natural philosophy, moral and intellectual philosophy, and French. 141 The spring of 1861 witnessed a flurry of activity at the North Carolina Military Institute as the Institution's faculty and cadets prepared for the impending conflict. One dramatic scene occurred when the cadets raised a secession flag, made by the ladies of Charlotte, over Steward's Hall so it could be seen by the passengers on the trains moving north out of South Carolina. James H. Lane, a member of Hill's faculty, destined to rise to the rank of General in the coming war, described what happened when the next locomotive passed by the campus. *". . . the artillery thundered its greetings to South Carolina as the train passed slowly by: the male passengers yelled themselves hoarse; the ladies waved their handkerchiefs and threw kisses to these brave boys."* 142

A mood of excitement and anticipation, sweeping across the South, engulfed Charlotte and the surrounding Southern counties at the beginning of the Civil War. On April 21st 1861 a local Confederate unit of volunteers known as the *"Charlotte Grays"* and members of the *"Sharon Riflemen"* were presented, with much ceremony and fanfare, a flag by the "belles" of Charlotte. Lizzie Alexander, a local Confederate supporter delivered a rousing speech on the occasion of their receiving the *"handsome flag"* from the local ladies, exclaiming: *"Permit me in the name of the ladies of Sharon to present you this Flag bearing the Lone Star as an emblem of North Carolina, to whom we now owe allegiance. . . Together with this token of our esteem and confidence we also entrust to you, brave sons of Mecklenburg, our dearest interests and hopes of security."* 143

Major Hill was summoned by the State's Governor to Raleigh and directed to organize the State's first military instruction camp. A tremendous number of eager volunteers had flocked from all over the State, followed shortly thereafter by the cadets from the North Carolina Military Institute. Marching as a body into Charlotte on April 26th 1861, the cadets of the North Carolina Military Institute boarded trains headed for the State capital for an imminent appointment with destiny. Major Hill brought with him to Raleigh his three professors; Lee, Lane, and McKinney - two of whom would fall in battle later at the head of North Carolina regiments and one of whom would become the successor of the noble General Branch as commander of one of North Carolina's best and bravest brigades. Hill also brought with him almost the whole corps of cadets, whose services proved invaluable as drill-masters of the ten thousand volunteers then in the camp of instruction of which Hill took charge. 144

To the people of North Carolina specifically, and the South in general, the State was but an evolution of the home, from whence sprang all that was pure and admirable in patriotism; where centered the love of family; whose ties were the strongest binding her people to earth. A blow at the State meant a menace at the home and, in such spirit, there was great resentment for what seemed to be an unholy intrusion upon their *"blessings of liberty."* History has shown that they did not desire to take from others the rights conceded to be theirs but simply claimed the privilege of withdrawing from a union *"founded to promote the general welfare"* but which had become so changed and altered that the creators could no longer recognize what once had been their creature. 45 As the state of affairs between Federal and North Carolina authorities continued to deteriorate, the leaders of the old North State gathered in convention to pass two resolutions: the secession of North Carolina from the Union and ratification of the Constitution for the Provisional Government of the Confederate States of America: *"We the people of the State of North Carolina, in Convention assembled, do declare and ordain, and ordain, and it is hereby declared and ordained, that the ordinance adopted by the State of North Carolina, in the convention of 1789, whereby the Constitution of the United States was ratified and adopted, and also all acts and parts of acts of the General Assembly, ratifying and adopting amendments to the said Constitution, are hereby repealed, rescinded, and abrogated. We do further declare and ordain that the Union now subsisting between the State of North Carolina and the other States, under the title of the United States of America, is hereby dissolved, and that the State of North Carolina is in the full possession and exercise of all those rights of sovereignty which belong and appertain to a free and independent State: Done at Raleigh, 20th day of May, in the year of our Lord 1861."*

The following ordinance was also passed: *"We, the people of North Carolina, in Convention assembled, do declare and ordain, and it is hereby declared and ordained, that the State of North Carolina does hereby assent to and ratify the Constitution for the Provisional Government of the Confederate States of America, adopted at Montgomery, in the State of Alabama, on February 8th 1861, by the Convention of Delegates from "the States of South Carolina, Georgia, Florida, Alabama, Mississippi, and Louisiana, and that North Carolina will enter into the federal association of States upon the terms therein proposed, when admitted by the Congress or any competent authority of the Confederate*

*States: Done at Raleigh, 20th day of May, in the year of our Lord 1861." -N. Y.
Times, May 26.* 146

The actions of this convention caused an immediate division among State
leaders. Another convention was convened on November 18th 1861 at Hatteras,
North Carolina, whereupon further legislation was enacted to decree: *"The
Provisional State Government for North Carolina was formally instituted on the
18th of November, by a Convention of delegates and proxies representing forty-
five counties of the State. The following ordinances were unanimously adopted:
By the people of the State of North Carolina as represented in Convention at
Hatteras, Monday, Nov. 18, 1861. Be it ordained by this Convention, and it is
hereby ordained and published by the authority of the same:*

*I. That this Convention, on behalf of the people of North Carolina, and
acknowledging the Constitution of the United States of America as the supreme
law of the land, hereby declares vacant all State offices, the incumbents of
which have disqualified themselves to hold them by violating their oaths to
support the Federal Constitution.*

*II. That the office of Governor of this Commonwealth having been vacated by the
death of John W. Ellis, and by the active treason to the Union of his
constitutional successor, Acting Governor Clark, therefore Marble Nash Taylor be
hereby appointed and declared Provisional Governor of North Carolina.*

*III. That the Constitution of this State and its amendments, together with the
statues and laws thereof, as contained in the Revised Code put in operation
January 1 1856, be declared continued in full force; also such subsequent acts
of the General Assembly as were not adopted in contravention of the National
Constitution, or in derogation of its authority.*

*IV. That the ordinance of the Convention which assembled at Raleigh on the 20th
of May last, proclaiming the secession of this Commonwealth from the Federal
Union, such secession being legally impossible, is of no force or effect; and said
ordinance, together with all other ordinances and acts of said Convention, or of
the General Assembly, made and done in pursuance of the treasonable purposes
of the conspirators against the Union, is hereby declared "ab initio - null and
void".*

*V. That whereas it is desirable that this State shall be represented in the Federal
Congress, and maintain her due weight in the councils of the Union, therefore
the Provisional Governor be directed hereby to order special elections, in
accordance with chapter sixty-nine of the Revised Code, as soon as practicable
and expedient, in any district or districts now unrepresented. And, in view of the
prevalence of armed rebellion and disorder in many portions of this*

Commonwealth, the Governor is hereby directed to issue his certificates of election upon presentation of such evidence as shall satisfy him of the fact of an election.

VI. That the Governor be authorized and empowered to fill such official vacancies by temporary appointment, and to do so such acts as, in the expedient for the safety and good order of the State.

The Convention adjourned, subject to be reassembled upon the call of the President." 147

Clearly, the State of North Carolina was a house divided and the inevitable course was set for conflict: Union v Confederacy; secessionist v loyalist; brother v brother. Upon the actions by the convention leading to secession from the Union and joining the Confederacy, D. H. Hill expedited his efforts to prepare the Carolinians for the coming conflict. 148

D. H. HILL

"had done as much hard fighting as any other general and had also displayed great ability in holding his men to their work by supervision and example."

[[General E. P. Alexander]]

Q15

CHAPTER VII

THE EMERGENCE OF LEE'S FIGHTING GENERAL

Daniel Harvey Hill's ancestral family tree placed upon him two major requirements; one that he should possess inner courage and two that he should live an unwavering life of Providence. Of these attributes he was fully possessive of both. Historians have never questioned that the brother-in-law Civil War Generals D. H. Hill and Stonewall Jackson were the two most led by Providence, not only during the war but throughout their entire lives – albeit the life of the latter would end fatefully, tragically and prematurely during the Battle of Chancellorsville by virtue of friendly musketry fire. 149 There is no argument that many Confederate Generals displayed great personal courage on the field of battle, thus rendering it nearly impossible to specify one to be designated as the *"bravest of the brave."* For to what standard does someone judge bravery? What measure can categorize one display of heroism over another? Clearly the adverb arguably must accompany any such declaration. But to determine the best *"fighter among fighters"* is not nearly as subjective and can be more easily judged by reviewing the official historical records of actions during Civil War battles. 150

It is without argument that Daniel Harvey Hill's accomplishments as a fighting General remain unsurpassed as recorded in the compilation of official records of the army of the Confederacy. There is little cause for subjectivity and less need for the adverb arguably when the designation of fighter is based upon thorough research and analysis of the historical official documents. Well before the termination of hostilities between the North and South, Hill had already solidified his position as the *"bravest man in the army"* by virtue of his courageous actions on the fields of battle during the Mexican War. 151 This notable characteristic of General Hill has been verified and conceded to him more frequently in the recorded histories of the Mexican War than was afforded any other Confederate General who participated in that conflict. It is the special purpose of this work, as previously stated, to exhibit the life and achievements of Daniel Harvey Hill as the courageous figure of Lee's Fighting General. Had he lived during another time in history recognition of his military expertise and amazing personal courage under fire would have certainly deemed him to be worthy of a seat at the round table of King Arthur's Court. In addressing the military career of D. H. Hill there is no speculation about his fierceness as a fighter and no premise to attach the word arguably to his designation as Lee's Fighting General.

D. H. HILL

"High and well deserved reputation as a hard fighter...seemed to go from choice into the most dangerous place he could find on the field."

[[Captain John Haskell – Longstreet's artillerist]]

Q16

A Soldier's Story

GREAT BETHEL

Listen now to the first-hand account of Private Frank I. Wilson –

Rifleman with the Buncombe Rifles of the First North Carolina Regiment

"In front of you stands an old Church, its roof greening with the moss of ages. From that humble building, for many generations, has gone up the sound of prayer, of praise and thanksgiving to Almighty God; and from that rude old pulpit, from time to time, for a long series of years, the Gospel has been preached: Christ and Him crucified, peace on earth and good will toward men. 152 *Look now to your left. That forest of tombstones, those numerous mounds – some red with the freshly upturned earth, and others green with the young grass, tell you that there is situated a section of the Great City of the Silent Dead. The rich with the lofty monumental column; the poor with the humble marble or still humbler head-rock; the old and the young; the saint and the sinner, are all on equality here, side by side, their bodies resolving into their original elements. Once they listened to the word of God in that old Church, some unto salvation, and some unto condemnation. Now they are dust, alike.*

How calm, how quiet, how peaceful is the scene! The old Church – the grave-yard – the tall old oaks waving their branches in the gentle breeze, and the tiny insects buzzing with a low murmur around – the sun just looking forth from his Eastern couch, silvering the dewdrops as they hang suspended from the leaves or fall in sparkling splendor to the earth. How the soft wind of the early morn soothes and cools the heated brow! What a tranquilizing effect all these things have upon the soul! How the mind retires, as it were, into itself, to reflect, to meditate, to worship! How thickly throng the thoughts of Time and of Eternity, of Life and Death; and how the senses are all mellowed and softened as we gaze upon the scenery around us! Involuntarily the mind mounts from nature up to nature's God, and the spirit feels chastened, though calm and refined. 153

Now look to your right. O God, what a contrast! There is a long trench dug in the earth, and beyond it, in the dense woods, you see muskets stacked. Close by these muskets you see men in uniforms – in warlike array – ay, in line of battle, ready at a moment's notice to seize their arms and hurl the leaden deaths against any approaching foe. Wide-mouthed cannon also, are gaping, as if impatient to commence the work of destruction. There are officers, with swords gleaming in the light of the newly arisen sun of this glorious June morning, moving from point to point; and there, in the centre of the line, waves proudly the Battle Flag – the Stars and Bars of a young nation just feeling the first throes of its birth. 154 *Recall for a moment the scene. Before you is the old Church; your left is the quiet graveyard; to your right, O Heaven! is WAR. Thus on earth mingles peace and strife; the Gospel and the sword; the sacred and profane; the quiet dead and the maddened living; the scenes of peace and the preparations for deadly conflict.*

But the sounds of a horse's hoofs are heard in the distance, coming up upon the right at rapid speed. A moment more and horse and rider appear, dash through our lines, and halt at a certain tent. The reins are dropped and the rider dismounts and enters the tent. 155 *'Colonel,' he said, 'the tale of the deserter is true. The enemy is advancing and will soon be upon us.' Orders are issued for the deserter to be brought before the Colonel, who thus addresses him: 'Your offense is pardoned. Go to your company, do your duty, and retrieve your character.' A few moments more, and a noble steed, with holsters at the saddle bow, is led up to that tent. A man comes forth, a small man in stature, but every muscle well developed. A glance shows that he is inured to hardships, that his frame is strong and wiry and capable of great endurance. His brow is slightly contracted, his lips compressed, and his whole air thoughtful; but there is a battle-gleam in his eyes, and determination marks every feature. He looks at his Adjutant and says: 'Captains to the centre.' He pats that gallant horse gently on the neck, strokes his forehead soothingly, speaks a few kindly words to him, and mounts. Slowly and thoughtfully he rides to the centre of the line. The*

Adjutant had done his duty, and the Captains are grouped together under that Battle Flag, anxiously awaiting him. 156

Let us look for a moment on that group of Captains. There stands a large eyed, bold and manly form, mildness beaming in his countenance but determination also stamped there. You see it mingling with his great good nature in the prominent eyes and in every feature. That is William W. McDowell, Captain of the 'Buncombe Rifles.' In peace he has been a lamb; in war he proved himself a lion. Beside him stands a tall, rough-hewed, but manly form, reminding you of one of the granite rocks of his native mountains. He is courteous and affable, and a kindlier heart never throbbed within a manlier breast. But look into his eyes; trace those long and boldly developed lines that seam his countenance; and you will read bravery even to desperate daring, written there. That is C. M. Avery, Captain of the ''Burke Rifles.' Alas! He has sealed his devotion to his country's cause with his life. 157 *Next to him is a form, not so tall, but well developed, with a tendency to corpulence. His light blue eyes bespeak a kindly nature, yet gleam with a light which tells you he possesses courage and decision, while that broad prominent under jaw indicates that he is persistent in his resolves, and not easily swerved from them. That is William J. Hoke, Captain of the 'Southern Stars,' from Lincoln County. By his side is a figure similar to his own, whose broad and placid face, just slightly browned and roughened by an Eastern sun and outdoor exercise, shows that with its predominant expression of good nature and friendly feelings, is mingled qualities firm and unswerving, untiring and persistent. In peace he was characterized for energy – and so in war. That is John L. Bridgers, Captain of the 'Edgecombe Guards.' I regret that I cannot portray the other Captains, as I have never seen them; but facts attest that they were brave and true men; and I mention their names with the names of their respective companies: D. A. Bell, Captain of the 'Enfield Blues,' Halifax county; Wright Huske, Captain of the 'Fayetteville Light Infantry,' Cumberland county; J. B. Starr, Captain of the 'Lafayette Light Infantry,' Cumberland county; R. J. Ashe, Captain of the 'Orange Light Infantry;' E. A. Ross, Captain of the 'Charlotte Grays.' And L. S. Williams, Captain of the 'Hornets' Nest Rifles,' both from Mecklenburg County.* 158

It is a fact not only somewhat remarkable, but highly gratifying, that all sections of North Carolina were represented in that one regiment. From the rugged mountains of the West, from the rolling and fertile lands of the Centre, and from the sea-washed sands of the East, are alike brave and alike entitled to that wreath of glory that now encircles their brows, and that North Carolina, through all her borders, has sons that will not only maintain her honor, but who have already, on many bloody fields, added intensity to the bright halo that has ever made radiant her untarnished fame.

Colonel Daniel H. Hill rides up to the assembled Captains and speaks:

'Comrades, a courier has just arrived with the certain intelligence that the enemy is advancing against us in force. We will fight him here. Repair to your respective companies and have them ready for battle. I will be with you again in a few moments.' 159

The captains return to their respective commands. A light touch of the spur and that noble horse springs forward, bearing his rider out into the thick woods. We will follow him. There stands the horse, now and then impatiently champing his bit, pawing the earth and tossing his head; but he loves his master too well to leave him. And where is that master? Look at the root of that great old oak, and you see him upon his knees. He is praying for strength, for guidance; and for victory. Above him waves the branches of the tall trees; the beams of the morning sun are peering as if were through loopholes in the dense green foliage, flickering over the earth as the gentle breeze stirs the overhanging boughs. What a lovely, what a pleasant, what a peaceable morning! Man may rage, but God ever smiles, heedless of the wrath of his puny creatures. 160 *Presently that kneeling form arises. Again he pats the neck of his steed, mounts, and rides back to his lines. How those few moments have changed his aspect! His brow is now smooth and serene, and his whole countenance is placid; but that stamp of determination, that high resolve, and that firmness of purpose, still mark every feature, and that battle-gleam still lights his eye. He rides along his lines and addresses his brave North Carolinians:*

'Soldiers, the enemy is approaching in heavy force. In one or two hours – perhaps less – you will be engaged in battle. Remember you are North Carolinians, and that the heretofore untarnished fame of your mother State is now in your hands. This battle is to be the first of a long series to be fought on the soil of Virginia, and you should be proud that you now have the opportunity to honor yourselves and to reflect additional glory on your native State. Repose in me, as your commander, the confidence I repose in you as soldiers, and victory shall this day perch upon your Battle Flag, no matter what the odds against us.' 161 *Thus he rides along, uttering these or similar words to each company, and he is answered with shouts, and assurances that they will stand by him to the death. Then his eyes flash, his countenance grows animated, for he knows the battle fever is raging in his ranks. He approaches the few Virginians in his command and addresses them: 'Virginians, you stand upon your native soil and the foot of the foul invader pollutes it. Show yourselves this day worthy representatives of your great State, and let us all unite to hurl back the foe that now advances to make us its prey. Remember the many great and good heroes of your State, and emulate their deeds. 'Give us liberty or give us death,' be your motto.'* 162 *Those gallant Virginians respond with cheers. The allusion to their great heroes has rekindled the fires of their patriotism, and they are ready for the fray.*

It is scarcely necessary for me to say that man was Col. Daniel H. Hill, a native South Carolinian, a brave and well educated soldier, and a Christian warrior. He doubtless has his faults, for no man is perfect; and whatever may be thought of some of his writings, none can doubt his qualifications for fighting. . . . 163

Listen! A low, deep, heavy, hollow sound is heard in the distance. It is the rumblings of wheels; the measured tread of long columns of armed men; the beating of iron hoofs on the hard ground; and various other sounds incident to the marching of a large army. Nearer and nearer approach these sounds, mingled with the rattling of muskets and the jingling of swords; and now comes into view column after column, their muskets, swords and bayonets gleaming in the sun, and the blue uniforms looking like a cloud of destruction about to burst and overwhelm our little band, now grasping their trusty arms. . . . 164 If the hearts of our little band fluttered faster than they did before, and if their blood coursed more rapidly through their veins than usual, fear was not the cause, but natural excitement that the calmest and bravest cannot wholly prevent. They may have grasped their arms more firmly – they may have compressed their lips more tightly, and their eyes may have gleamed with unusual light; but these things only indicated spirits undismayed and souls resolved. There was no quailing – they were nerved for the contest, and ready for it. 165 Suddenly from the Richmond Howitzers belches forth the iron deaths. The columns of the advancing foe are rent and torn, but the gaps are closed and on they come. All at once the leaden messengers are hurled from a thousand rifles and muskets, and they strew the ground with dead and wounded Yankees. Five times as many are hurled at our little Spartan band, but not a man is touched. One continued sheet of flame bursts along our front, and the work grows too hot for Yankee pluck, and they begin to show their backs. A shout goes up from our soldiers, and Yankee legs cannot outstrip our bullets. They fall at every step until beyond our reach, the Howitzers aiding the muskets in the work of death. 166

After a short breathing spell they again approach. Our dauntless heroes retire to their trenches. On come the gaudily dressed Zouaves, with yells like savages, and savages they were in all except disregard for personal safety. Like all bad men they were apparently reckless, but in fact were cowards. Little did they think that, like the sacrifices of ancient times, they were bedecked and ornamented for the slaughter; A few vollies throw them into disorder. They glory in the work of killing, but being killed is a very different thing. They could gloat with fiendish satisfaction over the blood of others; but their coward hearts cannot bear the idea of having their own veins drained. Many have been the helpless and unarmed victims that have fallen beneath their assassin strokes. But here there are two sides to the question. While they would deal death to others, their craven spirits cannot bear the thought of having the compliment returned. The whistling of bullets has no music for their ears, thought they could listen enraptured to the dying moans of the unoffending, slain for purposes of robbery or revenge. 167 *In vain their Colonel, Waldrop, tries to rally them. Elevating himself, with naked sword in hand, he curses them for cowards and tries to shame and exasperate them into bravery. Fool that he was, not to know that true valor dwells not in the bosoms of thieves and murderers. Fool that he was, not to know that such bosoms are insensible to shame. While waving his sword and heaping curses upon his flying scoundrels a ball from a North Carolina musket stretches him lifeless upon the ground. Those of his command able to run, ply their legs with might and main, scattered in all directions, and infusing their terror into others. They had physical force, but no true valor; the depraved are never brave. They are but beasts, and like all beasts, they shrink instinctively from danger, with a wild horror in which all reason, all manliness, all self-possession is lost.* 168

Meantime one of the Howitzers has been rendered useless, on another part of the line, by the breaking of a wire in the vent. Some hundreds of Yankees bravely rush upon the harmless piece and capture it. What a glorious deed! How renowned must they be in history! Have they not fearlessly rushed upon a piece of metal that will not shoot, and dauntlessly laid their hands upon it? Have they not won an elephant, and a dead one at that? Who can blame them for yelling and shouting over the thought of the undying fame that must now forever couple their names with those of the renowned heroes of history? 169 *Short lived congratulation! As bounds the lion upon the more ignoble beasts that are feasting upon the unresisting carcass provided for them by the valor of another, so springs Capt. Bridgers with his seventy five Edgecombe Guards, upon the jubilant Yankees. As flee the meaner animals with reckless fright, so flee these valiant captors of the inoffensive gun. A charge at them is all – upon them requires a fleetness of courage superior to that of fear – something rarely found. The gleam of bayonets was disgusting to their sight and they turned their backs to avoid seeing it, leaving behind them the prize for which they had expended so much breath in noisy shouts. But few of our men had been struck, and not a single one disabled.* 170

Very soon it was perceived that the Yankees were effecting a lodgment in an old house, from which they could very much annoy us. Capt. Bridgers called for volunteers to set fire to the house. Five men sprang forward, young Henry L. Wyatt the foremost among them, each with a brand in his hand. They made a dash for the house, and young Wyatt falls, struck in the forehead by a ball. Scarcely is he upon the ground before his slayer is shot down, and the Yankees speedily evacuate the house. Again repulsed, there is a halt in the battle storm. 171 *Colonel Hill rides along his lines, his face beaming with pride and joy, and is greeted with cheers. Every soldier feels himself a hero. That natural dread which all must feel when going into battle, has worn off, and now they feel invincible. Many of the dead have been borne off, but they can see many still lying where they fell, and they know their arms have been felt.* 172

In about half an hour the enemy again advances, from a different direction, having made a considerable circuit, with the intention of flanking our men and getting in their rear. But their columns plunge into a deep morass and they can neither advance nor retreat. Now does the carnival of death hold high revel in their ranks. In range of our marksmen, they fall by scores, some sinking into the slimy mud and water, the only graves they will ever know. All that can, struggle back, and make haste to put themselves out of reach of our guns. Like frightened sheep they scamper off, and infect their comrades with their own terror. A hasty, disorderly, and disgraceful retreat commences, our cannon accelerating their steps. Our men leap from their fortifications, and pursue the flying foe for several miles. The retreat becomes a rout and our victory is complete. 173 *Thus was hurled back in blood and shame the glittering hosts of Yankee chivalry! that went forth so proudly to capture that handful of 'ragged rebels.' How must old Beast Butler have felt when he saw his troops returning crest-fallen, whipped!* 174 *Our entire loss was one killed and seven slightly wounded; that of the enemy was about three hundred killed and as many more wounded. It is true that we had the advantage of position, but that would have availed us but little for our own superior valor and workmanship. Their balls, at times, flew thick and fast, but mostly far above the heads of our own troops, as if expecting to find them up trees.* 175

Let it be remembered that the first blood, shed in this war, in regular battle, was shed at the battle of Great Bethel; and let it also be remembered that the first blood of a Southern soldier that stained Confederate soil, was the blood of a North Carolinian – young Wyatt, who knew not the meaning of fear, and was insensible to danger when and where duty called. He was but a private soldier, but no braver spirit has more nobly perished on the battle field; whether clad in uniform or in humble garments. And from the day of his death the troops of North Carolina seem to have emulated his example. They have been among the bravest and most reliable troops in our armies, and have been excelled by none." 176

Such powerful words are very difficult to follow. Who can better describe, with such clarity, the wide range of emotions that the Officers and men of the First North Carolina Regiment must have experienced on that eventful day - the very first engagement of the bloody Civil War. Private Wilson was able to convey with so few words the knowledge he garnered as an actual participant of that historic moment. I am truly humbled before Almighty God by this soldier's story, his achievements and his unwavering devotion to his God, his country, and his comrades; as a fellow soldier, Carolinian, American, namesake to the

Hill family, and most importantly as a Christian; I salute him for his courage, bravery and gallantry.

Private Wilson's recorded account provides astonishing and thought provoking insight, not just into the character of D. H. Hill but into all other aspects of that moment in time. His writing generally requires a second, often third read by this author for there is so much within his story to comprehend. I trust you will absorb his message and apply his meaning to my writings as we continue with the Battle of Big Bethel.

BIG BETHEL 1861

CHAPTER VIII

On June 6th 1861 Colonel Hill was placed in command of the First North Carolina Volunteer Regiment under the provisions of Special Order 95, along with Colonel T. P. August and his Regiment of Virginia volunteers. 177 The Governor of North Carolina directed that the *"First Regiment of North Carolina Volunteers"* be formed and directed an election of field officers, resulting in the selection of D. H. Hill, C. O. Lee and J. H. Lane, respectively, to the offices of Colonel, Lieutenant-Colonel and Major. 178 The regiment included a small company of cavalry, a reinforcing battalion of infantry and a seven gun battalion of Richmond Howitzers under the command of Major G. W. Randolph; the latter would become Secretary of War. Colonel Hill's total force for the impending battle numbered 1,400 men. 179 He was ordered by the gallant Virginia Colonel John B. Magruder to make a reconnaissance in force toward the Union position at Fortress Monroe. 180

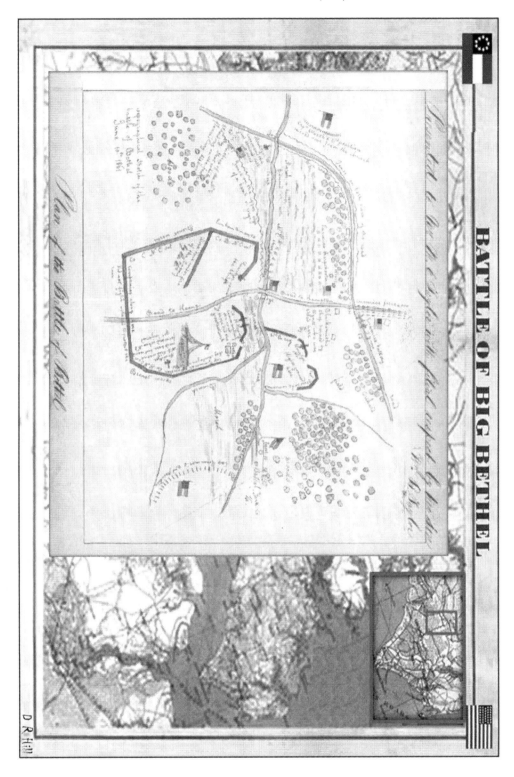

Receiving information that Union General Butler's forces were preparing to advance westward along the Peninsula, Colonel Hill fell back to Big Bethel church and occupied a suitable piece of ground for his initial fighting position. This piece of ground provided some natural tactical defensive advantages. There was a small branch of the Black river running along his front and right flank and an almost impenetrable forest bordering his immediate left. This afforded Colonel Hill a restricted avenue of advance for the enemy. [181] Using twenty-five spades and several hundred bayonets, Hill's men hastily fortified the position, constructing during the night some light earthwork entrenchments. Just prior to the conflict, Colonel Magruder joined Colonel Hill but did not interfere during the course of the battle with Hill's plans or his direction of the force. [182]

The Union General Butler started his advance with five thousand men, formed in three columns, totally confident that two of his detachments would travel via the two roads that passed north and south of Colonel Hill's position at Little Bethel. [183] There he planned to form a junction some two or three miles to the rear of the church where the two roads intersected; planning to first engage Colonel Hill with Colonel Duryea's Regiment of Zouaves along Hill's his front while his other columns united. From there he planned to press Colonel Hill's rear during the anticipated Confederate retreat. [184] Learning that a detachment of Federals was in the vicinity, Colonel Hill directed Lieutenant Colonel Lee with Company F, North Carolina Regiment to drive them back, while Major Lane's Company E, North Carolina Regiment was sent to drive off simultaneous pressure from another marauding party. This display of activity led General Butler, in command of the Federal army, to quickly organize a sizable force of 4,400 men and respond in kind, attempting to drive Colonel Hill's forces away from his vicinity. [185]

During the resulting battle, two Union detachments mistook each other in the darkness and engaged one another in a fierce skirmish. The Zouaves Regiment, instead of following immediately upon the heels of the fugitive rebels as General Butler had anticipated, turned instead to the rear and fled prematurely upon the sounds of musketry volleys to the front of their own reserve line. [186] General Butler continued to stage his forces in the immediate vicinity of Big Bethel as Colonel Magruder arrived with Cary's battalion of infantry and set the Confederate's battle array. [187] At nine o'clock on the historic morning of June 10th 1861 began the first battle of the Civil War. It was an intense fight, pitting the small Confederate forces of 1,200 men against the numerically overwhelming force of 7,500 Union soldiers. After a spirited round of preliminary skirmishing the main battle took place; lasting for two and one half hours and resulting in the complete rout of General Butler's forces; producing chaos and extreme confusion within the ranks of the Yankee troops. 188 The confident, high-spirited Rebel force pursued the surprised and wildly disorganized Yankees as they retreated; haphazardly discarding and scattering their guns, haversacks and knapsacks as they fled the field of the first battle, in great confusion and total disarray. 189

When the hostilities ceased and smoke cleared from the battlefield it was clear to the world that the tactics of Colonel Hill and the actions of the entire Confederate force were brilliantly successful, both in planning and execution. 190 The Federal losses reported by General Butler were eighteen killed, fifty-three wounded, and five missing. On the Confederate side the First North Carolina Regiment lost but one man killed - Private Henry Lawson Wyatt, and six men wounded; the Randolph's Howitzers also had three soldiers wounded in the fight. The Federals retired from the field of battle, foiled and utterly defeated. 191

From the Southern point of view, this first battle of the war raised enthusiasm throughout the South to a feverish pitch and brought great credit upon the soldiers engaged. Although the battle was a mere skirmish compared to the later battles it served to electrify the South, creating an air of confidence among the Confederate soldiers that would be carried with them into the coming, heavy combat at the Battle of Manassas. From the Northern perspective, the battle was nothing less than a major blunder and professional embarrassment for General Butler. 192 Word of the battle and the tremendous victory by the rebel forces spread like wildfire throughout the South, further elevating Hill's reputation as a seasoned combat veteran and extraordinarily brave officer. 193 Colonel D. H. Hill was already well known and highly revered as a soldier with an iron nerve who fearlessly rode unmoved across the field of battle with reckless abandon amid musketry volleys and cannonades of canister, shot and shell. He was quick to hold any laggards or deserters in contempt and would scold them in scathing terms. This was simply his true nature. 194

But those who knew him well were not surprised when, at battle's end, while others were feasting or carousing, D. H. Hill had fallen upon his knees and was returning thanks to Almighty God; whom he believed directed the course of every deadly missile hurled by the enemy with the same unerring certainty that ordered the movements of the multitudes of worlds in the universe, and into whose keeping he daily committed himself, his wife and little ones, his staff and his soldiers; prayerfully with the calm reliance of a child, that as a kind father God would provide what was best for him and them. 195 In a letter written after the battle to his wife, Isabella, Hill said: *"I have to thank God for a great and decided victory, and that I escaped with a minor contusion on the knee."* In another, he said: *"It is a little singular that my first battle in this war should be at Bethel, the name of the church where I was baptized and worshipped until 16 years old. The Church of my mother, was she not a guardian spirit in the battle averting the ball and the shell. Oh God, give us gratitude to Thee and may we never dishonor Thee by a weak faith."* 196

Learning of this great triumph, the North Carolina convention authorized the First North Carolina Regiment to inscribe the word *"Bethel"* upon their banner and it was proclaimed throughout the South that Colonel Hill and the Bethel Regiment had *"covered themselves with glory."* North Carolina's Governor Ellis recommended to the convention that Colonel Hill should be promoted to the rank of Brigadier General and that a full brigade be formed and placed under his command. When the North Carolina troops were turned over to the Confederate Government on August 10th 1861 Colonel Hill was the first officer of the State to be appointed a Brigadier General 197 by the newly installed President of the Confederacy, Jefferson Davis; and the First North Carolina Regiment was therein immortalized as the *"Bethel Regiment."* 198

"All hail to the brave sons of the Old North State, whom Providence seems to have thrust forward in the first pitched battle on Virginia soil in behalf of Southern rights and independence." 199

PENINSULA CAMPAIGN 1862

CHAPTER IX

Following his service at Big Bethel, Brigadier General Hill was assigned to the command of General Magruder and would again distinguish himself in combat during a series of engagements during the spring and summer of 1861, known as the Peninsula Campaign. 200 The Union's Army of the Potomac, under the command of General George B. McClellan, began the Peninsula campaign with a numerically superior army; comparatively to the size and composition of the Army of Northern Virginia, under the command of General Joseph E. Johnston. Both armies were comprised of brave and intelligent men but there was a great lack of combat experience within both. The ranks of both armies contained many men of military ability, as yet unknown to the world; many of whom were about to be sacrificed upon many of the same fields of battle where the soldiers of General George Washington and the French nobleman and soldier Jean-Baptiste Donatien de Vimeur, comte de Rochambeau had completed the glorious work of American emancipation. It was around Yorktown, already made celebrated by the submission of Lord Cornwallis, that the army of the Potomac was about to fight its first decisive battles.

W. S. HANCOCK

J. F. PORTER

J. B. McCLELLAN

H. HALLECK

J. HOOKER

PROMINENT UNION GENERALS
ARMY OF THE POTOMAC

A. DOUBLEDAY

J. POPE

J. A. DIX

A. E. BURNSIDE

E. SUMNER

H. W. SLOCUM

S. CASEY

J. F. REYNOLDS

W. E. FRANKLIN

Despite the historical associations of the Peninsula, this locality was but little known; a factor which created a dramatic effect upon the many battles fought during this campaign. Mistakes, blunders and miscalculations abound on both sides due to the lack of tactical information available to the commanders. The situation was further aggravated by a complete lack of topographical maps of the area. General McClellan's offensive initiative originated from Fortress Monroe; a Federal installation situated at the farthest point of the peninsula, approximately 115 kilometers in a direct line from Richmond. General McClellan's grand strategy called for a route of entrance toward the Confederate Capitol: bounded on the south by the James River and a vast estuary at Newport News; and at the north, first by an arm of the sea called York River, then by the Pamunkey, its principal tributary.

The region lying between these rivers may be divided into two parts. The first part forms a real peninsula between the salt tide water which ascend York River as far as West Point and the James River beyond City Point. This flat country is extremely wooded and thinly populated; is both sandy and marshy; and is intersected by countless bays. This part forms the peninsula of Virginia. The second part, extending between the Pamunkey and the James River proper to a distance far above Richmond, is covered with magnificent forests. This area is a little better cultivated than the former. Being populated here and there with residences of a few wealthy planters, it is divided longitudinally by the Chickahominy; a river rendered famous in the annals of American colonization by the romantic adventures of the traveler John Smith and the Indian maid Pocahontas. This water course flows through wooded swamps, where impenetrable thickets alternate with groves of tall white oak. The feet of these giant trees are buried in the swamp's ooze while their straight trunks rise to extraordinary heights. After a rain storm, the Chickahominy most often overflows its banks; spreading across the adjacent plans to form sheets of water, which at times is a kilometer in width. Accordingly, the peninsula's terrain presented multiple and formidable obstacles for maneuver and military operations by both armies and thereupon would soon occur many of the great battles of the Civil War.

YORKTOWN 1862

The Union General-in-Chief, George B. McClellan, advanced with his Army of the Potomac on April 2nd 1862, moving 58,000 men and 100 cannons from Fort Monroe up the Peninsula. General Magruder immediately maneuvered to intersect and engage General McClellan between the mouths of the Warwick and Poquosin Rivers, where the divide between these opposite flowing rivers is narrow. The Confederates established their sprawling defensive line behind the Warwick River, extending nearly 13 miles from the James to the York River. General McClellan appeared before this line of defense on April 5th 1861 whereupon his left immediately made a vigorous attack on the right of General Magruder's center. But the Confederate line responded with great authority, surging to quickly repulse the attack.

Taken aback from the spirited resistance of General Magruder's men, the Union General spent the next two days preparing for a siege of the Confederate defenses, distributing 100,000 men along their front, with numerous artillery batteries placed in support of the attack. General Magruder, with his small Confederate force of 11,000 men bravely held their ground as the Union lines pushed forward, endeavoring to break their defenses with overwhelming power.

J. B. MAGRUDER

D. H. HILL

J. E. JOHNSTON

PROMINENT CONFEDERATE GENERALS

YORKTOWN 1862

J. LONGSTREET

J. A. EARLY

G. T. ANDERSON

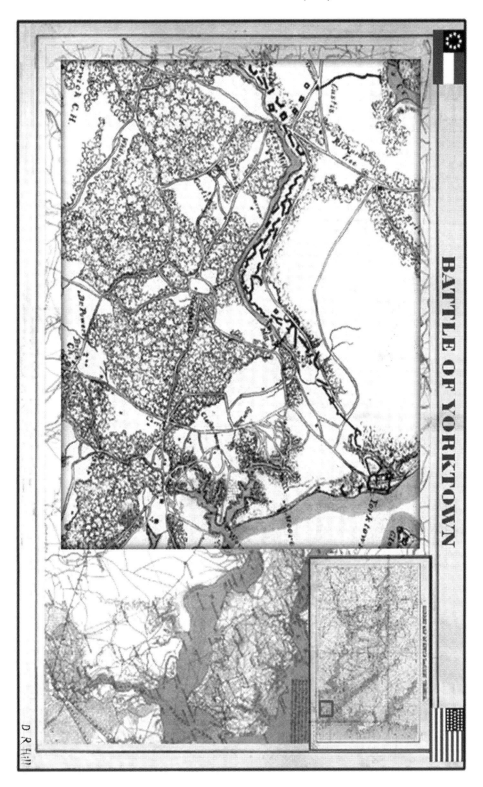

The staunch Confederate defense provided a bold front, giving General Joseph E. Johnston time to move his forces from the Rappahannock River and concentrate them on the Peninsula; effectively barring General McClellan and his army entrance to Richmond. The two armies continued to battle, with General Joseph E. Johnston leading them in a delaying action, pulling back from Yorktown toward Williamsburg. 201

On the afternoon of May 10th 1862 Brigadier General Hill found General Hancock directly to his front, beyond an open field and deployed within a thick stand of trees. The aggressive fighting style of Hill induced him to seek, and obtain from General Longstreet, permission to attack General Hancock's position; in an attempt to drive him from the field. General Hancock's artillery, well placed within a redoubt, was placing upon the troops of General Anderson a withering cannonade, causing great damage to the left of his line. About 5 p.m. General Hill advanced with two North Carolina Regiments and two Virginia Regiments of General Jubal Early's Brigade; taking personal charge of the right while General Early took charge of the left. The attack was bold as the charging rebels advanced gallantly across the open field. But entering the woods, their line became fragmented from the combination of withering fire and barriers within the dense forest, effectively stalling the assault. Generals Hill and Early rapidly reformed on General Anderson's line to strengthen their formation and battled the Union forces to a standstill until darkness fell upon the battlefield. At day's end, Confederate losses totaled 1,560 from their total force of 12,000 soldiers engaged in battle while the Union losses were 2,283 from their attacking force of 15,000 soldiers.

The results of this Williamsburg battle favored the Confederates. They were successful in holding their positions with great determination for the entire day. Their actions enabled General Johnston to fulfill his intent: an unmolested retrograde toward Richmond. Once again, General Hill's contributions were noteworthy, whereupon he received praise and recognition for his valorous fighting and leadership from General Johnston. 202

ASSIGNMENT TO THE DEPARTMENT OF NORTH CAROLINA

In September of 1861 General Hill was sent to Pamlico, North Carolina and placed in a command tasked to strengthen the defenses of the North Carolina coast. His respected military presence had been sought by several prominent North Carolina leaders as a means to inspire discipline and spirit within the Carolina troops. 203 Immediately upon his arrival, General Hill promptly set about realigning his forces to better posture them for the defense of North Carolina. 204 His service, albeit extremely brief, was very gratifying to the public men of the State, prompting the State to later ask for his return during another time of peril. 205 But on November 16th 1861 General Hill was suddenly ordered to report to the Army of Northern Virginia, at the behest of General Joseph E. Johnston 206 and a two weeks later he was appointed commander of a North Carolina Brigade and given command of the left wing of General Johnston's army, with his headquarters stationed in Leesburg, Virginia. 207

It was at this point in history that Brigadier General Hill would come to know another young brigadier who would rise to great fame for his exploits on the fields of battle as the greatest cavalry leader of the war, the daring and dashing James Ewell Brown, known as *"Jeb" Stuart;"* a man of unquestionable courage and charisma. However, all was not friendly between the two Generals from the very beginning of their working relationship and never did a personal relationship develop. There was a common and mutual dislike for one another from the very beginning that would only grow over the course of the Civil War; serving to flame the fires of controversy for D. H. Hill.

General J.E.B. Stewart was a Virginian who was held in high regard and great affection by other Virginians, especially Robert E. Lee, who considered Stuart to be his, and Virginia's, most beloved son. Conversely, General Hill was a revered hero of the Carolinas; cherished and adorned by many Southerners for his displayed gallantry during the Mexican War; highly respected by the young officers of the American army of that era as *"the bravest man in the army."* Of course, Hill's reputation as a fighter had only grown with his recognition as the newly hailed Hero of Bethel. 208

General J.E.B. Stuart was a man of great pageantry and flair, in dress and conduct; known to possess a fondness for lavish Southern galas, even amidst the conduct of the war's many campaigns. Conversely, General Hill was a man of strict Presbyterianism and unyielding in his faith. For D. H. Hill, with his rearing steeped in deep religious beliefs, considered frivolities such as partaking in activities of merriment and of hard drink to be detestable conduct for an officer, nay any man; he considered Stuart to be unsatisfactory, lacking in professional and personal conduct and not measuring up to his highly held standards for army officers' behavior. 209

Finally, General *"Jeb"* Stuart was a cavalryman - a branch of the army for which Hill held little regard and notable disdain. as evidenced by one of his famous quotes: *"You will never find a dead cavalryman with his spurs on."* 210

Given these considerations, D. II. Hill felt compelled to write his cavalry commander and provide a remedy for one of his major concerns with the cavalryman. Hill had noted with precision Stuart's loss of 194 soldiers during an earlier engagement with Federal troops at Dranesville, Virginia. Hill's mild, written rebuke was not an uncommon, fully justifiable action that any good Infantry Commander might take to mentor a supporting commander.

In a December 1861 letter, Hill he wrote to his cavalry commander:

"From what I have been able to learn, the enemy knew your strength and destination before you started . . . . I would therefore respectfully suggest that when you start again, you should disguise your strength and give out a different locality from that actually taken." D. H. Hill ended the letter: *"Excuse me the liberty I take, and believe me your sincere well wisher and friend."* Although mild in manner, this rebuke fueled a restrained dislike between the *"Carolinian"* and the *"Virginian"* that would grow as the war progressed. 211

Despite their unfriendly personal relationship, whether real or perceived, history records no evidence that this dispute diminished either of the legendary Generals' heroic accomplishments in any way.

D. H. HILL

"Intemperance or dissipation in any form was for him the unpardonable sin. D. H. Hill was a man of literary attainments, an assiduous student of Holy Scripture, and as a teacher of mathematics unsurpassed among American teachers."

[[Colonel Henry Elliott Shepherd]]

Q4

THE FORMATION OF D. H. HILL'S DIVISION

On March 26th 1862, after nearly 5 months of service with his North Carolina Brigade, commanding the left wing of Johnston's army, D. H. Hill was duly recognized for his valorous and gallant service when he received his commission as a Confederate Major General. 212 Marking this occasion, the Confederacy created the infamous Confederate D. H. Hill Division; an official unit designation which the division carried throughout the entire war, even when Hill was later reassigned to other duties and promoted to Lieutenant General. 213

For the next two historic years, D. H. Hill's Division would become an integral and immortal command of the Army of Northern Virginia. 214 The first decisive engagement for the newly formed D. H. Hill's Division occurred on May 4th 1862 during the Battle of Williamsburg. 215

D. H. HILL

"Stonewall Jackson repeatedly declared in my hearing that there was not...a man in the Southern Army, superior in military genius to D.H. Hill."

[[Colonel *James W. Ratchford*]]

Q17

WILLIAMSBURG 1862

The Confederate army's retrograde to Williamsburg began the evening of May 3rd 1862 with Jubal Early's brigade and the Twenty Fourth North Carolina Regiment assigned the duties of rear guard. 216 It had rained constantly for weeks and the roads, having been under high use, had become filled with mud and water ankle to knee deep. The Union forces had firm tactical control of both the James and York Rivers on either flank and intended to push up the York to get into the Confederate's rear. Orders called for General Joseph E. Johnston's Army of Northern Virginia to march to the Chickahominy at early dawn, with General Longstreet designated to bring up the rear. As General Hill's infantry slogged their way down the nearly impassable road, orders came to halt the march and return to Williamsburg. The Union's Army of the Potomac, under the command of General George B. McClellan, had approached and was aligning his forces to form a battle array in order to skirmish with the Confederate rear guard. General Johnston was not unwilling to turn and deal the Union forces a blow, if for no other reason, to demonstrate how, even in retreat, the morale of his army was good and as able to fight in retrograde as if on a victorious advance. General Hill directed his trains to continue on but ordered his infantry and some portion of his artillery to accompany his return to Williamsburg.

J. B. MAGRUDER

D. H. HILL

J. E. JOHNSTON

PROMINENT CONFEDERATE GENERALS

WILLIAMSBURG 1862

J. LONGSTREET

J. A. EARLY

L. McLAWS

The rain continued to fall and the distinct sound of battle could be heard as General Longstreet faced increasing pressure from Federal skirmish lines. General Magruder had directed the hasty construction of a cordon of redoubts, running from Queen's creek to the James River. The center of the Confederate line was Fort Magruder, a large, well constructed complex with closed earthworks, located on the main road from Williamsburg, Virginia. To the right, General Longstreet had moved to occupy the redoubts on the James River side with General Hill covering the potential avenues that might provide approach by the enemy. The left of the line was mostly unmanned - guarded by the treacherous and impassable swamps stretching along its front. 217 By afternoon of May 4th 1862 the Union vanguard arrived and pushed forward their cavalry against the positions of Generals McLaws, Semmes' and Kershaw's brigades. But overwhelming pressure by the Confederate forces caused the Union vanguard to retire.

The next morning intense skirmishing produced no more than an inconclusive outcome. General Hooker, being heavily reinforced by General Kearney, attacked the Confederate right with great energy. But his advance was met with even greater pressure and he was driven back and nearly routed. The battle raged throughout the day as General Longstreet firmly and successfully held the Confederate line, all but extinguishing the Federal's designs on the Confederate rear. 218 Union General *"Bull"* Sumner, acting in the capacity of General-in-chief for General McClellan at the time, had arrived early morning on May 5th 1862 with 30,000 men. But he chose to sit quietly down and across the Yorktown road, just out of sight and cannon range of the field of battle. He took little part in the battle unfolding around him and, despite the near rout of both Generals Hooker's and Kearney's forces, he declined to part with a single man to aid their cause. Union General Hancock, in an bold tactical move, actually moved into the empty redoubt on the Confederate left but, in a fortunate decision for the Confederates, General Hancock was commanded by General Sumner to return to his previous position. 219 General Hancock's strength of forces, while in the redoubt, was such that he could have wreaked havoc upon the Confederate line and, had he been allowed to do so, would have had an open road all the way to Williamsburg. Such an action would have placed the rear of General Longstreet in extreme jeopardy as well. Generals Hill and Early, both anxious for a fight, asked and received orders to assault General Hancock and drive him away. However, before they could launch their assault, General Hancock, acting upon orders from General Sumner, withdrew from the vacant redoubt for the evening. 220

At day's end, the Confederate defenders had beaten off every attack made upon them. Before the next morning, under the cautious proviso of General Johnston *"to be careful,"* the whole Confederate line was abandoned. Without delay, the brigades of General Hill and General Jubal Early, eager still for the fight, moved at the command of double-quick toward the front. The Confederate columns rushed forward nearly a mile down the Yorktown road then moved to file short to their left for another distance of about one-quarter mile. This difficult movement required the crossing of a newly plowed, soft and muddy field. Generals Hill and Early then positioned their forces, with Hill in the lead and taking charge of the right wing to form his battle line with the Fifth and Twenty Third North Carolina Regiments; General Jubal Early took charge of the left wing, forming a like array with his Twenty Fourth Virginia Regiment. Shortly thereafter was given the daring command of General Hill to *"load"* then *"fix bayonets."* 221

> ## D. H. HILL
>
> *"was a man of considerable capacity and always seemed to go from choice into the most dangerous place he could find on the field."*
>
> *[[Lieutenant General James Longstreet]]*
>
> Q2

As the line moved steadily forward, rifles at the ready, bayonets gleaming, there was an *"impatient valor and restlessness"* among the men. They advanced magnificently across the field with their alignment proper and true. But no enemy was yet encountered. With the crossing of the field accomplished, they then passed through the tangled woods, descending a steep hill and crossing a country road. From there they moved back into the forest and up another steep incline. Although breathless and weary, the high-spirited Rebel force continued their advance; still no enemy was to be found. Suddenly before them appeared a long, stretching cordon of redoubts. The Twenty Fourth Virginian Regiment fronted the large Union force, surprising them with a furious assault against the five full regiments, ten cannons and four thousand muskets of General Hancock. The Union troops suddenly found themselves positioned directly in front of the charging rebels, with their backs against the redoubts. The fighting was fierce as the Twenty Fourth Virginians, outmanned by the overwhelming Federal force before them at the redoubt, began to weaken and disorder began to fall upon their line; the two brigades assigned to the middle were nowhere to be found and the lone regiment covering the right wing had moved into position, but much too far to its right and well after the Twenty Fourth Virginia Regiment had already become decisively engaged. The Twenty Fourth Virginia Regiment found itself in what can best be described to any Infantry commander as a surrealistic nightmare: facing an overwhelming force – alone and unsupported. With complete surprise came the boldest of all commands from the officers up and down the Confederate line: *"double quick"* and *"charge."* Upon hearing the commands, be they insane, brilliant, or just a desperate act of survival, the courageous rebels charged with iron nerve and pressed forward toward the enemy. The Federals responded by applying overwhelming firepower, bringing oppressive, withering fire upon the gray lines. Showers of lead from Union musketry fire, combined with grape and canister of their field guns, were concentrated upon the Confederate officers and men as they fell dead and wounded on every side. Undaunted and despite the Union's devastating fire, the Rebel charge advanced with extraordinary enthusiasm, causing the enemy to falter. 222

General Early's horse was shot from beneath him and, in just another moment, he himself sustained a serious wound. Suddenly, from the Confederate right appeared the Fifth North Carolina Regiment, advancing with a great charge across the large field to join the fight. Having made adjustments to compensate for their initial misalignment, the men of the Fifth North Carolina Regiment moved with great gusto as they crossed the open field. But they quickly encountered horrendous musketry and cannon fire as the Union forces shifted a portion of their combat power to address the advancing regiment. Meanwhile, the daring charge by the Twenty Forth Virginia Regiment had advanced to within 20 feet of the Yankees, successfully pressing them backward to the most forward edge of the redoubt. Their success, however, came at an extreme cost as the withering Federal fire had so eviscerated the Virginians that nearly every other man had fallen. Then was heard the distinct order for the Union artillery to *"cease firing"* and *"limber up."* Suddenly there was great confusion within the Union ranks; their bayonets seem tangled and interlocked as they make off to the rear amidst calls from their officers to *"halt"* and *"stand ready men."* In a word, General Hancock's five regiments and ten guns had been attacked and driven off by a single Virginia regiment, to the point of being routed. Hence came the order from General Hill for the Confederates to withdraw, anticipating that the enemy would reform and retaliate with great effect. As the Fifth North Carolina Regiment pulled back across the open field to the cover of the tree line, the Twenty Fourth Virginia Regiment performed a left oblique movement into the woods to its left flank, retiring under cover without further damage. 223

Major General Hill, addressing the *"daring and dash"* of his two regiments, offered this commendation: *"The courage exhibited by the Fifth North Carolina and the Twenty Fourth Virginia made, too, a wonderful impression upon the Yankees, and doubtless much of the caution exhibited in their subsequent movements was due to the terror inspired by the heroism of these noble regiments. History has no example of a more daring charge. . . . It contributed largely to detain McClellan, to demoralize his troops and to secure our retreat from a vigorous and harassing pursuit."* 224

While personally leading his first line and attacking with utmost vigor, Generals Hill and Jubal Early were conspicuous for their gallantry and rendered upon General McClellan a staggering and bloody check. The opposing General there, *"the gallant Hancock,"* reported of the action that the 5th North Carolina Regiment and the Twenty Fourth Virginia Regiment *"deserved to have the word immortal inscribed on their banners."* Joseph E. Johnston's confidence in D. H. Hill grew ever stronger while General Longstreet reported of the action: *"Major General Hill, a hero of many battlefields, was conspicuous for ability and courage in planning the left attack."* 225

Always, D.H. Hill served with demonstrated valor and great efficiency in resisting any Federal advances and his reputation of absolute fearlessness continued to spread, securing for himself the growing respect and confidence of the entire army. 226 The written Official Records of the Union and Confederate Armies have recorded for immortality the undeniable evidence of General Hill's courageous fighting manner; from the very first moment he assumed command of a division in March of 1862 until his last courageous actions at war's end on the battlefield at Bentonville, North Carolina, in what would be the war's last battle: *"Hill's position, 'on every march' and 'in every battle,' with scarcely a single exception, is recorded in history, as within the official records of the Union and Confederate armies, that Hill was always to be found in a post of danger and honor."* General Hill's was the first division of Johnston's army to enter Yorktown and the last to leave; it was the charge at Williamsburg that Jubal Early described as *"an attack upon the vastly superior forces of the enemy, which for its gallantry is unsurpassed in the annals of warfare."* 227

SEVEN PINES 1862

On the eve of the Battle of Seven Pines, General Joseph E. Johnston had continued the retrograde of his Army of Northern Virginia from the Peninsula while General McClellan's Army of the Potomac methodically continued pushing the Confederates toward their capital in Richmond Virginia. At this juncture of the Peninsula Campaign it was the end of May 1862 and General McClellan was poised to cross the Chickahominy River with his numerically superior army; determined in his strategy to threaten Richmond. But the Union General-in-chief advanced with great caution in reaction to faulty intelligence that led him to believe he was greatly outnumbered by the Confederates.

On the morning of May 30th 1862 General Hill's troops were encamped in the vicinity of the Chickahominy, having just endured an overnight thunderstorm of unusual intensity that seemed to shake the heavens, openly exposing his men to the violent elements and a driving rainstorm. The seasonal late spring rains habitually rendered the low lying banks along the Chickahominy nearly impassable, turning them into swamps. 228 Early on May 31st General Hill prepared his forces for another decisive engagement, as it was the intent of General Joseph E. Johnston to attack the enemy's left that faced them directly across the Chickahominy. 229

J. LONGSTREET

D. H. HILL

J. E. JOHNSTON

W. H. C. WHITING

B. HUGER

PROMINENT CONFEDERATE GENERALS

SEVEN PINES 1862

S. GARLAND

R. E. RODES

G. B. ANDERSON

R. H. ANDERSON

A. JENKINS

G. PICKETT

L. A. ARMISTEAD

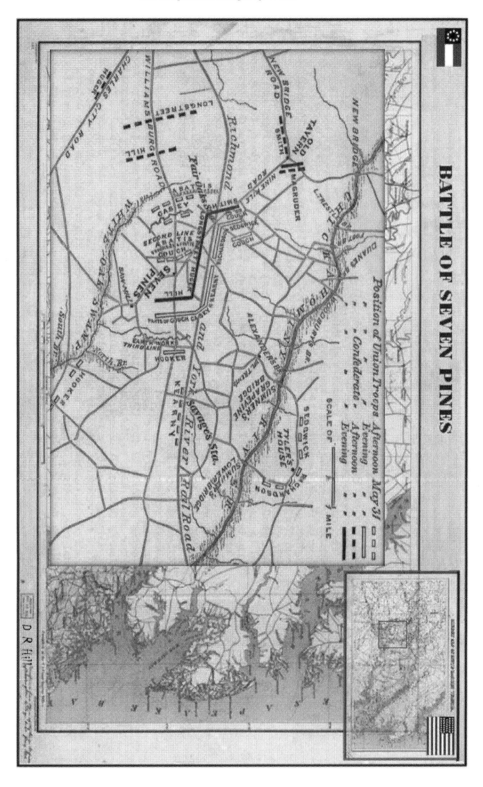

The pouring rainfall had swollen the stream above its banks and the entire area along the creek stood flooded with water. Many of the bridges had been swept away by the swift currents and General Johnston sought to use the weather to gain a tactical advantage. His plan was to launch a bold attack against the Union left, knowing that the swollen river and destroyed bridges would hinder any Union efforts to send reinforcements from their center and right. He would let the waters of God bind the Union's body and right arm while he would crush the left arm of his enemy. General Johnston would send General Huger down the Charles City road toward the Union's extreme left where he would outflank and turn the enemy; General Longstreet would send Generals Hill and Anderson to lead his forces down the Williamsburg road to engage the enemy's center front; and General Whiting would advance down the railroad and engage the enemy's right side. [230] In preparation for the coming engagement, General Hill instructed the brigades of Generals Garland and Rodes to send out pickets a few days before the battle to determine the size and composition of the enemy's force before him. General Garland was guarding the Williamsburg road while General Rodes was defending the Charles City road. General Hill ordered an armed reconnaissance and personally accompanied these officers whereupon he was satisfied that the enemy was not in force on the Charles City road. However he learned through the reconnaissance that there was a substantial, well fortified force along the Williamsburg road in the vicinity of Seven Pines and that the whole of Union General Keyes' corps had crossed the Chickahominy. [231] Communicating this information to General Johnson around noon on Friday May 30th he received a prompt reply, saying that General Johnston was satisfied by his report on the presence of the enemy in force to his immediate front and that the General-in-chief was resolute to attack, thus directing General Hill to serve with General Longstreet under his orders. [232] Upon receipt of orders from General Longstreet, General Hill moved his Division at dawn on May 31st 1862 along the Williamsburg road, in preparation to lead the attack upon the Yankees. However, General Longstreet's order clearly stipulated that he was not to begin the attack until relieved in position by the division of General Huger. Around 10 a. m. General Hill marched his men down the muddy Williamsburg road, arraying them in the woods to the right side of the road with General Anderson's men to the left, and waited anxiously for the signal to attack. But after an hour of waiting there were still no sounds of General Huger's guns to indicate that the battle had begun. General Longstreet was affronted by the slow pace of General Huger's advance. Around noon he concluded that General Huger must not yet be in position and decided to initiate the attack without further delay. [233]

Preparations for the attack were complete and the battle array set; General Rodes' Brigade was on the right of the road, supported by General Rains' brigade; General Garland was on the left, supported by General G. B. Anderson. 234 Preceding each wing of the attack was a regiment deployed as skirmishers. Having been long delayed in waiting for the relieving force, the Confederate right wing did not advance for a quarter of an hour after the left's movement. This delay resulted in exposing Generals Garland and Anderson to the lethal fire of the whole Yankee force. Recognizing the situation on the field, the right wing was hurried forward, moving handsomely to preserve the Confederate line, despite the difficult challenge of wading through mud and water, in many places 2 to 3 feet deep. 235 Precisely at 1 p. m., although General Huger had not yet arrived with his relieving force in accordance with the orders, the signal guns were fired and General D. H. Hill's Division moved off in fine style; General Rodes' brigade advanced along the right of the road, supported by General Rains' brigade; General Garland's brigade moved forward on the left, supported by G. B. Anderson. 236 It was a grand movement as the entire Confederate line advanced in superb fashion through the woods toward several Union brigades, tactically positioned along a series of well fortified redoubts and field works in the vicinity of Barker's farm. The 4th North Carolina Regiment courageously moved forward at the *"double quick"* and engaged the initial enemy defenders, effectively flanking and dispersing them to clear the way for the main attack. 237 Cannon shot and canister fire from the Union batteries tore through the trees, inflicting considerable loss upon the advancing troops, as Generals Hill and Anderson maneuvered their way forward through the woods toward the large open field that spread between the tree line and Barker's farm. But the cannons supporting General Hill's advance could not return the withering fire, being deeply mired in the mud along the Williamsburg road. Arriving at the edge of the woods, General Hill, drawing the uncontested hail of oppressive Union cannon fire, made the determination that further advance was impractical; Accordingly, he ordered his men into positions of defilade to escape the oppressive cannon fire until the line completely formed. General Hill was impatient to begin but, upon the advice of his men, he dismounted. However, instead of going to the rear, in typical Hill fashion, he quietly leaned upon his horse's neck and critiqued the enemy's fire; yet another display of his coolness under fire, representative of the Fighting General's fearless nature and a demonstrative example of why his soldiers would so boldly follow him onto any field of battle, against any foe

As the Confederate line finally began to take full form along General Hill's front, Generals Huger and Whiting had not yet expended a cartridge. The enemy, mistaking Hill's inaction for indecision, began to advance wherein they were instantly punished by a pummeling sheet of musketry fire, unleashed upon them as General Hill ordered the *"charge."* Given the absence of earthworks to the right and left, Hill directed his men to flank and attack their center. 238 General Hill detached General Rains to make a wide flanking movement, endeavoring to take the Yankee works in reserve, while General Rodes's Brigade moved steadily to the front. This flank attack was most opportunistic and proved to be of great importance. Before they reached the Yankee abattis, Generals Garland and Anderson had captured a 2-gun battery that had been enfilading the road with undulating fire. 239 Suddenly, finally, the Confederate cannons of Bondurant joined the fight and began placing murderous fire upon the Yankee's position, providing immediate relief for the advancing lines of infantry as the Union batteries shifted the bulk of their fire to counter-fire upon the now engaging rebel batteries of artillery. General Hill noticed a great commotion and much confusion in the redoubts as the Yankees began to evacuate the position. General Rodes took skillful advantage of this commotion and, amidst a chorus of rebel yells, moved his brigade forward in beautiful fashion; pushing forward through the low brushwood in front of the redoubt. Then, upon the signal of the flanking parties, these gallant men made a rush for the cannons; cleared them, entered pell-mell into the earthworks and bayoneted all who remained standing in opposition. 240

In the course of many Civil War battles, two distinct differences always seemed to emerge in the differing mannerisms and methods that *"Johnny Reb"* and *"Yank"* habitually displayed in their response to the command *"charge."* First was the line - their manner of alignment while in the attack. Upon the command *"charge,"* the Union soldiers would place great emphasis on preserving their alignment and spacing. On the other hand, the Confederate soldiers usually went into the charge at a run, with an everyman, more or less, for himself approach; The Union's methods often presented their soldiers as open targets for both musketry and cannon fire while the disjointed appearance of the advancing Confederate line, seeming to be most disorganized, often caused Union soldiers to mistakenly judge the approaching rebel line as disorganized when, actually, the Confederate attack would be extremely organized and often more daring in pitch and intensity. Second was the infamous *"rebel yell."* There was always an curious difference between the battle cries of the Union and Confederate soldiers. Veterans of the Civil War often spoke passionately of these two different, distinguishing traits. When attacking, the *"Yank"* would implore a normal cry, like: *"hurrah – hurrah – hurrah,"* a simple cheer which lacked stirring life. But the cries of *"Johnny Reb"* were yells of an intensely nervous description, every man for himself yelling *"Yai, Yai, Yi, Yai, Yi!"* - fierce shrieks made from each man's throat individually, and which can't be described or replicated except under the excitement of an assault in actual battle. 241

The Confederate advance was executed so rapidly and performed so fiercely, the Yankees abandoned six of their cannons. Quickly, General Rodes resourcefully turned them upon the retreating column with great effect, giving the Yankees a taste of their own canister and grape. The supporting Confederate cannons were drawn quickly into position and joined the fires of the six captured cannons; successfully repulsing an attempt of fresh Yankee troops to recapture the works. General D. H. Hill's Division had now captured eight pieces of artillery, the camp, a large number of tents therein, and the stores of a brigade. Their fierce assault had successfully driven the Yankees back 1 1/2 miles, forcing them to abandon a wide skirt of abattis, rifle pits, and redoubts. D. H. Hill's Division decisively defeated General Casey's division, including all the reinforcements that had moved forward in support of his line. Hill's men had satisfactorily pushed the entire complement of Union soldiers completely from the field, driving them into the woods and dismal swamps of the Chickahominy. 242

D. H. Hill's Division, having taken their first objective of the battle, had reformed rapidly and continued to advance successively through and past the Union positions, one after the other, exacting upon them a similar action and fate as with their capture of the first earthworks, advancing from redoubt to redoubt, as the battle continued to rage with great fury throughout the afternoon. The men's display of courage was simply magnificent as they advanced valiantly under continuous shell and grape. 243 Clearly possessing the initiative, General Hill continued to press upon the Yankees with great vigor, requesting that General Longstreet provide another brigade in order to exploit their success on the field. Within moments, the magnificent brigade of General R. H. Anderson moved to sustain the attack, bringing with him sufficient power to overwhelm the Yankees. General Anderson and the battle flags of the Louisianans and North Carolinians; General Jenkins and the flag of the South Carolinians; Generals Wilcox and Pryor with the flags of the Mississippians and Alabamians; merged their lines. The united force renewed their joint attack with a great shout of such immense proportion and volume the enemy for a brief moment ceased their firing. 244 General Anderson deployed his Palmetto Sharpshooters and the Sixth South Carolina Regiment to the extreme left, resolute to scour along the railroad and Nine-mile road with intentions to get in rear of the enemy. 245 But as General R. H. Anderson led them to within just a few yards of the enemy line, the Federals opened a murderous volley of fire upon them from their cover in the woods. The gallant men of General Anderson's command responded with great valor. With the support of extremely accurate fires from Confederate cannons that placed a devastating enfilade barrage upon the Union positions, Anderson's men launched yet another daring assault against the Federal line, casting them into great confusion whereupon they were soon in full retreat. With their lines joined and coordinated, General Hill's men continued the attack, facing a renewed strength and vigor from the freshly reinforced Union forces, vigorously attempting to breach the abattis that covered the front of their earthworks and served as protection for supporting Union batteries of artillery. While the enemy reinforcement's displayed much precision and neatness in their arrival, these fresh troops offered more numbers yet presented little more resistance that before. 246

By 4 p.m. General Hill, being in the lead of General Longstreet's corps attack, had driven the enemy down the Williamsburg road a mile through their camps; capturing along the way prisoners, stores, cannons, flags, redoubts and a whole Union bivouac and their standing tents. Still the battle raged and General Hill found himself far to the front of the Confederate's general line, creating a triangular formation with Hill's men at the point of the triangle and Generals Whiting's and Huger's at the corners of the triangle's base; having yet to make any attempt in the battle. Detecting the exposed positioning of General Hill's forces and estimating his position to be untenable, the Union forces mounted a spirited counterattack against his courageous but exhausted men. But General Hill, undaunted in his commitment to stand his ground, occupied one of the captured enemy's field works and turned their captured cannons upon them along with murderous discharges of Confederate musketry; throwing back the Union counter-assault. As darkness approached, General Johnston directed General Whiting to advance, in order, to draw Union fire and alleviate the pressure on General Hill.

With the additional support from General Whiting's movements, General Hill continued the attack, driving the Yankees completely off Barker's farm and from the surrounding openings pushed them into the woods. 247 General Hill directed the Brigades of Generals R. H. Anderson and Jenkins to vigorously pursue the fleeing enemy. Portions of General G. B. Anderson's brigade was deployed to join the pursuit, sweeping along the left of the road and driving brigade after brigade of the Yankees before them; in the process capturing two more cannon, several camps, with their commissary and quartermaster's stores intact. Finally, after dark, the attack reached a brief respite. The Confederate forces had, at this point, driven the enemy completely from the field of battle, pushing them over a mile beyond the main works of the Yankees at Seven Pines. 248

During the battle, the cannons of Dearing's battery placed in support of the attack by General Longstreet, had delivered a cannonade of deadly canister, grape and shell upon the enemy with devastating effect; performing their duty in a most heroic manner and contributing greatly to the total defeat of the enemy force to the front of General D. H. Hill's Division. 249 There were remaining in the woods on the right of the road, a strong Union force and General Hill was determined to drive them completely from the field as well. He quickly sent his adjutant to General Rains, who was positioned nearby, and issued him a written order to move farther to the right to take the Yankee in flank while General Rodes would move over the open ground for a frontal assault upon the Yankees in the woods. However, as General Rains was met with galling fire, his advance was checked, with a portion of his line repulsed by the Yankee line. In response, General Hill received additional support from General Longstreet with the arrival of General Kemper's brigade, who was sent by General D.H. Hill to move directly in support of General Rodes' frontal assault. However, General Kemper was unsuccessful in his support and General Rodes's men suffered extreme losses from the concentrated fires of the Union forces in the woods. By nightfall, nonetheless, the Yankees were driven out of the woods, with General D. H. Hill's Division taking undisputed possession of all the ground a mile around and in advance of the redoubt, which had been the objective of the attack. The tents and commissaries of the Yankee General Casey were found to be in excellent condition, providing excellent provisions for the men in General D. H. Hill's Division. The results of the assault produced a resounding victory on the field of battle, although his division had sustained casualties sufficient to weaken his combat power by one brigade in the process and his strength was now less than 9,000 men. But they had driven the Yankees decisively from the field with great authority; fighting fiercely with the odds against them two to one in numbers; with this disparity rendered even more formidable by the enemy's use of their abattis and earth-works. 250 In the darkness, General Whiting continued to press the enemy to his front into the woods, in the direction of the railroad. All the while, fierce cannonry continued to fall. General Johnston and his staff rode to the front and, while directing the attack, a piece of cannon shell wounded the General-in-chief severely in his groin. The shock stunned him and he fell from his horse, breaking two ribs, wherein he was evacuated from the field with expectations from the troops that he had been mortally wounded. Addressing the injury to General Johnston, a soldier from General Hill's command commented: *"Just to think that our best Generals will poke themselves in the front – Sydney Johnston was lost in that way, and I have see both Longstreet and Hill foolishly riding in front of the enemy not less than a dozen times to-day. Hill must be a shadow or an immortal, for he exposed himself often enough today to get his quietus a dozen times to-day."* 251

At daylight on the morning of June 1st 1862, General Johnston heavily reinforced General D. H. Hill's Division by bringing forward two additional Confederate divisions; Generals Huger and Heitzelman of General Longstreet's command; the remainder of General Longstreet's command included the brigades of Generals Pickett, Wilcox, Colston and Pryor who had moved into position. General G. W. Smith found himself decisively engaged along the Nine-mile road, while General D. H Hill resolved to concentrate his troops around the captured works, anticipating with great hope that the Yankees would attempt to retake them and issued orders to the advance brigades of Generals

Pickett, Pryor, and Wilcox to draw in their extended lines and form along the headquarters of Union General Casey. 252 But before these orders were received a furious attack was made upon Generals Armistead, Mahone, Pickett, Pryor, and Wilcox. General Armistead's men were very early pushed back and fled under extreme pressure, with the exception of a few heroic companies whose gallant officers maintained their ground against an entire brigade of attacking Yankees. General Mahone, being under strenuous attack as well, was forcefully driven back in great confusion. General Hill's men, except for the brigade of General Pickett, were forced to pull back and reorganize. However, in one of the most gallant displays of heroism on the field, General Pickett's men refused to yield their ground; against the odds of ten to one, for several hours longer, with a strong counterattack, retiring only after the Yankees had ceased to annoy him. The Yankees prudently chose not to reform for another attack and contented themselves for the balance of the day in a desultory fire of artillery, which hurt no one and was only attended with the gratifying result of stampeding the amateur fighters and the camp plunderers from Richmond.

With the Confederates successfully thwarting the vigorous Union assault, the enemy thought better of attacking their reorganized lines and withdrew in an organized fashion from the field. During the fight, the Confederates had captured ten cannons, 6,700 muskets and rifles in fine condition, ordnance, commissary, and a large quantity of medical stores, along with the 10 captured guns that had been removed the night before. With the Yankees occupying the ground to the rear of D. H. Hill's position along the Nine-mile road, he executed the delicate operation of withdrawing his men in the presence of a numerically superior Union force. This night withdrawal was extremely challenging due to road conditions. The thirteen Confederate brigades did not co-join until near midnight. Thus the delicate operation of withdrawing 30,000 men in the presence of a superior force of the enemy had to be expedited and performed before daylight. Aggravating the difficult night move, the heavy traffic of wagons and artillery caissons had converted the road into a condition of slush and mud holes, axle deep to the wagons and nearly impassable for infantry. Nonetheless, General Hill's men completed the move in fine order and regained their entrenchments by sunrise without leaving behind a single cannon, caisson, wagon, or straggling soldier. 253 As morning approached, anticipating a counter-attack in force, General Hill was ordered to pull his forces back to his original position from the previous day. It had been a glorious and victorious operation on the field of battle. Yet again, General Hill's command had performed with great valor and, by battle's end, the Division's gallant charge, Hill's men fighting with unsurpassed courage, served to demoralize the Union forces. Although the great majority of his men had never before been in battle, they distinguished themselves by infusing an undaunted spirit into the whole Confederate line.

After this decisive victory, under such difficult circumstances, not a brigade in the ranks seemed to entertain the remotest doubt of achieving ultimate success over the besieging army of Yankees. 254 But the grand plan envisioned by General Joseph E. Johnston had fallen inadequately short. The lack of speed and intensity with which General Huger had moved his troops caused great dismay within the leadership of the Confederacy, from General Longstreet, now the acting General-in-chief for the wounded General Johnston, up to and including President Jefferson Davis. Instead of crushing the left arm of the enemy and winning a decisive battle to set the stage for the complete destruction of the Army of the Potomac, the Union army, although bloodied and battered, was afforded the opportunity for yet another cautious withdrawal; denying General Johnston of his opportunity for total victory and the Yankees taking opportunity to reconstitute, reorganize, and rearm their troops for the next battle. 255 After the close of the Civil War, a Union officer wrote to General Joseph E. Johnson, asking the name of a Confederate officer who, on the right of his army at Seven Pines, had made himself most conspicuous for his daring and indifference to danger. The only mark of distinction which he could give General Johnston was that the officer rode a white horse. General Johnston replied that the officer to whom he was referring was D. H. Hill. Later, in writing to General D H Hill about the matter, General Johnston said: *"I drew my conclusion that your horse might very well have been taken for white and that no man was more likely to expose himself than you. Do you know that in Mexico the young officers called you the bravest man in the army?"* 256

Of the Battle of Seven Pines, Judge Avery wrote: *"no engagement of the war has given rise to more acrimonious censure and crimination than Seven Pines."* Then he added: *"The future historians who shall make up for posterity their verdict upon the controverted points as to the Battle of Seven Pines will find out one fact admitted by all of the disputants, that D. H. Hill was the hero of the occasion, and with his own gallant division, aided by two of Longstreet's Brigades, drove the enemy in confusion from the breastworks and turned their own guns upon them as they retreated."* 257 General D. H. Hill's Division had performed brilliantly throughout the Spring of 1862, as Union forces had labored to maneuver up the Peninsula between the James and York Rivers. Staunch Confederate pressure and resistance on the battlefield however served to stall the Union initiatives at every turn.

The Confederate General-in-chief of the Army of Northern Virginia - Joseph E. Johnson - had recently commended both Hill and his men for gallantry under fire and given them due recognition for their contributions to the army's success to date. Hill's reputation as a ferocious fighter continued to gain prominence and his notoriety continued to grow. Unfolding before Hill was the greatest conflict of arms of modern times. He had become revered for his bravery as a fierce fighter during Mexican War and his courage greatly acknowledged with the presentation of a golden saber that elevated him to hero status in the Carolinas; his military career had risen to even loftier heights at this juncture of the Civil War, marked with promotions from Colonel, Brigadier General, then Major General; he was bestowed with laudatory praise for his gallantry and heroism on the field of battle at Bethel, Yorktown and Williamsburg; the potential for even further greatness stood before him, as an open door, for which he seemed by Providence to enter and fulfill his destiny; with many hard fought battles that would surely come. But the severe wounding of General Joseph E. Johnston brought change that would impact Hill's career; command of Joseph E. Johnston's Army of Northern Virginia passed to the revered General Robert E. Lee. 258

D. H. HILL

"Hill's presence was always sufficient to give full assurance that we were in the right place and we had only to fight to win"

[[Colonel Walter Clark – 17th NC regiment]]

Q1

SEVEN DAYS 1862

Following the bloody engagements at Williamsburg and Seven Pines, General Hill and his gallant soldiers would next face a reconstituted, reorganized and resupplied Army of the Potomac during the Battle of Seven Days. During this span of seven days - June 25th thru July 1st 1862 – fierce and successive engagements would ensue; registering into the official records of the war five names as historical points of reference: Mechanicsville, Frayser's Farm, Gaines' Mill, Savage Station and Malvern Hill. 259 At this juncture of the Peninsula Campaign, the Army of Northern Virginia had inflicted over 50,000 casualties upon the Army of the Potomac. Notwithstanding the fact that General McClellan retained an overwhelming advantage over the much smaller opposing Confederate army, he was convinced that his army was lacking in sufficient troop strength and constantly sought more manpower and resources from the Federal War Department.

Further, General McClellan consistently demonstrated a tendency to overestimate Confederate capabilities and possessed a propensity to always err conservatively on the side of caution. The perceptive new Confederate General-in-chief Robert E. Lee understood this well and, over the course of General McClellan's tenure of command, would skillfully exploit this weakness repeatedly to gain the proverbial strategic upper hand. 260

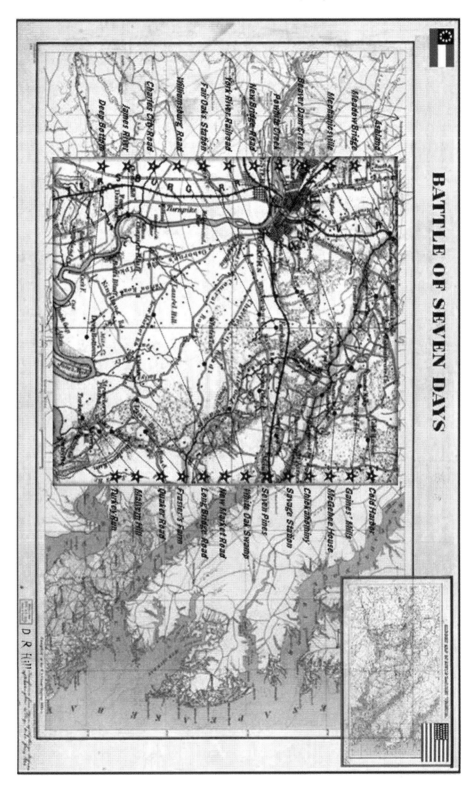

General George McClellan had positioned his large, reconstituted Union force in very close proximity to the Confederate Capital; so much so that the new Confederate General-in-chief Lee was undaunted in his intent to hurl General McClellan and his army back forcefully. 261

On the Confederate side of the ledger, one of General Lee's first actions as the new General-in-chief was to restructure the army by realigning the brigades within his divisions. General Lee acquiesced from the long-expressed expectations of the State Governors that their states' militia should remain together; a conscious effort to excite State pride and great enthusiasm within the ranks that would carry the boys through difficulties they might not attempt if joined with other troops. General Lee's restructuring of brigade alignment within divisions meant commanders would now have different troops under their command. It was a controversial step that raised the ire of many, not to mention Governor Vance of North Carolina. States' rights remained a driving influence within Confederate politics and, of course, the Generals of that day had to work within that sphere as well in their conduct of military operations. Immediately upon his arrival at his new headquarters, General Lee called a war council and summoned Generals Longstreet, A. P. Hill, Stonewall Jackson and D. H. Hill to go over the details of his plan of attack. 262 When the meeting was concluded and adjourned, all departed for their respective commands with a copy of General Order No. 75, issued by General Lee, to guide the conduct of the attack. 263

General Lee's plan was complex - requiring synchronization and timing through signals; and it was very risky due to his conscious decision to divide forces in the face of superior numbers and contiguously align them along the opposing enemy's line; but Lee's plan was efficient - providing clear instructions to his force. Importantly, it took advantage of General McClellan's weaknesses. As outlined in General Order 75, General Stuart's cavalry would precede General Stonewall Jackson on the march, initiating a sequential, organized move across the Chickahominy. Once across the river, the plan's battle array set the force: 264 General A. P. Hill would advance against the right flank of General McClellan at Mechanicsville, supported by General Longstreet, with General Jackson moving upon the rear of the same flank, supported by General D. H. Hill. 265 General Jackson's portion of the order read: *"Bearing well to his left, turning Beaver Dam creek and taking the direction toward Cold Harbor,"* after that to *"press forward toward the York River railroad, closing upon the enemy's rear and forcing him down the Chickahominy."* 266

General McClellan, having completed preparations for the Federal attack, advanced steadily upon Richmond and proceeded to fortify his positions along the banks of the Chickahominy River; determined to perfect his army's communications with its base of supplies near the head of the York River. The left wing of the Union army was established south of the Chickahominy between White Oak Swamp and New Bridge and was heavily defended by a line of strong works; access to which, except by a few narrow roads, was obstructed by felling the dense forests in front. 267 The Federal artillerist placed their heavy guns in fortified positions and strategically positioned them to provide effective covering fires upon the roads for a great distance. The Union army's right wing lay north of the Chickahominy, extending beyond Mechanicsville, and the approaches from the south side were strongly defended by fortified entrenchments. The Army of Northern Virginia was positioned between Richmond and the opposing Federal army. The divisions of Generals Huger and Magruder, supported by those of Generals Longstreet and D. H. Hill, were arrayed in front of the enemy's left while General A. P. Hill's division line extended from General Magruder's left beyond Meadow Bridge. 268

The command of General Jackson, including General Ewell's division, was operating in the Shenandoah valley and had succeeded in defeating the Federal forces under the command of Generals Fremont and Shields, effectively diverting the entire corps of Union General McDowell at Fredericksburg from uniting with General McClellan's forces; thus denying General McClellan the employment of nearly 40,000 able soldiers. To render this diversion more effective, and effectually mask his withdrawal from the Shenandoah Valley at the proper time, General Jackson was heavily reinforced by General Whiting's division, whose composition included General Hood's Texas brigade, and his own, under Colonel Law, and that of General Lawton from the South. 269

General Lee believed the enemy would attack Richmond by way of regular approaches. The strength of the left wing rendered a direct assault unwise, if not impracticable. It was therefore determined to construct defensive lines so as to enable a part of the army to defend the city while leaving the other part free to cross the Chickahominy and conduct operations on the north bank. General Lee was equally determined to sweep down the river on the far side, threaten General McClellan's communications with the York River, and force him to either retreat or give battle out of his entrenchments. The plan was submitted to President Jefferson Davis who was nearby and repeatedly on the field throughout the course of the plan's execution. 270

While Confederate preparations were in progress, General Stuart made his famous ride around the rear of the Federal army to determine its position and movements. As soon as the defensive works were sufficiently advanced, General Jackson was directed to move rapidly and secretly from the Valley, so as to arrive in the vicinity of Ashland by June 24th 1862. The enemy appeared to be unaware of General Lee's intent and, on June 26th 1862, attacked General Huger, without provocation, on the Williamsburg road; demonstrating

General McClellan's clear intention to secure his advance upon the Confederate capitol of Richmond. 271

D. H. HILL

"Because right is right, to follow right were wisdom in the scorn of consequences"

[[Colonel Henry E. Shepherd]]

Q22

General Lee had definitively established his order of battle with General Order 75. According to his directive, General Jackson was to march from Ashland on June 25th 1862 in the direction of Slash Church, encamp for the night west of the Central railroad, then advance at 3 a. m. on June 26th and proceed to turn Beaver Dam. General A. P. Hill was to cross the Chickahominy at the Meadow Bridge when General Jackson had advanced beyond that point, then move directly upon Mechanicsville. 272 As soon as the Mechanicsville Bridge should be uncovered, Generals Longstreet and D. H. Hill were to cross; with General D. H. Hill's division proceeding to support the advances of both Generals Jackson and A. P. Hill. 273 Afterward, the four commands were directed to sweep down the north side of the Chickahominy towards the York River railroad, with General Jackson on the left, in advance, and General Longstreet moving nearest the river and in the rear. Generals Huger and Magruder were ordered to hold their positions in the event of a assault by the Federal troops, to observe enemy movements and follow in vigorous pursuit should they retreat. General Stuart's cavalry was thrown out to conduct screening actions along General Jackson's left, guarding his flank and observing any enemy movements. 274

R. E. LEE

D. H. HILL

T. J. JACKSON

PROMINENT CONFEDERATE GENERALS

J. LONGSTREET

A. P. HILL

B. HUGER

R. RIPLEY

MECHANICSVILLE 1862

L. BRANCH

R. S. EWELL

W. H. C. WHITING

W. D. PENDER

Lieutenant General D. H. Hill (CSA)

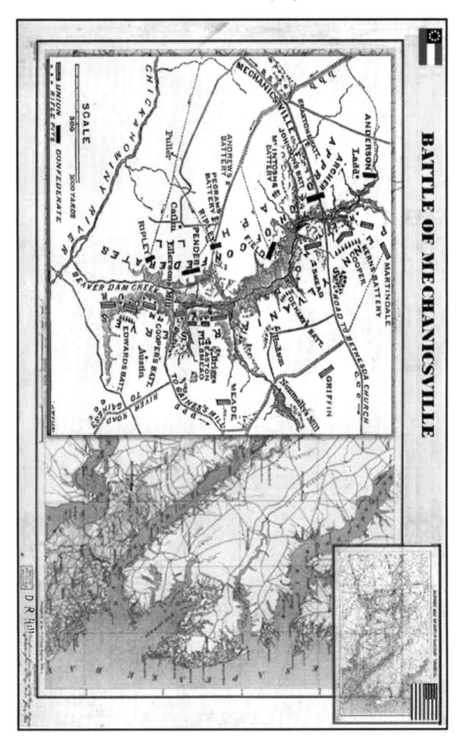

Brigadier General Pendleton was directed to employ the reserve Confederate artillery in such a manner to resist any approach of the enemy towards

~ 113 ~

Richmond; to oversee that portion posted to aid in the operations on the north bank; and to hold the remainder ready for use should further artillery support be required. 275 However, General Jackson met with unavoidable delay and the whole of General Jackson's command did not arrive at Ashland in time to enable him to reach the point as designated on June 25th 1862. Further aggravating General Lee's situation, Stonewalls movement on June 26th 1862 took much longer than had been anticipated, being further delayed by the enemy. 276 As a result of General Jackson's delay, General A. P. Hill did not begin his movement until 3 p. m. whereupon he crossed the river and advanced upon Mechanicsville. After a sharp conflict he drove the enemy from his entrenchments and forced him to take refuge in his works along the left bank of Beaver Dam, approximately one mile distant. 277 This enemy position was strongly fortified with the banks of the creek in front being high and almost perpendicular while direct approach required movement over open fields, providing little cover for the advance. Additionally, the Federal's position was further reinforced with covering fires of their artillery and a sizeable force of infantry entrenched upon the opposite side. The advancing Confederate troops had further difficulty crossing the stream as their progress was hampered by substantial impediments in the form of destroyed bridges and felled woods along the creek banks. 278

At this juncture of the battle it had been envisioned that General Jackson would have passed Beaver Dam, intent upon turning the enemy's right. However, the lack of concert caused by General Jackson's disrupted advance prevented General D. H. Hill's division from making their attack. 279 Generals Longstreet and D. H. Hill crossed the Mechanicsville Bridge as soon as it was uncovered and necessary repairs made but it was late before they reached the north bank of the Chickahominy. 280 General D. H. Hill's leading brigade, under the command of General Ripley, advanced to support the troops engaged and, at a late hour, united with General Pender's Brigade of General A. P. Hill's division; moving eagerly to turn the enemy's left. But his troops were unable in the growing darkness to overcome the obstructions. After sustaining a murderous fire of musketry and short-range cannonade he was forced to withdraw. The fire was continued until about 9 p. m. when there was finally a lull in the fighting. The Confederate troops had driven the enemy back and had seized control of the ground on the right bank, previously held by the enemy. 281

General Ripley was relieved at three p. m. on June 27th 1862 by two of General Longstreet's Brigades, which were then quickly reinforced. In expectation of General Jackson's arrival on the enemy's right, the battle was renewed at dawn and was conducted with great animation for about two hours. During the battle the Confederate line attempted to cross the creek but their progress was halted by a combination of fierce Union resistance and the impeding nature of the stream. Firmly holding their ground, the Confederates prepared to cross at another point nearer the Chickahominy. Before this crossing was accomplished, General Jackson successfully crossed Beaver Dam above, forcing the enemy to abandon their entrenchments and retire rapidly down the river; destroying a great deal of property in the process but leaving much in their deserted camps. 282

With the bridges over Beaver Dam repaired, the several columns resumed their march as prescribed in the order. The combined forces of Generals D. H. Hill and Jackson bore to the left, determined to cut off enemy reinforcements or intercept his retreat in that direction. Generals Longstreet and A. P. Hill advanced toward the Chickahominy taking many prisoners along the way; following a long line of abandoned Federal wagons and stores which marked the route of the hastily retreating Union army. As Generals Longstreet and A. P. Hill reached the vicinity of New Bridge about noon, General Lee had determined that the Federals had taken a defensive position behind Powhite creek, determined to dispute the Confederate's advance. General McClellan's army occupied a range of hills, with his right resting in the vicinity of the McGehee's house and his left near that of Dr. Gaines; on a wooded bluff which rose abruptly from a deep ravine. 283

This ravine was filled with sharpshooters, tactically positioned to take advantage of the cover provided by the banks for their protection. A second line of infantry was stationed on the side of the hill, directly behind an imposing breastwork of trees and positioned directly above and behind the first. A third occupied the crest of the hill and was strengthened with rifle trenches and crowned with artillery. The approach to this position required any attacking force to cross an open plain for a distance of nearly one quarter of a mile; exposing their entire line to a commanding triple line of musketry fire and concentrated fires of shell, grape and canister from multiple heavy Federal batteries, strategically positioned south of the Chickahominy. 284 In front of the Federal center and right, the ground was generally open; with the approach bounded on the side by dense woods; with impeding, tangling undergrowth and traversed by a sluggish stream which converted the soil into a deep quagmire. The woods on the farther side of the swamp were occupied by sharpshooters, tactically covering themselves with felled trees. This served effectively to increase the difficulty of passage and to detain advancing Confederate columns; under the fire of infantry that was massed on the slopes of the opposite hills and of the Federal batteries upon their crests. 285

In compliance with General Order No. 75, General Stonewall Jackson started his move to the vicinity of Mechanicsville; Generals Longstreet and D. H. Hill marched along the Williamsburg road and bivouacked on the Mechanicsville road while General Huger remained as the covering force to hold the right against a possible Union attack; General A. P. Hill advanced to the Meadow Bridge road, to the left of General Longstreet; and General Branch moved to the extreme left on the Brook Church road. 286 As General Stonewall Jackson pressed hard on the extreme left wing of the Confederate line to pressure the enemy's rear, General Branch's troops were decisively engaged holding the center of the Confederate line while General A. P. Hill's forces, having successfully crossed the Chickahominy, held the right of the Confederate line. 287

General A. P. Hill, leading the advance, had moved vigorously towards the York River railroad and had arrived in the vicinity of New Cold Harbor about 2 p. m. whereupon he was greeted with a decisive engagement by Federal troops. This contact prompted him to immediately form his line nearly parallel to the road leading from Cold Harbor towards the McGehee's house. Anticipating the imminent arrival of General Jackson and his proposed placement along the Confederate left, it was expected that his joining the line would cause the Federal's line to extend accordingly to address his line. 288 Under this impression, General Longstreet was held back until General Jackson's movement should begin. The principal part of the Federal army was now positioned on the north side of the Chickahominy. General A. P. Hill maintained his line, unbroken, and anxiously waited for General Branch's advance; eager himself to extend the vigorous attack upon the enemy to his front, in the direction of the small village of Mechanicsville. Although General Branch's progress had been steady he was still well back. General A. P. Hill, with 14,000 men - arms at the ready, was determined to push on and drive the enemy back, effectively clearing the way for Generals Longstreet and D. H. Hill. Although he had not received General Stonewall Jackson's signal that he was in position and ready to cooperate in a coordinated attack, General A. P. Hill took upon himself the responsibility to advance upon General McClellan's right. Later in his official report he stated that he feared a delay might *"hazard the failure of the whole plan."*

General A. P. Hill's advance was courageous, but very irresponsible. Although the attack was fierce and demonstrated with great effort, the Union defenses were nearly impregnable and the Union soldiers responded with great intensity, forcing the Confederates to fall back; harshly shattered by the infantry and withering shell, grape and canister fire that met them from the Union right. 289 General A. P. Hill's single division engaged this large force, driving the enemy back and assailing him in his strong position along the ridge. The battle raged fiercely, producing results of varying fortune, for more than two hours. At one juncture of the fight, three Confederate regiments pierced the Federal's line and pushed forward to the crest of the hill along the enemy's left, but they were soon forced to fall back under the pressure from overwhelming numbers. 290 The superior force of the enemy, assisted by concentrated and coordinated fires from his batteries south of the Chickahominy, pressured heavily the Confederate columns as they attempted to navigate the obstructions in their way. 291 Faced with these obstructions, murderous musketry fire and supporting cannonade, the Confederates were repelled. Though most of the men had never been under fire until the day before, they were rallied and, in turn, courageously fended off the advance of the enemy. Some brigades were broken while others stubbornly maintained their positions. But it soon became apparent that the enemy was gradually gaining ground. 292

With the planned attack along the Confederate's left being delayed by the length of General Jackson's march, and further hindered by the obstacles he encountered, General Longstreet was ordered to make a diversion in General A. P. Hill's favor by demonstrating a feint to the enemy's left. 293 In making this demonstration, the great strength of the enemy's position, already described, was discovered. General Longstreet perceived that, to render the diversion effectual, the feint must be converted into an attack. He decided, with characteristic promptness, to carry the heights by assault. His columns were quickly formed near the open ground and his preparations for the assault completed. 294 The battle raged as the Confederate forces unleashed a fierce, coordinated attack upon General McClellan's army; pursuing them vigorously and capturing several of their field works and cannons in the process. The fight pressed forward stubbornly from the Meadow Bridge. General Longstreet, sitting mounted and with his field glasses, watched the battle unfold from his elevated position on the south bank of the Chickahominy. The scene was majestic, yet horrific. The battlefield was partially obscured by clouds of dust and the thick smoke of cannon fire. He watched as the blue and gray lines thrashed against one another; the sounds of rattling musketry and deafening cannon fire echoing up and down the Chickahominy. The Union line began to falter as General Branch's soldiers continued their advance in the center of the line; crossing the green field and driving the enemy from their earthworks as enemy musketry fire steadily poured in upon them from the distant tree line. 295

Upon learning of General A. P. Hill's imprudent attack, General Hill was furious. Upon General Lee's realignment of forces, the flag of the First North Carolina Regiment, General Hill's famed Bethel Regiment, had been aligned with General A. P. Hill's command. Colonel Montford S. Stokes, commanding the First North Carolina Regiment, had led a heroic but desperate charge across an open field in the face of murderous fires but, to D. H. Hill's great sadness, fell mortally wounded in the process. 296 Learning of General A. P. Hill's precarious position on the battlefield, Generals Longstreet and D. H. Hill engaged the Federals in a fierce battle; pushing forward across the

Mechanicsville Bridge with their divisions and forming their lines at right angles with the Chickahominy. Meanwhile General A. P. Hill, having reformed his line, commenced his attack in the direction of the small village of Mechanicsville. 297

At this juncture of the battle, General Jackson finally arrived whereupon he and his right division, General Whiting's, took their positions to the left of General Longstreet's line. At the same time, General D. H. Hill's division formed to the Confederate's extreme left and, after a furious and bloody conflict, forced his way with great enthusiasm through the swamps and obstructions to successfully drive the enemy from the woods on the opposite side. 298 General Ewell's line advanced on General A. P. Hill's right and joined the furious engagement. The first and forth brigades of General Jackson's own division filled the interval between Generals Ewell and A. P. Hill. The second and third were sent to the right. The arrival of these fresh troops enabled General A. P. Hill to withdraw some of his brigades, greatly wearied and reduced by the long and grueling conflict. The Confederate line being now complete, a general advance from right to left was ordered. 299 On the right of the Confederate line, the troops moved forward with steadiness, undaunted by the withering fire from the triple lines of infantry on the hill, combined with the supporting cannonade delivering precision fires from both sides of the river, which burst upon them as they emerged upon the plain; a dreadful trail of dead and wounded soldiers marking the way of their courageous advance. 300

The enemy was driven with authority from the ravine to the first line of breastworks, over which the column of charging Confederates dashed; advancing to face the imposing entrenchments positioned on the crest of the slope. These were quickly stormed, resulting in the capture of fourteen pieces of artillery while the enemy was driven from the position and pushed deep into the field beyond. 301 Fresh Federal troops quickly arrived to augment the Federal forces as they fought mightily to rally their blue line and regain their entrenchments. But their efforts to rally were in vain. The Federals were hurled back with great slaughter until they reached the cover provided by the woods along the banks of the Chickahominy; wherein nightfall finally put an end to the Confederate pursuit. 302

Long lines of dead and wounded marked each stand made by the enemy in his stubborn resistance and the field over which he retreated was strewn with the slain. On the left, the attack was no less vigorous and equally successful. General D. H. Hill charged across the open ground to his front, with one of his regiments having first bravely carried a battery whose fire enfiladed their advance. 303 Gallantly supported by the troops on his right, who pressed forward with unfaltering determination, General D. H. Hill's division reached the crest of the ridge and, after a bloody struggle, broke the enemy's line;

capturing several of his batteries and driving the Federals towards the Chickahominy, in great confusion, until darkness rendered further pursuit impractical. 304

Union General Fitz John Porter, an artillerist and engineer, had prepared the village with great precision to nearly produce and impregnable defense; possessing a large number of constructed earthworks, greatly protected by placement of numerous cannon batteries. With darkness covering the field, a one-half hour cannon duel commenced between Confederate artillerist and General Porter's Union batteries; with showers of shells screaming through the night sky, lighting the faces of friend and foe as they exploded. General A. P. Hill's troops slugged their way toward the village as the entire town seemed to be ablaze; the burning barns, houses and stacks of hay lighting the evening sky. General Porter's cannons pummeled the advancing troops with concentrated fire while sweltering musketry fire from within the village ripped through their line; producing a devastating effect and, once again, pushing back General A. P. Hill's advance. 305 As the battle raged along the outskirts of Mechanicsville, General Ripley's brigade moved, as ordered by General Hill, farther to the left and to the front, in order to attack an entrenched position. This engagement would result in one of the bloodiest fights recorded during the entire war – fought with equal passion by both Union and Confederate soldiers. Union General Fitz John Porter had masterfully placed a battery of sixteen guns on the high ground to the right of the Mechanicsville road. The position was most formidable, situated on a rise of ground, covered with abattis, and defended by parapets supported by rifle pits. Beaver Dam creek ran along the front and left of the cannon emplacement. The brigades of Generals Pender and Ripley attacked this position with fierceness, and in concentration. General Hill ordered two of General Ripley's regiments, the Forty Fourth Georgia Regiment and his old Bethel Regiment, the First North Carolina, to maneuver on the right with General Pender while the Forty Eight Georgia Regiment and the Third North Carolina Regiment remained in front. 306

In a coordinated assault, the regiments moved forward; clearing the rifle pits and advancing to within 100 yards of the enemy's heavily fortified position. But the creek and the abattis remained as an impediment to further advance. Meanwhile, murderous musketry, shot, shell, and canister continued to pummel the Rebels. The Forty Fourth Georgia and First North Carolina Regiments were heavily depleted and thrown into great confusion, owing to the heavy loss of officers and their leadership. Likewise, General Pender's brigade was repulsed, sustaining similar, severe losses. 307

At this juncture, Rhett's battery of D. H. Hill's Division, having successfully crossed the broken bridge over the Chickahominy, took a position on the high ground to the immediate front of the enemy position. From there he proceeded to deliver sustained and devastating fires. For a moment, Rhett's cannons almost silenced the enemy's fire, providing a much needed lull for the assaulting forces. However, in retaliation, Rhett's cannons received an incoming barrage of counter-fire from Union batteries that inflicted much damage; killing many of his men and horses. Finally darkness engulfed the disputed position and at 10 p.m. firing from both sides ceased, effectively ending the battle without resolution but with each side having inflicted horrific carnage upon the other. Around midnight, the Union forces abandoned the position, destroying its contents as they departed. 308

The fight at Mechanicsville concluded with a tactical victory for General McClellan's Army of the Potomac while General Lee's Army of Northern Virginia had achieved none of their objectives. The execution of General Lee's complex General Order No. 75 was seriously flawed. The mission's success depended on precise execution, synchronization and timing by his commanders. But a sequence of miscues, and a little bit of old fashioned bad luck, threw the timing off for the entire scheme of maneuver; thus producing a seriously flawed execution of General Lee's intent. General Stonewall Jackson's delayed arrival, and General A. P. Hill's premature action before General Jackson was in proper position, sealed the fate of General Lee's plan. Instead of throwing the strength of 60,000 men against General McClellan's left wing, only five brigades, equating to about 15,000 men, actually engaged the Federals during the battle. The Confederates sustained nearly 1,500 casualties during the attack. However, despite General McClellan's tactical victory he once again demonstrated his tendency to overestimate Confederate capabilities and his tendency to err conservatively on the side of caution; withdrawing, yet again, cautiously in the face of victory. General Lee would use this strategic blunder to gain and hold the strategic upper hand as the next day of the Seven Days battles resumed with General Lee's attack upon General Porter at the Battle of Gaines' Mill. 309

D. H. HILL

"Do you know that in Mexico the young officers called you the bravest man in the army?"

[[Lieutenant General Joseph E. Johnston]]

Q3

MAJOR GENERAL WILLIAM EMMETT INGRAM

The Twentieth Century's Version of

ROBERT E. LEE

34th ADJUTANT GENERAL

of the Great State of

NORTH CAROLINA

GAINES' MILL 1862

On the morning of June 27ᵗʰ 1862 General Lee promptly ordered an attack to renew his efforts against the right flank of the Army of the Potomac. 310 Union Brigadier General Fitz John Porter's reinforced V corps was positioned on the northern side of the Chickahominy in a formidable defensive line. General Lee was determined to throw the full weight of his army, about 57.000 men in six divisions, upon the Federals. Generals Gregg and Prior, of General Longstreet's corps, successfully turned the enemy's left flank and carried, with the bayonet, what guns still remained in the Union batteries; in the front and to the right of Mechanicsville. In the meantime, the grand advance en echelon had begun. General Hill's troops marched by way of the Mechanicsville road to link up with General Stonewall Jackson's men, who were advancing from Ashland; with the Bethesda Church being designated as their point of junction. From there General Hill led the echelon toward Cold Harbor by way of Gaines' Mill. 311 General Lee's plan called to array the Confederate force with: General Longstreet on the right, along the Chickahominy swamp; General A. P. Hill on the immediate left of General Longstreet; then General Whiting, then General Ewell, then General Stonewall Jackson, with General Hill on the far left of the Confederate line; establishing a crescent formation extending from beyond New Cold Harbor, south toward Baker's Mills.

R. E. LEE

D. H. HILL

T. J. JACKSON

PROMINENT CONFEDERATE GENERALS

J. LONGSTREET

A. P. HILL

S. GARLAND

GAINES' MILL 1862

J. B. MAGRUDER

J. B. HOOD

R. S. EWELL

W. H. C. WHITING

W. LAWTON

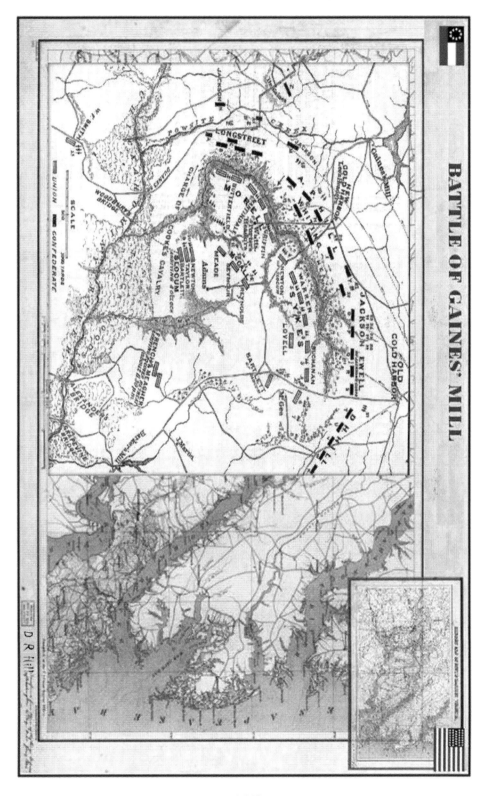

However, General Stonewall Jackson was once again delayed, preventing the full concentration of Confederate forces. 312 By 2 p.m., General Hill had positioned his forces in front of Old Cold Harbor: pressing forward through fallen timber and tangled brushwood, which the enemy had provided as an impediment for defense upon General Porter's right flank and rear; drawing heavy and effective fire from sharpshooters as they advanced. By design, General Hill's attack was to create a ruse de guerre and conceal the main attack by General Longstreet on the far end of the Confederate line. At 3:30 p.m. General Longstreet launched the main attack, driving the enemy down the Chickahominy. 313

At this juncture, General Stonewall Jackson had successfully maneuvered his forces north of Old Cold Harbor and, in characteristic Jackson style, purposely exposed his position to draw fire from the enemy; inducing them to reveal their positions. The furious Federal response that General Jackson received provided him with the confirmation he sought. General D. H. Hill's soldiers pushed the skirmishers from Gaines' Mill, effectively clearing the immediate line along the Powhite swamp. 314 Fully aware that General Longstreet was on his right, General Hill, exhibiting his usual ardor, made a daring dash across the Powhite swamp; successfully breaching the obstructions that had been emplaced and assaulting the strong batteries and entrenched lines of the Union center vigorously. General Hill's men fought with unequalled courage and determination while assaulting this strong enemy position. Their audacious assault caused General Porter to call for reinforcement of the line, to which General Slocum added his 5,000 men to the defense. 315 For two hours, D. H. Hill's men, though greatly outnumbered, fought to hold the position. But without support their single attacking line, against formidable obstacles, could not defeat three comparable lines of entrenched and barricaded infantry; tactically positioned one above the other, on a steep slope protected by fallen timber and having the ridge behind them occupied by heavy guns that poured upon them continuous shot and shell over the heads of the Union infantry. 316 At 4 p.m. General Longstreet was supposed to attack against General Porter's left, toward the Chickahominy at Turkey Hill. The crest of this hill, crowned with multiple Union batteries, was 60 feet higher than the plateau opposite, upon which General Longstreet had formed his line of battle. General Longstreet's men faced numerous, elaborate obstacles protecting the forward slope of Turkey Hill. General McClellan's heavy guns poured enfilade fire upon his attacking line, with devastating effect, from their positions south of the Chickahominy. Such were the conditions that caused General Longstreet to delay his attack for nearly three hours.

General Lee's frustration continued to grow. Once again, his plans to conduct a synchronized, coordinated attack to throw the entire weight of his army against General Porter's center front was being foiled by delays; first from General Stonewall Jackson and now General Longstreet. But General Lee's concerns would soon worsen and his situation would not improve. 317 General Stonewall Jackson, understanding the situation on the field, knew it appropriate to maneuver his forces to join the fight. Rapidly, he prepared to give exact instructions to one of his most trusted staff officers, Major Dabney; a directive to place his divisions on the march. But in another run of bad luck, Major Dabney fell ill from the strenuous exertions of the past several days of battle. This made it necessary for General Jackson to send him to the rear for rest and replace him with another messenger. Stonewall issued precise instructions to his new courier and dispatched him to ride, with all haste, to the right of the line; informing each division commander to bear to the left *in moving forward* thus bringing his line to successive action in echelon. 318 Unfortunately, the rider instructed the division commanders incorrectly. Instead of telling the commanders to *move forward*, he conveyed the message *"prepare"* to move forward. With no further explanation required, General Jackson's division commanders formed in echelon down the line, following the order explicitly, and prepared, but did not move forward. This, yet another conspicuous failure in communications, caused the loss of an hour or more of precious time. General Stonewall Jackson impatiently waited for the sounds of his cannons, signaling that his divisions were engaging the enemy's flanks and rear, per is order; by design to bring much needed relief to the Confederate center line. Major Dabney, noticing the delay, disregarded his physical ailments, mounted his horse and rushed down the line; correcting the confusion caused by the previous courier miscommunication and stirring the divisions promptly into action. 319

General Jackson's men responded with great enthusiasm; first General D. H. Hill's Division on the left, followed in sequence on the right by Generals Ewell and Whiting. Amidst the thunderous sound of cannons supporting the advancing divisions, a wild Rebel yell swept through the lines of Generals Longstreet and A. P. Hill: *"Jackson's come!"*

General Magruder contributed valiantly to the fight, holding the Union troops south of the Chickahominy as he marched and counter-marched his infantry in deceptive movements; all the while keeping his artillery in constant action. 320 General Porter, observing the change in the tide of battle, as the charging Confederate line rolled across his front and closed on his flanks, called for reinforcements. General McClellan directed Generals Franklin and Sumner to cross the river and reinforce his line. General Franklin's reply was that it was *"not prudent"* to do so and General Sumner, being greatly intimated by General Magruder, replied *"hazardous."* But the Union brigades of Generals Meagher and French dispatched 5,000 men across the river as reinforcements to General Porter's rear. 321

As the fierce battle of Gaines' Mill reached a fevered pitch, bravery, daring and heroism ruled the day for the Confederate army - all along the line. But never has there been a more heroic effort than the assault by the soldiers charging the Union line on this day; most notably the North Carolinians of General D. H. Hill's Division, the Georgians of General Lawton's Division, and the Texans of General Hoods Division. Fighting with great honor and distinction, these men stormed the heights at Turkey Hill and the McGehee's house, sweeping across the fences and ditches; through fallen timber and abattis and over entrenchments - which blazed with sheeted fire from the enemy's infantry and artillery.   These gallant fighters charged the entire Union front with an extraordinary display of heroism, losing one of every two men in the advance, but effectively rolling General Porter's line back in a sullen tide of defeat; becoming masters of the heights they had so bravely stormed. 322

With the Union line broken and the battle lost, the demoralized remnants of General Porter's corps retreated across the river during the night. The victory at Gaines' Mill saved Richmond for the Confederacy in 1862 and the resounding tactical defeat so unnerved General McClellan that he decided to abandon his advance on Richmond and launched an abrupt retreat toward the James River. 323

General Lee said: *"After a sanguinary struggle he [D. H. Hill] captured several of the enemy's batteries and drove them in confusion toward the Chickahominy creek until darkness rendered further pursuit impossible."* 324

It was widely recognized that it was General D. H. Hill's Division to whom the honor belonged for breaking the right of General Porter's line on that bloody day. *"The day was won with the bold and dashing charge of General Hill's infantry, in which the troops of Brigadier General Winder joined, the enemy yielded the field and fled in disorder."* During the fight, General D. H. Hill was asked, and granted permission to the request of Brigadiers Anderson and Garland, to move forward and attack the right flank and rear of the Union regulars. General Anderson's Brigade carried the flags of the 2nd 4th 14th and 30th North Carolina Regiments;   General Garland's Brigade carried the flags of the 5th 12th 13th 20th and 23rd North Carolina Regiments. During the assault, the Carolinians faced a Union battery with supporting infantry, positioned to enfilade them in their advance. General D. H. Hill dispatched two additional regiments which had become disoriented in crossing the swamp, to attack the infantry supporting the artillery, while the 20th North Carolina charged the battery to their front. The battery was captured and held long enough for the brigades of Brigadiers Anderson and Garland to advance across the plain. *"The effect of our appearance,"* says General Garland, *"at this opportune moment, cheering and charging, decided the fate of the day."* General Garland continued: *"The enemy broke and retreated and made a second stand, which induced my immediate command to halt under cover of the roadside and return the fire, when charging forward again we broke and scattered them in every direction. The ensuing confusion uncovered the left of the fortified line and left no obstacle between Hill and the McGehee house."* 325

Amidst all the great compliments earned by D. H. Hill's heroic actions during the Battle of Gaines' Mill, another event occurred which offers great insight into the true moral fiber of D. H. Hill, the man; it was not an action of combat, but rather an act of compassion that demonstrated a side of D. H. Hill's character of which the world generally knows so little - his warm sympathy for suffering and his lasting and steadfast fidelity to his friends. It happened that, during the night of the battle, several of Hill's soldiers captured two Union officers. Upon escort of these two prisoners to General Hill's quarters, Hill immediately recognized one to be an old army comrade from his days of service in Mexico; the other prisoner, Major Clitz, was also known, but to a lesser degree of friendship. Hill received both very kindly and sent for a surgeon to dress wounds sustained during the engagement by Major Clitz's.

General Reynolds, being in every respect ashamed that he had been caught off guard and captured while asleep, was comforted by General Hill, who reminded the fretful General that his gallant conduct in Mexico would serve to protect his good name. Both prisoners were paroled to report to General Winder at Richmond and furnished with the address of a personal friend of General Hill's who would willingly honor their drafts for money. Although such events were common during the Civil War, previous historical depictions of Hill that address this side of his character has been overlooked by historians. 326 If not for the injurious and detrimental nature of their comments, it would seem preposterous, even laughable, to acknowledge the expositors who were so critical of D. H. Hill's *"sharp tongue,"* while grossly ignoring so many of the positive aspects of this great Southern gentleman's nature and character. As with some great Greek tragedy, their expositions have implied that the life of *"Lee's Fighting General"* produced a sad outcome as some inevitable result of his personal flaws – that he was doomed to disaster from the outset.

Really? An iconic figure from our nation's past should be defined in this manner? If your measure of truth is based upon reliance of such expositions; presented by writers who neither knew the man nor experienced any fraction of the horrors he endured along his path through history, then I suppose a sarcastic attitude might be a criteria for defining one's life accomplishments. Perhaps you may be so judged. But, if your measure of truth is based upon historical facts, recorded in the annals of our nation's history and documented by leaders of unquestionable integrity - the likes of Robert E. Lee, Stonewall Jackson, Ole Pete Longstreet, and other iconic figures, then you will gain great enlightenment from this study of the heroic Confederate Lieutenant General Daniel Harvey Hill. If fault must be appropriated, place it squarely upon this author: for allowing the true accounting of D. H. Hill's greatness to be so long obscured within the monotonous and routine written OFFICIAL RECORDS and REPORTS of two armies: one long vanquished and the other long proceeded to other fields of battle in latter eras of our nation's ongoing history.

D. H. HILL

"Qualities of leadership which inspired the utmost confidence and loyalty in his soldiers and made him the idol of the Carolinas."

[[*James W. Ratchford*]]

Q30

SAVAGE STATION 1862

Early on June 29ᵗʰ 1862 Generals Longstreet and A. P. Hill were ordered to re-cross the Chickahominy at New Bridge and advance, by way of the Darbytown road, to the Long Bridge road. Confederate engineers Major R. K. Meade and Lieutenant S. K. Johnson, having been tasked to perform a thorough reconnaissance of the area, discovered that the works along the upper extremity of the Federal's line of entrenchments had been fully abandoned. General Huger immediately moved down the Charles City road, determined to take the Federal army in flank while General Magruder moved rapidly in pursuit, by way of the Williamsburg road, intent upon attacking the enemy's rear. [327]

General Jackson was directed to cross at Grapevine Bridge and move down the south side of the Chickahominy. Generals Magruder and Huger found the whole line of works deserted and large quantities of military stores, of every description, abandoned or destroyed. [328] General Magruder continued in pursuit, reaching the vicinity of Savage Station about noon, where he came upon the rear guard of the retreating Union army. Believing what he took to be an enemy advance, General Magruder halted and sent for reinforcements. [329] Accordingly, two brigades of General Huger's division were ordered to his support.

R. E. LEE

D. H. HILL

T. J. JACKSON

PROMINENT CONFEDERATE GENERALS

SAVAGE STATION 1862

J. LONGSTREET

B. HUGER

T. H. HOLMES

J. B. MAGRUDER

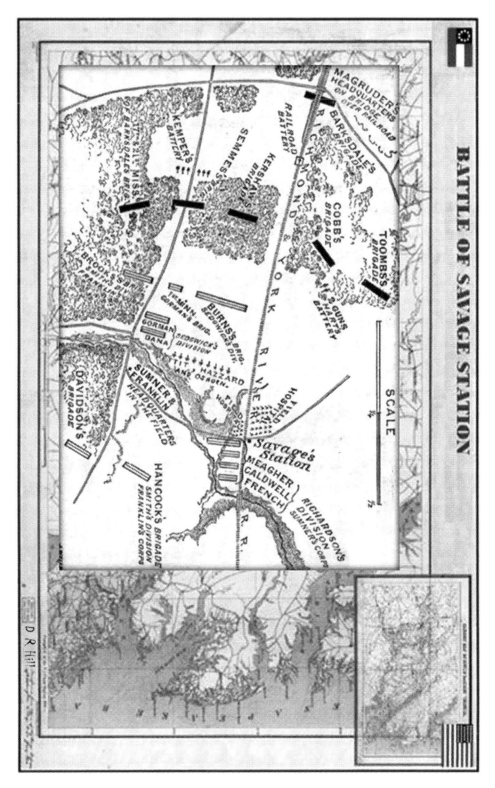

But they were later withdrawn when it became apparent that the force to General Magruder's front was not advancing. Rather, they were merely a covering force for the retreat of the Federal's main body.

General Jackson's route led to the flank and rear of Savage Station but he was once again delayed by the necessity of reconstructing Grapevine Bridge. Late in the afternoon, General Magruder attacked the enemy with one of his divisions and two regiments of another. 330 A severe action ensued, continuing for about two hours, until it's termination by nightfall. The Confederate troops displayed great gallantry and inflicted heavy losses upon the enemy but, owing to the lateness of the hour and in consideration of the small force employed, their result was not decisive and the Federal troops continued their retreat under cover of darkness; leaving behind several hundred prisoners while abandoning their dead and wounded into Confederate hands. 331 At Savage Station were found about twenty-five hundred men in a field hospital and a large amount of accompanying property. 332 The Federal's withdrawal had forced them to destroy large quantities of valuable stores, including necessary medical supplies for their sick and wounded. But these resources were merely traded for time for their retreating columns to cross White Oak Swamp without interruption; with their final act being the destruction of the bridge upon their departure. 333

D. H. HILL

"He was a skill-full officer, intelligent and keen eyed, stern to rebuke violation of orders and lack of discipline-a determined fighter-as the boys expressed it, "A fighter from way back."

[[Major William Smith, 14th NC regiment Anson Guards]]

Q24

When General Jackson reached Savage Station early on June 30th 1862 he was directed to pursue the enemy along the road used for his arrival while General Magruder was ordered to follow General Longstreet by way of the Darbytown road. 334 As General Jackson advanced, he captured such numbers of prisoners, and collected so many arms, that two regiments had to be detached for their security. Once again, his forward progress was stopped, this time by the hindrance of White Oak Swamp. 335 A large Federal force now occupied the opposite side and strongly resisted Confederate efforts to reconstruct the damaged bridge over the Chickahominy. Generals Longstreet and A. P. Hill, continuing their advance on June 30th 1862 soon came upon the enemy, strongly posted across the Long Bridge road about a mile from its intersection with the Charles City road. General Huger's route of entry led to the right of this position, with General Jackson's position to the rear. General Lee was induced to delay his attack until these two commands were in proper position. 336

On June 29th 1862 General Holmes crossed from the south side of the James River with part of his division and, the next day, moved down the river road until he came upon the line of the retreating Federals in the vicinity of Malvern Hill. 337

J. LONGSTREET   **R. E. LEE**   **D. H. HILL**   **T. J. JACKSON**

PROMINENT CONFEDERATE GENERALS

B. HUGER   **C. WILCOX**   **A. P. HILL**   **T. H. HOLMES**   **J. B. MAGRUDER**

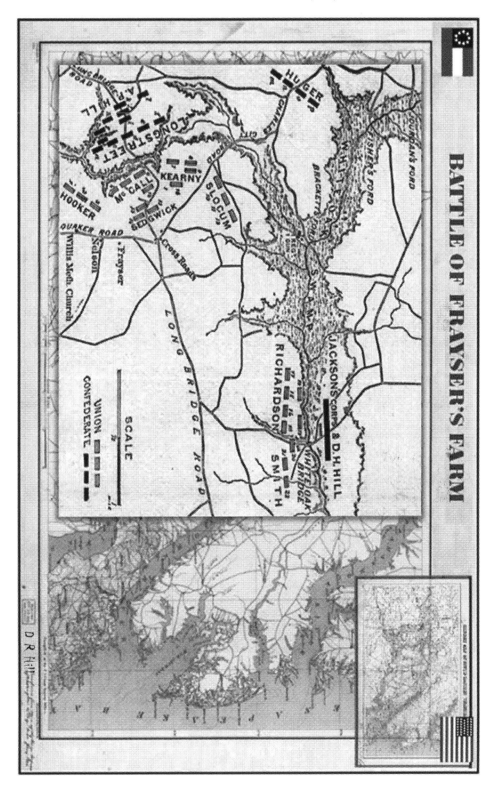

BATTLE OF FRASER'S FARM

Perceiving indications of confusion, General Holmes was ordered to open upon the Federal column with his artillery. His fires soon drew return counter-fire from a number of Federal heavy gun batteries, strategically posted and well supported by an infantry force superior to his own; 338 the cannonade was further assisted by the fires from gunboats in the James River that guarded this part of the Federal line. General Magruder, who at this juncture had reached the Darbytown road, was ordered to reinforce General Holmes. But being at a greater distance than had been supposed, he did not reach General Holmes' position in time for the attack. 339

General Huger reported that his progress was hindered; but about 4 p.m. firing was heard in the direction of the Charles City road, which was mistaken to be the signal acknowledging his approach. General Longstreet immediately opened with one of his batteries to give notice of his presence. 340 This brought on the engagement but General Huger, not coming forward and General Jackson having been unable to force the passage of White Oak's Swamp, placed Generals Longstreet and D. H. Hill in the unsteady position of being without their expected support. The superiority of numbers and advantage of position were clearly on the side of the Federals. 341

The battle of Frayser's Farm raged furiously until nine p. m. By that time, the Federal troops had been driven with great slaughter from every position except one; which was maintained only until their force was enabled to withdraw under cover of darkness. At the close of the struggle nearly the entire field remained in possession of the Confederate army; strewn with the enemy's dead and wounded. Many prisoners, including a General in command of a Federal division, were captured; along with several artillery batteries and over one thousands small arms. Had the other Confederate commands participated in a coordinated attack, as so desired and anticipated by General Lee, this battle would have proved most disastrous to General McClellan's army. 342

MALVERN HILL 1862

General D. H. Hill's Division next marched toward Savage's Station wherein he picked up a thousand prisoners; stragglers from the retreating Yankee army. During the process, General Hill's men gathered a large number of abandoned rifles, so many in fact that Hill was forced to detach the 4th and 5th North Carolina Regiments to escort the prisoners and the recovered arms to Richmond. 343 D. H. Hill had become convinced that an attack upon the concentrated Union army, so splendidly posted and with such a vast numerical advantage, both in soldiers and artillery, *"could only be fatal."* The Union defenses at Malvern Hill were positioned on a high plateau, stretching north from the lowlands along the valley of the James River, with its dominating high, steep hills; with Turkey Run being situated on the west and Western Run situated on the east. The Confederate line was fronted by a mile-wide stretch of open land – rolling and sloping toward the north where it ended in heavy forest, intersected by marshy streams; with only one good road leading through the forest out upon the plateau. General D. H. Hill's strategic and tactical concerns over attacking such an imposing defense were shared by many, including General Holmes, who remarked that it was: *"out of the question to attack the strong position of Malvern Hill from that side, with my inadequate force."* 344

R. E. LEE

D. H. HILL

J. LONGSTREET

T. J. JACKSON

PROMINENT CONFEDERATE GENERALS

L. A. ARMISTEAD

MALVERN HILL 1862

J. B. MAGRUDER

D. R. JONES

L. McLAWS

R. S. EWELL

W. H. C. WHITING

T. H. HOLMES

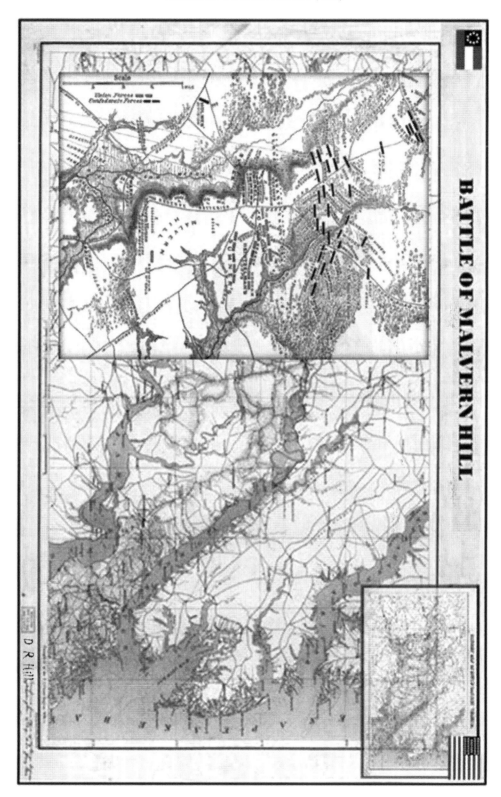

BATTLE OF MALVERN HILL

The march toward Malvern Hill met with much delay by the crossing of volumes of troops and elements of the Confederate trains. During one halt, Generals D. H. Hill, Lee and Longstreet met along the road near Willis' Church whereupon General Lee expressed to General Hill that: *"he bore grandly his terrible disappointment of the day before, and made no allusion to it."* General Hill in a previous conversation with Reverend L. W. Allen, a member of General Magruder's staff and a local man with great understanding of the area's terrain, described to him the area of Malvern Hill in great detail, noting it's striking features: *"it's commanding height, the difficulties of approach, it's amphitheatrical form and ample area, which would enable McClellan to arrange his 350 field guns, tier above tier, and sweep the plain in every direction."* 345

General Hill gave Allen's description of Malvern Hill to the other two Generals, presuming to say: *"If General McClellan is there in force, we had better let him alone."* Upon hearing this, General Longstreet laughed and said, *"don't get scared, now that we have got him whipped."* Hill did not share most of the other Generals' commonly held and over-confident assessment of the enemy's morale and disposition - upon which the command decision to attack Malvern Hill was made. General Hill openly opposed the attack before it was ordered and he would later criticize General Lee openly for ordering the attack with the now famous quote: *"It wasn't war, it war murder."* It is a criticism that was not taken well by many but one made earnestly from a man who held great contempt for disingenuousness. It was innate to Hill's nature to comment and voice his concerns, regardless of the listeners' rank or position. Hill's tendency to always express his view on matters of great importance, especially when the lives of his men were on the line, led to no one's exclusion, including General Robert E. Lee; such was the similar nature of another outspoken but legendary fighter of the twentieth century, General George S. Patton. General Hill would state later in the official report: *"It was this belief in the demoralization of the Federal army that made our leaders risk the attack."* 346 Without question, the fortifications around the Confederate Capitol at that time were very slight. General McClellan could have captured the city with very little loss of life. The want of supplies would have forced General Lee to attack him as soon as possible with all the disadvantages of a precipitated movement. But General McClellan seemed to have considered nothing of the kind; and as he continued his plans for a siege upon the hazard of Cold Harbor, he was bound to put every available man into that fight. 347

Early on July 1st 1862, General Hill's soldiers plodded their way through the swamp, advancing toward Malvern Hill with General Whiting's Division in the lead; but it was a difficult task and General Hill's elements of the march didn't arrived in position until just before noon. 348 The two generals spent some time reconnoitering and making tentative efforts with their artillery to determine the strength and position of the enemy. General Hill happened to notice General Stonewall Jackson as he provided a helping hand to Captain Reilly's North Carolina battery in an effort to push the battery farther forward. Suddenly, the battery was disabled from cannon fire as the surrounding woods became filled with shrieking and exploding shells. General Hill commented: *"I noted an artilleryman seated comfortably behind a very large tree, and apparently feeling very secure. A moment later a shell passed through the huge tree and took off the man's head."* Such was the lethality of the Union's rifled artillery. 349

General Whiting's Division moved, as directed by his orders, left of the Quaker Road with General D. H. Hill's Division going to the right; General Ewell's Division was placed in a reserve role. 350 The Divisions of Generals Magruder, Huger and McLaws were deployed even farther over to the right of D. H. Hill's Division; the divisions of Generals Longstreet and A. P. Hill were in reserve on the right wing and not engaged. 351 The terrain to the front of General Hill's position was formidable and much to the advantage of the Federals. Directly to his front the ground was open; varying in width from a quarter to half a mile and sloping gradually from the crest. The area was completely swept by the fire of Federal infantry and artillery. To reach this open ground, his troops had to advance through a broken and thickly wooded country; covered nearly throughout its whole extent by a swamp; passable at but very few places, with those being extremely difficult. The entire area was within range of Federal artillery batteries on the heights and supporting gunboats in the river; under whose relentless fire all maneuvers had to be executed. 352 Owing to ignorance of the country, the dense forests hindering necessary communications and the extreme difficulty of the ground, the whole Confederate line was not formed until a late hour in the afternoon. The obstacles presented by the woods and swamp made it impracticable to bring up sufficient quantities of cannons to oppose the extraordinary force of that arm employed by the Federals. The field itself afforded very few positions favorable for its use and none for its proper concentration. Clearly, General McClellan had total command of the battlefield's terrain. 353

General Lee's order of battle had called for General Armistead, from his position on the highest ground, to observe the Union line and, if there was any break in the Federal front, he should charge with a shout, followed by a simultaneous attack by others upon hearing his advance. Perhaps if all the Confederates had assaulted Malvern Hill in concert as General Lee had planned, the tide of the battle may very well have been less disastrous. However, of the ten divisions present, only the divisions of Generals Hill and those under General Magruder's command: General McLaws, General D. R. Jones and General Huger, dashed forward enthusiastically, but without the planned synchronism. 354

The order from General Lee's headquarters read: *"GENERAL D.H. HILL: Batteries have been established to act upon the enemy's line. If it is broken, as is probable, Armistead, who can witness the effect of the fires, has been ordered to charge with a yell. Do the same. R.H. CHILTON, A. A. G."*

Each of the other division commanders had received this order as well. 355 General Armistead, upon noticing a band of Union skirmishers, ordered three of his regiments to drive them from his front. *"In their ardor,"* said General Armistead, *"they went too far."* Hearing the sound of battle and shouting from General Armistead's men, General Hill believed it to be the concerted battle signal for the attack, and in obedience to his orders, attacked with a furious advance. But his courageous assault would be made by his division alone and wholly unsupported. 356 General Magruder, having the same order as General Hill, met with some delays and did not advance until he received a second issuance from General Lee to do so. Unfortunately for the men of D. H. Hill's Division, this second order would not arrive for over two hours, during which time they faced and fought the entire front of the Union army alone and unsupported. 357 To further aggravate the situation, the process to deploy supporting artillery was such that one battery should move up at a time, en echelon, to support the infantry in the attack; followed in succession by the next. But, as each battery arrived they was engaged by over fifty Federal pieces turned upon them, and each battery was crushed within a minute of their arrival. General D. H. Hill dashed toward the enemy with great vigor. But General Magruder failed to respond in kind, having met with some delays. It is of little wonder that General Hill would later criticize the management of this battle for it was the lives of his men that were placed so precariously on the line.

The Comte de Paris, who was on General McClellan's staff, recounted the gallant charge of D. H. Hill's Division: *"Hill advanced alone against the Federal positions . . . . He had therefore before him Morrell's right, Couch's division, reinforced by Caldwell's brigade; . . ..and finally the left of Kearny. The woods skirting the foot of Malvern Hill had hitherto protected the Confederates, but as soon as they passed beyond the edge of the forest, they were received by a fire from all the batteries at once, some posted on the hill, others ranged midway, close to the Federal infantry. The latter joined its musketry fire to the cannonade when D. H. Hill's first line had come within range, and threw it back in disorder on the reserves. While it was reforming, new {Confederate} battalions marched up to the assault in their turn. The remembrance of Cold Harbor doubles the energy of D. H. Hill's soldiers. They try to pierce the line, sometimes at one point, sometimes at another, charging Kearney's left first, and Couch's right; . .and afterward throwing themselves upon the left of Couch's division. But, here also, after nearly reaching the Federal positions, they are repulsed. The conflict is carried on with great fierceness on both sides, and, for a moment, it seems as if the Confederates are at last about to penetrate the very center of their adversaries and of the formidable artillery, which but now was dealing destruction in their ranks. But Sumner, who commands on the right, detaches Sickle's and Meagher's brigades successively to Couch's assistance.* 358 *During this time, Whiting on the left, and Huger on the right, suffer D. H. Hill's soldiers to become exhausted without supporting them. Neither Lee nor Jackson has sent the slightest order, and the din of the battle which is going on in their immediate vicinity has not sufficed to make them march against the enemy. . . . At seven o'clock Hill reorganized the debris of his troops in the woods; . . . . his tenacity and the courage of his soldiers have only had the effect of causing him to sustain heavy losses."* 359 Truly, the courage and valor demonstrated by D. H. Hill's Division's assault can only be described as sublime! Battery after battery was in their hands for moments during the fight, only to be wrested away by fresh troops of the enemy. 360 *"What might have been done if, but one division can perform such mighty acts of valor and heroism, had they had the cooperation of nine others?"*

General Lee's official report cited: *"Orders were issued for a general advance at a given signal but, the causes referred to, prevented a proper concert of action among the troops. D. H. Hill pressed forward across the open field and engaged the enemy gallantly, breaking and driving back his first line; but a simultaneous advance of other troops not taking place, he found himself unable to maintain the ground he had gained against the overwhelming numbers and numerous batteries of the enemy. D. H. Hill was therefore compelled to abandon a part of the ground he had gained after suffering severe loss and inflicting heavy damage upon the enemy. Prompt, vigilant, and obedient, he was always at his post at the appointed hour, and with the true conception of soldierly duty, moved upon order or signal of his superiors without waiting to count the cost. At Malvern Hill, as at Seven Pines, he charged the enemy under orders from the commanding general. The persistent pluck of his brave men, developed to the highest degree of his own unequaled coolness and courage, enabled him again to take and hold much of the enemy's outer line until after the last gun was fired."* 361

After much confusion and delay, General Magruder advanced heroically after sunset with his nine brigades to provide relief for the battered D. H. Hill's Division. Unfortunately, their attack was not synchronized and they were beaten in great detail. As each brigade would emerge from the tree line, the Federal guns, numbering from 50 to 100, would open upon them, tearing horrific gaps in their ranks; but for the heroism of these brave soldiers, they continued to press forward, although decimated for their valiant efforts. In recounting the attack of General Magruder's men, General Hill offered the full context of his infamous statement: *"Most of them had an open field, half a mile wide to cross and the fire of the heavy ordinance of the gun-boats in their rear. It was not war – it was murder."* 362

As nightfall approached it soon became difficult to distinguish friend from foe. The firing continued until after 9 p. m. with no decided result produced. A portion of the Confederate troops were withdrawn to their original positions while others remained on the open field; some resting within a hundred yards of the batteries that had been so bravely but vainly attacked. The general conduct of the Confederate troops was excellent; in many instances heroic. Noteworthy was the gallantry displayed early in the fight by D. H. Hill's division. The lateness of the hour at which the attack necessarily began offered the Federal's full advantage of their superior position, augmented by the natural difficulties that the terrain presented to the Confederate troops. 363

On July 2nd 1862 General Lee was informed that General McClellan had withdrawn his army during the night; leaving the ground covered with his dead and wounded and his route of exit displaying abundant evidence of a hasty retreat. A vigorous Confederate pursuit ensued but a violent thunderstorm prevailed throughout the entire day and greatly retarded the Confederate's efforts. The Federals succeeded in gaining Westover, on the James River, and came under the powerful protection of their gunboats. General McClellan's force immediately began to fortify their position, taking full advantage of the great natural strength provided by the terrain; their position flanked on each side by a creek and every avenue of approach to their front commanded by Federal's heavy guns in mounted entrenchments, further supported by their gunboats. 364

Given the enemy's disposition, General Lee determined an attack to be inadvisable. Owing to the condition of his troops, who had been marching and fighting almost non-stop for seven days, under the most trying circumstances, Lee ordered a general withdrawal; affording his men a much needed break. Several days were spent collecting arms and other property abandoned by the enemy. Finally, on July 8th 1862 General Lee's Army of Northern Virginia returned to the vicinity of Richmond. Under ordinary circumstances the Federal army should have been destroyed. The causes, many discussed here, were for a want of correct and timely information. This fact, attributable chiefly to the geography of the country, enabled General McClellan to skillfully conceal his withdrawal, adding much to the obstructions with which nature had beset before the Confederate's pursuing columns. The Federal's siege of Richmond had been denied them, and so too the ovarall objective of General McClellan's campaign. After months of detailed preparation and careful execution, at an enormous cost in men and money, the Army of the Potomac finally withdrew, in utter frustration. 365 Upon conclusion of the battle the

Confederate army had sustained double the casualties of the Union army; 5,650 casualties versus 2,214 Federal losses. Not only did the fourteen brigades engaged in the battle suffer, but so too suffered the inactive troops and the reserves who were too late arriving to be of assistance. Many casualties were sustained from the fearful artillery fire of Federal guns which reached all parts of the woods. Hence, more than half the casualties were from field pieces – an unprecedented effect of warfare for the Civil War era. [366]

An historical comment regarding Hill's open criticism of General Lee: After the war D. H. Hill was asked to write an article for the leading journal of that day, wherein he should detail the circumstances of the battle and offer his viewpoint that *"it wasn't war, it was murder."* Much to General Hill's great credit he offered this memorable and most eloquent reply: *"In my official reports. . . . I criticized the management of General Lee at Malvern Hill and South Mountain. He was then alive, my commander, and in the full tide of success. He is dead now and failed in his efforts. What I could and did do, when in the meridian of his power, I cannot do now."*

D. H. HILL

"In my official reports. . . . I criticized the management of General Lee at Malvern Hill and South Mountain. He was then alive, my commander, and in the full tide of success. He is dead now and failed in his efforts. What I could and did do, when in the meridian of his power, I cannot do now."

[[General D. H. Hill]]

Q25

This response stands today as the most poignant statement rendered, not only of the Battles of Malvern Hill and South Mount specifically, but of the entire Civil War in general. It is indicative of the perfect symmetry of this great man's characteristic features: an unflinching sense of duty that drove his dauntless courage accompanied by an unyielding steadfastness of purpose; his deep sense of loyalty, honor and integrity; and above all, his absolute determination for truth and honesty. Like many other great military leaders, he held an invincible fidelity to his convictions of honesty. Yes, he was openly critical of General Lee; for this he was convicted by many to be sharp of tongue. But his criticism was borne purely as the conviction of an honest man. A lesser man would have held his tongue rather than stick to his principles in order to forgo the accompanying wrath. But such conduct simply was not within General Hill's nature. He fought gallantly at the Seven Day's Battle but sustained nearly 40% loss of the 10,000 men that he had led onto the battlefield. It had been a bloody fight for which he and his men had been cited for great gallantry and valor in the Official Reports. But this congratulatory recognition was very costly as he and his men spent much of the entire next week burying the dead from the battle. 367

General Hill had first crossed the Chickahominy with 10,000 combat effective soldiers. Of these, 3,907 were killed or wounded and 48 were reported missing, either through capture or fugitives of the field. It was Hill's stated opinion that: *"throughout this campaign we attacked just when and where the enemy wished us to attack. This was owing to our ignorance of the country and lack of reconnaissance of the successive battlefields. Porter's weak point at Gaines' Mill was his right flank. A thorough examination of the ground would have disclosed that; and had Jackson's command gone in on the left of the road running by the McGehee house, Porter's whole position would have been turned and the line of retreat cut off. An armed reconnaissance at Malvern would have shown the immense preponderance of the Federal artillery, and that a contest with it must be hopeless. The battle, with all its melancholy results, proved, however, that the Confederate infantry and Federal artillery, side by side on the same field, need fear no foe on earth."* 368

One cannot be provided with a more resounding analysis of this battle than General Hill's preceding, first-hand account; rendered by a gallant soldier, an active participant in the conflict – *"Lee's Fighting General."* After the war much was written of D. H. Hill's contributions during the Battle of Seven Days. First, listen to General Hill's assessment of the Generals-in-chief, both Union and Confederate, then subsequently to other first-hand and creditable reports: *"Both commanders had shown great ability. McClellan, if not always great in the advance, was masterly in retreat, and was unquestionably the greatest of Americans as an organizer of an army. Lee's plans were perfect; and had not his dispositions for a decisive battle at Frayser's farm miscarried, through no fault of his own, he would have won a most complete victory. It was not the lease part of his greatness that he did not complain of his disappointment, and that he at no time sought a scapegoat upon which to lay a failure. As reunited Americans, we have reason to be proud of both commanders."* 369

On July 3rd 1862, just two days after the Battle of Malvern Hill, D. H. Hill wrote to his wife Isabella: *"I am perfectly well, never better. For eight days, I have not washed my face, have slept on the ground without a bed or blanket, have not taken off my boots or spurs, have been struck four times without being seriously hurt once. Surely, God even our God ought to be adored and worshipped."* 370

Judge Avery wrote: *"After that came the Seven Days' Battle. Each of these, of itself, was an epic. The army was then under General Lee. Gaines Mill was probably the most important of these engagements and D. H. Hill's Division struck a decisive blow at a critical moment. It was thus expressed by General Lee: "D. H. Hill charged across the open ground in front of him, one of his regiments having first bravely carried a battery whose fire enfiladed his advance. Gallantly supported by his troops on his right, who pressed forward with unfaltering resolution, he reached the crest of the ridge (above the McGehee house), and after a bloody struggle, broke the army's line, captured several of its batteries, and drove him in confusion beyond the Chickahominy until darkness rendered further pursuit impossible."* 371

General John B. Gordon wrote: *"was that of Lieutenant-General D. H. Hill, and the particular occasion which I select, and which aptly illustrates his remarkable faith, was the battle of Malvern Hill. At that time he was major-general of the division in which I commanded Rodes' brigade. He was my friend. The personal and official relations between us, considering the disparity in our ages, were most cordial and even intimate. He was closely allied to Stonewall Jackson, and in many respects his counterpart. His brilliant career as a soldier is so well known that any historical account of it, in such a book as I am writing, would be wholly unnecessary. I introduce him here as a most conspicuous illustration of a faith in Providence which, in its steadiness and strength and in its sustaining influence under great peril, certainly touched the margin of the sublime. At Malvern Hill, where General McClellan made his superb and last stand against General Lee's forces, General D. H. Hill took his seat at the root of a large tree and began to write his orders. At this point McClellan's batteries from the crest of a high ridge, and his gunboats from the James River, were ploughing up the ground in every direction around us. The long shells from the gunboats, which our men called "McClellan's gate-posts," and the solid shot from his heavy guns on land, were knocking the Confederate batteries to pieces almost as fast as they could be placed in position. The Confederate artillerists fell so rapidly that I was compelled to detail untrained infantry to take their places. And yet there sat that intrepid officer, General D. H. Hill, in the midst of it all, coolly writing his orders. He did not place the large tree between himself and the destructive batteries, but sat facing them. I urged him to get on the other side of the tree and avoid such needless and reckless exposure. He replied, "Don't worry about me; look after the men. I am not going to be killed until my time comes." He had scarcely uttered these words when a shell exploded in our immediate presence, severely shocking me for the moment, a portion of it tearing through the breast of his coat and rolling him over in the newly ploughed ground. This seemed to convert him to a more rational faith; for he rose from the ground, and, shaking the dirt from his uniform, quietly took his seat on the other side of the tree."* 372

CHAPTER X

THE DIX-HILL CARTEL – PRISONER OF WAR EXCHANGE

D. H. Hill was given a brief break from the rigors of war when, on July 14th 1862, he was designated to serve the Confederacy as an official emissary [373] to negotiate a general exchange of prisoners of war with Union authorities. [374] The Dix-Hill Cartel and prisoner of war issue remain today as one of the most overlooked and under researched topics of the Civil War. [375] Drawing from personal military experiences this author can solemnly report that there are no issues dearer to the true heart of any soldier than those surrounding the plight of our prisoners of war. My personal tenure of military service spanned the periods of our nation's history from the TET offensive in Vietnam through the surge of Operations Iraqi Freedom (OIF). During the former, I became determined to wear a POW bracelet as a constant reminder of colleagues captured on the field of battle.

Over a period of several years the old bracelet became quite tarnished and so worn from daily wear that it eventually broke into two pieces. Wearing this bracelet daily had become such an integral part of my soldierly regimen that I was immediately induced to have it repaired. Unable to find a vendor willing to do so, I was thrilled when my brother Dean repaired the bracelet with his arc welder. I was totally unconcerned with the cosmetics of the bracelet as the welding caused a huge black spot that blotted out a portion of the POW's engraved name. I personally regarded this item to be, not one of jewelry but, a symbol for the POW quandary. It became an essential part of my army uniform – along with my dog tags. I carried the bracelet with me during every military assignment for nearly 40 years. At the very end of 2010, after a negotiated accord between the governments of the USA and Vietnam facilitated the recovery and identification of his remains, this gallant POW, missing in action for more than 4 decades, finally came home – his mission complete and duty fulfilled. My personal experience, representing but a single illustration among thousands, provides soldierly insight to address the compassion associated with the issue. I can only suppose that the Prisoner of War issue was equally relevant in importance to both Civil War armies as it remains to our army today. General D. H. Hill played a significant role during the Civil War when, on July 14th 1862, he was entrusted by General Lee and the Confederate government, as an official emissary, to meet Union General Dix; empowered with full authority to negotiate for a general exchange of all prisoners taken and held or paroled by the respective armies; fully authorized to conclude any arrangement which provided for the exchange of prisoners upon terms of perfect equality. 376

D. H. HILL   **J. A. DIX**

In obedience to orders, he met on July 22nd 1862 with General Dix to formalize a negotiated cartel, stipulating that all prisoners of war thereafter taken would be discharged on parole until exchanged. General D. H. Hill and Union General Dix, having been commissioned by the authorities they respectively represented, made arrangements for a general exchange of prisoners of war, agreeing to nine articles: 377

Article 1 stipulated that all prisoners of war held by either party including those taken on private armed vessels, known as privateers, would be discharged upon the conditions and terms following: prisoners would be exchanged man for man and officer for officer; privateers to be placed upon the footing of officers men of the Navy. Men and officers of lower grades could be exchanged for officers of a higher grade, and men and officers of different services could be exchanged according to the following scale of equivalents: 378 A general commander in chief or an admiral would be exchanged for officers of equal rank, or for sixty privates or common seamen. A flag officer or major-general would be exchanged for officers of equal rank, or for forty privates or common seamen. A commodore carrying a broad pennant or a brigadier-general would be exchanged for officers of equal rank, or twenty privates or common seamen. A captain in the Navy or a colonel would be exchanged for officers of equal rank, or for fifteen privates or common seamen. A lieutenant-colonel or a commander in the Navy would be exchanged for officers of equal rank, or for ten privates or common seamen. A lieutenant-commander or a major would be exchanged for officers of equal rank, or eights privates or common seamen. 379 A lieutenant or a master in the Navy or a captain in the Army or marines would be exchanged for officers of equal rank, or six privates or common seamen. Master's mates in the Navy or lieutenants and ensigns in the Army would be exchanged for officers of equal rank, or four privates or common seamen. Midshipmen, warrant officers in the Navy, masters of merchant vessels and commanders of privateers would be exchanged for officers of equal rank, or three privates or common seamen. 380 Second captains, lieutenants or mates of merchant vessels or privateers and all petty officers in the Navy and all non-commissioned officers in the Army or marines would be severally exchanged for persons of equal rank, or for two privates or common seamen, and private soldiers or common seamen shall be exchanged for each other, man for man.

Article 2 stipulated that local, State, civil and militia rank held by persons not in actual military service would not be recognized, the basis of exchange being the grade actually held in the naval and military service of the respective parties.

Article 3 stipulated if any citizen, held by either party on charges of disloyalty or any alleged civil offense are exchanged, it would only be for another citizen; captured sutlers, teamsters and all civilians in the actual service of either party would be exchanged for persons in similar position. 381

Article 4 stipulated that all prisoners of war would be discharged upon parole in ten days after their capture and the prisoners currently held or taken thereafter would be transported to the points mutually agreed upon at the expense of the capturing party. The surplus prisoners not exchanged would not be permitted to take up arms again or to serve as military police or constabulary force in any fort, garrison or field-work held by either of the respective parties; nor as guards of prisoners, depots or stores, nor that would discharge any duty usually performed by soldiers, until exchanged under the provisions of the cartel. The exchange was not to be considered complete until the officer or soldier exchanged for had been actually restored to the lines to which he belonged. 382

Article 5 stipulated that each party, upon the discharge of prisoners of the other party, would be authorized to discharge an equal number of their own officers or men from parole, but would be required to furnish at the same time to the other party a list of their prisoners discharged and of their own officers and men relieved from parole, thus empowering each party to relieve from parole such of their furnished while keeping both parties advised of the true condition of the exchange of prisoners. 383

Article 6 stipulated that provisions of the aforementioned articles would be of binding obligation during the continuance of the war, irrespective of which party might have the surplus of prisoners, with the great principles involved being, first, the equitable exchange of prisoners, man for man, officer for officer, or officers of higher grade exchanged for officers of lower grade or for privates, in accordance with the scale of equivalents; second, that privateers and officers and men of different services would be exchanged according to the same scale of equivalents; third, that all prisoners, of whatever arm of service, would be exchanged or paroled in ten days from the time of their capture; if deemed practicable would be transferred to their own lines at that time; if not, they would be transferred as soon thereafter as practicable; fourth, that no officer, soldier or employee, in the service of either party, would be considered as exchanged and absolved from his parole until his equivalent has actually reached the lines of his friends; fifth, that the parole forbade the performance of field, garrison, police, or guard, or constabulary duty. 384

Article 7 stipulated that all prisoners of war held on either side and all prisoners thereafter taken would be sent with all reasonable dispatch to A. M. Aiken's, below Dutch Gap, on the James River, Va., or to Vicksburg, on the Mississippi River, in the State of Mississippi, and thereupon exchanged or paroled until such exchange could be effected, requiring that notice being previously given by each party of the number of prisoners it would send and specified the time when they would be delivered at those points respectively; further, should the vicissitudes of war change, the military relations of the places designated in the article to the contending parties would render the same inconvenient for the delivery and exchange of prisoners, other places bearing as nearly as might be the present local relations of said places to the lines of said parties would be by mutual agreement substituted. Nothing in this article prevented the commanders of two opposing forces from exchanging or releasing their prisoners on parole from other points as long as it was mutually agreed upon by both commanders. 385

Article 8 stipulated that, for the purpose of carrying into effect all articles of the agreement, each party would appoint two agents, to be called agents for the exchange of prisoners of war, whose duty it would be communicate with each other by correspondence and otherwise, prepare lists of prisoners, attend to the delivery of the prisoners at the places agreed upon and would carry out promptly, effectually and in good faith all the details and provisions of the entire agreement. 386

Article 9 stipulated that, in case any misunderstanding arose in regard to any clause or stipulation contained in the accord, it was mutually agreed that such misunderstanding would not interrupt the release of prisoners on parole, as therein provided, but would be made the subject of friendly explanations in order that the object of this agreement would neither be defeated nor postponed. 387

General Hill in the official records reported that scarcely had the cartel been signed when the Union military authorities commenced a practice of changing the character of the war *"from such as should become civilized nations into a campaign of indiscriminate robbery and murder."* His official report postulated that a general order, issued by the Union's Secretary of War on the very day that the cartel was signed in Virginia, directed Union military commanders to take the property of the Confederate people for the convenience and use of the army without compensation. 388

Subsequently on July 23rd 1862, General Hill submitted another official report detailing that: *"another general order issued by General Pope directed the 'murder of peaceful Confederate citizens as spies, if found quietly tilling their farms in his rear, even outside of his lines and one of his Brigadier-Generals, Steinwehr, last seized innocent and peaceful inhabitants to be held as hostages, to the end that they may be murdered in cold blood if any of his soldiers are killed by some unknown persons whom he designates as 'bushwhackers.' Some of the military authorities seem to suppose that their end will be better attained by a savage war in which no quarter is to be given and no age or sex is to be spared, than by such hostilities as are alone recognized to be lawful in modern times. We find ourselves driven by our enemies by steady progress toward a practice which we abhor, and which we are vainly struggling to avoid. Under these circumstances, this government has issued the accompanying general order, which I am directed by the President to transmit to you, recognizing Major-General Pope and his commissioned officers to be in the position which they have chosen for themselves that of robbers and murderers, and not that of public enemies, entitled, if captured, to be treated as prisoners of war."* 389

The President also instructs me to inform you that we renounce our right of retaliation on the innocent, and will continue to treat the private soldiers of General Pope's army as prisoners of war ; but if, after notice to your Government that they confine repressive measures to the punishment of commissioned officers who are willing to participate in these crimes, the savage practices threatened in the orders alluded to be persisted in, we shall reluctantly be forced to the last resort of accepting the war on the terms chosen by our enemies, until the voice of an outraged humanity shall compel a respect for the recognized usages of war. While the President considers that the facts referred to would justify a refusal on our part to execute the cartel by which we have agreed to liberate an excess of prisoners of war in our hands, a sacred regard for plighted faith which shrinks from the semblance of breaking a promise precludes a resort to such an extremity, nor is it his desire to extend to any other forces of the United States the punishment merited by General Pope and such commissioned officers as choose to participate in the execution of his infamous order." 390

Merely the tone of General Hill's written reports illustrates the passions stirred by what must have been most controversial negotiations over an extremely sensitive topic. Although his dialogue was very frank it was an internal document to the Confederacy. 391 However, many instances are officially recorded where the external communications between the Union and Confederate authorities became quite heated and accusatory, equally on both sides. While the tone of General Hill's letter portrayed him to possess that sharp tongue for which he has previously been cited, it also reflected his intolerance for any failure to meet his high threshold of honesty, integrity and honor. During the course of the war numerous prisoner exchanges were negotiated under the provisions of the Dix-Hill cartel; 392 often under the most contentious circumstances and generating heated communications at the very highest levels of military command. 393 Even the gentle giant, Robert E. Lee, was accused of using language deemed insulting to Federal authorities. One illustration was official correspondence between Generals Lee and Halleck wherein the latter wrote: *"your two communications of the second instant, with enclosures are received. As these papers are couched in language exceedingly insulting to the Government of the United States, I must respectfully decline to receive them.*

They are returned herewith. Very respectfully, your obedient servant, H. W. Halleck General-in-Chief, U. S. Army." 394

It is noteworthy to recognize that, while General Hill clearly possessed the skills necessary for articulation of the Confederate's position at the national

level, and although being fully entrusted to do so with great latitude on behalf of the Confederacy, clearly negotiations were not his forte. He was *Lee's Fighting General* – the Confederacy's Angel of Death! He was an accomplished man of brilliant intellect, capable of performing multiple roles at various levels of authority. But as to his greatest contributions to the Confederacy he was clearly at his very best seated in the saddle of a steed, brandishing his saber while leading his courageous soldiers into desperate battles under the chorus of Rebel yells, amidst the fog of war! It was of great service, equally to General Hill and to the Confederacy when, upon the successful completion of the Dix-Hill cartel, he was soon directed to reassume command of his beloved D. H. Hill's Division. Shortly after General Lee's engagement at the Second Battle of Manassas, the Army of Northern Virginia crossed the Potomac and General D. H. Hill was summoned to take command, once again, of D. H. Hill's Division.
395

MARYLAND CAMPAIGN 1862

CHAPTER XI

The armies of Generals McClellan and Pope had now been brought back to the point from which they set out on the campaigns of the Spring and Summer. The strategic objectives of the Army of the Potomac's Peninsula Campaign had been fustrating for them and the designs of the Federals on the Carolina coast had been thwarted by the withdrawal of their main body from North Carolina. 396 Northeastern Virginia had been freed from the presence of Federal soldiers up to the entrenchments of Washington D. C. Soon after the arrival of the Army of Northern Virginia at Leesburg, intelligence reports indicated that the Union troops, heretofore occupying Winchester, were now retired to the areas of Harper's Ferry and Martinsburg. This had effectively transferred the war from the interior to the frontier and provided the Confederate army with fortunate access to the plentiful supplies of rich and productive districts in the Shenandoah Valley. General Lee, desiring to inflict further injury upon General McClellan's Army of the Potomac, determined that his best course of action would be to advance his army into Maryland. 397

While Confederate operations in Maryland provided for a possible initiative, both tactically and strategically, General Lee's troops were poorly equipped for such an invasion. His army was extremely lacking in most of the materials of war. The Confederate troops were clothed poorly, thousands of them being destitute of shoes, and transportation assets to support the invasion were meager at best. Despite these deficiencies, General Lee still believed his army was sufficiently strong to hold the enemy along the northern frontier until the approach of winter should render any Federal advance into Virginia difficult, if not impracticable. There were also great expectations by the leaders of the Confederacy that the political environment in Maryland was such that the good citizens of that State would be supportive of, if not excited about, the presence of General Lee's Army of Northern Virginia. No matter how inferior the Federal leadership perceived the Confederate army to be, in comparison to their grand Army of the Potomac, General Lee was convinced that his invasion of Maryland would force the Federals to retain a substantial portion of their available forces in the Washington area; providing for military contingencies. 398

At the same time it was hoped that a Confederate military success might persuade the citizens of Maryland to desire the recovery of their liberty from an overreaching Federal Government. The difficulties that surrounded Marylanders were fully understood by General Lee and he anticipated their strong support of the Confederate's cause and believed that they would be very appreciative of Confederate assurances to provide the citizens of that great State with security and protection. Influenced by these considerations, the advance of the Army of Northern Virginia towards Maryland was put in motion. 399 General Lee's object in crossing the Potomac east of the Blue Ridge was to force the enemy, by threatening Washington and Baltimore, to evacuate Martinsburg and Harper's Ferry; and to establish his own lines of communication through the valley; then by advancing towards Pennsylvania to draw the enemy away from his own base of supplies. General Lee had not considered making a stand at South Mountain, probably not at any point north of the Potomac; but the continued occupation of Martinsburg and Harper's Ferry made it necessary to move directly upon the former place and to invest the latter, where both garrisons ultimately united.

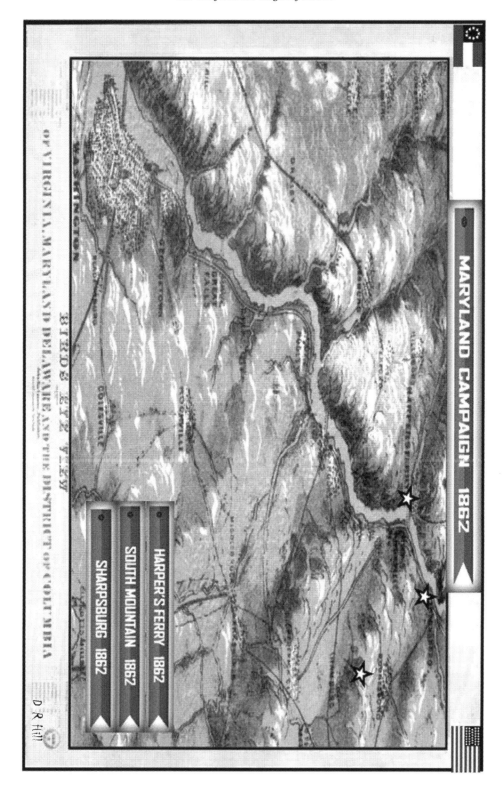

In consequence of the delay in reducing the garrison at Harper's Ferry it became essential to the safety of General Lee's army that General McClellan's entire force should be held in check for a whole day at the pass in the South Mountains; this strenuous assignment was given to D. H. Hill's depleted division, now numbering less than four thousand combat effective soldiers.

General Longstreet, with his whole force, estimated at four thousand, was positioned at Hagerstown, while General Jackson had disposed of his own command, including Generals McLaw's and A. P. Hill's Divisions, either with a view to an attack on Harper's Ferry or to cut off the retreat of its occupying force. Three days later McClellan, according to his own report, advanced to the attack at Sharpsburg with 87,000 men. General D. H. Hill, having reassumed command of his beloved D. H. Hill's Division, joined the Army of Northern Virginia once again on September 2nd 1862; 400 promptly advancing his troops during the period of the 4th through the 7th of September across the Potomac 401 and making camp in the vicinity of Fredericktown. 402

At this point in history the most controversial event of the entire Civil War transpired; the loss of Special Order 191, most commonly referred to as *"the lost dispatch."* A brief rundown of this event is provided here but this significant event holds such great historical importance that it warrants a detailed discussion and analysis; wherein an entire chapter has been devoted to the controversy in a later chapter. Such a separate and detailed accounting is required in order to provide you with the historical background and precise details necessary to gain a factual historical perspective of this most controversial issue of the entire war.

On September 9th 1862 General Lee issued Special Order 191, arguably one of the most risky and daring plans of the entire war. It contained the disposition and missions of his entire army, including their plans to move the following morning; describing in detail a bold Confederate action that would effectively divide General Lee's already small army in to four separate forces – all right under the nose of the Union's General-in-chief George B. McClellan. Beginning early on September 10th 1862 General Jackson was to go to Martinsburg, capture the garrison, intercept those seeking to escape to Harper's Ferry then return to the main body of the army at Boonsboro or Hagerstown. General Longstreet was to move to Boonsboro, with D. H. Hill's troops constituting the rear guard. 403

When Order No. 191 was issued, D. H. Hill had just rejoined the Army of Northern Virginia, having finished his work on the Dix-Hill cartel; he was temporarily assigned to the command of General Jackson. Thus, per standard military protocol, all orders received by General Hill after entering Maryland originated from General Stonewall Jackson. On September 9th 1862 General

Hill received his hand-written copy of Special Order 191 from General Jackson, significantly noting the receipt of no other copy thereof. Because the order provided such precise and classified details of the bold, yet risky, tactics of the Confederate plan, General Hill decided to retain personal possession of his copy of Special Order 191, as a measure of safeguard, instead of placing it with his other papers - as was routinely his practice. 404 Four days after General Lee issued Special Order 191 an Indiana private, B. W. Mitchell of the Twenty-Seventh Indiana Volunteers, found, in the vicinity of Frederick, three cigars wrapped in a paper which was addressed to General Hill. This paper was passed to General McClellan who found it to be a copy of Lee's Special Order 191. General Stuart, learning that General McClellan was in possession of this order, reported it to General Lee on the night of September 13-14th 1862. 405 As fate would have it, General Hill's decision to keep his copy of the order on his person would prove to be a most fortunate decision on his part; one that would later provide key supporting evidence demonstrating that neither he nor his staff ever received delivery of the copy of the Order; supposedly sent by courier from General Lee's headquarters but lost along the way. Thus, as later determined by formal Confederate inquiry, D. H. Hill and his staff could not lose that which was never in their possession. 406 Nonetheless, after reviewing the document, General McClellan was confident in its authenticity and most resolute to move decisively against General Lee's army.

At this juncture General McClellan supposedly made a legendary proclamation to one of his subordinates, wherein he reportedly exclaimed. *"Now I know what to do! Here is a paper with which, if I cannot whip Bobby Lee, I will be willing to go home."* From his reading of Special Order 191, General McClellan decided to attack D. H. Hill's Division at South Mountain, believing that General Longstreet was occupying the mountains, supported by D. H. Hill's division. General McClellan wrote General Franklin from Frederick City on September 14th 1862 just after he had read the *"lost dispatch,"* informing Franklin that General Longstreet was to move to Boonsboro and there halt with General D. H. Hill. General McClellan then directed Franklin to make his dispositions with an eye both to the relief of the garrison at Harper's Ferry and the capture of Generals Longstreet and Hill. Clearly the plan outlined in McClellan's letter is predicated upon his supposition that Generals Longstreet and Hill were together, constituting the main body of General Lee's army.

In another report to Union General Halleck, General McClellan estimated the Confederate forces to number 120,000 men. Given the contents of this letter, General McClellan was misled by his interpretation of Special Order 191 and his opinion supported by the skillful disposition of D. H. Hill's troops. General McClellan's report proved beyond all question that he believed the Confederate force to his front was some 30,000 strong; as recorded in the Official Records,

Series 1, Volume XIX, Part 1, p. 55. 407 General McClellan's overestimation of the strength of the Confederate force induced a slow-paced movement of his forces that provided General Longstreet sufficient time to come up in the afternoon, enabling General Hill the historic opportunity to confront and successfully block the whole Army of the Potomac assembled before him. 408 General Lee's decision to cross the Potomac east of the Blue Ridge was purposefully intended to present a strategic threat to the Washington and Baltimore areas, with expectations that the action would produce several favorable effects. The first expectation was to cause a Federal withdraw from the south bank where their substantial presence endangered the Confederate's lines of communications. Second, General Lee desired to gain some degree of safety for his soldiers who were engaged in the removal of Confederate wounded and the large quantities of captured Federal property acquired from recent battlefields. If his desired effects were attained, General Lee then proposed to move his army into western Maryland and effectively establish communications with Richmond through the valley of the Shenandoah. Once his communications were established, he would then proceed with his threat against Pennsylvania, determined to cause the Army of the Potomac to follow, thus drawing them from their base of supplies. 409

General Lee had anticipated that the Confederate's advance upon Fredericktown would lead to the evacuation of Martinsburg and Harper's Ferry, thus opening the lines of communications through the Valley. But when this did not occur, it then became necessary to dislodge the enemy, by force, from those positions before concentrating his army west of the mountains. 410 To accomplish this in a speedy manner, General Jackson was directed to proceed with his command to Martinsburg, drive the enemy from that place then move down the south side of the Potomac upon Harper's Ferry. Generals McLaws and R. H. Anderson's divisions were ordered to seize Maryland Heights on the north side of the Potomac and General Walker directed to take possession of Loudon Heights, on the east side of the Shenandoah, where it joins with the Potomac River. Upon reducing Harper's Ferry and clearing the Valley of the enemy, these commands were to then join the rest of General Lee's army at Boonsboro or Hagerstown. 411

HARPER'S FERRY 1862

The march of these troops began on September 10th 1862 in concert with movements by Generals Longstreet and D. H. Hill, who were ordered to cross the South Mountains and move towards Boonsboro. [412] General Stuart's cavalry remained east of the mountains to cover the army's movement, observe the enemy and slow down his advance. [413] Receiving reports that a considerable Federal force was approaching Hagerstown from the direction of Chambersburg, General Longstreet continued his march with all haste in order to secure the road leading to Williamsport; and also to prevent the removal of stores which were said to be in Hagerstown. [414] General Longstreet arrived at Hagerstown on September 11th 1862, leaving General Hill to take a position near Boonsboro, in support of the cavalry rear guard while arraying his forces to prevent any attempts by the enemy at Harper's Ferry to escape through Pleasant Valley. [415] The Federal army's advance was so slow and deliberate that General Lee believed his army had sufficient time to effectively reduce Harper's Ferry and afterward concentrate his troops; well before the arrival of General McClellan's forces would necessitate their engagement. [416] General Jackson marched with great vigor, crossing the Potomac in the vicinity of Williamsport on September 11th 1862; whereupon he dispatched General A. P. Hill's division directly to Martinsburg, disposing the remainder of his command to cut off any efforts by the enemy to retreat westward.

J. LONGSTREET

D. H. HILL

T. J. JACKSON

PROMINENT CONFEDERATE GENERALS

HARPER'S FERRY 1862

J.E.B. STUART

D. R. JONES

A. P. HILL

J. G. WALKER

L. McLAWS

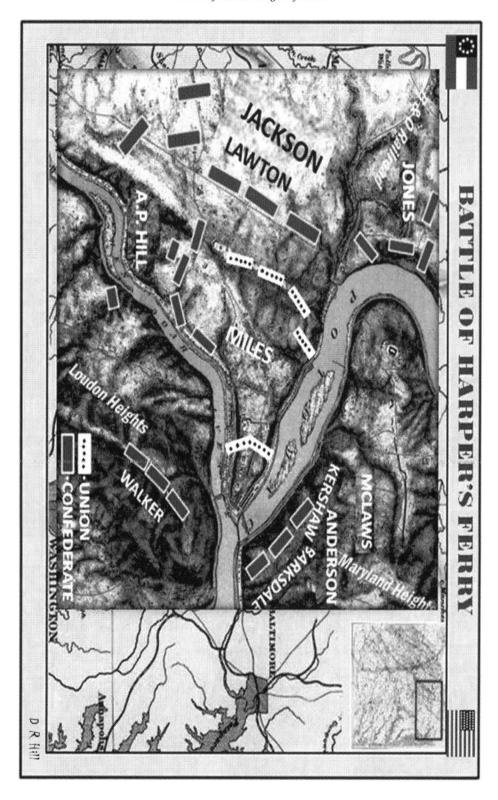

As General Jackson approached, the Federal troops evacuated Martinsburg and retreated to Harper's Ferry on the night of September 11th 1862. General Jackson entered Martinsburg on September 12th 1862, capturing some prisoners and abandoned stores. In the forenoon of the following day his leading division, under General A. P. Hill, came upon the strongly entrenched Union positions along Bolivar Heights, in rear of Harper's Ferry. 417 In preparation for his attack, General Jackson established communications with the cooperating forces of Generals McLaws and Walker; General McLaws had taken a position on the opposite side of the Potomac while General Walker was in the vicinity of the Shenandoah Valley. In accordance with the plan of attack, General Walker moved on September 13th 1862 and secured Loudoun Heights, subsequently positioning himself to support an advance upon Harper's Ferry.

General McLaws moved to Pleasant Valley on September 11th 1862 and, on the following day, arrayed his forces for the attack; directing General Kershaw to ascend the ridge, whose southern extremity is known as Maryland Heights, with orders to attack the strong Federal positions thereupon; assigning the brigades of Generals Semmes and Mahone the critical task of guarding the pass to his rear, through which he had entered Pleasant Valley; while disposing the remainder of his command to hold the roads leading from Harper's Ferry eastward through Weavertown and northward from Sandy Hook. 418

Owing to the rugged nature of the ground upon which General Kershaw had to operate, and for the want of passable roads to the heights, he was forced to use infantry alone. Decisively engaging the advance parties of the enemy on the summit of the ridge on September 12th 1862, he assaulted the heavily fortified works the next day. After a spirited contest the enemy was forcibly displaced, causing them to retreat, after spiking their heavy guns, to Harper's Ferry. By 4:30 p. m. General Kershaw was in possession of Maryland Heights. On September 14th 1862 a road for artillery was cut along the ridge and at 2 p. m. four guns opened fire upon the enemy from the opposite side of the river; subsequently the investment of Harper's Ferry was accomplished in short order. 419

SOUTH MOUNTAIN 1862

General McClellan's army approached the pass in South Mountain on the Boonsboro and Fredericktown road on the afternoon of September 13th 1862, determined to penetrate the mountains, reach the rear of General McLaws and intent upon relieving the Union garrison at Harper's Ferry. To prevent this from happening, General D. H. Hill was directed to guard the Boonsboro gap while General Longstreet was ordered to march from Hagerstown in his support. 420 Initially, General Hill deployed the brigades of Generals Garland and Colquitt to hold the pass but, upon determining that a considerable enemy force was near, he recalled the rest of his division. 421 At dawn on September 14th 1862 General Hill rose to face the imminent prospects of yet another fight – The Battle of South Mountain (or Boonsboro). This engagement was one of grand illusion and delusion. General George B. McClellan was under the illusion that he possessed a tremendous tactical advantage, being in possession of General Lee's Special Order 191. The Union General-in-chief was also under the delusion that *"the whole [south] mountain was swarming with Confederates."* 422 This misconception was wholly credited to General Hill's skillful tactical maneuvering which consistently provided, throughout the fight, an appearance of a significant Confederate presence whenever and wherever the Federals presented themselves.

S. GARLAND

D. H. HILL

J. LONGSTREET

PROMINENT CONFEDERATE GENERALS

G. B. ANDERSON

R. E. RODES

J. B. HOOD

R. RIPLEY

A. H. COLQUITT

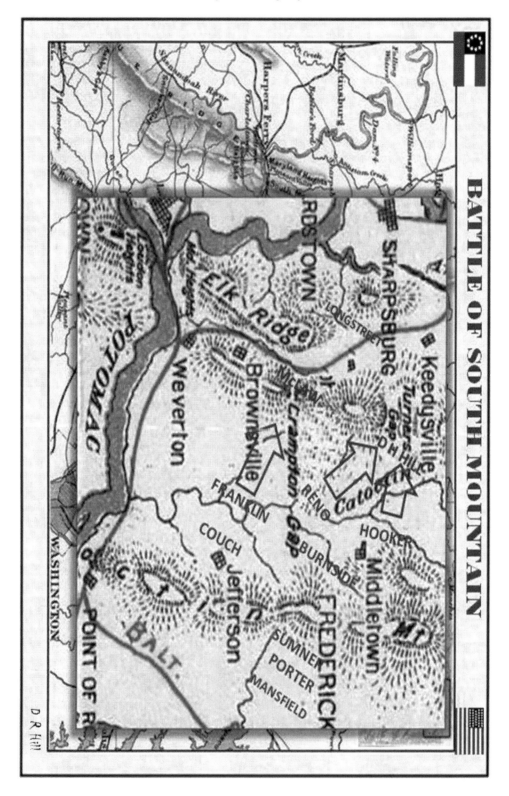

Whether through illusion, delusion or a combination of both, General Hill was able to craft and execute one of the most brilliant defensive operations of the campaign. His successful defense of the gaps along South Mountain saved the communications of General Lee's army, secured its concentration after General Jackson's capture of Harper's Ferry and rendered ineffectual General McClellan's assertion that he would *"whip Bobby Lee."* 423 General D. H. Hill's Division had been 22,000 strong, but for a heavy toll inflicted by battles, marches, lack of shoes, and many other attritions caused by the war, his force had been greatly reduced to only 5,000 combat efficient soldiers. General Longstreet was in the process of reinforcing him but the bulk of his units were still positioned in the vicinity of Hagarstown, some 13 miles away.

On September 13th 1862, General Hill was ordered by General Lee to position his troops to prevent the escape of the Federals from the besieged Harper's Ferry and also to guard the passes in the Blue Ridge mountain range near the small town of Boonsboro. 424 These military orders presented Hill with quite a dilemma; on the one hand he was to prevent the escape of the enemy from Harper's Ferry; on the other he was to prevent General McClellan's forces from gaining passage through the gaps in the South Mountains. General Hill faced the enormous challenge of how to cover the key points with so small a force. Understanding that all points were of great importance and that his coverage required a mobile and agile defense, he skillfully set the disposition of his small force in a manner that allowed him the ability to quickly engage and disengage, when and where they were most needed on the field. 425

General J. E. B. *"Jeb"* Stuart reported to General Hill that he had found little activity toward Turner's Gap and provided his assessment that two brigades would be sufficient to hold the pass. General Hill placed the brigades of Generals Garland and Colquitt accordingly and immediately ordered his other three brigades up from the neighborhood of Boonsboro. 426 He initially guided one brigade to Crampton's Gap, however once the enemy's main advance had formed to reveal that General McClellan's main attack would be through Turner's and Fox's Gap – vis-à-vis directly through center of his defensive position, he recalled that brigade. 427 A thorough and personal examination of the pass early the next morning convinced General Hill that his position could only be held by a large force and was wholly indefensible by a small one. Accordingly, he ordered up General Anderson's brigade. He also dispatched a regiment from General Ripley's brigade to hold another pass, some 3 miles distant, on his left. He felt reluctant to order up Generals Ripley and Rodes from the important positions they were currently holding until something more definitive was known of the strength and design of the Union forces arrayed before him. 428

Around 7 a. m. the enemy opened fire upon General Hill's right, pushing forward with a large force through the dense woods, seeking to gain a practicable road to the rear of General Hill's position. General Garland's brigade was dispatched quickly to meet this overwhelming force. General Garland valiantly thwarted the Union attack as he effectively held them at bay but his success came at a terrible cost; his brilliant effort cost the life of Garland – a *"gallant and accomplished Christian soldier"* who had no superiors and few equals in the service. 429 At the very onset of the battle, Colonel Ruffin of the Thirteenth North Carolina Regiment, who was standing beside General Garland when he was instantly killed, discovered a moment later that the other regiments of the brigade had retired, leaving only his command to bear the initial brunt of the entire leading element of General McClellan's force, totaling 30,000 men. Shouting commands to hastily realign his formation so that his force was facing to the rear, he instantly and defiantly ordered the regiment to charge. Despite great pain from a wound that he had sustained in the initial seconds of the engagement, Colonel Ruffin performed the Herculean feat of cutting his way, rearward, through the crowded rows of blue uniforms. 430 A few moments later the gallant colonel, being totally astonished that the maneuver had succeeded, was further dumbfounded to hear General Hill's expression of total glee upon discovering that General McClellan's *"whole Yankee army"* was approaching his front. General Hill quickly clarified his gleefulness however, revealing to the colonel that he was initially concerned that the movement upon his front was only a feint; further expressing concern that General McClellan's main body may have already passed through another gap, whereupon he would certainly throw the full weight of his main attack upon Generals Jackson and Lee. 431

General Garland's brigade was badly demoralized by their gallant leader's fall and the ensuing rough handling it had received. However, General Anderson's brigade arrived in a timely fashion to take the place of these much demoralized troops. Had the Union forces continued to press vigorously forward at this juncture of the fight, they most assuredly would have gained the main road. Providentially, however, they were either unaware of their success or themselves much too damaged to continue their advance. During the initial assault, the Twentieth North Carolina Regiment, under the skillful command of Colonel Iverson, had furiously attacked a Federal battery; killing all their horses and driving off the artillerist; thus rendering the battery of no further use to the Union forces. 432

Addressing cavalry operations, General Hill was initially concerned that General Stuart had suddenly withdrawn his command at daylight, except for the single regiment of Colonel Rosser. However, his concerns over cavalry support soon diminished when Colonel Rosser performed his duties in a most noble fashion. 433 General Hill watched from his elevated pinnacle on the mountain as a massive blue force of four advance corps from General McClelland's grand Army of the Potomac advanced steadily toward his position, with one corps forming before him, directly at the foot of the mountain. 434 At this defining moment, General Hill believed Providentially that the very hand of the Almighty was pulling forward the reigns of the Union cavalry and pushing upon the back of every blue uniform massing to his front.

The fate of the Army of Northern Virginia, and consequently the fate of the entire Confederacy, rested upon the gallantry and honor of General Hill's small band of fighters. Once this formidable fighting force numbered over 10,000, but attrition had reduced the ranks of D. H. Hill's Division to its current levels of fewer than 5,000 men. From the Battles of Seven Pines to Malvern Hill - not once had they turned their backs to the enemy. Yes, this small band believed within the full depth of their very souls that their leader, the *"bravest man in their army"* would require them to endure no sacrifice or face no danger that was not demanded by the inevitable exigencies of this desperate battle. 435 With God's help, General Hill would prevail in this battle, just as his General-in-chief had ordered him to do - at any sacrifice - even upon demand of his own life. He would have met death, not as the decree of fate but as the Providence of Almighty God who had brought him face to face with this desperate duty. 436 General Hill was set to release the *unbridled wrath* of the Confederacy's **Angel of Death** upon the Grand Army of the Potomac!

There were only two mountain roads practicable for artillery on the right of the main turnpike. The defense of the farther one had cost General Garland his life. General Hill now entrusted that task to Colonel T. L. Rosser's troop of cavalry whose forces were augmented with artillery and dismounted sharpshooters. 437 General Anderson was in a position to have the best view of the field and the supporting artillery of Bondurant's battery was deemed adequate to perform necessary artillery support for the defense. There was, however, a solitary peak on the left which, if gained by the Federals, would have given them complete control of the ridge commanding the turnpike. Tactically, possession of this peak was everything to the Union forces; but they were either extremely slow to recognize its significance or the importance of the peak escaped them completely. General Hill had a large number of guns from A. S. Cutts' artillery placed upon the hill to the left of the turnpike, designed to sweep the approaches to this peak. 438 From the position selected, there was a full view of the country for miles around. But the mountain was so steep that ascending columns were but little exposed to artillery fire. Notwithstanding the terrain, the artillerists of A. S. Cutts' battalion performed gallantly, providing supporting fires against the Union attackers. General Hill directed General Rodes to the left with orders to take control of the dominant peak previously mentioned and General Ripley was ordered to the right to support General Anderson. The attacking Union forces made several attempts to force a passage through the woods, right of and near the turnpike, but their advances were repulsed with great authority by the Sixth and Twenty-seventh Georgia Regiments and the Thirteenth Alabama Regiment of General Colquitt's brigade. [439]

It was now past noon and the Federals had been checked for more than five hours. But it was evident that they had amassed a large force on both sides of the road as General Hill's Signal corps confirmed heavy masses at the foot of the mountain. In answer to a dispatch from General Longstreet, General Hill urged him to move his troops forward with haste in order to further obstruct the Federal assault. [440] Generals Drayton and G. T. Anderson arrived around 3 p.m. with 1,900 men. General Hill was determined to preemptively engage the enemy force on his right before the Federals could launch their grand attack, which he anticipated would be against the left of his line. Generals Anderson, Ripley, and Drayton were called together and directed to move forward with all haste until they came in contact with General Rosser. In a bold move they were instructed to, upon establishing contact, *"change their flank, march into line of battle, and sweep the woods before them."* [441] To make possible their movements, General Hill tasked his supporting artillerists to bring forward a battery and provide a cannonade of shells upon the woods in various directions; intending to cause great confusion within the Union lines while providing a covering barrage for Confederate movements. General Anderson soon became partially engaged while General Drayton became decisively engaged. For unknown reasons, General Ripley *"did not draw trigger."* [442] The Fourth North Carolina Regiment of Anderson's brigade attempted to overrun the Federal cannon battery to their front but the assault was met with fierce resistance by the Federal troops and their gallant effort failed. Three Union brigades advanced rapidly, in beautiful order, against General Drayton; placing withering musketry fire upon them whereupon they were soon beaten and went streaming to the rear in total confusion. However, Generals Rosser, Anderson, and Ripley fought gallantly, firmly holding their ground and preventing the Federals from gaining positions to the Confederate rear. [443]

There was great deterioration occurring on General Hill's left. A division of Union troops had formed a strong line and was rapidly advancing in handsome style against General Rodes. General Hill directed his artillerists to turn every possible cannon and place concentrated fires upon the approaching Federal columns. But, owing to the steepness of the terrain and bad handling of the guns, the cannonade was not effective and inflicted very little harm upon the enemy's columns. General Rodes handled his brigade in a most admirable and gallant fashion, fighting with extreme valor for hours against vastly superior odds while maintaining the key-points of the position until darkness rendered a further advance of the Federals impossible. 444 Had General Rodes' men fought with less stubbornness a practicable artillery road to the rear would have been gained by the Yankees on the Confederate's left and the action would have cut off the Confederate's line of retreat. General Rodes' did not drive the enemy back or whip him, but with 1,200 courageous fighters, he held an entire Federal division at bay for over four hours without assistance from any one; losing in that time not more than one half mile of ground. 445 General Longstreet came up about 4 p. m., 446 accompanied by the commands of Generals N. G. Evans and D. R. Jones. 447 However, they took the wrong positions and, in their exhausted condition after their long march, they were quickly broken and scattered in the face of the enemy. General Hill's entire left was now openly exposed, giving the Federals an open avenue from which to push forward and seize the turnpike. 448 All available troops were gathered and placed in a hasty defensive line, behind a stone wall, with designs to resist any enemy approach upon the turnpike from the left. Encouraged by their successes in that direction, the Federals believed that it would be an easy matter to move directly up the turnpike; but they were greatly mistaken. Their advance was heroically met and bloodily repelled by the Twenty-third and Twenty-eighth Georgia Regiments of General Colquitt's brigade. 449 General Hood, who had moved in quickly on the right with his two brigades of noble Texans, pushed his skirmishers forward vigorously and drove back the Federals. The fierce fight lasted for more than an hour after nightfall then gradually subsided as the Federals retired from the line. 450

The battle of South Mountain remains, to this day, one of the *"most remarkable and creditable battles"* in the history of modern warfare. It was an absolute demonstration of heroism and courage by D. H. Hill's troops that provided such a fierce offensive – defense effort from dawn to 3 o'clock on September 14th 1862 – even to the point that the Federals remained of the mind that that they must be facing a substantial Confederate force of at least 30,000 men. By 3 p.m. General Longstreet's full complement of men had reached the field and joined with General Hill's forces to steadily drive the enemy back. After nightfall the Federal troops, despite a ratio of six Union soldiers for every one Confederate soldier, occupied no more ground than they had occupied before the attack's initial launch. 451

The official report by the Adjutant-General on General Anderson's staff summarized: *"It may be safely said that in its consequences, in the accomplishments of predetermined objects, and in the skillful disposition of small numbers to oppose overwhelming odds, it is without a parallel in the war. The division, unaided until a late hour in the afternoon, held in check the greater portion of McClellan's vast army endeavoring with battering-ram impetus to force its way through the narrow gap, and thereby afforded time for the concentration of our various corps, dispersed in strategic directions, in season for the bloody issue at Sharpsburg."* 452

The official report by the Adjutant-General on General Lee's staff summarized: *"The resistance made by General D. H. Hill at South Mountain deserves more than a passing notice. On the 14th of September, with the brigades of Rhodes, Garland, Colquitt, Anderson and Ripley, numbering in the aggregate less than five thousand men, for six or seven hours he successfully resisted the repeated assaults of two corps of the army under General McClellan (Burnside and Hooker's) fully 30,000 strong. About 3 p.m. he was reinforced. . . Thus it will be seen that a force of less than 10,000 men held McClellan in check for an entire day."* 453

Freeman, speaking of the climax of the battle when the enemy retired, said: *"D. H. Hill saw all this and rejoiced in it. Precisely that type of battle was his forte – hard combat where a man might fight with all his strength and cunning and not be responsible for strategy. In close, doubtful actions he was superb. No man seemed able to get more fire-power from a given number of troops."* 454

General McClellan had only days earlier proclaimed gleefully: *"Now I know what to do! Here is a paper with which, if I cannot whip Bobby Lee, I will be willing to go home"* His statement served to be only partial in truth for it wasn't Bobby Lee that General McClellan couldn't whip – he couldn't whip Bobby Lee's *Fighting General.* 455

General McClellan's proclamation did prove to be prophetic however. On November 7th 1862 President Lincoln would officially replace him as General-in-chief, ending General McClellan's military service to the Union. In a word, General McClellan's advance through the South Mountain gaps failed. General Lee stated in his official report: *"The resistance that had been offered the enemy at Boonsboro secured sufficient time to enable General Jackson to complete the reduction of Harper's Ferry."* 456 Had General McClellan gained passage through the South Mountains it would have enabled him to relieve the siege of Harper's Ferry and prevent a junction of Lee's separated divisions. But for the success of General Hill's defense of the gaps, General McClellan surely would have *"whipped Bobby Lee."* He could have decisively engaged his sizeable force to attack each of Lee's separated elements in detail. Additionally, he could have then advanced south and totally destroyed Lee's artillery and wagon trains parked in his rear. This would have driven a stake in the heart of General Lee's army and, most likely, would have delivered a fatal blow to the entire Confederacy.

The presence of the enemy at Crampton's Gap, however, suppressed the movements of General McLaws force. He retained the position that he had taken during the night of September 14th 1862 and remained there, determined to oppose any efforts by the enemy to advance towards Harper's Ferry until the defeat of that place was complete. Upon finding the enemy not able to attack, he gradually withdrew his command towards the Potomac. Deeming the roads to Sharpsburg on the north side of the river to be an impracticable avenue, he decided to cross the Potomac at Harper's Ferry and marched toward Sharpsburg by way of Shepherdstown. Owing to the condition of his troops, and other circumstances, his progress was slow and he did not reach the battle field at Sharpsburg until sometime after the engagement began on September 17th 1862. [457]

The Federal's effort to force the passage of the mountains had failed but information was received that another large body of Federal troops had moved through Crampton's Gap, only five miles in rear of General McLaws. Under these circumstances, General Lee deemed it prudent to retire to Sharpsburg where his army would be upon the flank and rear of the enemy should he move in force against General McLaws and where he could more readily unite with the rest of the army. [458]

General D. H. Hill's Division withdrew that night to Sharpsburg; having accomplished all that had been required of them – impeding the advance of the entire Army of the Potomac at Boonsboro sufficiently to enable General Jackson's reduction of Harper's Ferry.

SHARPSBURG 1862

The Battle of Sharpsburg, or Antietam as called by the Yankees, occurred in the span of 12 hours and resulted in the bloodiest battle of the Civil War. To this day it remains the bloodiest single day of battle in American history. General Hill's depleted and exhausted band of warriors, adhering to orders from General Lee, finally reached Sharpsburg about daylight on the morning of the September 15th 1862 459 after a long and demanding overnight march; 460 crossing the Antietam creek and taking a position on the west bank along the Boonsboro Road, along the range of hills between the town and the Antietam creek; 461 General D. H. Hill was positioned on the left nearly parallel to the course of that stream with General Longstreet positioned on the right of the road to Boonsboro. 462 The advance of the enemy was delayed by the brave opposition he encountered from Fitz Lee's cavalry and he did not appear on the opposite side of the Antietam until about 2 p. m. 463 Official information of the fall of Harper's Ferry and the approach of General Jackson was received soon after the commands of Generals Longstreet and D. H. Hill reached Sharpsburg on the morning of September 15th 1862, greatly revived the courage and morale of the troops. General Jackson arrived early on September 16th 1862 and General Walker came up later that same afternoon. 464

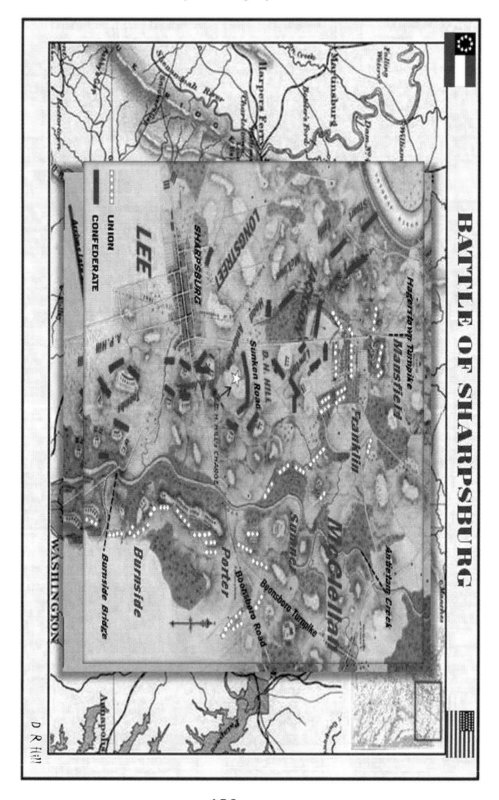

The Federals soon made their first appearance that day, but it was extremely haphazard with only small incidents of skirmishing and cannonading occurring. 465 On September 16th 1862 the artillery fire became warm and continued throughout the day. The enemy crossed the Antietam beyond the reach of Rebel batteries and menaced the Confederate's left. In anticipation of this movement, General Hood's two brigades had been transferred from the right and posted between D. H. Hill and the Hagerstown road. 466 General Longstreet held the position south of the Boonsboro turnpike and General Hill held the position on the right. General Hood's command was placed to the left of General D. H. Hill's Division with orders to guard the Hagerstown pike. 467

General Jackson was now directed to take a position on General Hood's left; forming his line with his right resting upon the Hagerstown road and his left extending towards the Potomac; protected by General Stuart with the cavalry and horse artillery. 468 General Walker, with his two brigades, was stationed on General Longstreet's right. 469 Just before sundown General Hill directed a cannon battery of Cutts' battalion to open upon the Union columns advancing toward the Hagerstown pike. At the same time, Colonel Stephen D. Lee brought up another battery farther down on the right and joined the cannonade, placing concentrated fires upon the Union advance. This offering of oppressive cannon fire effectively checked the enemy's forward movement and enabled General Stonewall Jackson to take his position on the field to General Hood's left. 470

As evening approached, the Federals opened more vigorously with their artillery and bore down heavily with infantry upon General Hood's line, but the attack was gallantly repulsed. At 10 p. m. General Hood's troops were relieved by the brigades of Generals Lawton and Trimble, of General Ewell's division, commanded by General Lawton. General Jackson's own division, under the leadership of General D. R. Jones, was on General Lawton's left, supported by the remaining brigades of General Ewell. 471 General D. H. Hill's depleted ranks had been further diminished by some additional straggling during the march from South Mountain and, on the morning of September 17th 1862, he had a viable force of but 3,000 infantry. 472 He did, however, have twenty-six pieces of artillery of his own and close to 50 pieces of Cutts' battalion, temporarily under his command. Positions were selected for as many of these guns as could be used but all the ground in front of his position was completely commanded by the long-range artillery of the Federals, strategically positioned on the other side of the Antietam creek. The moment a Confederate cannon would open fire, the Federals would respond with devastating counter-battery fire, pouring concentrated barrages upon the Confederate battery, methodically disabling or silencing the piece. 473

On the eve of the great Battle of Sharpsburg, General Hill and trusted Adjutant, and friend, Major Ratchford, were engaged in conversation; discussing preparations for the impending fight. Major Ratchford, himself never know to be shy in the face of any foe, but whose affection for his friend was unbounded, inquired: *"General, why do you expose yourself so recklessly? Do you never feel the sensation of fear?"* General Hill replied that he would *"never require my men to go where I did not know the ground or would not go myself,"* and that he had no fear of death if he met it in the line of duty. Major Ratchford then further inquired if he would not rather live than die. *"Oh, yes,"* replied General Hill, *"when I think of my wife and babies I would, but God will take care of them if he allows anything to happen to me."* 474

D. H. HILL

"impressed me as a zealous, unselfish patriot and great soldier, who knew not fear and shrank from no duty. His Christian faith was unbounded. He could always be found at the most dangerous place in the line, doing what he could to encourage and also protect the men."

[[Colonel Walter Clark – 17th NC regiment]]

Q26

GENERAL LEE AND DIVISION-COMMANDER
GENERAL D. H. HILL

Riding along the Confederate lines during a respite in the battle of Antietam.

At early dawn on September 17ᵗʰ 1862 General Lee's defensive lines prepared for another looming battle. General Robert E. Lee joined General D. H. Hill as they rode along Hill's line, positioned along and in the sunken road directly at the center of the Confederate line. The two Generals encouraged the men to stay calm and hold fast in the face of the coming enemy assault. As they passed the Sixth Alabama, General Hill's close friend Colonel J. B. Gordon shouted resolutely:

"These men are going to stay here, General, till the sun goes down or victory is won!" 475

[NOTE: This is an actual photograph of this historic moment in the history of the Sixth Alabama Regiment. Mounted on horseback you see Generals D. H. Hill and R. E. Lee and standing to their immediate left is General Gordon, making his famous proclamation. The photograph comes from the Memoirs of General Gordon and is a most treasured artifact by this author.]

Generals Lee and Hill continued on horseback along the line and were soon joined by General Longstreet. The three Generals then moved to take a position on a piece of high ground in order to study the enemy's battle array. General's Lee and Longstreet dismounted but General Hill remained in his saddle. General Longstreet commented: *"If you insist on riding up there and drawing fire, give us a little interval so that we may not be in the line of the fire when they open upon you."* Suddenly, General Longstreet observed a puff of white smoke through his field glasses and said: *"There is a shot for you."* Instantly a Federal shell struck General Hill's horse, cleanly removing both of the animal's front legs, sending the animal and Hill to the ground in a most awkward position; with the General partially entrapped by the carcass. After some degree of difficulty and brief delay freeing himself from his saddle, General Hill put the poor animal out of his misery, grabbed another steed and galloped quickly to rejoin his men; having observed a tremendous gathering of Union soldiers across the entire front of the Confederate line.

During the fighting at Sharpsburg, General Hill greatly distinguished himself, constantly exposing himself to enemy musketry and cannon fire, having no less than three horses shot under him. Of his conduct in that battle General Longstreet said: *"Generals D. H. Hill and Hood were like gamecocks, fighting as long as they could stand, engaging again as soon as strong enough to rise."* 476 477

As the early morning began to unfold, Union and Confederate pickets initially engaged one another but the skirmishes quickly escalated to become full battles. Union General Hooker initiated a bold attack, being reinforced with overwhelming power, to strike hard at General Jackson's line. General Hooker's attack advanced from the tree line whereupon General Jackson's men rose and delivered devastating volleys of extremely accurate musketry, tearing through the advancing blue line, surprising and initially staggering the enemy while Confederate batteries poured cannon fire upon them with devastating effects. 478 Federal cannons quickly responded with ferocious volleys, punishing General Jackson's men and laying them down in the cornfield rows with such effect that neither soldier nor single corn stalk stood in one entire section of the cornfield; leaving men and corn all to fall in one direction, that being away from and in line with the blast of the cannons. With this vicious Federal cannonade and accompanying infantry assault, General Jackson's line was broken, tearing a huge gap on General Hill's left flank. 479 Gallantly, the Texans of General Hood's Division moved rapidly forward to restore the line. General Hood's Texans always fought well and, in this effort, they were handsomely supported by Generals Colquitt and Ripley. Fighting was bloody and furious as the battle raged, with the lines pushing one another back and forth across the bloody field. 480

The enemy's artillery continued to descend vigorously from both sides of the Antietam, the heaviest fire being directed against the Confederate's left. Under cover of this fire, another large force of infantry attacked General Jackson's line. They were met by his troops with the utmost resistance and for several hours the conflict raged with great fury and alternating success. General D. R. Jones was compelled to leave the field and the command of General Jackson's division was delegated to General Starke. The troops advanced with great enthusiasm and the enemy's lines were repeatedly broken and forced to retire. Fresh Federal troops, however, soon replaced those that were beaten and General Jackson's men were in turn compelled to themselves fall back. It was at this juncture of the battle where the brave General Starke was killed; 481 General Lawton sustained a severe wound and nearly all the field officers along with a large proportion of his men were either killed or disabled. The Confederate troops slowly yielded to the overwhelming Federal numbers, falling back while stubbornly contesting every inch of the enemy's progress. General Hood returned to the field and relieved the brigades of Generals Trimble, Lawton and Hays, which had suffered severely from the Federal onslaught and incessant cannonade.

General Early, who succeeded General Lawton, was ordered by General Jackson to move with his brigade and take the place of Stonewall Jackson's old division, most of which had already withdrawn; its ammunition being nearly exhausted and its numbers greatly reduced. A small part of the division, being led by Colonels Grisgby and Stafford, united with General Early's brigade, as did portions of the brigades of Generals Trimble, Lawton and Hayes. 482 The raging battle continued with great zeal against General Stonewall Jackson on the left wing. The small commands under Generals Hood and Early fought valiantly, holding their ground against many times their own numbers of the enemy and under a murderous Federal cannonade. General Hood was reinforced by the brigades of Generals Ripley, Colquitt and Garland, under Colonel McRae, of General D. H. Hill's division and afterwards by General D. R. Jones' brigade, under General G. T. Anderson. 483 With great effort, the stubborn Federal's line was eventually broken and thrown back. But fresh numbers soon advanced to their support and they began to once again regain ground. The desperate resistance offered by the unyielding Confederate line, however, delayed the Federal's progress until the troops of Generals McLaws and Walker could be brought over from the Confederate right. The soldiers of General Hood's brigade, being greatly reduced in numbers and having entirely exhausted their ammunition, withdrew to resupply. Being relieved by General Walker's command, his gallant Texans immediately attacked the enemy in a most vigorous fashion, driving the entire Federal line back with great slaughter. Colonel Manning, commanding General Walker's brigade, pursued the fleeing Union soldiers until his advance was stopped by a strong fence; behind which was posted a large force of Union infantry and several batteries of supporting cannons. This gallant Colonel, too, was severely wounded and his brigade retired to the line on which the rest of General Walker's command had halted. 484

D. H. HILL

"The annals of war have not set before us a more heroic or dauntless soul. He excelled in the characteristics of invincible tenacity, absolute unconsciousness of fear, courage never to submit or yield, no one has risen above him, not even in the annals of the Army of Northern Virginia."

[[Colonel Henry Elliott Shepherd]]

Q8

Upon arrival of the reinforcements under General McLaws, General Early attacked the substantial Federal line directly in opposition to his front with great resolve. General McLaws advanced at the same time in a coordinated assault and the enemy was driven back in much confusion, closely pursued by the Confederate charge that pushed them well beyond the initial position occupied at the beginning of the engagement. The Federal troops renewed their assault upon the Confederate left several times but were successively repulsed, sustaining great loss upon each effort. The Federals finally ceased to advance their infantry and for several hours kept up a furious cannonade from their numerous batteries. But the Confederate soldiers firmly held their position with great coolness and courage. In typical fashion of General Stonewall Jackson, by the end of that day's fight he would push the Union forces back, eventually defeating three successive Federal corps throughout the course of the battle. 485

Suddenly, the enemy shifted the full weight of their main attack to the center of the line engaging General D. H. Hill's center front. 486 Immediately, General D. H. Hill was determined to rally his men in the bed of the old sunken road, nearly at right angles to the Hagerstown Pike; which had served as their position prior to the advance. 487 The onset of the enemy's assault pressed hard against Hill's line; the enemy's appearance seemed to be formidable and of great strength. But the rapid and accurate volleys of musketry from the enfilade positions along the lines of Generals Anderson and Rodes, combined with an intense Confederate cannonade, placed upon the enemy volumes of accurate fire; such that it caused great confusion and disorder in their line; forcing them to pull back. With the first line of the Federals broken, General Hill's men pushed rapidly forward, only to meet another line, and then another.

General Colquitt entered the engagement with 10 field officers but they were almost immediately decimated; 4 were killed, 5 badly wounded and the tenth officer had been stunned by a shell. General Garland's men had been much demoralized by the fight at South Mountain and the loss of their gallant General but still they fought with great passion. 488 Quickly, the enemy reformed and advanced against the center of General Hill's line toward the brigades of Generals Rodes' and Anderson with an even greater fury than before. Long and constant volleys resounded all along the entire line as the Union attackers pressed hard, resolute to break the Confederate line. One of General Hill's brigades, the Rodes' Brigade, had been decisively engaged since the first volley of the battle; having performed gallantly, fighting along with Anderson's Brigade, in the infamous *"sunken road;"* which would soon come to be forever known as *"the bloody lane."* Suddenly there was great confusion on the battlefield when Captain T. P. Thomson of the Fifth North Carolina cried out, *"They are flanking us."* 489 This cry spread like an electric shock along the ranks, bringing up vivid recollections of the flanking fire experienced at South Mountain. In an instant they broke and fell to the rear. Colonel McRae, though wounded, remained on the field and succeeded in gathering up some stragglers, personally rendering much efficient service while the Twenty-third North Carolina Regiment was brought forward by the gallant Lieutenant Colonel Johnston and posted in the old sunken road; joining the thick of the fight. 490

General Ripley's brigade had united with General Walker's line and had fallen back behind the ridge to the left and rear of the road. Three of General Hill's brigades had been broken and much demoralized and all of the artillery had been withdrawn from along the front of his line. Generals Rodes and Anderson were positioned in the sunken road and the stragglers gathered up by Colonel McRae had placed upon their left. 491 It was now apparent to General Hill that the Yankees were further massing to his front and that their grand attack would certainly be made upon his position in the center of his line. He sent several urgent messages to General Lee for reinforcements but before they could be offered General Franklin's entire Union corps attacked with great enthusiasm; marching in three parallel lines, with all the precision of a parade day, advancing upon General Hill's two center brigades. The magnificent Confederate soldiers, fighting from the defilade of the sunken road, placed upon the Federal troops a galling fire that pushed them back with great authority. Once again, General Franklin's corps advanced only to be again repulsed. The withering volleys of musketry forced the attacking Union soldiers to finally lay down behind the crest of the hill whereupon they began to place sustained fire upon the Confederate center line.

General Hill quickly grabbed a cannon battery and had them place enfilade fire upon the stalled Union line, producing favorable results and checking their advance for that moment. 492 Two of Colonel Cooke's batteries joined the Confederate cannonade and the massed and concentrated firing of shell, grape and canister had a withering effect upon the enemy's line; causing the enemy to stop, waver, and begin to fall back. *"In a few minutes they were sprinkling with canister the Union troops, who now had crossed the Sunken Road and were creeping forward, which made them hesitate."* 493

During this time, General R. H. Anderson reported to General Hill with a substantial force of some 3,000 to 4,000 men to reinforce his command. General Anderson was directed to form his line immediately behind General Hill's men who now formed the Confederate center along the sunken road. The addition of General Anderson's musketry aided greatly to bolster the Confederate line but, during this part of the engagement, that gallant and accomplished officer was grievously wounded and the command was delegated to General Pryor. Due to the concert of Confederate actions, the enemy's fire had now nearly ceased and, but for an unfortunate blunder of Lieutenant Colonel J. N. Lightfoot of the Sixth Alabama Regiment, no farther advance would have been made. 494

General Rodes had observed a Confederate regiment lying down in his rear and not engaged. With the fire being somewhat random and slack, he went to the disengaged troops and learned they belonged to General Pryor's brigade; he determined that, in compliance with the orders of Lieutenant Colonel J. N.

Lightfoot, they had been halted by due order and not by dereliction of duty. General Rodes, quickly locating General Pryor, informed him as to their conduct whereupon he immediately ordered his men forward. 495

As General Rodes returned toward his own brigade, he met Lieutenant Colonel Lightfoot of the Sixth Alabama Regiment who exclaimed that the right wing of the regiment was exposed to a terrible enfilade fire; which the enemy was enabled to deliver by their gaining somewhat upon General G. B. Anderson. In response, General Hill ordered General Rodes to throw the full weight of his right wing back and out of the sunken road. But for great confusion upon the field, instead of executing the order, he moved briskly to the rear of the regiment and gave the command, *"Sixth Alabama, about face; forward march."* Major Hobson, of the Fifth North Carolina Regiment, seeing this, asked him if the order was intended for the whole brigade. He responded, *"Yes,"* and thereupon the Fifth North Carolina Regiment and the other troops on their left retreated, absent of undue enemy pressure. 496 Unfortunately General Rodes did not see their retrograde movement until it was too late to rally them; by his reasoning he explained: *"Just as I was moving on after Lieutenant Colonel Lightfoot, I heard a shot strike Lieutenant Birney (aide), who was immediately behind me. Wheeling around, I found him falling, and that he had been struck in the face. I found that he could walk after I raised him. I followed him a few paces and watched him until he reached a barn, a short distance in the rear, where he first met someone help him in case he needed it. As I turned toward the brigade, I was struck heavily by a piece of shell on my thigh. At first I thought that the wound was serious; but finding, upon examination, that it was slight, I turned toward the brigade, when I discovered it, without visible cause to me, retreating in confusion. I hastened to intercept it at the Hagerstown road. I found, though, that with the exception of a few men from the Twenty-sixth, Twelfth, and Third, and a few under Major Hobson, of the Fifth (not more than 40 in all), the brigade had disappeared from this portion of the field. This small number, together with some Mississippians and North Carolinians, about 150 in all, I rallied and stationed behind a small ridge leading from the Hagerstown road."* 497

Despite the confusion adjacent to his line, General G. B. Anderson's men still nobly held their ground along the sunken road. But the enemy quickly began to pour in through the gap created by the inadvertent retreat of General Rodes' men. The ensuing assault by Union General Bull Sumner's troops brought murderous enfilade fires upon the Confederate line positioned along the sunken road, decimating them to the extent that the Confederate dead were stacking up as cordwood along the lane, which would aptly become known as the *"bloody lane,"* a term that today remains synonymous with the Battle of Sharpsburg, or Antietam. During this onslaught of Union troops, General

Anderson himself was mortally wounded and his brigade was totally routed by the attacking Union soldiers. Colonel Bennett of the Fourteenth North Carolina Regiment and Major Sillers of the Thirtieth North Carolina Regiment bravely rallied a portion of their men. 498 But there were no other troops nearby to help hold the center, except a few hundred that were quickly rallied from various brigades.

The Federals advanced across the old road which General D. H. Hill's Division had held earlier in the morning. The rallied Confederate troops of Boyce's South Carolina battery took a strong position in the cornfield and immediately launched a spirited volley upon the Union columns. The fires continued with great enthusiasm, although exposed to a terrible direct and reverse fire from the long-range Federal guns across the Antietam. A caisson exploded but the undaunted battery unlimbered and continued to place murderous volumes of grape and canister fire upon the Union troops, driving them back in great disorder. 499 However, the unfortunate misinterpretation of orders in General Rodes' Brigade, wherein the command to turn his flank in order to face the withering Union fire had been mistaken to be a call for a general retreat, caused the unfortunate withdrawal from their position. This created the huge gap in the Confederate line. This was a most regrettable error which was immediately capitalized upon by the Federal troops and exploited greatly to their tactical advantage.

In the confusion of any pitched battle, a tactical error of this magnitude will generally result in one of two outcomes: either an opportunity for victory or a foundation for defeat. When engaged in heated battle, the manner in which a leader handles peril often becomes a true test of his metal, leadership and competence. Instantly, General Hill would be subjected to this very test – a trial of exceeding magnitude and one upon which the lives of his men and possibly the fate of the Confederacy could well depend. But this man, the consummate *"fighter from way back,"* was up for the challenge.   Swiftly, decisively he sprang into action; employing a battery of South Carolina cannons to set the fire of grape and canister upon the advancing Union forces. Of General Hill's actions, Freeman wrote: *"If Harvey Hill realized that the rout and ruin of the Army of Northern Virginia might come then and there, on his front, he did not exhibit any anxiety. Neither did 'Old Pete.' Fuming in the carpet slippers his injured heel compelled him to wear, Longstreet rode or hobbled in search of men and guns to mend the gap in the line. D. H. Hill found in a cornfield Boyce's South Carolina Battery, which was awaiting orders. Cheerfully Boyce's men dashed into the open and began to unlimber,"* 500

It was on this September day, in a field of corn, covered with blood that Daniel Harvey Hill would reach his defining moment in history – attaining the pinnacle of his military career by performing one of the greatest acts of valor and courage in the annals of modern warfare. His valorous actions this very day would once and for all bestow upon him citation of his name as *"Lee's Fighting General."* Two Divisions of General Bull Sumner's corps advanced to the Sunken Road with great vigor in an attempt to wrest away the initiative of the battle and seize complete tactical advantage on the field. General Hill quickly observed the changing tide of the battle and, sensing a great opportunity, immediately sought to regain the initiative instead for a Confederate tactical advantage.   He was now confident that the Yankees were in a full state of demoralization and he believed within his heart and soul that, given just a single regiment of fresh men, he could drive the whole of them back across the Antietam. 501 Quickly he rounded up about 200 men who told the General that they were willing to advance to the attack, but only if he would personally lead them in the fight. The courage of any soldier to grab a musket and lead a small group of volunteers into a desperate battle against overwhelming odds is, within itself, a true definition of heroism; but for a general officer to act accordingly defines that man as one with whom any good soldier would follow *"to the gates of hell and back."*

D. H. HILL

"There was never a better soldier or a man better qualified to judge of the merits of one. The clash of battle was not a confusing din to him, but an exciting scene that awakened his spirit and his genius."

[[Colonel Walter Clark – 17ᵗʰ NC regiment]]

Q27

In one of the most gallant actions of the entire Civil War, if not the annals of modern warfare, General D. H. Hill grabbed a musket and, in a most valorous display of heroism, charged the formidable Federal line – leading his men from the front – as the courageous volunteers followed with an awe inspiring chorus of rebel yells. General Hill led the advance in this most courageous act of offense, emblematic of his most valorous charge of the entire war. The onset was furious; nothing seemed to overpower the impetuosity of General D. Hill in close quarter assault – his men imitating his actions, fighting beside him both left and right. It was the pure boldness of the brave men who, but with great difficulty, fought desperately with every fiber of their being to stand fast and unyielding to hold the Confederate's ground. But their valiant effort was met with murderous volleys of Union musketry that sent sheet after sheet of deadly lead shearing through the charging line; breaking and decimating them with devastating effect.

During the melee, Major Hobson and Lieutenant J. M. Goff of the Fifth Alabama Regiment, imitating the leadership of General Hill, courageously demonstrated an equal level of valor in the face of that withering enemy fire during this charge. 502 Inspired by the courage and valor of General Hill's assault, Colonel Alfred Iverson of the Twentieth North Carolina Regiment; Colonel Christie of the Twenty-third North Carolina Regiment; and Captain Garrett, Adjutant J. M. Taylor and Lieutenant Isaac E. Pearce of the Fifth North Carolina Regiment likewise gathered up an additional 200 men and launched a courageous second assault to the right against the Federals in flank. Their initial push drove the Union troops back a short distance, but in the face of withering fire, they too were also repulsed.

Although the two attacks were repelled, the bravery displayed by these two small but undaunted groups of heroes during their remarkable charges invoked a sobering effect upon the enemy. The Union troops were completely deceived by the boldness of the two attacks and were so induced to believe that there must be a much larger force in front of them. Based upon their assessment of the Confederate's strength at that point on the field, they made no further significant attempts to break the Confederate line along the center of General Hill's line. 503 By about 2 p.m. the attack against D. H. Hill's Division in the center of the field came to an end and the now exhausted Union soldiers withdrew from the center. But the Battle of Sharpsburg was not yet over. Hostilities shifted to the right wing; lightly defended by a small force comprised of General D. R. Jones' Division; now reduced to only two regiments and an equally depleted General Toomb's Brigade. General Lee's beleaguered army had fought gallantly throughout the entire day but by four o'clock the battle was nearly lost. 504

At this juncture, Union General Burnside's corps was massing his men to attack the right of General Hill's line; determined to deliver a final, decisive blow that would win the battle, and the day, for the Army of the Potomac. A heavy Union column advanced vigorously, at a double-quick pace, up the Boonsboro pike. To counter the force, General Hill ordered up some 200 or 300 men, under command of Colonel G. T. Anderson, to a position located on the top of the hill commanding Sharpsburg. But they were immediately exposed to murderous enfilade fire from a Federal battery positioned near the church on the Hagerstown pike; forcing them to retire to another hill which provided a more suitable position. A small force of about 30 men under the command of Lieutenant Colonel W. H. Betts of the Thirteenth Alabama Regiment remained to support General D. H. Hill's Division artillery, under Generals Jones, R. A. Hardaway, and Bondurant. 505 As the advancing Union columns were allowed to come within easy range, a murderous cannonade delivered a sudden storm of grape and canister upon them with devastating effect, driving them back in total confusion. The fires from Betts' men were so fierce that General Burnside reported that he had engaged heavy Confederate columns on the hill. General D. H. Hill wrote in the official report of the battle: *"It is difficult to imagine how 30 men could so multiply themselves as to appear to the frightened Federals to be a composition of three heavy columns."* 506

On General Hill's extreme right, however, the Federals met with greater success as they crossed the Antietam, driving the Confederates before them. General D. R. Jones' men had fallen back nearly to the road in rear of Sharpsburg as the Union troops continued to advance in fine style to the crests commanding the town. If they had advanced only a few hundred yards more they would have effectively cut of the line of retreat for General Hill's entire division. In reaction, General Hill directed the cannons of Carter upon this imposing force of Federals whereupon he opened upon them three guns, aided by two additional cannons of Donaldsonville Artillery. 507 The cannon firing was performed beautifully and the Union columns, at a distance of some 1,200 yards, were routed by the cannonade alone, without the aid of musketry fire. General Hill recorded in his official report: *"This is the only instance I have ever known of infantry being broken by artillery fire at long range. It speaks badly for the courage of Burnside's men."* 508

Seizing the initiative, General Hill's troops quickly launched a daring attack upon the Federal's extreme right, driving back the whole corps of General Burnside. At this juncture of the battle, General Hill observed a noteworthy Union movement of a rather nonsensical character, worthy of mention. General Hill reported in his official report: *"General Pryor had gathered quite a respectable force behind a stone wall on the Hagerstown road, and Col G. T. Anderson had about a regiment behind a hill immediately to the right of this road. A Maine regiment, the Twenty-first, I think, came down to this while wholly unconscious that there were any Confederate troops near it. A shout and a volley informed them of their dangerous neighborhood. Their Yankee apprehension being acute; the idea was soon taken in, and was followed by the most rapid running I ever saw."* 509

As the battle continued to rage on the right of the Confederate line, General Lee was stationed in person where General Toombs' Brigade was fighting valiantly to halt the onslaught of Federal troops. The fight was harsh and the Confederate's efforts were hard pressed to hold the enemy along the Antietam creek. A fierce battle waged at the old rock bridge over the creek, known today as the Burnside Bridge, with charge after Union charge beaten back; so to the extent that the whole of the bridge was completely covered with fallen soldiers, both Union and Confederate. After a grueling struggle the Union forces finally prevailed and moved with great authority against the Confederate positions; posted along the high ground overlooking the Antietam creek. But just as the Confederate's line began to wilt under the relentless pressure, exciting news reached the beleaguered Confederate troops that General A. P. Hill was on the way. 510

General A. P. Hill arrived upon the field, with his battle ready troops, having just completed his march from Harper's Ferry. 511 The news of his arrival quickly spread along the entire Confederate line, instilling within the Rebels new vigor and providing a sudden shift in tactical advantage to the Confederates. General A. P. Hill, in compliance with General Lee's orders, moved rapidly to reinforce General D. R. Jones, accompanied by the brigades of Generals Archer, Branch, Gregg and Pender, the last of whom was placed on the right of the line.

Flushed with success, the reinvigorated Rebel line moved forward forcefully to assault the opposing Federal force, immediately arresting their progress and causing their line to waver. General D. H. Hill's batteries were thrown forward and united their fires with those of General D. R. Jones', to great effect, from the left of the Boonsboro road. 512 At this moment General Jones ordered General Toombs to charge the flank, while General Archer, supported by Generals Branch and Gregg, moved upon the front of the Federal line. The enemy made a brief resistance then broke under the pressure of the Confederate charge; retreating in confusion towards the Antietam, pursued vigorously by the troops of Generals A. P. Hill and D. R. Jones, until the retreating Union soldiers reached the protective covering fires of their batteries on the opposite side of the river. 513 During this attack the brave General Branch was killed while gallantly leading his brigade.

It was now nearly dark and the Federal artillerist had massed a number of batteries to sweep all approaches to the Antietam. The corps of General Porter, which heretofore had not been engaged, now appeared to contest the Confederate's advance. At this juncture of the fight, the Confederate troops were much exhausted and greatly reduced in numbers by fatigue and casualties sustained during the conduct of the bloody battle. Under these circumstances, General Lee deemed it to be inadvisable to push for further advantage in the face of fresh Federal troops, their numbers greatly exceeding the number of his own. Accordingly, the Confederate General-in-chief recalled his forces to reform on the line originally held by General D. R. Jones. 514 While the attack on the Confederate center was progressing, General Jackson was directed to maneuver his men in an effort to turn the enemy's right. But he found himself facing a substantial, well defended Federal line that extended nearly to the Potomac, and strongly supported with artillery, such that he deemed further action to be reckless, choosing to abandon the operation accordingly.

Finally, the repulse on the right of the line finally brought a welcomed end, by both armies, to the engagement. Upon the conclusion of this protracted and bloody conflict, every Federal effort to dislodge the Confederates from their positions had been defeated, inflicting upon them severe losses. 515 In consideration of the difficult nature of the conflict: wherein General Lee's troops had been so decisively engaged; having experienced great privations of rest and food; long marches, without shoes over mountain roads; his army felt the great effect of attrition within its ranks. Further frustrating the force, these causes had compelled thousands of brave men to absent themselves, and many more had done so from unworthy motives. 516 Given all sources for the depletion, this great battle of Sharpsburg was fought by less than forty thousand men on the Confederate side, all whom had undergone the greatest labors and hardships in the field and while on the march. Nothing could surpass the determined valor with which the Army of Northern Virginia engaged the large, fully supplied and equipped Army of the Potomac; the results reflecting the highest form of credit upon the officers and men engaged. The Confederate artillery, though much inferior to that of the Federal cannons, in the number of guns and weight of metal, rendered most efficient and gallant service throughout the day and contributed greatly to the repulse of the attacks on every part of the line. 517

Regarding the fighting along Burnside's bridge, Mr. Freeman said: *"Above the din of battle could be heard the fox-hunters call, the wild 'rebel yell.' Red banners were following stars and stripes. Ragged boys in butternut leaped over prone bodies in blue. The roar of the guns on the heights swelled to a pitch of triumph. Yard by yard the Union line sagging and gapping but unbroken, fell back to the shelter of the low ridges near the creek. Slowly, after sunset, the fire died away. By nightfall the ghastly action ended. To the bark of the gun succeed the wail of the wounded."* 518

D. H. HILL

"No tribute can do justice to the unknown and unrecorded dead. Most of them exiles from home and family; men who had endured every hardship, trial, and privation for so long a period, but to find at last nameless graves, uncheered by the world's applause and uninfluenced by the hope of distinction, they sacrificed ease, comfort, happiness, life itself, upon the altar of their country."

[[General D. H. Hill]]

Q28

As nightfall closed in on the battlefield, General Hill's troops were found to be positioned in the center, only 200 yards to the rear of their initial position which they held at the start of the day. The Confederate forces had successfully held two thirds of the battlefield, including the ground gained by General A. P. Hill on the right. The only ground lost was in the center, where the Union main attack had been made, and where there had been the most severe fighting, resulting in the heaviest losses to both armies. Upon the occasion, General Hill reported in his official report: *"The skulkers and cowards had straggled off, and only the bravest and truest men of my division had been left. It is true that hunger and exhaustion had nearly unfitted these brave men for battle. Our wagons had been sent off across the river on Sunday, and for three days the men had been sustaining life on green corn and such cattle as they could kill in the fields. In charging through an apple orchard at the Federals, with the immediate prospect of death before them, I noticed men eagerly devouring apples."* 519

The conduct in battle by General D. H. Hill's Division demonstrated that, despite the human hindrance of hunger and fatigue, his officers and men fought most heroically and with great distinction upon the two battlefields in Maryland. His famed division had sustained horrific casualties: 3,000 men of the less than 9,000 men engaged at Seven Pines; 4,000 men of the 10,000 men in the battles around Richmond. But at Sharpsburg, the loss was 3,241 men in two battles alone, out of less than 5,000 men engaged. 520 The total effect of these devastating battles equated to nearly two-thirds of his division's entire force. Official reports recorded 925 men to be missing. Undoubtedly a large number of the missing fell into the hands of the Federals when wounded, but there were 2,316 men reported killed and wounded, equating to nearly 50% of the men taken into action. The losses inflicted upon the officer corps were staggering: one Brigadier General was killed and one seriously wounded; three brigade commanders were seriously wounded; four colonels were killed and eight seriously wounded; one Lieutenant Colonel was killed and seven were wounded; two Majors were killed and two were wounded. There were but thirty four field officers present during the battles, and only nine left when the fighting was over. The mortality was equally great among company commanders, and several regiments who were left under command of lieutenants. 521

Speaking of his soldiers' courage and resolve General Hill said: *"Still, the stubborn spirit of the men was not subdued. From 1,500 to 1,700 were gathered together, on the morning of the 18th, and placed in a position more sheltered than the one occupied the day before and would have fought with determination, if not with enthusiasm, had the Federals made yet another advance."* 522

General Hill's assessment of the Battle of Sharpsburg provides poignant insight: *"The battle of Sharpsburg was a success so far as the failure of the Federals to carry the position they assailed. It would, however, have been a glorious victory for us but for three causes:*

First - The separation of our forces; Had McLaws and R. H. Anderson been there earlier in the morning, the battle would not have lasted two hours, and would have been signally disastrous to the Federals.

Second - The bad handling of our artillery; [Confederate cannons] could not cope with the superior weight, caliber, range, and number of the Yankee guns; hence it ought only to have been used against masses of infantry. On the contrary, our guns were made to reply to the Yankee guns, and were smashed up or withdrawn before they could be effectually turned against massive columns of attack. An artillery duel between the Washington Artillery and the Yankee batteries across the Antietam on the 16th was the most melancholy farce in the war.

Third - The enormous straggling; the battle was fought with less than 30,000 men. Had all our stragglers been up, McClellan's army would have been completely crushed or annihilated. Doubtless the want of shoes, the want of wood, and physical exhaustion had kept many brave men from being with the army; but thousands of thieving poltroons had kept away from sheer cowardice." 523

Although some expositors have obsessively criticized General Hill for his sharp tongue, most often without offering a forum for rebuttal, there can be no question of the gallantry and valor displayed by Lee's Fighting General during the Battle of Sharpsburg. Perhaps if his critics would with full candor consider the context of horrific battle and its devastating effects upon the veterans thereof; possibly if they would reserve criticism – annotating their absence from active participation in the fight;   maybe if they could fathom the tremendous sense of personal loss that accompanies burying a fellow soldier in an unmarked grave, recently fallen before you. If by God's grace you are someday honored and privileged to lead courageous soldiers to battle, only to witness their untimely demise under the mantle of your leadership might you, too, on occasion be inclined to be of sharp tongue?

Consider General Hill's dutiful, yet most difficult, reporting of the battle's aftermath: *"In this sad list we have specially to mourn many distinguished officers. Brigadier-General Garland was killed at South Mountain-the most fearless man I ever knew, a Christian hero, a ripe scholar, and most accomplished gentleman. Brigadier General G. B. Anderson was mortally wounded at Sharpsburg-a high-toned, honorable, conscientious Christian soldier, highly gifted, and lovely in all the qualities that adorn a man. Colonel C. C. Tew, Second North Carolina Regiment, was one of the most finished scholars on the continent, and had no superior as a soldier in the field. Colonel B. B. Gayle, Twelfth Alabama, a most gallant and accomplished officer, was killed at South Mountain. Colonel W. P. Barclay, Twenty-third Georgia, the hero of South Mountain, was killed at Sharpsburg. There, too, fell those gallant Christian soldiers, Colonel Levi B. Smith, Twenty-seventh Georgia, and Lieutenant Colonel J. M. Newton, of the Sixth Georgia. The modest and heroic major [P.] Tracy, of the Sixth Georgia, met there, too, a bloody grave. The lament Captain [W. F.] Plane of that regiment, deserves a special mention. Of him it could be truly said that he shrank from no danger, no fatigue, and no exposure. Major Robert S. Smith, Fourth Georgia, fell, fighting most heroically, at Sharpsburg. He had received a military education, and gave promise of eminence in his profession. Captain James B. Atwell, Twentieth North Carolina, deserves to live in the memory of his countrymen for almost unsurpassed gallantry. After having greatly distinguished himself in the capture of the Yankee battery at South Mountain, he fell, heroically fighting, at Sharpsburg. Brigadier-General Ripley received a severe wound in the throat from a Mini-ball, which would have proven fatal but for passing through his cravat. After his wound was dressed, he heroically returned to the field, and remained to the close of the day with his brigade. Brigadier-General Rodes received a painful contusion from a shell, but remained with his command. Colonel McRae, commanding brigade, was struck in the forehead, but gallantly remained on the field. Colonel Bennett, Fourteenth North Carolina Regiment, who had conducted himself most nobly throughout, won my special admiration for the heroism he exhibited at the moment of receiving what he supposed to be a mortal wound. Colonel [W. L.] De Rosset, Third North Carolina, received a severe wound at Sharpsburg, which I fear will forever* deprive the South of his most valuable services. Colonel F. M. Parker, Thirtieth North Carolina, a modest, brave, and accomplished officer, was severely wounded at Sharpsburg. Colonel J. B. Gordon, Sixth Alabama, the Chevalier Bayard of the army, received five wounds at Sharpsburg before he would quit the field. The heroic Colonel [B. D.] Fry, Thirteenth Alabama, and Colonel [E. A.] O'Neal, Twenty-sixth Alabama, who had both been wounded at Seven Pines, were once more wounded severely, at Sharpsburg, while nobly and Major [R. D.] Redden, Twenty-sixth Alabama, were both wounded at South Mountain, the former severely. They greatly distinguished themselves in that battle. Lieutenant Colonel J. N. Lightfoot, Sixth Alabama, and Lieutenant Colonel [William A.] Johnston, Fourteenth North Carolina, were wounded at Sharpsburg, the latter slightly. Major [S. D.] Thurston, Third North Carolina, received a painful contusion, but did not leave the field. Lieutenant-Colonel Ruffin, Thirteenth North Carolina, remained with his regiment on South Mountain after receiving three painful wounds. Lieutenant Colonel [W. H.] Betts, Thirteenth Alabama, was slightly wounded. Lieutenant Colonel [C. T.] Yachry, Twenty-seventh Georgia, had just recovered from a severe wound before Richmond to receive a more serious one at Sharpsburg. Lieutenant Colonel [E. F.] Best and major [J. H.] Huggins, Twenty-third Georgia, gallant and meritorious officers, were severely wounded at Sharpsburg." 524

Commenting on the actions of General Hill, Colonel Henderson said: "*From before 10:00 until 1:00 o'clock the battle raged fiercely about the Sunken Road which was held by D. H. Hill and which witnessed on this such preeminence of slaughter that it has since been known by the name of 'Bloody Lane.' Here, inspired by the unyielding courage of their leaders, fought the five Brigades of D. H. Hill, with R. H. Anderson's Division and two of Walker's Regiments; and here Longstreet, confident as always, controlled the battle with his accustomed skill. He [D. H. Hill] did not have a regiment – not one, fresh or blown – but would not the still unwounded soldiers attack? One answered that he would go if Hill would lead. Instantly Hill accepted his offer. Soon he had some 200 in a crude, uneven line. D. H. Hill seized a rifle; shouted a command and started forward. It was fine but it was fruitless. So small a force could not get far in the face of the fire the Unionists poured into it. D. H. Hill reluctantly had to recall his volunteers. The same fate was met by an attack organized by some of the North Carolina Colonels and delivered on the right center.*" 525

General Lee said in his official report: "*The attack on our left was speedily followed by one in heavy force on the center. This was met by part of Walker's Division and the Brigades of G. B. Anderson and Rodes of D. H. Hill's command, assisted by a few pieces of artillery. The enemy was repulsed and retired behind the crest of a hill, from which they kept up a desultory fire. At this time, by a mistake of orders, General Rodes' Brigade was withdrawn from its position* *during the temporary absence of that officer at another part of the field. The enemy immediately passed through the gap thus created and G. B. Anderson's Brigade was broken and retired, General Anderson himself being mortally wounded . . . . The heavy masses of the enemy again moved forward, being opposed by only four pieces of artillery, supported by a few hundred men belonging to different brigade, rallied by General D. H. Hill and other officers, and parts of Walker's and R. H. Anderson's commands, Colonel Cooke of the Twenty-seventh North Carolina Regiment, of Walker's Brigade, standing boldly in line without a cartridge."* "At this critical moment, when the enemy was advancing on Cooke," reported General Longstreet, "a shot came across the Federal front, plowing the ground in a parallel line, then another and another, each nearer and nearer their line. This enfilade fire was from a battery on D. H. Hill's line, and it soon beat back the attacking column." 526*

Judge Avery summarized Hill's service to the Army of Northern Virginia succinctly with one sentence: *"At Sharpsburg the last, as in every previous engagement in which D. H. Hill participated with that army, no figure was more conspicuous and no line firmer than his."* 527

At days' end the bloodiest battle in American history was over. Before the battle General McClellan had real expectations of producing an outcome that would give the Federals reason to thank God for a great victory. Ironically, General Lee, with the same level of sincerity, had similar expectations for producing an outcome that would give the Confederacy reason to thank the same God for having granted to them a great victory. Both men being of faultless integrity and unquestioned sincerity, it was hardly possible for both to be victors on that occasion. 528 On this day, the results of this fierce fighting resulted in a disastrous defeat for General McClellan's army and, combined with the licking his men had taken at South Mountain by General Hill's small band of warriors, General McClellan would soon face predictable replacement by President Abraham Lincoln as Commander of the Army of the Potomac. But this Confederate victory, although a remarkable feat given their accomplishments against such overwhelming odds, came at a very heavy price. They had won the fight but lacked the numerical and physical strength to follow up in order to gain the tactical and strategic advantage that had been afforded to them by their victory. 529

General McClellan had passed upon yet another opportunity to move boldly and decisively whereupon he could have crushed General Lee's army at that moment in history. The Union General-in-chief had been under the delusion that the whole of the Confederate army was defending the gaps at the South Mountain; 530 but it was a severe misconception that had prevented him from crushing General Lee's army at that time.

Shortly after the battle of South Mountain, as the two armies camped along the Antietam creek, planning their strategies for the coming battle of Sharpsburg, the Union General missed yet another opportunity to crush General Lee's army. General Lee had little more with which to fight than the seriously worn and depleted forces of Generals Hill and Longstreet; whose troops were completely exhausted from the fighting at South Mountain and their following overnight march to the Antietam creek. General Lee was lacking the combat power of General Stonewall Jackson's men as they had not yet arrived upon the field. Further, he was lacking the additional power of General A. P. Hill's men whose planned arrival was well after General Jacksons. On the other hand, General McClellan had in position sufficient Union corps to sweep across the Antietam creek and capture every existing remnant of General Lee's army camped therein. But again, he failed to act boldly and decisively; deciding not to attack immediately thus allowing time for General Lee to place upon the field a substantial force. It is without question that, had the battle of Sharpsburg been fought in the absence of General Stonewall Jackson's men, the Confederate forces would have been routed. 531

It is of little wonder that many of General McClellan's most faithful supporters were beginning to believe that before he could be persuaded to attack the enemy, his methods of operation required that his aide-de-camp must ride to the front, take off his hat, and politely ask the Confederates: *"Gentlemen, are you ready?"* They might have added, with equal truth, if not politeness, that his indecisiveness was the same as *"Giant Stupidity:"* *De mortuis nil nisi bonum* will not do when we are discussing matters of history, otherwise we should be indebted to speak nothing but good of Caligula. 532

Let's consider another great battle of military history as a frame of reference to understand the significance of fighting General Lee's army at the Battle of Sharpsburg - had there been the absence of General Stonewall Jackson. Why did The Duke of Wellington await Napoleon Bonaparte's attack at Waterloo knowing that if Field Marshall Gebhard Leberecht von Blucher did not come he would be defeated? History has provided a simple answer: because Wellington had the same confidence in the old Prussian Field Marshall that General Lee had in General Stonewall Jackson. 533 Further, there was an even more striking difference between the task performed by Field Marshall Blucher and that accomplished by General Stonewall Jackson just days earlier at Harper's Ferry. The Prussian Field Marshal had only to steal away and leave Marquis de Grouchy to fight the air, as it were, while General Jackson not only defeated the forces he was sent to neutralize, but captured the whole of them, officers and men, horses and artillery, quartermaster, commissary, and ordnance stores. Had General McClellan possessed some of General Stonewall Jackson's *"gumption"* he would hardly have waited for General Lee to be thus reinforced, but hurrying up his tardy regiments, he would have hurled all the troops he had in hand at General Lee's weakened army that were being concentrated at Sharpsburg. 534

Continuing with comparisons of these two battles of Waterloo and Sharpsburg, the obvious points on the field for Lord Wellington and Napoleon were Hogomont, La Hayne Sainte, and the sunken road of Ohain. The latter, however, is somewhat hidden in the mists of the past and its existence even largely dependent upon the tradition due to its reference by Victor Hugo. Similarly obvious points on the field at Sharpsburg are the *"sunken road"* and the bridge now known as the *"Burnside Bridge."* The former was the *"bloody lane"* whereupon General Hill achieved the pinnacle of his military career as *"Lee's Fighting General."* After the battle was over there was no spot on that field that presented a more horrible appearance than the *"sunken road"* and the adjoining area whereupon General Hill led his famous, desperate charge. The roadway along the lane was literally filled with dead men and the slopes that approached it were covered with windrows of the harvest of death. Likewise, the bridge, known today as the Burnside Bridge, was probably the next most important position. Before the attacking Federals attempted to reach, cross, then exit the bridge, they were at all times exposed to point-blank fire from the Confederates, tactically posted on the Sharpsburg side, in a sort of a natural *tete de pont*, but reversed. That is to say, it defended the opposite end from that which a regular *tete de point* would. 535

During the fiercest fighting along the sunken road, officers and men had fallen like autumn leaves, all along the line; yet they remained *"dressed on the centre"* where their colors had flown while they continued to load and fire as regularly as if at target practice. This offered striking evidence of maintaining discipline during a fight and an example of heroism worthy of the best and bravest." 536

During the Battle of Sharpsburg, there was no great display of strategy or grand tactics on the part of either of the Generals-in-chief; as they have long since passed beyond the reach of praise or criticism, there so shall they rest. But posthumous honors are easily bestowed upon all those gallant men who lost their lives in this epic battle. In performance of their heroic deeds, the soldiers of the Confederacy stand as magnificent figures - attired in their dingy Confederate uniforms of gray and butternut, splashed with the crimson tide of that mighty fight along the banks of the Antietam creek. And special honor is granted to one courageous fighter who survived the perils of this battle, to fight yet another day as *"Lee's Fighting General:"* a formidable fighter who rose to the very top of his profession of arms - illumining the military horizon with splendor: his sincerity unquestioned, his courage unchallenged, his name and fame immutable, immaculate and immortal. 537 Given the challenges facing

General Lee's Confederate army, with respect to the overwhelming numerical advantage held by General McClellan's Army of the Potomac, the Battle of Sharpsburg was perhaps the greatest victory achieved in the gallant history of the Army of Northern Virginia. General Robert E. Lee's Army, with just 35,000 men, decisively defeated General McClellan's numerically superior Federal troops, consisting of 87,000 men.

After waiting a day for an anticipated Federal counterattack, General Lee ordered the move of his army to positions south of the Potomac River, where his embattled Army would spend the last few days of September and much of October 1862 in reconsolidation and reconstitution of his army. As the Confederates could not look for a material increase of strength, and the enemy's force could be largely and rapidly increased, it was not thought sensible to wait until he should be ready again to offer battle. [540] Consequently, General Robert E. Lee withdrew his army to the south side of the Potomac, crossing near Shepherdstown, without loss or Union interference. [541]

In November 1862 D. H. Hill's Division was ordered to lead the march to Fredericksburg for yet another appointment with destiny: The Battle of Fredericksburg. [538] During this march, a large number of General Hill's men had been barefooted since the return of General Lee's army from Maryland; yet he accomplished the unusual feat of marching 200 miles in twenty days without leaving on the way a single straggler, whereupon General D. H. Hill's division took a reserve position upon arrival in the vicinity of Fredericksburg. [539] That day passed without any demonstration on the part of the enemy, who from the reports received, was expecting the arrival of reinforcements. During the early days of December 1862, Lee's Army of Northern Virginia occupied the high ground just behind the city of Fredericksburg, Virginia, taking up entrenched defensive positions in preparation for the next major engagement of the campaign. Lee's army would again face the Federal forces of the Army of the Potomac on the field of battle during the period of December 11th - 15th 1862; this time facing the Union Army under the command of Major General Ambrose E. Burnside – Lincoln had replaced General McClellan after his failures at the South Mountain and Sharpsburg where his proclamation that he would *"whip Bobby Lee"* had fallen measurably short, thanks in large part to the contributions of *Lee's Fighting General* and D. H. Hill's Division. [542]

D. H. HILL

"in action & under fire he commands the admiration & respect of everyone."

[[Major James N. Edmondston]]

Q7

CHAPTER XII

MILITARY DEPARTMENT OF NORTH CAROLINA

In February 1863 General Hill offered his final adieu to his old D. H. Hill's Division and, at the special request of North Carolina's Governor Zebulon Vance, General Lee released General D. H. Hill from the Army of Northern Virginia, 543 whereupon he was appointed to assume command of the District of North Carolina. 544

At this juncture of the Civil War, Union forces were in control of New Bern, Washington and other places in Eastern North Carolina. From these towns the Federal troops frequently made sudden marches out into the countryside to overawe the people and destroy their crops. These movements were very damaging, not only to the residents of North Carolina, but to General Lee's army in Virginia as well. The Federal raids and other incursions in eastern North Carolina were effectively disrupting the flow of supplies that were desperately needed to support the Army of Northern Virginia. Concerns over the security and sustainability of the railways leading from the ports of Wilmington and Charleston were of mutual concern and importance to the State of North Carolina, the Commonwealth of Virginia and the Confederate government. Additionally, the residents of Governor Vance's great State had been extremely vocal about so much attention being given to the defense of the Commonwealth of Virginia, in their view, often at great expense to Carolinians. 545 This growing pressure induced the Governor to find a strong leader to assume command of the District of North Carolina. North Carolinians were insistent upon someone who would deal with the Yankee perpetrators. These were major concerns that Governor Vance argued effectively with the Confederate government to successfully gain General Hill's appointment to the Department of North Carolina. General D. H. Hill was clearly the most distinguished North Carolinian within the Confederate armies. When *Lee's Fighting General* finally arrived in his adopted home State, the citizens held great expectations that he and Governor Vance would *"drive the Federal forces out of the State or to shut them up in the towns."* 546

Z. VANCE

But General Hill quickly learned that the army of the District of North Carolina was not properly staffed, manned, and resourced; being extremely lacking in the capabilities required kick the enemy out of North Carolina. However, utilizing what limited resources that were provided to him, he was able to strike a number of hard blows against the Federal troops in eastern North Carolina - effectively limiting the Federal raids and allowing the long wagon trains to resume their resupply to General Lee's army in Virginia. 547 The relationship between Governor Vance and General Hill immediately became one of mutual respect; a great relationship that would last long after the war. General Hill had absolutely no political aspirations as his strength was that of a skilled fighter. He was always proven to be most effective when mounted on his steed, courageously charging Yankee lines while leading his beloved Confederate soldiers into desperate battle. Now he found himself in a new arena where he was required solve many challenges, not by the sword, but through discssions with politicians. This new assignment might have been be fatal to his military career but his unique and special relationship with Governor Vance allowed him to perform effectively and accomplish great things for his beloved State. Foremost in his relationship with Governor Vance was his respect for the Governor's battlefield service to the State as a soldier. 548 *Lee's Fighting General* considered military service to be the most honorable duty one could perform for his beloved State of North Carolina specifically and to the Confederacy in general. As such, the General held Governor Zebulon Vance in highest regard. After all, the two men had much in common. 549 Zebulon Vance, too, was a Carolinian; born in the mountains near Asheville, NC on May 13th 1830. The two men's experiences during childhood were in stark comparison, both growing up in genteel poverty, both educated at home by their mothers, and both having developed the same sense of pride in service to their State and, subsequently the Confederacy. Both had been provided the opportunity to become learned men; Harvey's formal education at the United States Military Academy produced a career soldier while Zebulon Vance's education at The University of North Carolina at Chapel Hill produced a competent attorney.

In 1854, when he was only twenty four years old, the Whigs elected young *"Zeb"* as a member of the United States Congress, thus becoming the youngest member of that respected body. He was again elected to another term in 1860 but his term would be shortened with the coming of the Civil War. When the controversy arose between the North and South over secession, Zebulon Vance was a strong Union man. He had developed into quite a charismatic speaker who had become known, affectionately, as the *"Mountain Boy"* from Carolina. His colorful speeches were always filled with amusing and appropriate anecdotes and he could deliver the most memorable speeches from the stump; always gaining favorable responses and spoken compliments such as: *"You ought to have heard young Vance. He is the greatest stump speaker that ever was – the greatest that ever was!"* 550 But when the war began, in spite of his efforts, Vance declared that he would stand by the South. *"If,"* he said, *"war must come, I prefer to be with my own people. If we have to shed blood, I prefer to shed Northern rather than Southern blood. If I have to slay, I had rather slay strangers than my own kindred and neighbors."* 551 It was this firm position of support for the Confederacy that was a common thread for Harvey and Zebulon. But D. H. Hill most respected Zeb, not for his speaking skills, but for his actions. Young Zebulon Vance left the United States Congress and returned to his home in Buncombe County, whereupon he raised a company of sturdy mountain men and was elected Captain of the Rough and Ready Guards.

In May 1861, he led his Rough and Ready Guards down to Raleigh, North Carolina where they joined other North Carolina troops. It was this venue whereupon Major D. H. Hill and Captain Zebulon Vance first came to establish their friendship. Major D. H. Hill was further impressed with Captain Vance as the war progressed and Zebulon was elected Colonel of the 26th North Carolina Regiment. It was during his leadership that Colonel Vance distinguished himself as a fighter during the Battle of New Bern. 552 On March 14th 1862 during the Battle of New Bern, Colonel Vance demonstrated himself to be a very brave and skilful officer. Nothing but Colonel Vance's personal courage and leadership saved his 26th North Carolina Regiment from destruction as they were attacked by an overwhelming Union force. He led his men in a glorious fight that earned him the respect of many, including his men who would follow him *"into the jaws of certain death"* if he would only lead the way. 553

Colonel Vance would continue his distinguished service to the Confederacy during the great battles around Richmond where he led his men with great skill and notable courage. He was so daring in battle that his men were afraid he would be killed. Begging him not to expose his life so recklessly, they forcefully asserted to him that North Carolina could not afford for him to be killed, for in August the people were going to elect him governor. But Colonel Vance, being an accomplished fighter, much like General Daniel Harvey Hill, refused to shun any danger to which his men were exposed. Every time they went into battle, he rode at their head, cheering and encouraging them. It was this fighting spirit that D. H. Hill so admired in the man – making him one to whom D. H. Hill would grant his utmost respect and loyal support. 554 In August 1862, while fighting in Virginia at the head of his regiment, he was elected Governor of North Carolina. Although he did not ask for the office, when the people had chosen him he felt obliged to accept. Colonel Vance resigned from the Army of Northern Virginia, traveled to Raleigh, North Carolina, and on September 8th 1862 began his duties as Governor of the great State of North Carolina. 555

Affording the mutual respect that only one soldier can give to another, General D. H. Hill began his term at the Department of North Carolina - being of like mind with Governor Vance. Their mutual respect for one another, their loyalty to North Carolina and their determination to protect and defend her people formed the basis for their tremendous working relationship. This mutual admiration and soldierly respect would serve them well in the discharge of their duties. 556 Working closely together, the two men were able to keep the ranks of North Carolina's Regiments full. Through their combined efforts, North Carolina sent more soldiers to the Confederate army than there were voters in the State and they kept her soldiers better clothed and better fed than the soldiers of any other Southern State. 557 Many a poor, ragged soldier had shoes on his feet, a blanket to protect himself from the snow, and a piece of bacon once a week because of the painstaking support that their close personal and working relationship produced.

After a great period of service, working hand in hand with Governor Vance to advance North Carolina's cause, General Hill was ordered in the early part of 1863 to move his headquarters from North Carolina to Petersburg Virginia whereupon the organization of his Department, and its assigned responsibilities, were greatly enlarged. 558 His duties were also expanded to include responsibilities for the overall defense of Confederate installations in the vicinity of the James River. General Hill labored energetically to perform his duties, spending much time reviewing the defenses within his area of responsibility. 559 When General Lee's Army was in Pennsylvania the Federals, under General Dix, advanced up the Peninsula from Yorktown. The people of Richmond and the heads of the Confederacy's governmental departments there became greatly alarmed over the safety of the City. General Hill was ordered to transfer all available troops from south of the James and afterward assume command of the forces defending Richmond. Shortly after assuming command General Hill confronted and defeated General Dix at Bottom Bridge, driving him all the way back to where he had started at Yorktown. This action served to restore, not only the confidence of the people of Richmond, but most political and military leaders of the Confederacy as well. Judge Avery reported that many Committees of grateful citizens of Richmond visited General Hill's Headquarters often to express their thanks for his conduct of their defense. 560

D. H. HILL

D.H. Hill and Stonewall Jackson taken under accurate Federal artillery fire during White Oak swamp fighting

"Fast riding in the wrong direction is not military, but is sometimes healthy."

[[General D. H. Hill]] June 30 1862

Q23

CHAPTER XIII

PROMOTION TO LIEUTENANT GENERAL

On July 13th 1863 General D. H. Hill was visiting the home of Mr. Poe, a relative of Edgar Allen Poe, when President Jefferson Davis galloped up to the home on horseback, exclaiming in an excited manner: *"Rosecrans is about to advance upon Bragg; I have found it necessary to detail Hardee to defend Mississippi and Alabama. His corps is without a commander. I wish you to command it."*

General D. H. Hill replied: *"I cannot do that as General Stuart ranks me."*

"I can cure that," answered President Davis, *"by making you a Lieutenant-General. Your papers will be ready tomorrow. When can you start?"*

"In twenty four hours," replied General Hill. Before leaving, President Davis provided his views on the subject to the new Lieutenant General and left him with parting words of congratulations. 561 In recognition for General Hill's gallantry and distinguished service to the Confederacy, and upon the order of President Jefferson Davis, Daniel Harvey Hill was promoted to the rank of Lieutenant General. Judge Avery recounted the event: *"About the 10ᵗʰ day of July, 1863"* President Davis called at General D. H. Hill's quarters three miles east of Richmond, and after many kind and complimentary comments upon his conduct as an officer during the preceding year, informed him that he was appointed a Lieutenant General." 562

D. H. Hill was given orders to report without delay to General Joseph E. Johnson, near Vicksburg, Mississippi. 563Lieutenant General Hill, along with his staff, set out immediately for his new assignment. While en route, when Hill reached his home in Charlotte, North Carolina, he was notified that his destination had been changed and he would report for duty to General Braxton Bragg at Chattanooga, Tennessee where he would assume command of a corps in General Braxton Bragg's army at Chattanooga. 564

D. H. HILL

"Do you know that in Mexico the young officers called you the bravest man in the army?"

[[Lieutenant General Joseph E. Johnston]]

Q3

LIEUTENANT GENERAL D. H. HILL'S CORPS

The next major engagement for the newly promoted Lieutenant General D. H. Hill would be the Battle of Chickamauga - the greatest battle, except perhaps for Gettysburg, fought in the Civil War. Early in September General Bragg prepared to engage his Army of Tennessee against Union General Rosecrans' Army of the Cumberland. Soon, General D. H. Hill would find himself engaged in another desperate battle, one of great historical importance, for himself and the Confederacy. This pitched and bloody battle would produce for the Confederacy a great victory on the field of battle that would establish a military high water mark for the Confederacy. But General Braxton Bragg's failure to capitalize on the Confederate victory and exploit the gains earned on the field of battle would soon render the victory to be a barren one. General Bragg's serious mistakes would create the *"Controversy at Chickamauga"* that cost him the confidence of his subordinates, his command of the Army of Tennessee, and would surround D. H. Hill in his third and final controversy of his military career. 565 At the beginning of the Civil War, General D. H. Hill was asked the question, *"Who of the Federal officers are most to be feared?"* D. H. Hill replied: *"Sherman, Rosecrans and McClellan. Sherman has genius and daring, and is full of resources.*

G. H. THOMAS   **W. S. ROSECRANS**   **U. S. GRANT**   **T. CRITTENDEN**   **W. T. SHERMAN**

PROMINENT UNION GENERALS
CHICKAMAUGA AND BENTONVILLE

I. PALMER   **H. VAN CLEVE**   **G. GRANGER**   **T. J. WOOD**   **A. McCOOK**

Rosecrans has fine practical sense, and is of a tough, tenacious fiber. McClellan is a man of talents, and his delight has always been in the study of military history and the art and science of war." Grant was not once thought of. The light of subsequent events thrown upon the careers of these three great soldiers has not changed my estimate of them; but I acquiesce in the verdict which has given greater renown to some of their comrades. It was my lot to form a more intimate acquaintance with the three illustrious officers who I foresaw would play an important part in the war. I fought against McClellan from Yorktown to Sharpsburg (Antietam), I encountered Rosecrans at Chickamauga, and I surrendered to Sherman at Greensboro, N. C. – each of the three commanding an army. D.H.H. 566

Lieutenant General D. H. Hill arrived in Tennessee to find General Bragg's Army of Tennessee camped along the Tennessee River, where he reported in on July 19th 1863. Lieutenant General Hill received from General Bragg the warm welcome of a comrade who had served as Hill's commander during the Mexican war and had observed his gallantry and knew of his reputation as *"a fighter from way back."* The cordial and enthusiastic greetings from two old classmates from West Point, A. P. Stewart and Pat Cleburne, also gave cause for great optimism for the new Lieutenant General in this, his new assignment. 567 General D. H. Hill had not seen General Braxton Bragg since he was the junior Lieutenant in Lieutenant Bragg's battery of artillery at Corpus Christi. The other two lieutenants in the battery were George H. Thomas and John F. Reynolds; all four having been colleagues and friends. Reynolds had been killed fighting at Gettysburg only twelve days before General D. H. Hill's new assignment; General Thomas, the strongest and most pronounced Southerner of the four, was now Union General Rosecran's most revered subordinate. Such was the nature of this war – pitting brother against brother, friend against friend.

General D. H. Hill's initial interview with General Bragg did not go well. General Bragg was unusually silent and reserved, appearing to be gloomy and despondent. The strained relationship between General Bragg and many of his subordinates was commonly known to be unpleasant. General Bragg had also alienated and distanced himself from the rank and file, largely due to his many retreats – actions that reduced the enthusiasm which soldiers feel for their successful generals and which induces them to obey orders without question. *"The one thing a soldier never fails to understand is victory, and the commander who leads him to victory will be adorned by him, whether that victory has been won by skill or by blundering, by the masterly handling of a few troops against great odds, or by the awkward use of overwhelming numbers."* 568

General D. H. Hill was assigned to command General Hardee's old corps, 569 consisting of Generals Cleburne and Stewarts divisions, with his headquarters located at Tyner's Station, 570 a few miles east of Chattanooga, along the Knoxville railroad. 571 Shortly upon arrival, and in great anticipation of the battle, D. H. Hill's respected chief of staff, Colonel Archer Anderson offered an introductory address to the corps men, saying: *"The corps of Hardee had lately gained as a commander a stern and dauntless soldier from the Army of Northern Virginia in D. H. Hill, whose vigor, coolness and unconquerable pertinacity in fight had already stamped him as a leader of heroic temper. Of the religious school of Stonewall Jackson, his earnest convictions never chilled his ardor for battle, and in another age he would have been worthy to charge with Cromwell at Dunbar, with the cry, 'Let God arise and let his enemies be scattered.'"* 572

Late August of 1863 found General Rosecrans on the march with his Union Army of Cumberland moving from Chattanooga, southwest through the gaps of Missionary Ridge. The Union chief had mistakenly expected General Bragg's army to be in full retreat toward Georgia when he abandoned Chattanooga but he soon found the Confederate Army of Tennessee consolidating their forces in preparation for an attack. Rosecrans responded and proceeded to concentrate his own forces wherein both armies would soon face one another in battle array on either side of the Chickamauga creek.

The Federal forces, on August 21st 1863, made their presence known on the west bank of the Tennessee River with a cannonade; firing randomly upon a small village just east of the river. 573 By August 29th and 30th 1863, General Rosecrans, with two of his corps commanders, Generals McCook and Thomas, using Lookout Mountain to mask their movements, crossed the river unopposed about thirty five miles south of Chattanooga into Wills Valley; establishing his headquarters at Trenton. A few days before the crossing, General Bragg had said petulantly: *"It is said to be easy to defend a mountainous country, but mountains hide your foe from you, while they are full of gaps through which he can pounce upon you at any time. A mountain is like the wall of a house full of rat holes, ready to pop out when no one is watching. Who can tell what lies hidden behind that wall?"* said General Bragg, pointing to the Cumberland range across the river. 574 On September 7th 1863 General Rosecrans ordered General McCook's corps through Winston Gap to cross Lookout Mountain and position his forces in the area of Alpine, east of the mountain. He sent General Thomas, through Stevens' and Cooper's Gaps, to occupy McLemore's Cove; a narrow valley between Lookout and Pigeon Mountains. The ease of General Rosecran's movements, being without opposition, had been made possible by General Bragg's withdrawal from Chattanooga; another controversial retreat by General Bragg. His concession of Chattanooga had been a tactical error: by holding the city he would have effectively neutralized General Crittenden's corps while rendering any possible link up between Generals Rosecrans and Burnsides to be impossible. But of greater impact was the strategic error: Chattanooga was a key objective for the Confederacy - to lose the city was to effectively lose all of east Tennessee, south of Knoxville. Whatever General Bragg's thought process, he had completely abandoned Chattanooga by August 8th 1863 and General Crittenden gained possession the very next day, without expending a single cartridge, shell or soldier. Criticism continued to grow with General Bragg's decision to make yet another uncontested retreat. 575 His failure to outperform General Rosecrans in the complex details of strategic planning would prove to be the major source for criticism of General Bragg; based upon two major strategic flaws in his performance and leadership:

First, he failed obtain, or possess, the essential information and knowledge to be sufficiently aware of the battlefield; both tactically and strategically. Second, he failed to provide the quality leadership necessary for supervising and executing his orders. *"No General ever won a permanent fame who was wanting in these grand elements of success, knowledge of his own and his enemy's condition, and personal superintendence of operations on the field."* 576 As an illustration, you will note through study and analysis that General Bragg failed to attack General Negley's division in the cove on September 10th 1863 due to his lack of knowledge of road conditions, existing obstructions at Dug Gap, and the enemy's position and disposition; reaffirming the importance of knowing battlefield conditions. 577

On the morning of September 13th 1863 General D. H. Hill was informed that General Polk had been ordered to attack General Crittenden at Lee and Gordon's Mills, and that the artillery reserves and trains were specially entrusted to the corps of General D. H. Hill. General Breckenridge was ordered to guard the roads leading south from Lafayette; General Cleburne was directed to guard the gaps in Pigeon Mountain. But a second lost opportunity occurred when General Bragg failed to execute an attack, despite the strong urging by General Pegram to do so. In his official report General Bragg, addressing this failure, quoted the following order, his first, General Polk thereby instructing him to attack as proffered by General Pegram: *"General: I enclose you a dispatch from General Pegram. This presents you a fine opportunity of striking Crittenden in detail, and I hope you will avail yourself of it at daylight to-morrow. This division crushed, and the others are yours. We can then turn again on the force in the cove. Wheeler's cavalry will move on Wilder so as to cover your right. I shall be delighted to hear of your success."* General Bragg then restated that this order was twice repeated, at short interval, with the last dispatch being: *"The enemy is approaching from the south- and it is highly important that your attack in the morning should be quick and decided. Let no time be lost."* 578 General Bragg then elaborated upon his explanation, stating that he had received a message from General Pope that he had taken up a strong defensive position and requested that he should be heavily reinforced. General Bragg replied to General Pope that he should not put off the attack, reminding him of the attack's importance. However, the critical failure was General Bragg's personal decision not to depart for the battle line until the next morning; wherein he was surprised to find that General Pope had made no advance upon the enemy. General Bragg's actions are extremely problematic, from a perspective of military leadership.

During the execution phase of any active operation, it is of critical importance that the General-in-chief should be in the center of his marching columns that he may be able to give prompt and efficient aid to whichever wing may be threatened; when a great battle is to be fought, the General must be on the field of battle to ensure that his orders are executed and to take advantage of the ever changing phases of the conflict. This is, by definition, military leadership. One the other hand, as fulfillment of one's leadership responsibilities, a General cannot send one message from a distance of ten miles, much less four messages, to execute a daring attack at daylight, which he was never to witness. General Crittenden could have been no more exposed to attack. On March 11th 1863, he had divided his force of three brigades, placing Generals Palmer's and Van Cleve's brigades at Ringgold, a distance of twenty miles from Chattanooga; of critical tactical importance was his placement of his third brigade, commanded by General Wood, a full ten miles away from Ringgold in the vicinity of Lee and Gordon's mills – in a great position of vulnerability; alone and unsupported for nearly two days. General Crittenden marched and counter-marched with such extraordinary coolness and such a nonchalance manner that his movements to which, in the annals of warfare, there is no parallel. Had General Bragg afforded his army the able leadership so expected for a man in his position of authority, as General-in-chief, he would have been present on the field of battle, leading his soldiers to cease a great tactical advantage given to him by is enemy; effectively crushing the forces of General Crittenden and winning a great tactical victory with far reaching strategic implications. Instead, by squandering yet another great opportunity, General Bragg permitted General Crittenden to consolidate his forces, forming a disposition to move against his defenses on Missionary Ridge just a few short days later at the Battle of Chickamauga. 579

In response to criticism for this failure General Bragg, in his official report, charged General Polk with failure to crush General Crittenden's forces while in their isolated positions at Ringgold. However, upon study and critical analysis of the situation on the battlefield at that time, it must be noted that General Pope was ordered to *"take a position on a specific spot – Rock Spring – thence, if not attacked, to advance by daylight on the 13th of September, and assume the offense against the opposing forces,"* which were expected to come from the direction of Ringgold. *However, if you closely examine the location of units on the field you will see that General Crittenden was at Gordon's Mill, behind the Chickamauga, on the evening of the 12th. The order was simply impractical and could not have been accomplished under any given circumstance."* General Crittenden, being totally unaware of his hazardous position, crossed unopposed at the mills and united with General Wood late on September 12th 1863, General Bragg, considering the wide dispersion of Federal forces and their confronting him at so many points, fell into great confusion – *"with the popping out of the rats from so many holes."* General Bragg knew he was encircled by the enemy, he just didn't know *"who they were, their strength, or their plans."* 580 As the battlefield continued to slowly take shape for the coming battle along the Chickamauga creek, considering it to be more a process of evolving when compared to the rapidly developing battlefields he had grown accustomed to while serving in General Lee's Army of Northern Virginia's area. General D. H. Hill recalled a comment he once made to General Patton Anderson: When two armies confront each other in the East, they get to work very soon; but here you look at one another for days and weeks at a time." General Anderson replied with a laugh:*"Oh, we out here have to crow and peck straws awhile before we use our spurs."* The time for crowing and pecking straws was now about over. 581

On September 16th 1863, General Rosecrans had his forces well in hand, extending from Lee and Gordon's Mills to Stevens' Gap, in a line running from east to southwest and covering a length of about eleven miles. General Bragg held the gaps in Pigeon Mountain and the fords to Lee and Gordon's Mills.

Each of the Confederate corps commanders was positioned to effectively turn the left flank of their respective enemy. General Bragg had crossed the Chickamauga at points north of Lee and Gordon's Mills but, in doing so, risked fighting with his back to the river – a risky position should his line be forced to the rear. On the other hand, should he be successful in the attack, he faced the possibility of cutting General Rosecrans off at the Tennessee River and, possibly, retaking Chattanooga. 582 General Bragg's plan of attack placed General Polk in charge of the right wing, which included the corps of General's Hill and Walker; and General John Hood holding the left wing with the corps of Generals Hood and Buckner until Longstreet's arrival.

General Lee had dispatched Longstreet to the Army of Tennessee as part of the Confederacy's overall war strategy but his arrival was still pending. General Bragg had assumed that if the strength of the enemy's extreme left, under the command of General George H. Thomas, could be driven from the Lafayette road, the enemy's communication with Chattanooga would be cut off and the retreat and ruin of the enemy would be inevitable. 583 General Bragg had labored in developing the rapid restructuring of his army and had personally developed his plan of attack, to the exclusion of input from his Generals and staff, and the practices and procedures he used in preparing and issuing orders was greatly lacking in efficiency, when compared to the efficiency of General Lee's staff, to which General Hill had become accustomed. General Bragg's plans seemed to be more intent on a hurried approach rather than a concentrated effort and the manner of Bragg's delivery, considering that he waited until the end of the 1st day of the battle to reveal his concept to his Generals, seemed totally disjointed to Hill: 584 *"Want of information" in General Bragg's headquarters was in striking cont rast with the minute knowledge General Lee always had of every operation at his front, and I was painfully impressed with feeling that it was to be a haphazard battle. * * * Whenever a great battle is to be fought, the commanding general must be on the field to see that his orders are executed and to take advantage of the ever changing phases of the conflict."* 585 *My sympathies had always been with Bragg. I knew of the carping criticisms of his subordinates and the cold looks of his soldiers, and knew that these were the natural results of reverses, whether the blame lay with the commander or otherwise. I had felt, too, that this lack of confidence or lack of enthusiasm, whichever it might be, was ominous of evil for the impending battle. But ignorance of the enemy's movements seemed a still worse portent of calamity. — D.H.H."* 586

General Rosecran's risks were facing the prospect that General Bragg's forces could, in fact, force him to retreat to the Tennessee, cutting him off, capturing his army and the retaking of Chattanooga. But he had General Granger's corps in reserve, holding the strong defenses at Chattanooga and his army also held the gaps in Lookout Mountain. General Rosecrans, adjusting to the field as General Bragg had set his battle array, countered his positioning of forces by moving General McCook to take the place of General Thomas at Pond Spring; Thomas moved to relieve the two brigades of General Crittenden at Crawfish Springs; and he moved General Crittenden to position his forces to the left of General Wood at Lee and Gordon's Mills, in order to protect the road to Chattanooga. Thus this was the plan:

"1: On September 18th 1863, General Bushrod Johnston's column, on crossing at or near Reed's Bridge, will turn to the left by the most practicable route, and sweep up the Chickamauga toward Lee and Gordon's Mills;

2: General Walker, crossing the Alexander's Bridge, will unite in this move and push vigorously on the enemy's flank and rear in the same direction;

3: General Buckner, crossing at Tedford's Ford, will join in the movement to the left, and press the enemy up the stream from General Polk's front at Lee and Gordon's Mills;

4: General Polk will press his forces to the front of Lee and Gordon's Mills, and if met by too much resistance to cross will bear to the right and cross at Dalton's Ford or at Tedford's, as may be necessary, and join the attack wherever the enemy may be;

5: General D. H. Hill will cover our left flank from an advance of the enemy from the cove, and, by pressing the cavalry in his front, ascertain if the enemy is reinforcing at Lee and Gordon's Mills, in which event he will attack them in flank;

6: General Wheeler's cavalry will hold the gaps in Pigeon Mountain, and cover our rear and left, and bring up stragglers;

7: All teams, etc., not with troops should go toward Ringgold and Dalton beyond Taylor's Ridge. All cooking should be done at the trains; rations when cooked will be forwarded to the troops;

8: The above movements will be executed with the utmost promptness, vigor, and persistence." 587

If this order had been issued on any of the preceding four days it would have totally thrown General Rosecrans into great confusion and would have had an extremely high probability of producing a tremendous tactical victory on the field. Even if the order had been issued just 24 hours in advance of the attack, it would have produced most favorable results in the attack. However, the order was not issued appropriately or in a timely and procedurally correct manner.

General Hill's corps, consisting of Generals Breckinridge's and Cleburne's divisions, was on General Polk's far right. But there was much confusion when General Polk gave orders to Generals Breckinridge and Cleburne but failed to give a copy to General Hill, assuming that General Bragg would pass it along. The delay and inefficient manner with which General Bragg was supervising the battle was again in stark contrast to the efficiency exercised by General Lee and his staff. This caused great confusion in the delivery of orders to affect a timely, coordinated attack. And the noticable absence of General Bragg's presence on and around the battlefield was extremely unsettling to General Hill, having become so accustomed to the command presence that General Lee so aptly displayed before his army. 588 Lieutenant General Hill expressed his concerns from the outset: *"The opposing forces at Chickamauga were almost evenly divided, with the Confederates and Federals each placing approximately 50,000 men on the field of battle. The Federal forces were a little over that number and the Confederate forces somewhat under, but there was not a difference of more than three or four thousand men on the respective sides."* 589

D. H. HILL

"He was the very "Ironsides" of the South – Cromwell in some of his essential characteristics coming again in the person and genius of D. H. Hill."

[[Henry Elliott Shepherd]]

Q11

CHAPTER XIV

THE BATTLE OF CHICKAMAUGA

On September 17th 1863 General D. H. Hill was directed to move his corps at daylight the next morning, in rear of General Polk's corps, toward Lee and Gordon's Mills. 590 A demonstration was to be made at that point by General Polk while the rest of the army would cross a little farther down the Chickamauga creek. 591 General Cleburne's division was drawn up in line of battle at the Anderson's house on September 18th 1863 and General Breckinridge was sent to guard the crossing at Glass' Mill. Just prior to sundown, General D. H. Hill's cavalry pickets were attacked by a considerable Union force, driving them back and successfully advancing across Owens' Ford. General D. H. Hill quickly led the column of General Adam's brigade to engage the advancing Union force but their advance stalled along the line in front of General Childress. 592 Early on the morning of September 19th 1863 General Adam's brigade was withdrawn to Glass' Mill. At this juncture General D. H. Hill was determined to create a diversion. General Helm's brigade unleashed a ferocious ten gun cannonade that placed a large volume of withering fire upon the Yankees with devastating effects; producing fire that was unusually accurate and extremely deadly.

PROMINENT CONFEDERATE GENERALS

J. PEGRAM

P. E. CLEBURNE

D. H. HILL

E. F. CHEATHAM

B. BRAGG

B. JOHNSTON

J. S. NEGLEY

T. HINDMAN

S. E. BUCKNER

CHICKAMAUGA 1863

J. WHEELER

J. G. WALKER

L. McLAWS

A. STEWART

L. POLK

J. PATTON ANDERSON

J. B. HOOD

J. C. BRECKENRIDGE

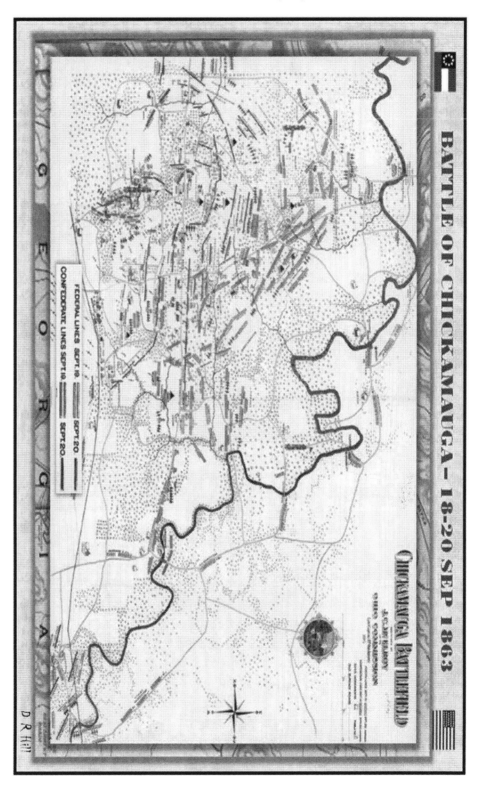

The ground was still scattered with unburied Union soldiers from previous days of fighting and 11 horses lay near the position of the Yankee battery. 593 In the afternoon General D. H. Hill received an order to personally report to General Bragg at Thedford's Ford with further instructions to hurry forward General Cleburne's division to that same location. When General Breckenridge's division arrived at Thedford's Ford, he was placed in relief of General Hindman at Lee and Gordon's Mills. General D. H. Hill, upon reporting to the commanding general, learned that while the Confederate troops had been moving up the Chickamauga creek, the Union forces had been moving down the creek. This action produced an opportunity for Union forces to outflank the Confederates and they successfully drove back the Confederate right wing with great enthusiasm. General D. H. Hill responded with directions to General Cleburne to take a position on the extreme right and initiate a counter-attack with all haste. General Cleburne set his battle line and just after sundown they advanced in magnificent style, pushing the Yankees back some three quarters of a mile. During the assault, General Cleburne's troops captured 3 cannons, a number of caissons, 2 stands of colors and upward of 300 prisoners; all the while sustaining but minor losses; The greatest loss of Confederate soldiers fell chiefly upon General Wood's brigade as they encountered withering musketry fire crossing an open field to later engage the Union's log breastworks along the edge of the open field's opposite side. 594

General D. H. Hill's artillerists, Captain Semple and Lieutenant Key, moved their batteries forward, under cover of darkness, to within 60 yards of the Yankee line and opened fire, with devastating effects upon the enemy. General D. H. Hill had placed the other cannon batteries of the division on his right flank, wherein they delivered murderous enfilade fires upon the Yankee line. General D. H. Hill, in his official report, stated: *"I have never seen troops behave more gallantly than did this noble division, and certainly I never saw so little straggling from the field."* 595

The decisive action closed between 9 p.m. and 10 p. m. on the late evening of September 19th 1863, wherein it was deemed unwise to pursue the fleeing Union soldiers in the darkness. The Confederate line had become considerably deranged as a result of the violence of the fight. Having totally seized the momentum of the battle, General D. H. Hill talked with General Cleburne and each of his brigade commanders, as tactical readjustments were made to the line; discussions designed to determine the best potential tactical strategy to exploit the situation on the field. 596 General D. H. Hill left at 11 p. m. to locate General Bragg at Thedford's Ford, at the location orders for the day had stated his headquarters would be. Although a considerable distance of nearly 5 miles to the ford, General D. H. Hill was without orders for the next day and he deemed it necessary to find the commanding general to confirm his intent.

Along the way, General D. H. Hill learned from some soldiers that General Breckinridge had repositioned his line, pulling up from Lee and Gordon's Mills. General Hill immediately dispatched a rider to find General Breckinridge and instruct him to position his division at once to General Cleburne's right. 597

Around midnight, General D. H. Hill received unusual instructions from General Bragg's Adjutant that his corps had been placed under the command of General Polk, functioning as their wing commander, and that General Polk wished to see him that night at Alexander's Bridge; at a considerable distance of some 3 miles from his current location. After a lengthy night ride, General D. H. Hill arrived at Alexander's bridge in the middle of the night. Unable to locate General Polk, he continued his ride forward to the line of battle, arriving there a little after daylight. 598 General Breckinridge had not yet placed his division in position, in line with instructions from General Polk's, wherein he granted General Breckenridge permission to rest his troops for the night due to the wearied condition of his men. 599 General D. H. Hill had issued repeated and urgent orders to his corps, in regard to keeping rations for three days constantly on hand, but owing to difficulties resulting from the previous day's ferocious fighting some of the men had been without food the day before. Rations for the day were cooked and on hand but had not yet been issued. The order was immediately given by General D. H. Hill to for their prompt issue. 600

At 7.25 a.m. on the morning of September 20th 1863 General D. H. Hill received a written order from General Polk but addressed to his division commanders, directing them to advance at once upon the enemy. General Polk had issued the order directly to the brigade commanders because he couldn't locate the corps commanders and, with time being of the essence, wanted to initiate an assault upon the enemy. General D. H. Hill immediately replied to the note, saying *"Brigadier General Jackson's brigade was at right angles to my line; that my men were getting their rations, and that they could finish eating while we were adjusting the line of battle."* General Polk, very soon arriving upon the field, made no objection to this delay. 601

At 8 a.m. General Bragg himself came upon the field, informing General D. H. Hill for the first time that an attack had been ordered at daylight. At this juncture however, there had been absolutely no essential preparations for battle and, in fact, in obedience to military protocol and principles of military leadership such essential provisions could not have been made without the presence of the General-in-chief. There had been no reconnaissance of the enemy position; the Confederate's own line of battle had not yet been adjusted - part of the line was at right angles to the rest; there was no cavalry coverage along the flanks; and of great importance, there was no battle intelligence on the location or composition of the enemy; for no orders had yet fixed the strength or position of the enemy reserves. 602

General D. H. Hill's own line had been arranged north and south to correspond to the position of the enemy in order to parallel the enemy's line. General Cheatham's division was practically at a complete right angle to General D. H. Hill's line but was declared to be correctly positioned by the General-in-chief Bragg. This division was later discovered by General Polk once the battle began to be in rear of General Stewart's division, where he took immediate action to remove them. Moreover, General Kershaw's brigade, of General McLaw's division, was found to be positioned between Generals Stewart and Cheatham. The battle alignment was greatly disorganized and in total confusion, highlighting to General Hill the tremendous value of and great appreciation for General Lee's efficient processes regarding the issuance of official military orders. 603

Around 8.30 a.m., General D. H. Hill received a report from his extreme right that a very strong enemy line was extending across the Reed's Bridge road, at nearly right angles to his line. Immediately, General Adams was directed to push back the enemy's line of skirmishers which he accomplished in a most handsome manner. General's D. H. Hill, Forrest and Adams performed a reconnaissance of the field and found that the Confederate line extended well beyond the Union's line, that their flank was covered for a great distance by infantry skirmishers but and that no cavalry was visible. 604 During the previous night's fight, General D. H. Hill had determined there to be great tactical advantage in outflanking the Union line. Accordingly, he had placed General Breckinridge on the right of General Cleburne; in order to turn the log breastworks – where the Union troops were heard working to improve their position through the night. General D. H. Hill's corps was now positioned on the extreme right of the Confederate line of infantry. General Forrest had moved his cavalry forward to guard the Confederate flank and had dismounted a portion of his men to act as sharpshooters. 605

At this juncture of the battle a general advance was ordered. As the right was to begin the action, General Cleburne was directed to dress by General Breckinridge. As soon as the movement began, General D. H. Hill dispatched a note to General Polk, reminding him that the corps was in single line without reserves; and if the enemy was successful in breaking any one point, the entire line would be broken. 606 At 9:30 a. m. General Breckinridge advanced with General Adam's brigade on the right, General Stovall's brigade in the center, and General Helms' brigade was on the left. The Union skirmishers were driven rapidly and within about 700 yards the left portion of the breastworks were encountered by General Helms. 607

Two heroic efforts to take them were repulsed, and that noble officer General Helms, *"ever ready for action,"* in the language of his division commander, *"endeared to his command by his many virtues, received a mortal wound while in the gallant discharge of his duty."* 608 With their gallant commander fallen, General Helms' brigade was then withdrawn 200 yards to the rear. Unfortunately, this withdrawal created a gaping hole in the left of the Confederate line, invoking memories of the gap at Sharpsburg's bloody lane. As with the unintended withdrawal at Sharpsburg, this gap proved to be most disastrous for the rest of the day's engagement. The Union troops, recognizing the broken line, quickly seized the tactical initiative and began to pour forces into the opening with extreme swiftness, securing a position from which they immediately began to place devastating crossing fires upon the Confederate troops as they attempted to swing round upon their left. 609 Upon learning that Union General Gist's brigade was in his corps rear, General D. H. Hill dispatched a rider with a message to General Walker to bring forward a brigade, in all haste, to fill the gap made by General Helm's withdrawal. But this request was misinterpreted and instead of getting this single brigade from General Walker, his two entire divisions came forward, accompanied by General Polk. The brigades of Generals Walthall and Gist were then directed to fill the gap but nearly an hour's time was lost since the repulse of General Helm's troops; giving the Union forces ample occasion to securely post in the gap. General's Walthall and Gist were immediately met with a withering frontal and flanking fires which threw their brigades into great confusion, causing them to be driven back ahead of time. 610

Upon the repulse of General Helm's brigade, General Breckinridge proposed, and General D. H. Hill cordially approved, a change of front for his two right brigades, directing them to swing round on the flank and engage the rear of the Union position. 611 In the meantime, Generals Adams and Stovall advanced with great enthusiasm, driving back two lines of Union skirmishers; General Stovall halted at the Chattanooga road. General Adams, after dispersing a regiment and capturing a battery, successfully advanced to cross at Glenn's farm, whereupon he halted;   General D. H. Hill then rode to the command of Generals Adams and Stovall, on the right, to direct the fight on that portion of the field. 612

At this juncture it was evident, from the comparatively slight enemy resistance encountered, and having no viable threat into his immediate front, that the Confederate line had extended well beyond the enemy's left. General D. H. Hill at once ordered these brigades to make their front perpendicular to the original line of battle; positioning the Confederate line with the left of General Adams and the right of General Stovall resting on the Chattanooga road. From there General D. H. Hill ordered them to advance upon the flank of the enemy. Slocomb's cannon battery, which had previously provided superior and devastating fires upon the enemy's position, was posted favorably on the ground west of the road to support the movement. The advancing brigades courageously moved forward in fine order across the open field and into the woods beyond. 613

General Stovall soon encountered the extreme left of the enemy's breastworks, which, retiring from the general north and south direction of his entrenchments, extended westerly nearly to the Chattanooga road. 614 After a fierce and well-contested conflict, General Stovall was checked and forced to retire under great pressure. General Adams, on the west of the road, had engaged two lines of the enemy that had been greatly reinforced and had reformed nearly at right angles to the troops facing his main line of works. The enemy's front line was routed, but it was found to be impossible to break the second, owing to their being strongly supported by a devastating cannonade of canister, grape and shell upon the attacking Confederate troops. After a bloody struggle, which reflected great honor on the brigade's efforts, General Adam's troops were forced back under tremendous pressure and in great confusion. Here General Adams, well known for his judgment on the field as well as his courage, was severely wounded and fell into the hands of the enemy. Lieutenant-Colonel Turner, of the Nineteenth Louisiana, was also wounded and the gallant Major Butler, of the same regiment, was mortally wounded. 615

General Stovall had advanced under the withering musketry volley and cannonade fire to gain a foothold beyond the angle of the enemy's works. General Adams had audaciously advanced still farther, being actually in rear of the entrenchments. For want of a good supporting line to General Stovall's division at this moment there would probably have been achieved decisive results; the engagement on the Confederate right had inflicted heavy losses upon the enemy and compelled the Union line to weaken other parts of their line in their efforts to maintain this critical point. 616 General Adam's brigade quickly reformed behind and under the covering fires of Slocomb's battery, which performed with great gallantry; immediately repulsing the enemy with the precision delivery of a rapid and well-directed cannonade of canister, grape and shell. Under Slocomb's covering fires, General Adam's whole division fell back to a ridge parallel to and overlooking the Chattanooga road. 617

The faultiness of the Confederate plan of attack was now but too apparent. Perhaps never before in the history of war had an attack been made in a single line without reserves or supporting force. It was most unfortunate that the Confederate attack was directed to the front, against such strong and well defended breastworks. The important results caused by two brigades on the flank proved that, had General Bragg's army been moved under cover of the woods a mile farther to the right, the whole Federal position would have been turned and an almost bloodless victory achieved. A simple reconnaissance before the battle, deem always essential during such conflicts, would have shown the practical nature of such a movement and the tremendous tactical advantage that might have been attained. 618 While General Breckinridge had to encounter the difficulty of decisively engaging two lines with just his single one, General Cleburne had the still more difficult task of attacking the heavily fortified breastworks along his entire front; and of disentangling his troops mixed up with those of the left wing; all owing to the want an adjustment to the line of battle before the action began. 619

General Cleburne's gallant men suffered greatly in their bloody battle at the enemy's breastworks. From their initial assault upon the breastworks, five hundred men were killed or wounded by enemy fire in only a few minutes. Upon the repulse of General Cleburne's gallant men, noting that General Lowrey's regiment had already been forced to retire, General Cleburne ordered the brigade still farther back to reform. General Deshler's brigade was moved to the right flank, with all intention of connecting his brigade with General Polk's left, attempting to fill the huge gap existing in the center of the line by the withdrawal of General Wood. However, General Cleburne was unable to connect with General Polk's left as the enemy had already turned his left had driven them back; wherein he quickly concluded that, for General Polk to retain his position would be a useless sacrifice of life. 620 General Cleburne ordered General Deshler's brigade to fall back with the rest of his line and, with his and General Wood's brigade, General Cleburne then took up a strong defensive position - some 400 yards in rear of the point from which they had been repulsed. General Deshler's brigade had moved forward toward the right of the enemy's fortified works, but could not advance beyond the crest of the low ridge from which General Lowrey had been repulsed. General Cleburne therefore ordered General Deshler to take cover behind the ridge and to hold his position as long as possible. This engagement was the first battle in which General Deshler had the honor of commanding as a general officer; it would also be his last as the gallant General fell when a cannon shell passed fair through his chest. 621

General Polk's entire corps failed in its attack; General Breckinridge was compelled to fall back a short distance and General Cleburne still farther after a heavy repulse; but the fierceness of their assault had a most important bearing upon the issue of the battle. Upon review of the Official Reports for the battle of Chickamauga, it is clear that Union General Rosecrans gave the Confederate Army credit for having a plan of battle designed to seize the road between his position and Chattanooga - believing that the Confederates intentionally moved on his left, wherein he detached largely from his right in order to secure his line of retreat. This withdrawal of an entire division produced a gap, permitting General Longstreet's troops to pour through the opening. 622 A heavy pressure upon the Confederate forces, when first disordered by the repulse, might have been serious but the left wing immediately engaged the enemy, forcing Generals McCook and Crittenden to flee in great disorder in the face of the audacious assault. 623

After General D. H. Hill had reformed his line, he reported in person to General Polk, informing him that he wished to renew the attack when the gap between Generals Breckinridge and Cleburne was filled, and that not less than a brigade would be required to do so. General Polk promised to have it filled, selecting General Jackson's brigade for the mission. However, General Jackson's brigade never moved forward to occupy the gap, instead taking a position opposite and far in rear. 624 General Polk had directed General D. H. Hill to take charge of all the attacking forces. General Walker's corps, responding to orders, advanced in beautiful order, gaining an important advantage on the field. The Chattanooga road was successfully seized once more as a Confederate cannonade poured tremendous volumes of precise fire upon the Yankee's rear, achieving devastating effects. Unfortunately, the Confederate left had become very disorganized by the slanted fire from the unfilled gap and the right brigade, instead of being formed across the road, aligned itself parallel to the road instead. This resulted in exposing the Confederate troops to unmerciful enfilading fires that produced a withering effect upon their advance. The Confederate line pressed the Union right of their line with great zeal, initially forcing them back. But this resulted in some of the troops being pushed to the rear of General Walker's right and his whole force was driven back. 625

This second repulse from the Chattanooga road, though unfortunate, probably saved the occupying troops from destruction. General Forrest reported to General D. H. Hill soon after the repulsion that a heavy Federal column was advancing in all haste from the direction of Chattanooga. General Forrest's active scouts soon brought in some prisoners who provided information that General Granger's corps was passing. Immediately, the attacking Union forces threw a skirmish line toward General D. H. Hill's corps, strongly indicating the prospects for a flank attack; whereupon immediate preparations were made accordingly. Confederate artillery opened upon the marching Union column, causing them to divide; with one portion moving to the left of the corps and the other portion advancing upon General Cleburne. Cleburne engaged the confused formation eagerly, placing upon them a storm of shot and shell; driving them back in even greater confusion. 626

It was now 3.30 p.m. and General Polk ordered a general advance. There was some delay as attempts were made to recall officers that had been dispatched, in vain, seeking such an order. 627 General Polk pulled General Cheatham's division and placed him in support of General Breckinridge, who initiated the assault with great authority; his brave men charging eagerly forward, amidst a chorus of rebel yells in a most daring manner. At the same time, two brigades of General Cheatham's command moved to the left of General Breckinridge and established connection with the line of General Cleburne. General Forrest moved his cavalry forward rapidly, determined to seize the Chattanooga road while General Breckinridge swept southward down the road and in rear of the breastworks. As the whole line was moving forward a message was received from General Cleburne that General Polk had successfully carried the northwest angle of the Union works, at the point where Generals Helms, Walthall, and Gist had been repulsed earlier in the morning. 628

General Breckinridge's second attack was not attended with the challenging difficulties that had been ever present during the morning assault. His left wing was effectively driving the Union forces everywhere. The tide of battle had clearly shifted to the distinct advantage of the Confederate forces. General Polk had secured the troublesome angle of the breastworks while General Forrest's cavalry was wreaking thundering havoc on his right - the enemy's left. General Gist, of General Walker's command, had successfully maneuvered his way to the enemy's rear while Colonel Govan, commanding Liddell's brigade had successfully seized the Chattanooga road. 629 The whole corps halted as it approached the Chattanooga road, taking up a line parallel to the road; anticipating the presence of a large enemy force in the thick wood to their front. There was also concern for a possible accidental engagement between the two wings of General Bragg's army, as General Longstreet was known to be pressing northward, although his exact position was not known, while the entire right wing was pressing southward. Upon personal examination of the tactical situation on the field, General D. H. Hill determined that there was no significant enemy presence to his immediate front and that General Hood's division had halted at a right angle to the road, at a very close distance to the left of his line. 630

Never, perhaps, was there a battle in which the troops were so little mixed up and in which the organization was so little disturbed. The corps was well positioned to resume the fight at dawn the next morning; with the ranks being thin but with great morale and high spirits. However, instead of exploiting the tremendous tactical advantage on the field with a bold continuance of the assault, D. H. Hill's corps was assigned, the next morning, the dutiful task of burying the dead and gathering up arms. It was a tremendous squandering of one of the greatest opportunities of the entire Civil War. 631

General D. H. Hill had engaged his corps in accordance with the orders for the second day of the battle enduring great confusion surrounding the time for the attack and the timing of signals that would start the offensive. During the attack, General Breckinridge's two right brigades had made an impulsive charge, breaking the left of the Union General Thomas and successfully crossing the Lafayette road. With a composition of only 2,000 infantry troops and a single battery of artillery, in one of the boldest actions of the entire war, General Breckinridge had swung his line around at a right angle to that of the enemy and swept down upon their flank; the left of General Breckinridge's line had encountered a network of extremely fortified earthworks, as had General Cleburne's whole line; with both facing a stiff resistance of the Union forces before them. The charge then reached a finishing point. If the Confederate assault could have produced another advancing line to fill the gap, they would have achieved a decisive victory before noon and might have pushed the enemy across the Tennessee River or even forced their foe into total surrender. But for the want of orders granting them permission to do so, the opportunity was lost for Generals Walker and Cheatham to strike the lines. Despite the pleading of D. H. Hill and the swearing of Walker, no orders were forthcoming and General Bragg was nowhere to be found to issue them. 632

Scarcely had the decimated forces of D. H. Hill reformed when, all too late, General Walker finally went forward with another single line. But they were hurled abruptly back by fresh Union troops that the enemy had rapidly massed upon his left, countering the design developed by General Bragg's ill-managed movement. Meanwhile, General Cheatham had not been allowed to budge an inch or fire a gun; restricted by the absence of authority by order to do so. Thus, the attacking force was driven back and cut to pieces in horrific fashion for want of a present, active, moving head to strike with the two arms of the right wing at one time. The fierce onslaught of D. H. Hill's corps had failed, as had the gallant and fearless charge of General Walker; noting the action recorded in the official records stipulating that: *"as a chain is no stronger than its weakest link, so a single advancing line is no stronger than its weakest point."* 633

Splendid conduct had been demonstrated by the troops on the Confederate right and the fierce manner of the attack. The great uneasiness that had been inspired by General Breckinridge's bold charge of the morning had borne fruit, however, in an entirely unexpected way; his bold actions led the enemy to mass so much of their force behind General Thomas. Generals D. H. Hill and Forrest had been awe inspiring to their soldiers as they gallantly rode up and down in front of the Union line, taunting the enemy and drawing fire upon the young troops who followed closely at their heels. As the battle raged, General D. H. Hill had continued to attack the enemy vigorously, producing a great and controlling effect; not just only on the mind of the Union's General-in-Chief, but upon the minds of his subordinates, echelons deep. His daring attack had engendered such foreboding that it caused a rushed transfer of Union troops from the right to the left that invoked great confusion and swayed the conduct of Union forces on the battlefield. Thunderous artillery fire and the roar of musketry had continuously placed a withering fire upon the Confederate positions. Despite General D. H. Hill's dispatching of one messenger after another, begging for official orders from General Bragg, seeking his permission to form lines and make a general advance upon the right and left wings of the enemy, his efforts were futile. 634

Several hours had passed and, unable to find General Bragg or determine the location of his headquarters, Generals Longstreet and D. H. Hill had conferred and mutually agreed to assume joint command responsibility and ordered an immediate pursuit by General Forrest, with the assurance that they would seek General Bragg's permission to push forward and support the gallant General Forrest at early dawn the next morning. But due to their inability, through diligent inquiry, to communicate with General Bragg, they were unable to detail the infantry support necessary to adequately support Forrest's pursuit of the enemy.

At this juncture, if General Forrest had been provided the infantry support that he required, he would have been positioned to bring upon the single division of General Thomas an attack that could have secured a decisive flanking action, perhaps the surrender of his division, or possibly driven him completely out of the gap on Missionary Ridge. Facing no further obstructions, the Confederates could have moved on the road all the way to Chattanooga and Nashville in order. 635 The profound strategic importance of the tactical initiatives that had been successfully gained on the field of battle, through notable gallantry by the men, simply escaped General Bragg's comprehension. When finally he was located and informed of the situation on the field, General Bragg could not believe the enemy was defeated and would not issue orders for pursuit. 636 General Polk finally gave in to the relentless pleas from General D. H. Hill and permitted him to take charge of the forward movement of three lines, General Walker in front, his own corps composing the second and General Cheatham the third. The advancing column had directed its main attack upon the left. The fighting had been fierce and quickly had become spontaneous. There had been a momentary wavering of the brigade on the right, but the attacking Confederate forces had seized the initiative and had overwhelmed the breastworks of General Thomas; catching 5,000 prisoners in the angle. A thunderous chorus of cheers had erupted that could be heard for miles. At this moment in history, the Confederacy had achieved its military high water mark for the entire Civil War. But General Bragg had convinced himself that the battle had not yet been won. General Longstreet said later that it had never occurred to him General Bragg would require a written report of the triumph, for anyone within five miles of the field would have know of the great victory by the great chorus of rebel yells and thunderous roar of the troops.

After the battle it was cited by General Longstreet that General D. H. Hill's attack upon the enemy's left, being of such notable strength, produced such a sense of foreboding in the minds of the Federal's General-in-Chief Rosecran and his subordinates that it produced such alarm as to cause their hurried transfer of Federal troops from left to right; thus enabling General Longstreet to cease the initiative from the Union disorder, double up the Union right, and completely drive General Rosecrans from the field of battle. The victorious Confederates captured fifty-one pieces of artillery and fifteen thousand muskets, while five thousand Union prisoners were taken. 637

The Controversy at Chickamauga – for the Confederacy, a fleeing moment of grand opportunity was gone forever. General Bragg could have seized this historic occasion and reaped the fruits of a grand victory at Chickamauga; his Army of Tennessee could have taken great advantage the attainment of a milestone event, so monumental that it could have restored confidence lost upon the fields of Gettysburg and Vicksburg; and the General-in-chief could have reclaimed the mantle of prestige for the whole of the Confederacy. Instead, General Braxton Bragg found his army scattered along the face of Missionary Ridge, waiting for the enemy to transform Chattanooga into an invincible haven and eventually uniting the consolidated forces of Generals Grant and Sherman with the reorganized army of General Thomas to later overwhelm and crush his army. The long list of delays during the battle was indeed costly. Complicated by General Bragg's inability to grasp the situational awareness of the battle, his unwillingness to accept General Pope's battle assessment, and his eventual delays in issuing timely orders so desperately needed by his corps commanders, led to the greatest squandering of a Confederate victory of the entire Civil War. 638

But General Braxton Bragg's greatest failure, above his many conspicous errors at Chickamauga, was his failure of leadership. Compare General Bragg's actions, before – during – and after Chickamauga, including his attempts to place blame elsewhere, to the leadership provided the Confederacy by one of it's greatest leaders, General Thomas J. *"Stonewall"* Jackson. Here are the words of his friend and mentor, General D. H. Hill: *"Invidious critics have attributed many of Stonewall Jackson's successes to lucky blunders, or at best to happy inspirations at the moment of striking. Never was there a greater mistake. He studied carefully (shall I say prayerfully!) all his own and his adversary's movements. He knew the situation perfectly, the geography and the topography of the country, the character of the officers opposed to him, the number and material of his troops. He never joined battle without a thorough personal reconnaissance of the field. That duty he trusted to no engineer officer. When the time came for him to act, he was in the front to see that his orders were carried out, or modified to suit the ever-shifting scenes of battle."* D. H. H. 639

After the battle was over, the Confederate generals were deeply grieved and resentful that their great victory, achieved with such severe losses in officers and men, was frittered away by General Bragg. While the gallant fighting at Chickamauga produced a great military victory, it came at a tremendous cost in human treasure of so many courageous sons of the Confederacy.

It was at this juncture that, through an agreement formed by great frustration, General Buckner drew up and Generals Polk, Longstreet, Hill, Buckner, Cleburne, Cheatham, Brown, and other generals united to sign a detailed statement of facts and recommendation, by petition, to President Jefferson Davis calling for the appointment of another General-in-Chief. The petition stated that the commanding general Braxton Bragg had lost the confidence of his army and asked that he be transferred to another command and replaced by a more acceptable leader. 640 This demonstrated lack of confidence in his leadership by his subordinate Generals angered General Bragg. The fury of controversy surrounding the petition prompted a personal visit by the Commander-in-Chief, President Davis. 641 When President Davis arrived he summoned all the Generals who were signatories of the petition. In a manner, most unusual, President Davis conducted an open inquiry; questioning each signer of the petition while in the presence of all others, including General Bragg who sat quietly in a corner and listened intently as each subordinate General was asked to clarify and expand upon their allegations against him. 642 General Bragg's presence effectively caused a suppressive air that made it difficult to speak candidly with the President. Upon conclusion of the inquiry, President Davis met privately with General Bragg and was convinced that D. H. Hill was the primary instigator and most active promoter of the plan to get rid of Bragg as the General-in-chief. Subsequently, both the President and General Bragg determined to assign responsibility for the whole sin of the insubordination of the inferior officers of that army upon General D. H. Hill. 643

Hill harbored no unkind feeling toward Bragg, and at the time of the petition, had reluctantly reached the conclusion that it was his duty to join his comrades in urging General Bragg's removal. Hill believed that it might be possible to find a leader like Stonewall Jackson; one who could overcome superior numbers by vigilance, speed, and strategy. Although the overwhelming preponderance of supporting evidence in fact surrounding the controversy at Chickamauga clearly proved that Hill wasn't the primary instigator, as Bragg asserted, the unusual manner in which the inquiry was handled by the President provided little opportunity for anyone to oppose General Bragg. This left General Hill to take the brunt of Bragg's retaliation. 644 Immediately after President Davis' visit, General Bragg requested that General Hill not be reassigned to his Army, *"for want of prompt conformity."* Generals Breckenridge and Cleburne, with passion and great effort, personally urged the

President to retain General Hill as their Corps Commander. But their ardent pleas fell upon deaf ears and President Davis removed Lieutenant General D. H. Hill from the Army of Tennessee at the request of General Bragg. 645 Immediately following General Bragg's reprisals, General D. H. Hill immediately called for a Court of Inquiry, to ensure that the failures of General Bragg would not place a grim judgment upon either his military record or the Hill family name. But the War Department replied that no charges existed against him, thus there was no occasion for a Court of Inquiry. 646

The situation was a totally frustrating experience for D. H. Hill. Upon what sound reasoning was there reason for punishment in the absence of any charges? 647 There came from within the War Department a series of resistant actions regarding General Hill's pursuit of a new assignment, one appropriate with his rank as Lieutenant General. General Joseph E. Johnston, who had always held D. H. Hill with great respect and admiration, asked that General Hill be immediately assigned to his Army. But in formal bureaucratic fashion, he was notified that D. H. Hill could not be assigned as a Lieutenant General without displacing officers currently assigned. 648 Instead of an assignment, D. H. Hill was directed, in a insincere manner, to merely report monthly to the office. However, this obstacle was soon removed upon notice that, while the entire construct of the Confederacy was tumbling down upon the South, their bravest Fighting General sat obediently to men, exposed to no peril, rather seated in the comfort and safety of the War Department building. Meanwhile, General Hill again applied for assignment and the Adjutant General notified him that if he wanted service he would have to accept it at his previous rank. 649 General Hill stated that he was perfectly willing to do so but requested that it be accompanied with a written military expression of confidence in his capacity, gallantry, and his fidelity; otherwise his usefulness with the troops might be impaired. This request was laid before the President whereupon he said: *"He could see no reason for not granting Hill's request."* However, when it came to working out the administrative details of the order, the Adjutant General could find no precedent for such and made no effort at all to grant his request. 650

Later in 1864, General Hill would be reassigned to the Army of Tennessee, by then under the command of General Joseph E. Johnson. 651 Ironically, D. H. Hill would reunite with General Braxton Bragg on the soil of his native state, leading the final remnants of North Carolina regiments in their last hopeless charge against the forces of General Sherman in their last fight, the Battle of Bentonville. 652 On November 25th 1863, just a little over one month after giving him his full support, General Braxton Bragg was routed by General U. S. Grant at the battle of Missionary Ridge. The Confederate victory at Chickamauga was indeed a decisive victory; but the Union victory at

Missionary Ridge was even greater. With hindsight being 20/20, President Davis soon realized that he should **not** have retained General Bragg as the head of the Army of Tennessee after Chickamauga. In a conciliatorily expression to D. H. Hill, the former President, writing in his book *"Rise and Fall of the Confederate Government"* offered great praise upon General D. H. Hill commending him for his ability, zeal and courage; within Davis' post war writings, not one disparaging allusion was made toward D. H. Hill. Judge Avery wrote: *"It is but just to President Davis, as well as to General Hill, to state that there was good reason to believe that the former, in his last days, became convinced that General Hill was not the author of the petition, or the principal promoter of the plan for Bragg's removal, and that it dawned upon the Great Chieftain that the retention of Bragg was the one mistake of his own marvelous administration of the Government of the Confederacy. When Johnson and others criticized the President, General Hill, then editing a magazine that was read by every Confederate, indignantly refused to utter one reproachful word, even in his own vindication."* 653

Again, just as General Hill would have no part of criticizing his former General-in-chief Robert E. Lee about the Battle of Malvern Hill, the nature of this great man would not allow him to offer one reproachful word, even in his own defense. In reverence to Lieutenant General D. H. Hill, the world must truly know how thoroughly he retained the confidence, respect and admiration of the officers and men of the Army of Tennessee. Their feelings are reflected in the following letters, written by courageous men well qualified to reflect the opinion of both officers and men in that Army; men who followed D. H. Hill's leadership and fought valiantly under his command at the Battle of Chickamauga: 654

Letter from General Cleburne: *"Allow me also to express to you the sincere regard and high confidence with which in so short a time you succeeded in inspiring both myself and, I believe, every officer and man in my command."* 655

Letter from General Breckenridge: *"I saw you for the first time on my way to this army from Mississippi, when my division became a part of your corps, and I have had more than one occasion to express my admiration for your fidelity to duty, your soldierly qualities, and your extraordinary courage on the field. It may gratify you to know the opinion of one of your subordinates, and to be assured that, in my opinion, they are shared by his division."* 656

Letter from General Clayton: *"I have been in the military service since the 6th of February 1861, and I have never been under a commander to whom I and my command formed so strong an attachment in so short a space of time. In the camp we were not afraid to approach you, and on the field you were not afraid to approach us and even go beyond us. This feeling was universal among privates as well as officers and to a greater degree than I have ever known toward anyone except perhaps General Stuart."* 657

Letter from General M. P. Lowrey, afterwards Governor of Mississippi: *"So far as I have heard an expression from the officers and men of this corps, you services with us have been most satisfactory. In the camp and on the march your orders were received and obeyed with the most cordial approval and with the greatest pleasure. The warm devotion that has been created in so short a time will not die while memory lives."* 658

 Letter from General L. E. Polk: *"In behalf of myself and brigade, allow me to express to you our high appreciation of your uniform kindness in all of your official intercourse with us, and to say to you that although you have not been long with us, you have gained our love, confidence and respect. And that it was with great regret that we heard of your being taken away from us. And in being so taken away our confidence in you as a soldier, gentleman and patriot has not been in the least diminished. We part with you, General, with the greatest regret, and hope some new field may be given you for the display of that generalship that led us to victory at Chickamauga."* 659

CHAPTER XV

GENERAL SHERMAN'S MARCH TO THE SEA

Union General William T. Sherman marched from Atlanta, Georgia on November 16th 1864. After expelling the city's residents and burning a good portion of their city, he headed toward the Carolinas in his famous march to the sea; intent upon linking up with General Grant's army to crush the remainder of the Confederacy's armies. With the Army of Tennessee now crushed, after devastating retreats before Franklin, it now found itself behind, instead of in front of General Sherman's advancing forces; thus leaving no substantial Confederate forces to oppose his March to the Sea. General Sherman had established a new base, where communication with the sea was open to him, while General Hardee, the Confederate commander resisting General Sherman's march, initially established a defensive line; extending from the Savannah River to James Island, beyond Charleston, stretching for just over 100 miles. 660

General Sherman's march northward from Savannah began early in February 1865. His army moved in two columns; one threatening Augusta and the other Charleston, each of which cities the Confederates tried to defend. 661 President Davis acknowledged in his post Civil War writings that, instead of pursuing such a policy, all the Confederate forces in the Carolinas and Georgia ought to have been concentrated in Sherman's front. General Hampton also tells us in the official records that such was the opinion of General Beauregard, but does not know why it was not done. 662 General Hardee, operating from Charleston with only had a handful of unorganized troops, quickly deemed it totally impractical to attempt holding this long line. Consideration was given to abandoning Charleston and concentrating every available man in front of General Sherman in order to contest his passage of the rivers and swamps that were in his line of march. 663

As General Sherman marched through South Carolina, he sent General Kilpatrick against the Confederate forces in Augusta. But General Kilpatrick was soundly defeated at Aiken South Carolina on February 11th 1865 by General Wheeler, thereby saving the city of Augusta for the Confederacy. However, the beautiful capital of South Carolina, Columbia, did not escape the wrath of General Sherman's forces. As he approached the city, the modest Confederate force of only 5,000 men retreated before him. The Mayor of Columbia met the advancing Federals and surrendered the city, *"with the hope that, as no resistance had been offered, it would be protected from pillage and destruction."*

During that night the greater part of Columbia was burned. The city was full of helpless women, children and invalids; many of whom were driven from their homes - to which the torch was applied. An effort was made by General Sherman to shift the blame upon General Hampton by declaring that by *his* orders the cotton in the city was set ablaze and that the burning cotton was the cause of the inferno. But General Hampton denied strongly that any cotton was set ablaze by his orders. He also denied that the citizens set fire to bales of cotton or that any cotton was on fire when the Federals entered the city. The people of Columbia, both white and black, furnished abundant testimony to the fact that Columbia was burned by the Federal soldiers. General Slocum admitted as much when he said: *"I believe the immediate cause of the disaster was a free use of whiskey, which was supplied to the soldiers by citizens with great liberality. A drunken soldier with a musket in one hand and a match in the other is not a pleasant visitor to have about the house on a dark, windy night."* However, he did say that he did not believe it was done by General Sherman's orders. General Sherman, in his memoirs said: *"The army having totally ruined Columbia, they moved on toward Winnsboro."* There is no doubt that the Federal soldiers burned the city and that they were never punished for their actions, whether or not it was ordered by General Sherman. 664

On the same day that General Sherman entered Columbia, the decision was made to evacuate Charleston, South Carolina as General Hardee withdrew to the vicinity of North Carolina and established defensive lines along the Pee Dee River. General P. T. G. Beauregard directed General Stevenson to march toward Charlotte North Carolina; General Cheatham, with his division from the Army of Tennessee, advanced from Augusta and was moving to take a position along the west side of the Congaree and Broad rivers. 665 General Lee, who had at this late day been made General-in-chief of all the armies of the Confederacy, called upon General D. H. Hill's old mentor and friend, General Joseph E. Johnston, to take command of all the forces in the Carolinas; with orders to consolidate and reconstitute a viable fighting force, then drive back General Sherman. 666 General Johnston, now sufficiently recovered from the serious wounds sustained during the Battle of Seven Pines, was assigned on February 23rd 1865 to assume command of these widely dispersed and disorganized forces; charged with the formidable task of reforming the shattered Army of Tennessee. General Johnston first set about the task of organizing the remnants into a cohesive force to oppose General Sherman which, by his estimation, would soon be somewhere in the vicinity of Fayetteville, North Carolina. 667 He took immediate, vigorous actions to perform the part assigned him, rapidly consolidating the withdrawing Confederate commands: General Hardee's command from the Charleston garrison; Generals Stevenson's and Cheatham's divisions from the Army of Tennessee; and General's Hampton's and Wheeler's cavalry, who had been skirmishing frequently with the Federals, attempting to suppress their advance. 668 General Hoke's veteran division from the Army of Northern Virginia also joined him before the concentration had been affected.

Meanwhile, General Sherman continued his march, entirely unobstructed, except for spirited fights on March 8th 1865 at Kinston North Carolina, on March 16th 1865 at Averysboro, North Carolina and also meeting some resistance from Confederate cavalry moving eastward from Fayetteville toward Goldsboro. General Johnston recognized that, unless some form of decisive action was taken, Generals Sherman and Grant would soon join forces and unite their armies to overwhelm the depleted and exhausted Army of Northern Virginia. He preferred to attack the Federals before all their forces could be united but was aware that the forces of General Cheatham's division would not arrive in time to join such a fight. All circumstances considered, General Johnston was faced with one of two courses of action: Course of Action 1 - he could attempt to rapidly transport his infantry by rail to Virginia and reinforce General Lee, thus enabling the possibly to strike a decisive blow on Grant's left flank, or course of action 2 – he could throw his small force against the army confronting him, with the hope of crippling, if not defeating General Sherman.

There was great risk involved with either course of action but General Johnston determined the latter to be the Confederacy's best chance, and perhaps their only hope. Thus, the decision was made that, in the face of General Sherman's overwhelming force, General Johnston would take possession of a battlefield, at a site of his own choosing, to confront General Sherman. His field of choice was at Bentonville, North Carolina. [669] In hasty preparation for the looming battle, he dispatched General Hampton ahead, accompanied by General Butler's division of cavalry, to occupy a strong position at Bentonville and hold it until the infantry and artillery could come up. [670]

"Black Magic of the Hip Shoot"

"Charge 5, Green Bag; base quadrant 240, 11 minus charge C Factor 6;

"left 100, drop 50, fire for effect"

to the guns -

"Deflection 3206, Quadrant 237"

"FIRE!"

In tribute to the legendary Chief of Smoke

First Sergeant John D. Williams

Bravo Battery, 1st Battalion (SP) 113th Field Artillery

NCARNG

BENTONVILLE 1865

On the night of March 18th 1865 General Johnston reached Bentonville and on the early morning of March 19th 1865, the battle began as General Johnston's men engaged the leading column of General Sherman's advancing army. Generals Bragg and Hoke, placed in tactical positions on the Confederate left, successfully repulsed the initial Federal advance while the gallant General Hardee led a courageous charge on the right; forcing the Union forces back for some distance. That night Sherman's whole army was united directly to General Johnston's front. For two days General Johnston and his hastily consolidated force of 20,000 men held in check General Sherman's 70,000 men. 671 During a successful Confederate charge on March 21st 1865, led by General Hardee, General D. H. Hill participated courageously in the final military engagement of his memorable career, fighting with same fiery spirit as always exhibited, courageously leading his men in one last desperate and successful charge against the Union army. 672

W. W. LORING

W. J. HARDEE

D. H. HILL

J. E. JOHNSTON

B. BRAGG

PROMINENT CONFEDERATE GENERALS

BENTONVILLE 1865

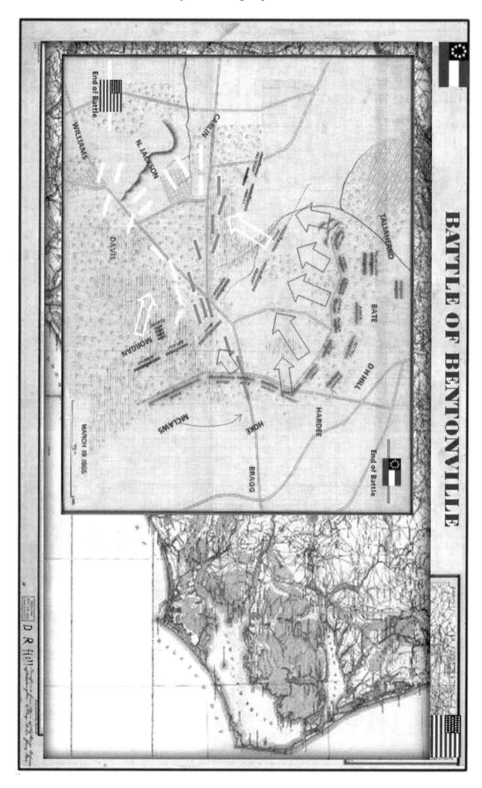

It is noted with great sadness that the son of the gallant General Hardee, a noble lad of just sixteen, fell mortally wounded during this last great battle of the Civil War. 673 General Johnston, in his official report, rendered the following general account of the battle that occurred on March 19th 1865:

"General Bragg's were formed across it [the Goldsboro' road] at right angles, and the Army of Tennessee on their right, with its own strongly thrown forward. The ground in our front, north of the road, was open; that on the south of it, covered with thickets. We had but one road through dense black-jack for our movements, so that they consumed a weary time. While they were in progress a vigorous attack was made on General Bragg's left. Lieutenant-General Hardee was instructed to send one division to its support and the other to the extreme right, and with the latter and Stewart's troops to charge as they faced, which would bring them obliquely upon the enemy's left and center. General Bragg's troops were to join in the movement successively from right to left-In the meantime the attack upon General Bragg was repulsed with heavy loss, and another made on Stewart's corps, commanded by Major-General Loring, by whom the enemy was quickly driven back. These two affairs showed that the Fourteenth Corps was in our immediate front. It was near 3 o'clock before Hardee's troops were in position on the right. He then made the charge with characteristic skill and vigor, well and gallantly seconded by Stewart, D. H. Hill, Loring, and the officers under him. Once, when lie apprehended difficulty, Hardee literally led the advance. The Federals were routed in a few minutes, our brave fellows dashing successively over two lines of temporary breastworks, and following the enemy rapidly, but in good order. A mile in rear the Fourteenth rallied on the Twentieth Corps in a dense growth of young pines. In this position the Federal right rested on a swamp and was covered by entrenchments. Our troops continued to press the enemy back, except on the left, where we were held in check by the Entrenchments just mentioned. Their progress was very slow, however, from the difficulty of penetrating thickets in line of battle. About 6 o'clock the Federal force was so greatly increased . . . that it seemed to attempt the offensive, but with little effect. They were able to hold their ground until night only by the dense thickets and breastworks. After burying our dead and bringing off our own and many of the Federal wounded, and three pieces of artillery (a fourth was left because we had not horses to draw it away) we returned to our first position." 674

During the fight on March 19th 1865, General D. H. Hill led the remnant of North Carolina regiments, under the command of General Hardee, for what would be their last battle of the Civil War. During the fight, General Hill's men launched an attack across an open field, exposing themselves to withering fire as they covered a distance of three hundred yards. The attack, starting at quick time, turned into a furious assault, complete with a chorus of rebel yells as they accelerated their pace with the command double quick. With great daring and a tremendous display of valor, D. H. Hill's men drove the enemy from the cover of their entrenchments, forcing them into full retreat, where they were pushed back to join their second line. After firing a few volleys, General D. H. Hill, leading yet another charge across the field, pressed forward until his men reached the second enemy entrenchment; now manned by Union soldiers consolidated from both their first and second lines. In one, final unheralded display of courage, General D. H. Hill dashed over the enemy's breastworks on horseback in front of his men; pursuing the enemy completely from the field of battle. 675

As the sun set upon the Bentonville battlefield, so too, set the sun upon *Lee's Fighting General's last fight.* General Daniel Harvey Hill, the Confederate *Angel of Death* prominently mounted upon his steed, saber drawn, charged the Yankee's blue line in this, his final assault, as always – leading from the front – his gallant soldiers into one final, desperate battle. General D. H. Hill ended his contributions to the war on the battlefield at Bentonville the same way he had begun the war on the battlefield at Big Bethel;   a daring assault achieving a dearly won victory. 676 Later that evening, General Johnston withdrew the remnants of his beleaguered Confederate forces across the rain-swollen Mill Creek. The next morning, Union forces pressed against General Johnston's retrograde to the vicinity of Hannah's Creek, but eager to link up with other Union elements in Goldsboro. General Sherman broke contact with General Johnston's forces and continued his march.

In the fighting at Bentonville, Union forces sustained 1,527 casualties; General Johnston's command sustained a loss of 2,606 men, with a large number of those being soldiers who recognized the end to be near and simply returned to their homes. Meanwhile, General Sherman added the forces of Major Generals John Schofield and Alfred Terry to his command. After two and one half weeks of rest, his army departed for its final campaign which concluded with Johnston's surrender at Bennett Place on April 26 1865. 677

Although the Battle of Bentonville was a tactical victory for General Joseph E. Johnston's army, it was a strategic loss. Following the Confederate's strategic defeat at Bentonville, N.C. on March 21st 1865, the Confederate army of Gen. Joseph E. Johnston, beleaguered and depleted, dutifully followed Sherman's resumed march northward April 10th 1865. En route General Johnston received word of General Robert E. Lee's surrender at Appomattox. This ended all hope of joining General Lee to oppose the invaders of the Carolinas. During a meeting with General Sherman at the James Bennett place near Durham, North Carolina on May 3rd 1865, General Joseph E. Johnston's once proud army finally lay down its arms and closed hostilities east of the Mississippi River. 678

As an avid student of military science, I know nothing in military history that resembles the close of the Civil War. No more bitter and stubborn conflict was ever waged between different nations or different parts of the same nation; a libation upon our national conscience that requires remembrance - that we should never again commit to another war of fratricide. Millions of men had taken arms, one against the other; myriads had perished on each side and countless treasure had been expended. Yet in a moment, the mighty struggle ended and peace was proclaimed throughout the land; leaving the exhausted South completely at the mercy of the victorious North.

D. H. HILL

"It would be great presumption in me to criticize any movement directed by General Johnston, in whose skill and generalship I have always entertained implicit confidence, and I should not now venture to express an opinion as to the propriety"

[[General D. H. Hill]]

Q9

CHAPTER XVI

THE LOST DISPATCH

The loss of Special Order 191, most commonly referred to as *"the lost dispatch"* was the most litigious event of the entire Civil War. Controversy reigned supreme for decades after the war, notwithstanding facts surrounding the incident; whereas a formal process of Confederate military inquiry was conducted, replete with affidavits; wherein it was found that not a single basis in fact established that General D. H. Hill, or anyone on his staff, ever received the disputed copy of the Order from General Lee's headquarters; and whereas, it was established that D. H. Hill could not lose that which was never in his possession. The colleagues of General Lee and D. H. Hill, being the other Confederate generals – all men of great valor - who knew of D. H. Hill's integrity, fully accepted his word upon face value and the supporting testimony provided through affidavit by his staff. But a specific expositor by the name of Mr. E. A. Pollard, greatly lacking in diversity and unprejudiced points of view, either through incompetence, incredulousness, or both, gained great notoriety by crafting many written versions of history that suited his interests, with great defamation of Hill's character, and great pleasure for anyone espousing Northern leaning viewpoints.

Handwritten Copy of SO 191 – Drafted by General Stonewall Jackson (Page 1)

Special Thanks for the Courtesy shown by North Carolina State Archives {{PD-1923}}

Handwritten Copy of SO 191 – Drafted by General Stonewall Jackson (Page 2)

Special Thanks for the Courtesy shown by North Carolina State Archives {{PD-1923}}

For some it seemed permissible to elevate the stature of some Virginians if by means of denigrating other southern states, notwithstanding the greater sum and total of NC grave markers upon Virginia's soil than of Virginian markers, or markers of any other southern state. 679

From this expositor's pen, a great web of conspiracies grew that proposed all sorts of wild theories and despicable possibilities to explain the loss of Special Order 191. One theory suggested that General Lee purposely lost the order to create a ruse de guerre – a tactic to deceive his Union adversary, General McClellan for strategic and tactical advantage; yet another theory proposed that the dispatch's loss must certainly be the sinister work of a Union spy – performing their secrecy-cloaked duty – a believable idea at that time perhaps, for it was a common practice used by both sides during the war, to gain critical components of battlefield intelligence. 680 But in the final analysis of every controversy, true historians mandate that, with every proposed theory, there must be provided sufficient unquestionable evidence, objective not subjective proof, to substantiate their claims; or have their own creditability called into question, wherein their proposed theories shall be submissively dismissed. Given this rigid standard to guide real historians, to the great exclusion of prejudiced expositors, we arrive upon the most significant pronouncement of this entire book. You, as the reader, must ask yourself this question: *"to whom should I assign responsibility for the loss of General Lee's Special Order 191?"* To answer this question and resolve this most litigious controversy, you must make that determination for yourself: *"Do you believe D. H. Hill's account and accept it to be factual? Or, do you simply take Lee's Fighting General to be a fool and a liar."*

In the process of writing this book, this author invested more time and effort into the personal research and investigation of the circumstances surrounding the *"lost dispatch"* than all other topics included in this book combined; after years of study and application of critical thought, I have come to one very simple yet absolute conclusion: If you seek the answer to this mystery, you need to look no further than the first person, written account of Lieutenant General Daniel Harvey Hill.

So, offered for your review is an historical extract of General Hill's account of this controversy. Examine his first-hand account carefully. Either you will believe him to be a distinguished man of irreproachable integrity or you will deem him to be the greatest liar of the Civil War and convict him upon your judgment alone – not upon opinions of elucidation postulated by expositors who themselves had no first-hand knowledge of, or participation in, the event. 681

Respectfully presented herewith, I offer the narrative of General Hill:

"The Historian must be conversant with his subject, patient in the investigation of facts, impartial in weighing conflicting statements, unprejudiced, dignified, and truthful. The lack of anyone of these qualities is fatal. Hence it has happened that during the twenty-three hundred years since the "Father of History" wrote his nine books, there has only been found here and there a name deemed worthy to be dignified with the noble title of Historian. Hence it has happened that of the millions of histories poured upon the public in this long interval, only one, here and there, has come down to our time.

Nor is it difficult to see the cause of this failure. The history of mankind has been little else than a history of the wars that have desolated countries and wasted human life. These could, of course, only be intelligibly described by those who understood military language and military movements. We could not expect one to write a treatise on jurisprudence, who was ignorant of the phraseology and the principles of law. We could not expect one to lecture on the proper treatment of disease, who had never studied chemistry, anatomy, physiology and their associated branches. We would be shocked at the presumption of him, who should attempt to proclaim the truths of the gospel without having studied the Bible. We would laugh at him, who would attempt to write a description of a naval combat without even understanding nautical terms.

At the close of the Mexican war, a distinguished authoress, who wished to write its history, held a consultation on the subject with an officer, who subsequently held a high rank in the Federal army. He said to her frankly, "Madam, I know not what obstacles genius may enable you to surmount. For my own part, I would not attempt to write a naval history without understanding the alphabet of naval science. You may be able to write a military history without understanding the alphabet of military science."

The world is not so complaisant, and it always expects that those, who first described battles by land and sea, shall understand, at least, the nomenclature of war. The more general historians may abridge the details thus furnished and incorporate the abridgement with the social, religious, political and literary annals of the nation, whose history he is writing. – Thus Thucydides was a distinguished soldier. Xenophon had an important command in the memorable retreat of the "ten thousand." Caesar, the historian, was also Caesar, the greatest captain of his age. Sallust, the historian, was a member of the military family of Caesar.

Even Gibbon was a profound student of military science, and was two years and a half in military service. When we wish to read something valuable, touching the wars of Napoleon, we take up the history of General Jomini, the Napoleon au Tribunal de Caesar, the Dispatches of Wellington, Napier's Peninsular War, &c., -- books written by military men, understanding the subject *of which they treat. So for an account of a particular battle, as Waterloo, we may be entertained by the vivid description of the great French novelist, but we look for authentic facts to Gneisenau, Beamish, Jones, &c. Thus too, in our own first great rebellion, we rely upon the statements of the loyal Tarleton and the rebels Greene and Lee. As they wrote about what they saw with their own eyes, or knew of their own personal knowledge, we feel sure that their dates and events are correct, thought a partisan coloring may be thrown around the latter. Therefore, their books have lived, and will live, while the sensational stories of mere book writers have perished long ago.*

The general history of the second American rebellion must be a most difficult task, since three millions of men were called out on one side, and about half a million on the other. 'Tis a stupendous undertaking to comprehend fully fifty gigantic battles, and two hundred lesser combats of no little magnitude. The reports of regiments, brigades, divisions, corps and armies, must be read and digested, and how many thousands of these there will be! Next, the histories of each, and of all these bodies of men must be read and digested. (At present, not one a thousand has been written.) Next, the archives, of the respective Governments at war, must be carefully studied, that their policy may be understood in projecting certain campaigns, which culminated in certain great battles. It is plain that if this vast material was all gathered together and placed before the general historian, he would have a work of many years in collating, weighing, examining, rejecting and digesting. It is equally plain that if either the material is wanting, or the patient and intelligent investigation for years is wanting, the book may pay the historian, but it will never pay the reader.

If we wish the history of our Confederate struggle to be correctly written, we must encourage the writing of the histories of the smaller commands, -- regiments, brigades, etc., etc. General Longstreet has made a move in the right direction in selecting a competent officer to write the history of his corps. Let each corps commander do the same thing. The writers so selected would exert themselves to draw out the histories of the subordinate commands, and would, at any rate, get all the official reports of the subordinate commanders in their respective corps. From the several corps histories in any one army, (as that of Northern Virginia) the historian for that army may gather his materials and write his book. – And from the histories of the several armies, the general historian may gather the materials for the history for the whole – combining with the military, the civil and political annals of the period of war. Should the proper interest in this subject be excited among our people, the corps historians might hope, in four or five years, to get the subordinate histories, from which their own could be compiled. This is all that we can expect in this generation. The general history must be the task of our descendants. Perhaps in a quarter of a century, when the passions and prejudices evoked by the war shall have subsided; come calm, dignified, impartial man of learning, industry and ability, may gather together the materials furnished in the manner suggested, and from them produce a truthful history of the great rebellion. The wisest statesman of the South has well said that this is not the age for the history of the Confederate struggle.

We suppose no one will question the correctness of the principles we have laid down, or deny that the qualities enumerated above are essential to the historian. But measured by this standard how immeasurably will all the war books yet produced fall short! Most of them have been written by civilians ignorant of the first rudiments of military science, who never heard the whistle of a hostile shot, and to whom the strategy of a campaign and the tactics of the field are alike incomprehensible. One of these writers is a civilian, who exalts to the skies a certain division for its gallantry at Gettysburg and attributes the disaster there to the cowardice of a certain brigade, and yet the cowardly brigade lost more men than the heroic division! Another writer, (a clergyman) in his biography of a noble partisan officer, has to describe the movements of Jackson's corps, in which there are many North Carolina soldiers. But the whole volume contains but one allusion to the brave soldiers from that State – "here the 21st N. C. regiment suffered heavily." At the very time this clergyman was composing his book at Winchester, Va., the Memorial Association of that city were inviting Gov. Vance of North Carolina to address them, and giving as a reason for their invitation that their Cemetery contained more graves of soldiers from North Carolina than from any other State – a fact which might be said of every burying ground in Virginia. – The wise reader will throw aside as worthless, books bearing the marks of prejudice and partiality, as well as of ignorance of the subject. What shall be said then of the historian, whose chief merit, it is claimed, consists in his prejudice and partiality? The "Old Guard" for November, under the editorial head, says of Mr. E. A. Pollard: "He is partial, prejudices, dogmatic, determined – the very man to write contemporaneous history. He represents evidently the thoughts, hopes and passions of a particular set, and when the materials he gives are used by the future writer of history, there is no danger of their receiving more than their proper weight. He does not in the least attempt to disguise his prejudice, or conceal his hatred. His dislike of Jefferson Davis is particularly plain. It is like part of his style. It crops out in every direction." (The italics in the extract are or own.) This is certainly strange doctrine. Unfairness has never before been commended as an excellence in any writer, and surely least of all in the historian. – "Truth is in order to goodness" is a well-known maxim of Lord Bacon; and when the competency of the author is not in dispute, he is valued just in proportion to our belief in his honesty and truthfulness.

Mr. E. A. Pollard, though an ardent advocate of the war, was, we believe, never under fire, and we might question the ability of a man to describe all the battles of the four years' struggle, who was never a witness of one. But we do not propose to discuss his competency, and will confine ourselves to exposing his prejudices and his inaccuracies. It has been the desire of the Editor of this Magazine not to obtrude upon his readers the part he himself acted in the war, but as Mr. E. A. Pollard has made certain statements with reference to him, which are matters of general and not merely of personal interest, he thinks there is no violation of good taste in replying through his own columns. To prevent misapprehension, he will drop the Editorial we and speak in the first person. Believing that life was too short to be wasted in reading a history of the war, a quarter of a century in advance of the time, when a truthful history could be written, I had not read a single line of the "Lost Cause," by Mr. E. A. Pollard, and did not know until very recently, when my attention was called to it by a friend, that in speaking of a dispatch from Gen. Lee at Frederick, Maryland, addressed to me, which was lost by someone, he used the following language: "A copy of the order directing the movement of the army from Frederick had been sent to D. H. Hill; and this vain and petulant officer, in a moment of passion, had thrown the paper on the ground. It was picked up by a Federal soldier, and McClellan thus strangely became possessed of the exact detail of his adversary's plan of operations."

I will make upon this extraordinary statement of Mr. E. A. Pollard three remarks. First. The harsh epithets which he applies to me are unworthy of the dignity of the historian, and prove a prejudiced state of mind. Second. If I petulantly threw down this order, I deserved not merely to be cashiered, but to be shot to death with musketry. – And it seems strange that Gen. Lee, who ought to have known the facts, as well as Mr. E. A. Pollard, never brought me to trial for it. 'Tis still stranger that Mr. Davis, nearly a year after the alleged occurrence, promoted me to a Lieutenant- Generalcy, and sent me to command a corps at Chickamauga. Third. If Mr. E. A. Pollard cannot prove this statement by trustworthy eye-witnesses, who saw this petulant act of throwing down the dispatch, he could be convicted of slander in any respectable Court of Justice in Christendom. But there is not the shadow of truth in his charge, and he has therefore perpetrated a gross and unprovoked slander.

General McClellan states that a dispatch, of General Lee, directed to me was found near Frederick, Maryland, and that he gained most important information from it. There can be no doubt then, that such a dispatch was lost. – But it is obviously unfair to assume that a paper with my name on the envelope was necessarily lost by me in person. Might it not have been lost in Gen. Lee's own office? Might it not have been dropped by his courier in carrying it to me? As the Adjutant is keeper of all orders, might it not have been lost by my Adjutant? Who has the right to assume that the loss was through my own carelessness? Who, without evidence, can presume to charge me with throwing it down in a fit of passion? I challenge Mr. E. A. Pollard to produce a single witness, who saw the act.

There are some circumstances which will satisfy any unprejudiced mind that I am not responsible for the loss of the dispatch. My division was the first to cross the Potomac, which it did at Cheek's ford, upon a verbal order, and with no knowledge whatever of the object of the expedition. We crossed one afternoon about 3 o'clock, and were engaged till the same hour the next day in destroying the Chesapeake & Ohio canal. I then learned that Gen. Jackson had crossed and wished to see me. After a rapid ride, I found him at the head of his division examining a map held by Captain (afterwards Colonel) E. V. White, who still lives. He said, "You have been placed under my orders, I wish your division to join me, to-night, near Frederick." I returned and brought up my division that night. General J. was disabled the next morning by his horse falling back upon him, and I was put in charge of the corps. I rode forward and joined Captain White's scouts, and together, we crossed the bridge over the Monocacy, and went first to the telegraph office. For the next two or three days, we drew all our supplies and received all our orders through General Jackson. It seems to me very improbable then, that General Lee would send an order directly to me. -- Official etiquette required it to be sent through Jackson, and if the celebrated order of Sept. 9th (the one McClellan found) was not sent thus, it was in violation of usage. I have the certificate of my Adjutant (who is still living) Major J. W. Ratchford, that no order ever came to the division from General Lee. I have no recollection of any myself. But I have in my possession now (and it has been shown to many persons) a copy of this very lost order of Lee, which is in General Jackson's own hand-writing. He did not trust it to be copied by his Adjutant, and with like care, I carried it in my pocket and did not trust it among my office papers. It was right and proper that I should have received this order from Jackson, and from no one else, and I have no recollection of getting one from General Lee's office direct. My Quarter-master, Major John D. Rogers, (now residing at Middleburg, Virginia,) writes to me that while at Frederick, he received all the orders in regard to his wagon train, supplies, &c., through Gen. Jackson's Quarter-master. It seems to me utterly incomprehensible that all orders should have come through the usual official channels, except this one, the most important of all.

There is a mystery about this order, at Frederick, which would seem to indicate that there was something wrong in the manner of transmitting it, or treachery in the persons carrying it. General R. H. Anderson commanded an independent division (unlike mine in that respect) and yet he received no copy of the celebrated order. He writes to me that he is perfectly sure of this, and Gen.

Chilton (Chief-of-Staff to General Lee) is equally certain that the order was sent to all the Major Generals. But without attempting to unravel the mystery, I will content myself with pronouncing the charge of Mr. E. A. Pollard to be wholly untrue. It will be difficult for that gentleman to explain why I preserved with so much care, Jackson's copy of Lee's order, and threw away so contemptuously the order itself, coming directly from the Head-quarters of the Army.

I first heard of the lost dispatch and the unkind comments made upon it by some pen-and-ink warriors, when I was on my way from the Department of North Carolina to defend Richmond from the attacks of troops coming from Fortress Monroe to capture the Confederate Capital, during the absence of Lee's army in Pennsylvania. As part of Mr. E. A. Pollard's history was written during the war, it may be that while I was risking my life for the defence of Richmond he, secure in his office, was penning this most unjust and unprovoked slander. I next heard of this aspersion upon me when I was at Chattanooga, just before the battle of Chickamauga. Fearing that there might be a stain upon my memory, if I fell in the approaching battle without some explanation of the mystery, I wrote home that the copy of Lee's order, which governed me in all I did while in Maryland, could be found among my papers, having been sent home by a private hand while we were encamped on the Opequon. It was found precisely as indicated. As my statement made after the battle was very generally copied, it seems strange to me that Mr. E. A. Pollard never saw it.

I will next examine the allegation that the loss of the dispatch was a serious damage to the Confederate cause. It will not be difficult to show that it was just the reverse. The celebrated order of Lee is in these words: "The army will resume its march to-morrow, taking the Hagerstown road. Gen. Jackson's command will form the advance, and after passing Middletown, with such portion as he may select, take the route beyond Sharpsburg, cross the Potomac at the most convenient point, and by Friday morning, take possession of the B. & O. R. R., capture such of the enemy as may be at Martinsburg, and intercept such as may attempt to escape from Harper's Ferry."

"General Longstreet's command will pursue the main road as far as Boonesboro, where he will halt with the reserve, supply and baggage trains of the army."

"General McLaws, with his own division and that of General R. H. Anderson, will follow Gen. Longstreet, on reaching Middletown, will take the route to Harper's Ferry, and by Friday morning, possess himself of the Maryland Heights, and endeavor to capture the enemy at Harper's Ferry and vicinity."

"General Walker, with his division, after accomplishing the object in which he is now engaged, will cross the Potomac at Cheek's Ford, ascent the right bank to Lovettsville, take possession of Loudoun Heights, if practicable, by Friday morning Key's Ford on his left, and the road between the end of the mountain and the Potomac on his right. He will, as far as practicable, co-operate with Gen. McLaws and General Jackson in intercepting the retreat of the enemy."

"General D. H. Hill's division will form the rear guard of the army, pursuing the same road taken by the main body. The reserve artillery, ordinance, and supply trains will precede General Hill."

"General Stuart will detach a squadron of cavalry to accompany the commands of Generals Longstreet, Jackson, and McLaws, and with the main body of the cavalry, will cover the route of the army, and bring up all stragglers that may have been left behind."

"The commands of Generals Jackson, McLaws, and Walker, after accomplishing the objects for which they have been detached, will join the main body of the Army at Boonsboro or Hagerstown."

"Each regiment on the march will habitually carry its axes in the regimental ordnance wagons for the use of the men at their encampments to procure wood, &c."

Now observe the cautious order does not give the composition and strength of our forces. It speaks of Jackson's "command" without naming the divisions of which it was composed.   Thus, A. P. Hill, Early, and Starke, -- division commanders – are not mentioned.   So, likewise, it speaks of Longstreet's command, without naming Hood, Jones, or Evans (division commanders.) McClellan simply learned from it that Lee had divided his army, sending part to capture Martinsburg and Harper's Ferry, and leaving Longstreet and myself to guard the mountain passes, parks of artillery and wagon trains. McClellan would have been the most inefficient of generals, could he not have gained that information in a friendly country from his own scouts and spies. He tells us too, that he learned of the leaguer of Harper's Ferry by the roar of artillery some days before it fell. A staff officer of McClellan (Colonel Abert) informs me that the firing was heard on the Catoctin (Harper's Ferry) before the Federal army left Fredrick. McClellan's cavalry and scouts were surely active enough to inform him that a portion of Lee's army was not a Harper's Ferry, even if the country people (generally Union men) gave him no information. The important fact gained by finding Lee's order was, that Lee had divided his forces; in every other respect, the order mystified and deceived him. I have too much respect for McClellan's administrative ability, which was of the highest order, to believe that he could not have gained this one fact without Lee's order in his pocket. The merest blunderer, at the head of an army, could learn that much about his antagonist.   Even Banks, or Butler, or poor Schenck could have organized cavalry and scouts to be efficient enough to discover that a portion of Lee's army *was in front, while the roar of his cannon was heard far off towards Harper's Ferry.*

Notice that Lee's order was calculated to deceive McClellan in two important particulars. 1st. It taught him to believe that Jackson would not go to Harper's Ferry. But that active officer, after the capture of Martinsburg, hastened to Harper's Ferry and took an important part in its reduction. 2nd. It taught him to believe that Longstreet was at Boonsboro, just at the foot of South Mountain, whereas he was at Hagerstown, 17 miles from South Mountain, when the battle began at the latter place, on the morning of the 14th September. To this false information is doubtless due the salvation of the Southern army. Had the battle of Boonsboro (or South Mountain) been lost early on the morning of the 14th, our army would have been cut in two, the whole of our artillery and vast wagon trains (parked in the valley beyond Boonsboro) would have been list. Probably the sun of the Confederacy would have set on that day. It is scarcely probable that we could have ever supplied the loss of such immense materials of war. My division had been reduced by battle, marches, want of shoes &c., from 22,000 to 5,000 men, and I had several miles of mountain passes to guard. McClellan had 80,000 well-armed, well-equipped and well-trained soldiers. He could have crushed my little squad in ten minutes, but for the caution inspired in him by the belief that Longstreet was there. -- Lee's order deceived him, too, about Jackson's whereabouts, and doubtless the apprehension, that ubiquitous partisans had returned from Martinsburg, as directed by Lee's order, and which he had time to do, made McClellan still more guarded in his approaches. Certain it is that my little handful repelled his attacks with ease until 3 P. M. At that hour, a Serg't Major in one of Rodes' regiment (a Northern man by birth) deserted to the enemy and asked with astonishment why they were so cautious, as only a few thousands were holding the passes. -- The attack upon us was now made with some vigor, but in the meantime Longstreet's troops had come up, and through utterly exhausted by their forced march, they aided in maintaining the position till after night-fall. We then withdrew without losing a gun, a wagon or an ambulance.

Mr. E. A. Pollard is pleased to call the battle of Boonsboro the Thermopylae of the war, and he pays a merited tribute to my gallant division. Nowhere in the war were such tremendous odds encountered. The few, who stood on that mountain top on that bright Sabbath morning, were the bravest of the brave, and the vast masses of the enemy sent no chill of terror to their hearts. Amazement at the feebleness of the assault of the immense hosts, and not fear, was the predominant emotion in their minds. But while even to this day, the recollection of their courage and devotion sends a thrill to my heart, candor compels me to say that they could not have resisted for ten minutes, the tremendous odds against them, had not the Federal Commander been paralyzed by the false impression derived from that very dispatch, the capture of which he deemed so important a prize. In going to Harper's Ferry from Martinsburg instead of returning to Boonsboro, General Jackson acted on his own responsibility and in violation of Lee's order. McClellan, misled by that order, no doubt, thought Jackson at Boonsboro. His great caution then was due to the natural error, (into which he had been led by using the order as his guide,) that he was fighting Longstreet and Jackson, when he was only fighting my small force. It was this error which saved Lee from destruction; and in the inscrutable Providence of God the loss of the dispatch prolonged the Confederate struggle for two more years.

I have shown, 1st, that the charge of Mr. E. A. Pollard of my having thrown down Lee's dispatch in a fit of passion is a gross slander: 2nd, that it was proper that Lee's order should have come to me through Jackson and that I have still in my possession Jackson's copy of that order: 3rd, that if Lee's order was sent to me directly, neither myself nor Staff know anything of the order was a benefit and not an injury to the Confederate arms. There are living witnesses, who can substantiate all my statements, while Mr. E. A. Pollard cannot produce a single person, who saw the act which he slanderously ascribes to me.

Men are notoriously bad judges of their own characters, and it is therefore useless for me to say that I think that my gentle accuser is mistaken in pronouncing me to be vain and petulant. But I must believe that the eminent historian himself has similar characteristics. It does seem to me that it savors somewhat of vanity for a penny-a-liner for the Richmond press to sit in judgment upon Confederate President, Cabinet, Congress and all the civil dignitaries of the land, and like Jove on Mount Olympus hurl his thunderbolts at them all. It does seem a little vain for a man, who never saw a single battle-field to attempt to describe so many hundreds of battles, and tell what were the errors in the conduct of them all. It looks very much like vanity for a man, who does not know the alphabet of military science, to criticize officers of every grade, from the Commanding General to the lowest subaltern. In fact, I think that it would be great presumption in Mr. E. A. Pollard to criticize the military career of one of Lee's corporals or drummer boys. As for petulance, bless my life: it is amazing that Mr. E. A. Pollard can bring the charge against any one, when his book is nothing but one big mass of petulance against Mr. Davis and all others, who have incurred his petulant displeasure. I have received a large number of letters from Southern officers, pronouncing Mr. E. A. Pollard's book to be a libel upon history. Among these writers, are the men the most honored at the South. One of them (a full General) has sent an elaborate and a crushing review of that blundering and prejudiced volume, which claims to be a history. I do not believe that a single respectable officer or soldier can be found, who will pronounce it accurate, reliable, and trust-worthy.

I will now show that Mr. E. A. Pollard is either too prejudiced or too inaccurate to be relied upon as a historian. I will confine myself to the battles in which I, myself, was engaged, because I know more of them than of any others, and because I wish to prove that he has shown a personal dislike to me, inconsistent with the grave character of the historian. In referring to the battle of Seven Pines, Mr. E. A. Pollard says: "Through the thick woods, on marshy ground, in water in many places, two feet deep, Longstreet's regiments moved on, brushing off occasionally a cloud of skirmishers that disputed their passage. As they came upon the enemy's works, a sheet of fire blazed in their faces. It was sharp, rapid work. Some of the regiments crept through the low brush wood in front of the redoubt, and at a given signal from the flanking parties, made a rush for the guns, cleared them, and entering pell-mell into the earthwork, bayoneted all who opposed them." Where did Mr. E. A. Pollard stumble upon all this stuff? Longstreet did not have a single regiment engaged in capturing Casey's earth- works. They were carried by my division without any support whatever -- the first instance in the war, so far as I know, of the storming of earthworks. The enemy attempted to retake his works, and Longstreet sent me R. H. Anderson's brigade, which behaved most nobly, and a few detached regiments, which were not engaged. That night, Longstreet sent up all his division, and next day (June 1ˢᵗ,) sent me also Huger's division. I thus had the immediate command of three divisions on that day, and received no orders from any source whatever. That night, we withdrew by Longstreet's order, because the attack on the Nine Mile road had failed, exposing thereby our flank and rear. Rodes' brigade was the first to occupy Casey's entrenchments, though he did not lose so many men as G. B. Anderson, or Garland. The flanking parties gave no signal, no guns were cleared, (a new term in military science!) and no Yankees were bayoneted. I am sorry to spoil Mr. E. A. Pollard's fancy sketch.

Four divisions were selected by General Lee to turn McClellan's right flank on the Chickahominy. They were commanded by Longstreet, Jackson, A. P. Hill and myself. McClellan cast all upon the chances of success at Gaines' Mill, and lost. It was this battle which hurled McClellan out of his entrenchments before Richmond, and drove him to the shelter of gun-boats, on the James river. Surely then no truthful account could be given of so important an action, which does not tell of the part played by each of the four attacking divisions. But Mr. E. A. Pollard does not mention my division at all in connection with this great fight! Was its role in the great drama so insignificant that the historian could pass it over in silence? I think not. The charge, which it made across an open field, a fourth of a mile wide, raked in flank by a battery, and torn in front by numerous batteries and thousands of rifles, was never surpassed in gallantry. The French Princes on McClellan's staff state that the Federal army was first broken on its right flank – just where my division attacked. Gen. Garland, one of my brigade commanders, in his official report thus speaks of the charge across the field.

"The effect of our appearance at this opportune moment upon the enemy's flank, cheering and charging, decided the fate of the day. The enemy broke and retreated." Gen. R. E. Lee, (who ought to be as good a judge as Mr. E. A. Pollard, as to who should be mentioned and who should not) thus alludes to this decisive charge. "D. H. Hill charged across the open ground in his front, one of his regiments having first bravely carried a battery, whose fire enfiladed his flank. Gallantly supported by the troops on his right, who pressed forward with unfaltering resolution, he reached the crest of the ridge, and after a bloody struggle, broke the enemy's line, captured several of his batteries, and drove him in confusion toward the Chickahominy, until darkness rendered further pursuit impossible." -- General Jackson, under whose eye my division fought, pays it a still more handsome tribute. If Mr. E. A. Pollard had not read Lee's and Jackson's reports, when he wrote his book, he failed to get that information, without which he should not have attempted to play the part of the historian. If he had read them, and omitted altogether to notice one of the four divisions engaged in the most important battle of the first three years of the war, he must have done so through a prejudice unworthy of the historian. He may take either horn of the dilemma. In the biographical sketch with which Mr. E. A. Pollard honors me, he charges me with attacking prematurely at Malvern Hill. -- The truth is that I obeyed Lee's signal and advanced, but those on my right and left did not. Gen. R. E. Lee ought to be as good a judge of my conduct as Mr. E. A. Pollard. In his report of Malvern Hill, Lee says: "A general advance was to be made at a given signal. On the left, D. H. Hill pressed forward across the open field, and engaged the enemy gallantly, breaking and driving back his first line; but a simultaneous advance of the other troops not taking place, he found himself unable to maintain the ground he had gained against the overwhelming odds and numerous batteries of the enemy."

Who is right, Mr. E. A. Pollard in calling my attack premature or Gen. R. E. Lee in saying that it was made at the appointed signal? There is a very curious instance of Mr. E. A. Pollard's prejudice, in his account of the battle of Sharpsburg. Gen. Lee was pleased in his report of that battle to compliment some personal exertions of mine, at the most critical period of the fight. He says: "The heavy masses of the enemy again moved forward, being opposed only by four pieces of artillery, supported by a few hundreds of men belonging to different brigades, rallied by Gen. D. H. Hill and other officers."

Mr. E. A. Pollard, in speaking of the same imminent crisis, says: "The heavy masses of the enemy again moved forward, being opposed only by four pieces of artillery, supported by a few hundreds of men, belonging to different brigades."

Mr. E. A. Pollard copies Lee's report verbatim till he comes to the personal compliment and then he flies off at a tangent! Well does the "Old Guard" say of Mr. E. A. Pollard: "He does not in the least attempt to disguise his prejudice or conceal his hatred!" The most remarkable instance of Mr. E. A. Pollard's inaccuracy, through either ignorance or prejudice, is to be found in his account of the operations preceding the battle of Chickamauga and of the battle itself. I believe that this was the bloodiest battle of the war, and one of the greatest in modern history. I commanded one of the four corps engaged on the Confederate side. It was longer engaged and suffered more proportionally than the other three. It had for its Major Generals those noble heroes, John C. Breckinridge and Patrick R. Cleburne. Its Brigadiers, its Field and Company Officers, its rank and file were inferior to none in the world. The high reputation of its officers, the unblemished record of its soldiers, the glorious part taken by it in the action — all these entitled its Corps Commander to consideration enough to be correctly reported. But Mr. E. A. Pollard makes but two allusions to me and these are both egregious blunders. In speaking of an order from General Bragg to attack a detachment of the enemy in McLe More Cove, Mr. E. A. Pollard says: "The attack was delayed; a day was lost, and with it the opportunity of crushing a column of the enemy; and, when Hindman, with whom Gen. D. H. Hill had contumaciously refused to co-operate, and who had therefore to await the junction of Buckner's command, was at last ready to move, Thomas had discovered his error, retreated to the mountain passes, and thus rescued the Federal centre from the exposed position in McLe More Cove."

Now there is not one word of truth in the statement that I contumaciously refused to co-operate with General Hindman. General Bragg intended to surprise the enemy at daylight on the morning of the 10th of September, and designated Cleburne's division of my corps to co-operate with Hindman. I was aroused just before day on that morning by my Chief-of-Staff, Col. Archer Anderson, (now living in Richmond, Va.,) who showed me Bragg's order, and called my attention to the extraordinary fact that it had been four hours and three-quarters from the time of its issue, till its reaching me. I carried it to Gen. Cleburne, (whose division was ordered to move) and found him sick in bed. Two of his regiments were absent, the roads were heavily obstructed with timber in his front, cut down by our forces, and requiring hours to remove them. Some of his troops would have to march nine miles; some, thirteen miles; and other, fourteen miles to reach the point of junction with Hindman. He said to me, "as it is impossible to execute the order, it would be foolish to attempt it." I promptly notified Gen. Bragg of the state of things and he selected Buckner's division to take the place of Cleburne's, as Buckner was nearer to Hindman and had no obstacles to encounter. Bragg, in his order to Buckner says: "Gen. D. H. Hill has found it impossible to carry out the part assigned to Cleburne's division." What Gen. Bragg calls impossible, Mr. E. A. Pollard calls contumacious. It would seem that General Bragg ought to be as good a judge of contumacy as Mr. E. A. Pollard, and he certainly was too strict of a disciplinarian to let an infraction of orders go unpunished. When he wrote his official report of the battle of Chicamauga, his *feelings toward me were not kind, but he was too just a man, even to insinuate any reflection upon my conduct.*

Not content with putting this absurdity in one book, Mr. E. A. Pollard, repeats in his "Lee and his Lieutenants," with the addition that on account of this McLe More Cove affair, I was relieved from duty with the Army of Tennessee!! I did not know this fact before I saw it in Mr. E. A. Pollard's book, and doubtless it will surprise General Bragg as much as myself. As General Hindman had been arrested, by General Bragg, for this McLeMore Cove affair, and as there was a probability of misapprehension and misstatement, I applied to General Cleburne for a paper setting forth his recollection of my interview with him. I append this letter dated 15th October, 1863, a little more than a month after the occurrence, when his recollection was fresh on the subject.

"I remember very distinctly the morning of the 10th September last, on which you received orders to unite with Gen. Hindman at Davis' X Roads, and attack the enemy at Stephen's Gap. On that morning, two of my brigades, less two regiments, were stationed at LaFayette, Georgia; the third was on Pigeon Mountain, holding Catlett's Gap, Dug Gap, and Blue Bird Gap. The two absent regiments were of Polk's brigade, had been holding the fords of the Tennessee River and had not yet rejoined from detachment. To have united my division (or rather the portion of it at La Fayette, and the Gaps,) at Dug Gap, would have taken several hours -- in addition, my information from our cavalry was that Dug Gap was heavily obstructed with fallen timber, which it would take a considerable time to remove. Davis' X Roads, the point of junction with Hindman, was between nine and thirteen miles from LaFayette, and more than fourteen miles from Catlett's Gap, via LaFayette, the only practicable road then known to us. I learned from Colonel Archer Anderson, that the order for the movement was received by him at 4 ½ a.m., on the 10th ult., and the time specified in the order for the junction with Hindman at the Cross Roads was that same morning. With these facts before me, I am convinced that Gen. Bragg's order could not have been carried out, and that the contingency existed which (under the terms of the order itself,) made it your duty to postpone the movement."

Gen. Cleburne's letter is now before me and I have given every word of it, verbatim, the italicizing, however, is my own. It will be seen that he says that General Bragg's order could not be carried out, and that under the circumstances, it became my "duty to postpone the movement." It is well known that Gen. Cleburne was a very rigid constructionist of orders, and that no man in the Confederate service, more strictly obeyed his orders to the very letter. But General Cleburne pronounced the non-compliance with the order a duty. Mr. E. A. Pollard calls it "contumacy!" -- Whose opinion is the most valuable, that of the great soldier, who poured out his heart's blood for the Confederacy, or that of

Mr. E. A. Pollard, who never saw a battle-field? On a question of military duty, and military etiquette, the opinion of Gen. Cleburne ought to be as valuable as that of Mr. E. A. Pollard.

The other allusion to myself by Mr. E. A. Pollard is an insinuation that the delay in attacking on the morning of the 20th September was due to me. If Mr. E. A. Pollard had read the official reports of Generals Bragg and Polk he would have known that the insinuation was unjust. If he had not read them, he ought not to have attempted to write an account of the battle. But, although Mr. E. A. Pollard has been studious to avoid all reference to me (save in this unfair insinuation,) a comparison of his account of the battle with my official report of it will show that he has followed my report very closely and has gained many of his facts from it! I am constrained, therefore, to attribute his unfairness to malice and not to ignorance.

I will now close by a reference to the sentiments of my corps towards myself. This may seem to savor of that vanity with which my gentle accuser charges me. -- But as I have been silent on this subject for four years, the candid will attribute a reference to it now to the desire to repel slander and not to unworthy egotism. The Major Generals of my command, Breckinridge and Cleburne, went to Mr. Davis and made an earnest appeal to him to retain me with the Army of Tennessee, and accompanied their request with flattering references to my services. After my connection had been severed with that Army, those two noble officers sent me, of their own motion, letters full of regret for my separation from the corps and of kind appreciation of my character as a soldier. And after my return to the east, the surviving Brigadiers of the corps sent me similar letters. Even Mr. E. A. Pollard cannot cast the suspicion of interested motives upon tributes paid under such circumstances. The writers had been with me in camp, on the march and on the battlefield, and it is reasonable to suppose that they could form as correct an opinion as Mr. E. A. Pollard in his snug office at Richmond "snuffing the battle from afar."

It has given me no pleasure to expose the blunders, inaccuracies, prejudices and misrepresentations of this burlesque upon history. -- But having earnestly attempted to do my duty to my native country in the hour of her sore trial, I am not willing that my reputation should be blackened and my name made odious among my countrymen, through the malice and unfairness of one, who encountered no dangers, endured no hardships and suffered no privations for that "Lost Cause," of which he so presumptuously claims to be the historian. I am still less willing, that the glorious services of as gallant a division and as gallant a corps as the sun ever shone upon, should be ignored, slurred over, or feebly reported because the commander of the division and corps is not in favor with the eminent historian!

The private soldier can gain no laurels to adorn his own brow. -- He identifies himself with his regiment, his brigade, his division and his corps, and the reputation and glory of each become his own. A slight to the command is felt as keenly by the private as by the general officer aye, more! For the officer has his individual distinction, which the private has not. A wrong to a corps, division, or lesser body of men, is a wrong to all the private soldiers thereof, and it is the more unpardonable when done through malignity towards the commander and in the sacred name of truth and history." [682]

Imbued with an earnest devotion to the cause, which rose on occasion to the height of enthusiasm, D. H. Hill did not hesitate to denounce in unmeasured terms those who evaded duty in our armies, when the conditions were such as to plainly demand the active service of every able-bodied son of the South. In reading his words, you have now been afforded his viewpoint and can draw from his oratory your conclusion: Do you believe D. H. Hill's story and accept it to be factual? Or, do you simply take him to be a fool and a liar?"

As the reader, if you accept his story then you may now answer the question: *"to whom must I assign responsibility for the loss of General Lee's Special Order 191?"*

CHAPTER XVII

PRIDE AND PREJUDICE

AN AUTHOR'S EXPOSITION

As we conclude our study in the life of D. H. Hill as a soldier, and before we proceed with our study of his life after the war, it is important to reiterate my distinct purpose for this entire study. From the beginning my intent has been to fully address the total character of this man in all the critical attributes which constitute the abiding test of his true greatness. At this juncture, we have studied his unquestioned military heroism and clearly established him to be among the bravest of the Confederacy's brave. We have learned of the events and circumstances which led to his emergence as *Lee's Fighting General*. Further, we have addressed the two most litigious events of the entire Civil War, providing sufficient historical and empirical data from which to draw final resolution for the lost dispatch and the controversy at

Chickamauga. But before we continue to study his life as a Christian, Father, College President and my namesake, I want to conclude his military career by addressing one final issue: the charges by past expositors that D. H. Hill was *sharp of tongue* - expositions which have served to effectively exclude General Hill from the collective consciousness of our Nation's proud military history and deny him the fame for which he so rightly deserves.

As with any good literary motif, these expositors injected a recurring element of symbolism in their writing; subjecting their readers to extremely negative innuendos about D. H. Hill; primarily applying a vastly overstated and symbolic significance to his sharp tongue while hypothesizing that this aspect of his character should be considered as his most prevalent and defining trait – eclipsing his well-documented accomplishments of valor and gallantry on so many fields of battle. Their repetitive motifs produced further expositions which served to perpetuate their overarching literary theme; a contentious, often pernicious mood, that portrayed Daniel Harvey Hill as a petulant person: specifically culpable in the loss of Special Order 191; completely responsible for General Bragg's failures at the Battle of Chickamauga; and most blameworthy of all Generals for the defeat of the Confederate armies and the fall of the Confederacy. These continuing expositions, promoting their motifs, were clearly designed to suit varying personal reasons and served to build a narrative of *idyllic notions* that some Southern Generals should be elevated to the *level of Sainthood* while others should bear the brunt of public dismay over the tragic fall of the Confederacy.

Consider the motifs in Shakespeare's play *Macbeth* wherein he used a variety of narrative elements to shape his audiences' perceptions; he echoed the phrase *"fair is foul and foul is fair"* to invoke the concepts of good and evil; his play also featured the central motif of the washing of hands which effectively produced verbal images of the movement of the actors. Similarly, many post Civil War expositors used a continuing postulation of their recurring motifs, associating D. H. Hill with the nefarious aspects of the war's two great litigious acts: the lost dispatch and controversy at Chickamauga; asserting to a shattered and grieving Southern class that it was palatable to adopt their narratives of idyllic notions, greatly to the expense of many – like ole "Pete" Longstreet and Daniel Harvey Hill. These two southern heroes were both excoriated greatly after the war by these expositors, none of whom "pulled trigger" during any engagement of the conflict. Using their freedom of literary expression, one of the most sacrosanct elements of our nation's constitution to this day, they systemically weaved together the thematic complexities of their idyllic notions. Shakespeare consistently connected the recurring motif of *eyes* throughout Macbeth to a constantly changing flow of images, and often violent manipulations, in order to call into question the ability to accurately perceive and understand reality. Such was the effort by these expositors to call into question their readers' abilities to accurately discern the true nature and character of D. H. Hill.

The absolute truth and reality of the Civil War is found through intense study of horrific combat upon its many fields of battle; many desperate and bloody struggles - fought by men of valor and distinction, both North and South. The realities that we must understand – and the conclusions that must be drawn – must be grounded in the realities of historical fact; unarguable truths that are accurately recorded in the archives and annals of military history – written in the OFFICIAL RECORDS and REPORTS of both great armies. These reports and records are foundational in the construct of this Study in Bravery and Southern Valor -*Lee's Fighting General.*

I want of offer a few existential truths to provide a direct correlation between the expressions of historical fact against the idyllic notions of these expositors. I am compelled to provide documented historical reports from witnesses with first-hand, direct knowledge of Daniel Harvey Hill and his actions. As the reader, you can draw your own conclusions through application of comparative analysis and critical thought; examining both the documented historical records of the annals of the Civil War in consideration of the expositors' motifs. First, consider this one infamous quote by Robert G. Kean: *Hill's snarling "so regularly and acerbically at the world around him" caused Lee-"perhaps the personally least contentious general officer commissioned on either side"-to form a negative opinion of him.* This quote has been referenced often by many expositors to support their efforts to define the sarcastic tongue of D. H. Hill to be his most predominant personal character trait.

Okay, who exactly was Robert Garlick Hill Kean? He was a Virginia lawyer and Civil War bureaucrat whose wartime diary provided these expositors access to his view of the inner workings of the Confederate government during the War. Kean enlisted as a private in the Confederate army but was taken to be the aide of his wife's uncle, George W. Randolph, whom he followed into the War Department at Richmond; wherein he eventually became the chief of the Bureau of War. This man never *pulled trigger* on the field of battle, yet these expositors so quickly and often cited his criticism of D. H. Hill to support their allegorical assertions. It is this man, the chief of the Bureau of War who handled the controversial issues surrounding Lieutenant General D. H. Hill's promotion and post-battle assignment, or lack thereof, resulting from the controversy at the Battle of Chickamauga. Robert Kean was a Virginian; his memoirs were edited by a Virginian. It is without question that he avidly supported efforts to postulate a pro-Lee, pro-Virginia perspective. So, consider this in your comparative analysis and critical thought as you examine other famous quotes about General D. H. Hill; comments provided by first-hand witness who possessed intimate knowledge of Hill's true character and who actively participated in many of the great battles of the Civil War – pulling trigger often.

D. H. HILL *"Hill's presence was always sufficient to give full assurance that we were in the right place and we had only to fight to win."* -- [[Colonel Walter Clark – 17ᵗʰ NC regiment]] Q1

D. H. HILL *"was a man of considerable capacity and always seemed to go from choice into the most dangerous place he could find on the field."* --[[Lieutenant General James Longstreet]] Q2

D. H. HILL *"Do you know that in Mexico the young officers called you the bravest man in the army?"*-- [[Lieutenant General Joseph E. Johnston]] Q3

D. H. HILL *"Intemperance or dissipation in any form was for him the unpardonable sin. D. H. Hill was a man of literary attainments, an assiduous student of Holy Scripture, and as a teacher of mathematics unsurpassed among American teachers."* -- [[Colonel Henry Elliott Shepherd]] Q4

D. H. HILL *"never a more pluckier or determined fighter."* -- [[General James Longstreet]] Q6

D. H. HILL *"in action & under fire he commands the admiration & respect of everyone."* -- [[Major James N. Edmondston]] Q7

D. H. HILL *"The annals of war have not set before us a more heroic or dauntless soul. He excelled in the characteristics of invincible tenacity, absolute unconsciousness of fear, courage never to submit or yield, no one has risen above him, not even in the annals of the Army of Northern Virginia."* -- [[Colonel Henry Elliott Shepherd]] Q8

D. H. HILL *"Qualities of leadership which inspired the utmost confidence and loyalty in his soldiers and made him the idol of the Carolinas."* -- [[Colonel James W. Ratchford]] Q10

D. H. HILL *"He was the very "Ironsides" of the South – Cromwell in some of his essential characteristics coming again in the person and genius of D. H. Hill."* -- [[Henry Elliott Shepherd]] Q11

D. H. HILL *"His absolute unconsciousness of danger was enough to thrill the ordinary brain with a sort of vertigo as it revealed itself in the most phenomenal situations or supreme crises."* -- [[Colonel Henry Elliott Shepherd]] Q12

D. H. HILL *"Upon one occasion, his horse being shot under him, as he was in the act of writing an order, holding the paper in his hand, steed and rider sank to the earth and without the relaxation of a muscle or a movement of the head, he finished the order, handed it to a courier, as calm and unconcerned as if reviewing the battalion of cadets in the grounds of the Institute at Charlotte."* -- *[[Colonel Henry Elliot Shepherd]]* Q13

D. H. HILL *"Fancy a man in whom the grim determination of a veteran warrior is united to a gentle tenderness of manner . . . . affix a pair of eyes that possess the most indisputably honest and kindly expression; animate him with a mind clear, deep and comprehensive, and imbued with a humor as rich as it is deep and effective; infuse man and mind with a soul which in its lofty views compels subordinates of the material to the spiritual, and holds a supreme trust in the wisdom and goodness of the Almighty – is zealous in the discharge of duty, and looks with scorn on all that is mean and sinful. Add to all these a carriage that is indomitable, and a love of truth and honor which is sublime, and you have the earthly embodiment of D. H. Hill."* -- *[[NC Supreme Court Justice - Colonel A. C. Avery]]* Q14

D. H. HILL *"had done as much hard fighting as any other general and had also displayed great ability in holding his men to their work by supervision and example."* -- *[[General E. P. Alexander]]* Q15

D. H. HILL *"High and well deserved reputation as a hard fighter...seemed to go from choice into the most dangerous place he could find on the field."* -- *[[Captain John Haskell – Longstreet's artillerist]]* Q16

D. H. HILL *"Stonewall Jackson repeatedly declared in my hearing that there was not...a man in the Southern Army, superior in military genius to D.H. Hill."* -- *[[Colonel James W. Ratchford]]* Q17

D. H. HILL *"....a capable, well read soldier, and positively about the bravest man ever seen. He seemed not to know peril and was utterly indifferent to bullets and shell...."* -- *[[General G. Moxley Sorrell]]* Q18

D. H. HILL *"Like Jackson he was, too, a born fighter – as aggressive, pugnacious and tenacious as s bull-dog, or as any soldier in the service, and he had a sort of monomania on the subject of personal courage."* -- *[[General G. Moxley Sorrell]]* Q19

D. H. HILL *"In a portrayal of the character of Daniel Harvey Hill his all-prevailing moral courage first reveals itself with its correlated traits: absolute loyalty to truth, frankness, ingenuousness, an incapacity to play the hypocrite, effacement of self, and insensibility to fear. In this rarest of human virtues he was preeminent; his ethical creed might be concisely embodied in the language of a poet."* -- *[[Colonel Henry E. Shepherd]]* Q21

D. H. HILL *"Because right is right, to follow right were wisdom in the scorn of consequences"* -- *[[Colonel Henry E. Shepherd]]* Q22

D. H. HILL *"He was a skill-full officer, intelligent and keen eyed, stern to rebuke violation of orders and lack of discipline-a determined fighter-as the boys* expressed it, "A fighter from way back"; -- [[Major William Smith, 14th NC regiment Anson Guards]] Q24

D. H. HILL *"impressed me as a zealous, unselfish patriot and great soldier, who knew not fear and shrank from no duty. His Christian faith was unbounded. He could always be found at the most dangerous place in the line, doing what he could to encourage and also protect the men."* -- [[Colonel Walter Clark – 17th NC regiment]] Q26

D. H. HILL *"There was never a better soldier or a man better qualified to judge of the merits of one. The clash of battle was not a confusing din to him, but an exciting scene that awakened his spirit and his genius."* -- [[Colonel Walter Clark – 17th NC regiment]] Q27

D. H. HILL *"In a portrayal of the character of Daniel Harvey Hill his all-prevailing moral courage first reveals itself with its correlated traits; absolute loyalty to truth, frankness, ingenuousness, an incapacity to play the hypocrite, effacement of self, and insensibility to fear. In this rarest of human virtues he was preeminent; his ethical creed might be concisely embodied in the language of a poet."* -- [[Colonel Henry Elliott Shepherd]] Q29

D. H. HILL *"Qualities of leadership which inspired the utmost confidence and loyalty in his soldiers and made him the idol of the Carolinas."* -- [[*James W. Ratchford*]] Q30

AUTHOR'S EXPOSITION

In fairness to these expositors, quotes addressing D. H. Hill with negative connotations do exist. In one instance, General Robert E. Lee confided in *private communications* that General Hill was *". . . an excellent executive officer, he does not seem to have much administrative ability. Left to himself, he seems embarrassed and backward to act."* Using this quote out of context, many expositors have portrayed D. H. Hill as being "backward to act." But when the comment is taken in its full context a completely different conclusion is made. General Robert E. Lee knew D. H. Hill to be a *fighting general*, not an administrator or War Department bureaucrat. He understood that General D. H. Hill was most effective mounted upon his steed, saber in hand, leading the charge of an assaulting Confederate line in bloody battle. He clearly and repeatedly expressed his feelings on this matter; several instances are noted in this manuscript by his direct quotes and numerous others are in the archives of his personal memoirs, OFFICAL REPORTS of the Army of Northern Virginia and the OFFICIAL RECORDS of the Union and Confederate Armies.

With D. H. Hill, as with every other General Officer assignment or reassignment made by General R. E. Lee, Hill's capabilities were fully considered and placement by official order was made in the best specific interest of Lee's command and the general welfare of the Confederacy. Yes, controversial issues, such as D. H. Hill's open criticism of his decisions at Malvern Hill, may have offered abundant opportunities to punish or chastise his *fighting general,* perhaps in some spiteful way. But any suggestion that General Robert E. Lee, perhaps the most honorable and just man of the nineteenth century, would have made critical command decision based upon such trivial criteria, has no understanding of strategic leadership.

Any senior military officer will acknowledge that the criterion for determining their career path is based wholly upon their professional competence: experience acquired through extensive education and training – well documented through meritorious performance at various levels of command. Simply stated, this *is* the criterion for military personnel actions; selection for command, promotion, et al. These considerations have always mandated full compliance; not only during my lengthy tenure of military service [a period spanning from the Vietnam conflict to the surge phase of Operation Iraqi Freedom] and they were certainly were no less stringent during the Civil War. To suggest that General Robert E. Lee would act in such a petulant, unprofessional manner is offensive, not only to myself, but to our entire profession of arms. Thus, it is understandable that many are equally offended by expositions which promulgate *idyllic notions* that D. H. Hill acted in a petulant manner.

Due diligence and empirical research are required to understand the military processes involved in wartime general officer placements and assignments; It's a little know, and ostensibly reported, fact that General Stonewall Jackson was merely an eyelash away from being relieved of command – purportedly for marching his men in excess during a specific road march – an action which nearly led to his resignation from the Confederate army; General Jackson's notable tardiness in several instances during the conduct of the Battles of Seven Days were extremely problematic and caused General Lee some degree of anguish; General Lee had, in hand, the written resignation of General D. H. Hill – a factor of great influence in the corporate decision by the Confederacy's leadership when they acquiesced to Governor Vance's stern request for Hill's assignment to the Department of North Carolina; General Magruder was formally admonished by General Lee for his poor performance during a specific battle; wherein allegations were made of his improper use of morphine to deal with a medical issue; General Hood, a man renowned for his bravery and aggressiveness, bordering at times on recklessness, was practically eviscerated by some expositors for his decisive defeats during the Atlanta and Franklin-Nashville Campaigns; General Bragg, with his leadership wholly supported by President Davis during the conduct of the Battle of Chickamauga, was relieved shortly thereafter for his conduct and disastrous results of the ensuing battle of Missionary Ridge – notwithstanding his noted inefficiency and poor demonstration of performance as the General-in-chief of the Western Campaign, he would later be re-elevated to the position of General-in-chief of the Army of Northern Virginia when General Lee was elevated to be the Supreme Commander of the Confederacy.

Something critical is missing in the preceding paragraph. There are no end notes provided by this author to support the exposition of that specific paragraph. Employing a most effective ploy, used by my esteemed US Army

War College professor [Colonel Phil Thompson], my allegorical statements are submitted for your critical analysis. You may totally dismiss them as being unsupported by historical documents, accept them to be fact, or you can challenge yourself – as Professor Thompson habitually challenged me – to invest some time into the required due diligence necessary to either confirm or refute the paragraph [in part or in whole]. This challenge is extended to you with the same level of veracity that Colonel Thompson habitually exacted upon my entire War College Seminar Group. My reasoning for extending this challenge is to emphasize to every reader the true importance of empirical research when writing of all things historical. It was so easy, yet so harmful for Mr. E. A. Pollard to author his expositions, so greatly lacking in diversity and unprejudiced points of view. His disingenuous tendencies as an historical revisionist caused great personal injury to the name of *Lee's Fighting General* and effectively suppressed the promulgation of General Hill's military heroism for nearly one and one-half century, denying him of the fame for which he is most deserving. Can you imagine the injurious nature of such expositions if written of our innumerable great heroes of the Civil War?

As part of my empirical research for this book I conducted numerous surveys, addressing a wide range of Civil War topics; interviewing a large cross-section of adult Southerners - indiscriminate of their ages, genders, and professions. One specific survey is noteworthy and warrants citation herein. When surveyed, a great majority of the people questioned recognized General Robert E. Lee instantly when shown his portrait. A lesser but substantial number of people correctly identified a portrait of Stonewall Jackson. But sadly, of the one hundred people questioned, not a single person could identify the portrait General D. H. Hill. The culmination of my empirical research produced a resounding confirmation of the injurious effect that expositors, such as Mr. E. A. Pollard, can and do have upon the honorable recording of our nation's history. Thus, I conclude this personal exposition with no more than one great expectation: that General D. H. Hill will finally receive due recognition for his bravery and Southern valor and that he will finally be granted his deserving and notable place of prominence at the table with our other great American military heroes.

CHAPTER XVIII

LIFE AFTER THE WAR

"COMRADES: . . . I earnestly exhort you to observe faithfully the terms of pacification agreed upon; and to discharge the obligations of good and peaceful citizens, as well as you have performed the duties of thorough soldiers in the field. By such a course, you will best secure the comfort of your families and kindred, and restore tranquility to our country."

J.E.J.

General Joseph E. Johnston
General Order No. 22 683

The surrender of General Joseph E. Johnston's Confederate Army to General William T. Sherman at the Bennett Place near Durham, North Carolina on April 26th 1865 marked the end of the Civil War for General D. H. Hill. Just seventeen days earlier, General Lee had surrendered at Appomattox and within one week, General Richard A. Taylor would be forced to give up his troops in Alabama. When General Kirby Smith's Trans-Mississippi Army at New Orleans capitulated exactly one month later, all hostilities of the Civil War were finally and officially concluded.

General D. H. Hill was mustered out of the Confederate army under the auspices of Federal parole at Greensboro, North Carolina on April 26th 1865. 684 Under the terms of surrender, it was specified that Confederate soldiers be allowed to take possession of on hand supplies; sufficient to enable their return home and a start at life anew. General D. H. Hill, having appropriated an army ambulance and a pair of mules, joined his brother, Colonel William M. Hill, and the two beleaguered officers made their way toward the General's home in Davidson College, North Carolina.   That ninety mile wagon ride must have been the most agonizing trip of D. H. Hill's life.

For the past four years, he had devoted his heart and soul to serving the Confederacy and had fought gallantly for the cause. 685 It had been a brilliant effort – in fact, the greatest effort in the annals of modern warfare. As a young officer, General D. H. Hill had emerged from the Mexican War with the reputation as the *"fighter from way back."* After innumerable citations for gallantry on Civil War fields of battle, he had now become legendary as *"Lee's Fighting General."* Within the hearts and minds of the Union ranks he had become the legendary Confederate *"Angel of Death."* But the fight was now over - and it was a losing effort. The South had been defeated; that valiant cause for which he had so often risked his life was utterly lost. During the conflict, he had witnessed the terror that horrific warfare produces - death, devastation, depravity, – every conceivable wantonness that only mankind can bring upon itself. But now, life would change for the General and all other returning soldiers. He was headed home to his wife and six children to resume another daunting task: serving as patriarch for his beloved Hill family and providing for their welfare. 686

Upon arrival home, General Hill gave the appropriated ambulance and mules to his brother, bidding him a fond farewell for his continued long journey to his home in Mississippi. At this juncture, General D. H. Hill was faced with the task of contemplating his next career move. He had little interest in returning to Davidson College as a professor but he was a prolific reader and a masterfully talented writer. Given his experience as an author, having published three books, and with the help of his brother-in-law James P. Irwin, who had acumen for business, they decided to publish a magazine appropriately called *"The Land We Love."* 687

The magazine was devoted to literature, agriculture, and military history and met with phenomenal success; quickly growing in circulation and popularity to become the most read magazine in the region. During that era, few Southern homes were without a copy and, as circulation increased, so expanded its readership and distribution well beyond the boundaries of the South. The magazine provided insightful articles on agriculture while covering other subjects such as education, politics, and local news. Of course, the magazine provided General Hill a perfect forum to present his editorial perspective on military history. The magazine's readership was eager to hear the old General's point of view on the many battles in which he participated. Plus, a host of other distinguished writers frequently contributed their insightful articles on a variety of topics. The magazine provided a much sought after voice for Southerners struggling to cope with the Confederacy's collapse, the defeat of their army and the contentious intrusion by the Federal government into all aspects of their daily lives; especially the pervasive political and socio-economic impact that the Federals had imposed upon the South's economy. With abject poverty being status quo for the region, viewpoints conveyed through The Land We Love fit nicely with the resident's Lost Cause ideology; and the articles were always quite supportive of their plight. 688

For the first six months as the magazine's editor, General Hill advocated for his readership to maintain the moral high ground; promoting efforts to restore the piedmont area of the Carolinas; socially, culturally, and economically. Initially, the General supplied the majority of published articles, addressing matters of military history. But, upon his request, many former Confederate Generals began to furnish their perspectives, adding great depth and substance to the articles by providing first-hand accounts; personal reminiscences from men, many now legendary, who actually stood the lines of many engagements and spoke with clarity regarding the authenticity of their articles, paying great homage to historical accuracy. The readership was eager to gain this first hand insight expounding, in accurate detail, so many of the war stories that had become iconic within Southern culture. 689

Ever the advocate for education, General Hill's editorials continually postulated the importance of education and training to develop the South's resources; citing as essential the develop of competent, well-trained workers - including but not limited to area farmers, miners, engineers, blacksmith, and machinists. The General took great pleasure in corresponding with a number of his military acquaintances, recalling many shared wartime reminiscences and contributing to a steady stream of correspondence by many veterans that served to provide an historical foundation for many of the events in which they played such a major role. General Hill was always insistent upon having his commanders, at every level, commit their action to written reports, feeling that the only true expositions of military history should be written by the soldiers to whom the duty fell to fight the battle, not a group of educated civilian historians, lacking in the required knowledge of the science of warfare and the understanding of military protocol. He would often liken an historian's account, written without having participated in the battle or event for which he writes, to that of a doctor who would operate without the benefit of having attended a medical school; or a lawyer who would defend a client without having attended a school of law. 690

General Hill was emphatic in his expressions of love for the old North State, noting with unease that written histories of other state's regiments were starting to establish an historical record without benefit of creditable input from regimental commanders of North Carolina, commenting: *"It is unfortunate for North Carolina that none of her own sons has attempted a history of the war. There was scarcely a corporal in the ranks of the North Carolina troops, who could not write a more truthful history than any yet put forth."* 691

The Land We Love continued to grow in readership and stature, as one of the few creditable sources for accurate portrayals of historical events; gaining a long and growing long list of endorsements from most creditable veterans of the Civil War. Generals P.T.G Beauregard and General John Bell Hood wrote that General D. H. Hill's magazine had *"claims upon our people as a home monthly, representing our own sentiments and feelings. To the late Southern soldier, the 'Land We Love' has peculiar attractions; it is the acknowledged organ of the late Confederate Army; it preserves the record of the heroism and devotion of our soldiery, and is now almost the only channel by which the truth of history can be vindicated."*

Such public endorsement by men of great stature within the South spoke directly to General D. H. Hill's editorial integrity. Included upon their written endorsement were the names of seventy-six additional, distinguished Southerners whose similar endorsements were provided, with each a signatory; including such names as General Breckinridge, General Johnston, General Early, and his old friend from his days in command of the Department of North Carolina, Governor Zebulon Vance. 692 General D. H. Hill's obdurate editing style, being uncompromising in principles and proclaiming integrity and historical accuracy to be sacrosanct, confirmed his character to be beyond reproach; as an editor, a soldier and a Christian man. The first supposed *"historian"* of the Lost Cause - Mr. E. A. Pollard– who once campaigned vigorously to impugn General D. H. Hill's integrity, even while the blood of soldiers in D. H. Hill's Division was still spilling forth on many battlefields, had later been humiliated, discredited and silenced, resulting in the loss of his professional creditability. The Land We Love, having gained in creditability and statue, became the most trusted, premiere publication of reference for reporting war editorials. General D. H. Hill and his magazine continued to gain broad recognition and prominence from Northern editors and readers as well. The reissue of his book, Crucifixion of Christ in a Presbyterian periodical also contributed greatly to the General's renown as an author and editor. 693

Daniel Harvey Hill was an erudite and modest man who lived without the slightest form of pretentious of character; the construct of his character was defined by his stern sense of duty and a resolute intolerance for inefficiency, pretense and ostentation. Yet he was a compassionate man who reflected a love of humanity, charity – in fact and in judgment, a contented and happy mind, and these qualities were reflected through is literary works. But he was also a very private man, whom his family and closest friends found to be very caring, possessing a sharp wit, keen intellect, and an ever present sense of humor. Often, during trying times in his life, he would summon strength to face adversity, reliant upon these noble qualities. But it was his profound religious convictions that most defined the General's character and it was from God whom he summoned when, on November 10th 1866 he lost his beloved five year old son James Irwin to sickness. He and his family mourned deeply over the loss of their child but through God's grace, their intensely-held faith sustained them. The passing of young James Irvin profoundly affected him and, for several months, concerns for family outweighed concerns for the magazine, wherein he spent less time performing editorial duties. 694

After three years at the editorial helm, General D. H. Hill sold his interest in The Land We Love. This marked the end of one editorial endeavor but the start of yet another when he established a weekly newspaper, based in Charlotte, North Carolina appropriately titled, The Southern Home. Debuting on January 20th 1870, this new publication was devoted to agriculture, industrial development and marketing issues of the State. 695 Initially, the paper insightfully addressed reigning issues of the day, exhorting very popular views within the small farming communities and was extremely accommodating of the Grange movement; a fraternal organization for farmers that encouraged them to band together for their own economic benefit. 696

The Southern Home's editorials supported this agenda, which included resisting railroad monopolies and pushing for rural mail deliveries. However, as the South continued to struggle under Reconstruction, the Southern Home's commentary predominantly address his reader's concerns the greater local issue of the day. There was a virulent antipathy throughout the South toward the influences of the many Carpetbaggers, a pejorative term used by the locals to describe Yankees who moved to the area during the

Reconstruction era after the Civil War. They were aptly named for their propensity to carry carpet bags, a form of luggage common for that era, and considered to be nothing more than insidious Northerners who were hell bent upon exploiting Southerners through questionable practices. Using the paper as a political forum, D. H. Hill successfully turned the editorials of his paper into the voice of the people crying out against these *"oppressors and their home allies;"* invoking journalistic denunciation of the corrupt and brutal Federal mandates during the Reconstruction. The General was personally credited for creating an *"Army with Banners"* in the fight for the restoration of home rule. 697

D. H. HILL

"If not General D. H. Hill, to whom would you trust your life in combat?"

-- D. R. HILL – Brigadier General
D. H. Hill's Division XXI {Provisional CSA}
Author – *Lee's Fighting General*
US Army (retired)
Hill Namesake

PRESIDENT OF ARKANSAS INDUSTRIAL UNIVERSITY

In June of 1877, General D. H. Hill accepted the prestigious post, President of Arkansas Industrial University in Fayetteville, known today as the University of Arkansas; reflecting his philosophical commitment to educating the youth to whom the responsibilities lay for building the New South. The General and his family arrived in Fayetteville, Arkansas on September 1st 1877 to a cordial welcome and settled comfortably into the local community. 698

Prior to his arrival, the General had never been in Arkansas and his only prior contact with Arkansas people had been a military association with that state's soldiers during the war. The General was greatly revered by the people of Arkansas for his distinguished service to the Confederacy, having led several Arkansas Regimental flags into battle during his command tenure with General Lee's Army of Northern Virginia. Also, one of his divisions, commanded by General Cleburne's, contained more Arkansas soldiers than any other division in the Confederate armies, and they proved to be ferocious fighters for General D. H. Hill's corps at Chickamauga. General Hill's esteemed reputation lent great creditability to the young institution and, in return, his personal affection for the fine fighting men of Arkansas produced a sensing that he would feel at home with the people of Arkansas. 699

Upon his arrival, the General found a small institution, poorly financed, with a small but excellent faculty and a fine, earnest student body; but one without discipline or control. He immediately set about the task of building the fledging Arkansas Industrial University into a respected institution, supplanting many existing policies and installing the type of reform that served him so favorably during his tenures at Davidson College: including the demerit system and mandatory Sunday school attendance. As two of the school's early historians put it, Hill's tenure *"was characterized with the Christian spirit."* Holding dear to his philosophy regarding college discipline, the new President was quick to expel several male students for drunkenness, despite the young men's renown as members of prominent Arkansas families. Holding firm to his principles, General Hill did not back down, drawing corollaries with other schools, and convinced his Board of Trustee's that he should exclusively handle internal affairs concerning curriculum and discipline. Notwithstanding the old General's staunch disciplinary standards, he developed great rapport with the student body and took his role seriously in preparing them for survival in post antebellum America. *"Knowledge is power,"* he told the graduating Class in 1881 and that his expectation of them was great, also warning the young men that success at Arkansas Industrial University did not automatically guarantee riches, but that their exhibited *"perseverance and pertinacity"* would serve them in good stead as adults.

When he went there, the Arkansas Industrial University ranked at the very bottom of the list in attendance for Southern colleges. During his tenure as President, the school steadily improved, reaching a ranking of third among the other Southern colleges, both in attendance and scholarships. But in 1881 the General and his family suddenly suffered another personal family tragedy when their beloved youngest daughter, Harriet, contracted diphtheria and passed while visiting relatives in North Carolina. The loss was devastating; of such magnitude that the General and his wife, Isabella, never fully recovered from the shock. Once again he and his family would mourn deeply over the loss of another young child. But through God's grace, their intensely-held faith again sustained them. 700

No feature of Hill's character was more intensely developed than his affection for his children; pervading every phase of his nature. When God took James Irwin and Harriet, he dedicated the creations of His genius and scholarship, as a monument to their memory. 701 After eight years of devoted service as the President of Arkansas Industrial University, citing declining health and being quite fatigued from the continual effects of the stressful position; aggravated by a bout of pneumonia and remorseful over the death of Harriet, the General submitted his resignation, to be effective with the end of the coming spring semester of 1885. His crowning achievement during his tenure was the positive influence that he was able to instill within the student body. Having earned their respect, the students were highly devoted to the General and sought to emulate his high ideals and sense of duty. Upon his resignation, and the acceptance thereof, the University's Board of Trustees passed the following resolution:

"   *   * We feel in parting with General D. H. Hill we are losing one who has been a blessing to our State and a strong support to this University. And we here put upon record our high appreciation of his unwearied and abundant labors and his deep devotion to duty. We feel that it would be hard to find his equal and high moral worth and strong Christian character united with fine literary culture and scholarly attainments. In the hearts of his old students scattered throughout the length and breadth of the State he has erected a monument of his eminent worth and ability."* 702

The years spent in Lexington had been professionally rewarding. Conversely, the family had also seen its share of troubles, notably the loss of their youngest daughter and issues with the General's health; specifically his bout with pneumonia and generally issues habitually associated with the aging process. However, the Hill family was blessed during their stay with the birth of three additional children: Robert Hall Morrison Hill, Eugenia Hill, and Randolph Hill. 703

PRESIDENT OF GEORGIA MILITARY & AGRICULTURAL COLLEGE

In 1885, General D. H. Hill accepted the call to preside over the Georgia Military and Agricultural College. 704 The move to Macon, Georgia provided a milder, more favorable climate and placed the General much closer to his friends and family living in North Carolina. The slower pace of living in the small Southern town, combined with a less rigorous work environment, was most agreeable to the General and it provided him with more time for reminiscence and writing about his Civil War experiences. General Hill found his work experience there to be most congenial. It offered him a very influential position from which he could construct and implement policy for the college while providing time to pursue one of his great loves; teaching. He relied heavily upon his son, Daniel Harvey Junior, who was on the faculty at the college, to handle the laborious and mundane administrative details that accompanied the position. 705 The position also provided time for reminiscence of past; and anticipation of future events for his children. Ever the prolific writer, the General corresponded often with his children, sharing his optimism for their bright future and exhorting them to remain steadfast to uphold Hill family Christian duties; to observe the Sabbath; to avoid getting into debt, as did his father; to avoid lending money to others; to refrain from smoking and chewing tobacco; and insisting they write home more often. 706

Nearing the end of his life, General D. H. Hill took great pride and solace in the Christian growth and maturity of his children. Harvey Junior was advancing in his career as a college professor, teaching English at North Carolina Mechanical and Agricultural College in Raleigh, North Carolina, known today as North Carolina State University – destined to gain prominence as an author and distinguished educator in his own right;   and honored in memoriam with the Daniel Harvey Hill Junior Library of North Carolina State University's library; his youngest son Joseph Hill would complete law school and establish a successful law practice – also destined to gain prominence as a State Supreme Court Justice in the Great state of Arkansas; his oldest daughter, Eugenia, married Thomas J. Arnold and reared a wonderful family, worthy of sustaining the reputation of the Hill family name - Eugenia became a writer of great distinction on numerous religious subjects, many of which were published in Presbyterian papers and church periodicals.; his other daughter never married but was an accomplished artist –   and became a most successful teacher of art in schools and colleges. She too was much beloved in a large circle of kindred and friends. Suffice it to say of the three sons and the son-in-law, that each attained distinction in his own field and each was recorded on Who's Who in America. 707

 As General D. H. Hill neared completion of his final tenure with the College, his health declined rapidly. He had suffered for quite some time with chronic illnesses, but symptoms of stomach cancer made all aspects of his life increasingly difficult. Coping daily with the pains and discomforts associated with the illness, through sheer personal determination and fortitude, he still continued to teach; putting forth an appearance before his students. 708 General Hill taught mathematics over a span of thirteen years, another two years he devoted to teaching Military Science; becoming a master in each. He was familiar with the campaigns of all the great Captains in history and could describe them with as much detail as he could describe one of Lee's campaigns. It can be asserted with assurance that few teachers ever taught successfully in so many fields of culture. He had been constant writer and speaker - an original thinker who seldom chose to follow the beaten path. His opinions, and there were many, were always a result of thought and study; often expressed in terse but clear language. Unmoved in the presence of danger and schooled to hide his emotions at suffering, he reserved only bitter scorn for cowardice and treachery.

But after a long, distinguished career as an educator, General Hill resigned his post with the Georgia Military and Agricultural College in June of 1889; notifying the Board of Trustees of his medical prognosis and informing them that he would not live throughout the year. With his tenure fulfilled, General Hill and Isabella returned to his home in Charlotte, North Carolina. 709

CHAPTER XIX

THE FINAL JOURNEY HOME – *"Nearly There"*

General D. H. Hill returned to his beloved North Carolina to spend his final days. Surrounded by close family and friends, the General made it known to all that he was patiently awaiting his Master's call - a call he knew would not be long delayed. Although feeble in body, his mind remained keen and alert and his sense of humor undiminished. He took great comfort knowing that Isabella was with him and enjoyed staying in constant touch with his children; either through correspondence or visits. Just two days before his death, he sat on the front porch of his home *"talking cheerfully in the sunshine for about an hour."*

On his last day on Earth, the General drifted in and out of consciousness. But Harvey Junior and his sister were able to make out his final phrase from their father's lips – *"nearly there."* 710

In his personal life, which the world did not see, there was sweetness, light and beauty; and the real tenderness of his nature has left an unfailing memory within generations of his beloved Hill family. Indeed it may be said of him that no purer citizen, no more unselfish patriot, no braver soldier ever trod the path of duty. On September 24 1889, Lieutenant General Daniel Harvey Hill, **"Lee's Fighting General"** passed away – a beautiful end to a beautiful life. 711

EPILOGUE

FINAL REPORT: TO LIEUTENANT GENERAL D. H. HILL

"THE HISTORICAL ACCOUNT OF "LEE'S FIGHTING GENERAL"

REPORT OF: BRIGADIER-GENERAL D. R. HILL, COMMANDING,

D. H. HILL'S DIVISION   XXI [[CSA-PROVISIONAL]]

HEADQUARTERS

D.H. HILL'S DIVISION – XXI (CSA-PROVISIONAL]]

CHARLOTTE, NC

24 SEPTEMBER 2012

MEMORANDUM FOR: Lieutenant General D. H. Hill [[C.S.A.]]

GENERAL D. H. HILL: WITH GREAT PERSONAL REGARD AND IN DEFERENCE TO YOUR DISTINGUISHED SERVICE TO THE CONFEDERACY, I PROUDLY REPORT, WITH THIS BOOK'S PUBLICATION, THAT MY MISSION STANDS FULFILLED AND COMPLETE

IAW YOUR INSTRUCTIONS, THE OFFICIAL RECORD OF YOUR MILITARY SERVICE HAS BEEN VALIDATED; YOUR VALOROUS ACCOMPLISHMENTS DULY RECORDED IN THE HISTORICAL ARCHIVES;   AND YOUR OUTSTANDING SERVICE TO THAT GREAT CAUSE FULLY ACKNOWLEDGED.

IN STRICT COMPLIANCE WITH YOUR WRITTEN DIRECTIVE, DETAILING YOUR CRITERION FOR THE CONSTRUCT OF THIS MANUSCRIPT, I HAVE ENDEAVORED TO FOLLOW YOUR INTENT EXPLICITLY; TO GAIN SOLDIERLY INSIGHT INTO THE REBELLION SO AS TO APPROPRIATELY STUDY THE MILITARY SCIENCE OF THE FIGHTS; AND TO ASCRIBE CONTEXT TO THE ENVIRONMENTS OF YOUR BATTLES.

IN RECONNAISSANCE AND PREPARATION FOR THIS MISSION I HAVE WALKED UPON THE MANY SACRED FIELDS OF YOUR CAMPAIGNS: BETHEL, YORKTOWN, WILLIAMSBURG, SEVEN PINES, SEVEN DAYS, BOONSBORO, SHARPSBURG, CHICKAMAUGA AND BENTONVILLE; IN PRAYERFUL REVERENCE AT THE MANY POINTS OF DECISION AND CULMINATION AT EACH FIELD I HAVE:

STOOD WITHIN THE DEFILADE OF THE BLOODY LANE AT SHARPSBURG WHERE THE GALLANT ANDERSON FELL; WALKED UPON THE ADJACENT FIELD WHERE YOU SO GALLANTLY MADE YOUR DESPERATE CHARGE; CROSSED THE BURNSIDE BRIDGE AND CONTEMPLATED TACTICS OF THE *tete de point*; STOOD UPON SOUTH MOUTAIN AND WALKED THE TERRAIN OF RODES OBSTINENCE AND GARLAND'S DEMISE; CLIMED THE HEIGHTS OF MALVERN HILL AND NAVIGATED THE SWAMPS OF THE CHICKAHOMINY; WALKED THE BANKS OF THE CHICKAMAUGA CREEK AND THE HEIGTS OF MISSIONARY RIDGE; AND CROSSED THE SPAN OF YOUR OPEN FIELD AT BENTONVILLE;

FROM MY DESK I HAVE READ THE FULL COMPLIMENT OF OFFICIAL REPORTS OF BOTH ARMYS' ARCHIVES; FROM GENERALS-IN-CHIEF TO THE REGIMENTAL COMMANDERS ALL; I HAVE PONDERED YOUR WRITINGS AND THE WRITINGS OF THE DISTINGUISHED MEN OF YOUR ERA, LEARNED AND HONORABLE EVERY ONE; WHO KNEW YOUR FACE *AND* THE *FEEL OF THE TRIGGER* – TAKING THEIR PERSEPCTIVE ALONE TO COLLATE THE EMPIRICAL DATA FOR RESEARCH;

I HAVE HUMBLY WALKED, WITH GREAT HONOR AND PRIVILEGE, UPON TWO BATTLEFIELDS OF MY OWN ERA AND EXPERIENCED THE GREAT PERSONAL LOSS OF COMRADES;

AS DID YOU, I HAVE SEIZED THE MANY OPPORTUNITIES AFFORDED BY THE MILITARY TO GAIN ENTRANCE TO, AND AN EDUCATION FROM, THEIR INSTITUTIONS OF HIGHER LEARNING; AND I HAVE BEEN AFFORDED THE GRAND HONOR OF, AND EXPERIENCES ASSOCIATED WITH, TENURES OF PLATOON, BATTERY, BATTALION, REGIMENTAL AND BRIGADIER COMMAND.

YET THERE IS WITHIN ME AN OVERWHELMING SENSE THAT MY WRITINGS ARE NOT PLENARY IN NATURE, BUT MERELY A STARTING POINT FOR CONTINUED STUDY; THAT SOME CALM, DIGNIFIED, IMPARTIAL MAN OF LEARNING, INDUSTRY AND ABILITY WILL FOLLOW MY EXAMPLE AND EXPOUND UPON MY WRITINGS HEREIN; FURTHER ENLIGHTENING FUTURE GENERATIONS WITH AN EVEN MORE DETAILED EXPOSITION OF THE HISTORY OF THE GREAT REBELLION.

IT HAS BEEN MY GREATEST HONOR AND PROFOUND PRIVILEGE TO COMPLETE THIS MISSION OF YOUR BIDDING. MAY GOD CONTINUE TO BLESS YOU, AND GUIDE YOU, FOR SURELY HIS FACE IS NOW BEFORE YOU!

*   *   *   *   *

VERY RESPECTFULLY,

YOUR OBEDIENT SERVANT

//D.R.H.//

BIOGRAPHICAL SKETCH OF THE AUTHOR:

DR. DANNY R. HILL

Brigadier General – D.H. Hill's Division [[XXI-Provisional]]

Commanding General; US Army (Retired) & Family Namesake

D. R. Hill was born September 5th, 1949, in Union County, NC – within a 25 mile radius of the locations of D.H. Hill's birth, childhood home, professorships with the North Carolina Military Institute and Davidson College; he entered the US Army in 1968 as a private and advanced through the NCO corps attaining the rank of Staff Sergeant; graduating with honors from the North Carolina Military Academy [[successor institution of D. H. Hill's North Carolina Military Institute]] he was commissioned Second Lieutenant, Infantry in 1973 with unit assignment as platoon leader to NCARNG unit bearing lineage and honors of the First North Carolina's "Big Bethel" Regiment, including the "Big Bethel" battle streamer" – the "immortal" First North Carolina Regiment - first commanded by Colonel D. H. Hill; his military service totaled 41 years [[August1968-September2009) and included a total of twelve years in command at the brigadier, regimental, battalion, company, and platoon levels; his assignments ranged from platoon, company & battery level to 3 star command; twice he was called to the battlefield in the defense of our nation; he was highly decorated with his highest honor being the US Army's Legion of Merit medal; he is a graduate of the US Army War College [Class of 2004], the US Army Command & General Staff College, and all four Officer Advance Schools of Infantry, Armor, Artillery, and Engineer. He holds his Ph.D. in Management, M.B.A.; Masters in Strategic Studies; Bachelors and Associates Degrees in Business; he is married and continues to raise his Christian family under the same devout Presbyterian faith as is the custom in the Hill families. On this date, he proudly serves as the Provisional Commanding General – D. H. Hill's Division XXI – [[Provisional]] and responsible for the perpetuation of the Division's heritage and the memory of the gallant soldiers of that distinguished command through the website [[www.LeesFightingGeneral.com]]

Library of Congress

TXu 1-822-427

ISBN-13: 978-0615671697

ISBN-10: 0615671691

www.LeesFightingGeneral.com

Manufactured in the United States of America

Library of Congress Cataloging-in-Publication Data

Hill, D. H. (Daniel Harvey), 1821-1889.

Lee's Fighting General: Lieutenant General Daniel Harvey Hill CSA

A Study in Bravery and Southern Valor

Edited by D. R. Hill

Illustrated by D. R. Hill

PUBLISHED 2012 -- THE CONFEDERATE PRESS

Charleston, South Carolina

IN MEMORY OF

THE SOLDIERS OF D. H. HILL'S DIVISION

WHOSE HEROISM ELICITED THE HIGHEST ADMIRATION

AND UTMOST RESPECT OF THEIR

COMMANDING GENERAL

LIEUTENANT GENERAL DANIEL HARVEY HILL

THEREFORE, IN RECOGNITION AS HIS HUMBLE NAMESAKE,

I DEDICATE THIS BOOK;

IN DOING SO

I OFFER THIS EARNEST HOPE AND SOLEMN PRAYER:

SHALL THEY ENDURE THEIR SACRIFICES

WITH THE MEMORY OF THEIR GLORY

ACKNOWLEDGEMENTS

MAY GOD BESTOW UNTO THEM SERENITY, JOY AND HIS BLESSING:

HEATHER *MY WONDERFUL WIFE WHOM I MOST ADORE;* **MARY ALICE** *MY SISTER; A LADY BY GOD'S GRACE BUT D,H, HILL'S EQUAL IN ALL TRAITS– GREAT SHALL BE HER REWARDS IN HEAVEN;* **MY CHILDREN ALL;** *ANGIE; JONATHAN; TOMMY LEE; HANNAH; DILLON; KARA; DANIEL; MY PRIDE & JOY; MY DAD -* **W. T.** *- AS SUCCESSFUL WITH AGGREGATE AS WILLIAM HILL WAS WITH IRON ORE; MY MOM -* **ANNIE LEE** *- EQUAL TO THE BEAUTIFUL NANCY IN EVERY RESPECT; FIRST SERGEANT* **JOHN D. WILLIAMS** *MY TRUE MENTOR-BLACK MAGIC–LEGEND AND PRIDE OF BRAVO BATTERY; PVT* **CHARLES W. HILL;** *WWI VETERAN– WOUNDED IN FRANCE- HERO OF 119TH INFANTRY; COLONEL* **BILLY HILL;** *HERO OF THE FIRST REBELLION; LIEUTENANT GENERAL* **D. H. HILL;** *HERO OF THE SECOND REBELLION; 2LT* **TOMMY BOOTH** *(RIP); MY BEST FRIEND–TAKEN FAR TOO SOON; MSG* **JACK DANDRIGE;** *MY FRIEND THE ARTILLERIST-FROM CHILDHOOD THRU IRAQ TIL TODAY;* **JAMES "FOXX" REDDISH;** *MY MOST LOYAL FRIEND;* **DEAN HILL;** *MY OLDER BROTHER–WOULD HAVE ASKED TO BE NO MORE THAN TO BE A PRIVATE IN D. H. HILL'S DIVISION BUT WORTHY OF A GENERALSHIP;* **PAYTON PARK** *MY FRIEND – WITH PERSONAL CHARACTER AS D. H. HILL; COLONEL* **JOHNNY ALLEY;** *MY FRIEND AND THE BEST DAMNED BRIGADE COMMANDER OF 'EM ALL; LIEUTENANT GENERAL* **BILL INGRAM;** *OCS-14 CLASSMATE–UNDAUNTED!-OF WHOM I AM MOST PROUD; MAJOR GENERAL* **WILLIAM E. INGRAM SR**; *20TH CENTURY'S ROBERT E. LEE; BRIGADIER GENERAL* **KEN NEWBOLD;** *MY GREATEST SUPPORTER TO WHOM I WAS HIS "SQUEAKY WHEEL;" MAJOR GENERAL* **SKIP MCCARTNEY;** *MOST KNOWLEGABLE GENERAL WITH WHOM I HAD THE HONOR TO SERVE; MAJOR GENERAL* **JIM MALLORY**; *I FOLLOWED HIM TO THE BATTLEFIELD TWICE–I WOULD DO SO AGAIN UPON HIS CALL; MAJOR GENERAL* **GEORGE GOLDSMITH;** *TWENTIETH CENTURY'S LONGSTREET; MAJOR GENERAL* **DOUG ROBERTSON;** *A BRILLIANT COMMANDER–THE GENTLEMAN GENERAL; COLONEL* **"BOBBY JOE" GOSS;** *HIS EXAMPLE LED ME FROM CORPORAL TO COLONEL; COLONEL* **JACK MIDYETTE;** *SUPREME ARTILLERIST AND MOST HONORABLE SOLDIER; COLONEL* **TOMMY WILLIAMS;** *GENERAL PATTON'S EQUAL IN AUDACITY; COLONEL* **BILL KEETER;** *A SUPERB LEADER AND FRIEND; COLONEL* **RALPH LYON;** *A GREAT FRIEND AND COUNCELOR- STRAIGHT SHOOTER; COLONEL* **MONT HUNTER;** *MY CHILDHOOD FRIEND AND WARTIME CONSIGLIERE; COLONEL* **CHARLIE CROSBY;** *EQUALED THE NOBLE RATCHFORD AS DEPUTY COMMANDER DURING MY BRIGADIER AND TWO REGIMENTAL COMMANDS; COMMAND SERGEANT MAJOR* **JIM DUNLAP** *(RIP); TO WHOM I WAS HIS "DARING YOUNG LIEUTENANT" AND HE MY GREAT FRIEND; SERGEANT MAJOR* **DON POPE;** *REVERED AMONG ALL*

INFANTRYMEN; SERGEANT MAJOR **JERRY SHORE;** *ALWAYS A SMILE – AN UNWAVERING FRIEND - "AQUA-MELONE"; COMMAND SERGEANT MAJOR* **LOUIS STABEL;** *MOST PROFESSIONAL NCO WITH WHOM I HAD THE HONOR TO SERVE; SERGEANT FIRST CLASS* **BOB ALEXANDER** *(RIP); HE HELPED ME SURVIVE "THE EARLY YEARS AS STAFF SERGEANT;" MASTER SERGEANT* **LAWRENCE ARIAL;** *"MY GOOD BUDDY" WHOM I RESPECT GREATLY;STAFF SERGEANT FIRST SERGEANT* **JIM SHOLAR**; *MUSH – THE GLUE THAT FIRMLY HELD BRAVO BATTERY TO ITS HIGHEST STANDARD;* **DAVID BOOTH** *ARTILLERIEST WORTHY OF GUN CHIEF FOR THE GALLANT PELHAM; TO COLONEL* **SONNY SIMPSON** *50% HILL - 100% WARRIOR - OF WHOM I AM EXTREMELY PROUD; SERGEANT MAJOR* **MYRIAM GONZALEZ;** *A GREAT LEADER AND LOYAL FRIEND; COMMAND SERGEANT MAJOR* **"COWBOY" LANE;** *GREATLY ADMIRED-HE "ITCHED" FOR THE FIGHT AS DID D. H. HILL; SERGEANT FIRST CLASS* **BOBBY RIVERA**-*MY PERSONAL SECURITY NCO IN IRAQ–AN NCO TO BE FEARED AND REVERED; DR.* **RICHARD STARNES;** *DESTINED TO BECOME A FINE GENERAL; COLONELS* **MATT** *AND* **BUDDY HOLBERT;** *PROFESSIONAL SOLDIERS - DOUBLE TROUBLE FOR AL QAEDA; MAJOR* **DAVID BLAND;** *AS SKILLED WITH TECHNOLOGY AS A PALMETTO SHARPSHOOTER;* **GRADY HILL** *HIS MUSIC PLEASES AS THE HARP OF KING DAVID;* **LIB HILL SIMPSON** *ISABELLA'S EQUAL IN EVERY RESPECT; FAMILIES OF* **DR. A.P. KITCHIN** *AND* **MYRON WEBB;** *THE TRUEST HILL FAMILY FRIENDS;* **PAUL GALE JR** *(RIP); A BRILLIANT AND INSPIRATIONAL MAN; MASTER SERGEANT* **MARVIN SHERRIN** *(RIP); PATTON'S PRIDE – WWII; MY MOST CHERISHED FRIEND FROM CHILDHOOD TO THIS DAY:* **PATRICIA JANE BOOTH**:*) MY EAST ELEMENTARY MAFIA;* **DON SKINNER**; **MIKE YOUNG; LINDA MILLS; RONNIE ROLLINS; RICHARD WINCHESTER; LANNY STACK; LINDA KESIAH; DANA JACKSON; FRANK GOODWIN; DEDRIA IRVIN; DON RATLIFF; FLOYD LOCKAMEY;** *et al; COLONEL* **PHIL THOMPSON** *MY WAR COLLEGE PROFESSOR–CLASS OF 2004; WHO TAUGHT ME THE IMPORTANCE OF CRITICAL THOUGHT; COLONEL* **TOM CATHEY**; *THE BRAVEST MAN WITH WHOM I EVER SERVED;* **SEVEN SOLDIERS** *WHOM I DIRECTED TO THE BATTLEFIELD BUT DID NOT RETURN (RIP); HEROS ALL;* **MY SOURCES**; *WITHOUT THE EMPIRICAL HISTORICAL DATA PROVIDED THIS ACCURATE DEPICTION OF HISTORY COULD NOT HAVE BEEN POSSIBLE;LET US ALL REMEMBER: WHILE WE MAY SURMISE MUCH ✝ HISTORICAL FACTS REMAIN AS SACROSANCT AS OUR FAITH, OUR FAMILIES, AND OUR ARMY VALUES;*

D.R.H.

HISTORICAL RESEARCH

Validation of this manuscript for historical accuracy has been the author's foremost priority. All assertions contained herein are based upon valid historical documents of the Civil War era; citations all predate [[PD1923]] and are restricted to provide only 1st hand accounts by expositors intimately familiar with the life and career of D. H. Hill; the great majority of citations were extracted directly from the OFFICIAL RECORDs of the Union and Confederate Armies and General Robert E. Lee's OFFICIAL REPORTs of the Army of Northern Virginia. All other citations are attributable to reputable veterans of the Civil War era, with full disclosure and reference available in the bibliography. The overarching pretext has been to validate the character of Lee's Fighting General through application of pure citations of recorded historical data and to invalidate postulated, speculative expositions wholly lacking in diversity and unprejudiced points of view – unjust postulations that have obscured this man's achievements from the recorded annals of modern warfare.

It is the intent and purpose of this manuscript to correct a great injustice placed upon the honor of D. H. Hill specifically and the Hill Family name in general. Through the application of critical thought and comprehensive research, this manuscript stands to wholly exonerate Lieutenant General D. H. Hill [C.S.A.] of the two litigious events adversely affecting the memory of his name: the Lost Dispatch and controversy at the Battle of Chickamauga – citing historical records that clearly vindicate him in the former as having no involvement in the event and exonerate him in the latter from General Braxton Bragg's conduct of the Battle of Chickamauga. History is obliged to remove the inaccurate postulations surrounding both of these litigious events and judge D. H. Hill wholly by the nature of his character, the heroism of his service and the deeds of his life - proclaiming him deserving of past due recognition for his gallantry, heroism, and great service to both the Union and Confederate States of America. May God Rest his Soul.

D.R.H.

D. H. HILL

"Fancy a man in whom the grim determination of a veteran warrior is united to a gentle tenderness of manner . . . . affix a pair of eyes that possess the most indisputably honest and kindly expression; animate him with a mind clear, deep and comprehensive, and imbued with a humor as rich as it is deep and effective; infuse man and mind with a soul which in its lofty views compels subordinates of the material to the spiritual, and holds a supreme trust in the wisdom and goodness of the Almighty – is zealous in the discharge of duty, and looks with scorn on all that is mean and sinful. Add to all these a carriage that is indomitable, and a love of truth and honor which is sublime, and you have the earthly embodiment of D. H. Hill."

[[NC Supreme Court Justice - Colonel A. C. Avery]]

Q14

END NOTES

1 D. H. Hill Grave Monument (1889): Davidson College Cemetery, Davidson, NC – Inscription

2 The Annals of the War (1879): Alexander K. McClure {{PD-1923}} p. 196

3 Southern Historical Society Papers (1885): Vol. XIII & XIV James I. Robertson {{PD-1923}}; p. 125

4 Lives of Distinguished North Carolinians (1898) William Joseph Peele {{PD-1923}} p. 529//Southern Historical Society Papers (1885): Vol. XIII & XIV James I. Robertson {{PD-1923}} p. 117

5 The Land We Love (1868) D. H. Hill (1899); Vol. V – May-Oct 1968; Charlotte, NC – Jas. P. Irwin & D. H. Hill; (1868); p. 272

6 Life of Robert Edward Lee (1906): Henry E. Shepherd {{PD-1923}} full text

7 OFFICIAL RECORDS (OR) of the Union and Confederate Armies (1902): {{PD-1923}} SERIES: I VOLUME: XIX CAMPAIGN: Antietam SERIAL: 028 PAGE: 0281

8 D. H. Hill Papers, NC Archives (1915): [[NC Archives]]

9 The Land We Love (1867-68): Vol. IV, Nov-Apr 1867-68; Daniel Harvey Hill {{PD-1923}} p. 272

10 Holy Bible (1843): Scofield {{PD-1923}} p.593; p.522

11 Lives of Distinguished North Carolinians (1898) William Joseph Peele {{PD-1923}} p. 524

12 D. H. Hill Papers, NC Archives (1915): [[NC Archives]]

13Life and Character of Lieutenant General D. H. Hill (1893): Alphonso C. {{PD-1923}} p. 5

14 The American Generals (1855): John Frost {{PD-1923}} p. 178

15 The Congregationalist (1873): R. W. Dale; J. G. Rogers {{PD-1923}} pp. 43-52

16 The Granite State Monthly (1918): Vol. XIII Otis G. Hammond {{PD-1923}} p. 41

17 The American Generals (1855): John Frost {{PD-1923}} p. 177-178

18 History of South Carolina (1920): Yates Snowden {{PD-1923}} p.384

19 History of South Carolina (1920): Yates Snowden {{PD-1923}} pp.384-385

20 History of the Presbyterian Church of Bethel (1938): Rev. R. A. Webb p. 13

21 The American Generals (1855): John Frost {{PD-1923}} pp. 177-179

22 King's Mountain and its Heroes (1881): L C. Draper; A. Allaire {{PD-1923}} pp. 218-219

23 Col. William Hill's Memoirs of the Revolution (1921): William Hill, AS Salley {{PD-1923}}

24 Lives of Distinguished North Carolinians (1898) William Joseph Peele {{PD-1923}} p. 525-526

25 Col. William Hill's Memoirs of the Revolution (1921): William Hill, AS Salley {{PD-1923}} pp. 11-34

26 Col. William Hill's Memoirs of the Revolution (1921): William Hill, AS Salley {{PD-1923}}

27 Lives of Distinguished North Carolinians (1898) William Joseph Peele {{PD-1923}} p. 524

28 D. H. Hill Papers, NC Archives (1915): [[NC Archives]]//Biography of Daniel Harvey Hill pp. 2-7

29 Life and Character of Lieutenant General D. H. Hill (1893): Alphonso C. {{PD-1923}} p. 5

30 Lives of Distinguished North Carolinians (1898) William Joseph Peele {{PD-1923}} p. 525

31 D. H. Hill Papers, NC Archives (1915): [[NC Archives]]//Biography of Daniel Harvey Hill Lieutenant General, CSA (1886): Joseph M. Hill {{PD-1923}} pp. 2-7

32 Lives of Distinguished North Carolinians (1898) William Joseph Peele {{PD-1923}} p. 525

33 *D. H. Hill Papers, NC Archives (1915): [[NC Archives]]//Biography of Daniel Harvey Hill Lieutenant General, CSA (1886): Joseph M. Hill {{PD-1923}} p. 8*

34 *Confederate Veteran Magazine (1917): R. A. Cunningham Vol. XXV {{PD-1923}} p. 366*

35 *Lives of Distinguished North Carolinians (1898) William Joseph Peele {{PD-1923}} p. 525*

36 *Makers of North Carolina History (1911): R. D. W. Conner {{PD-1923}} p. 223*

37 *Makers of North Carolina History (1911): R. D. W. Conner {{PD-1923}} pp. 223-224*

38 *Southern Historical Society Papers (1885): Vol. XIII & XIV {{PD-1923}} C. D. Fishburne p. 423-443*

39 *Makers of North Carolina History (1911): R. D. W. Conner {{PD-1923}} p. 224*

40 *D. H. Hill Papers, NC Archives (1915): [[NC Archives]] {{PD-1923}} D. H. Hill to wife, Isabella*

41 *D. H. Hill Papers, NC Archives (1915): [[NC Archives]]//Biography of Daniel Harvey Hill Lieutenant General, CSA (1886): Joseph M. Hill {{PD-1923}} p. 8*

42 *Col. William Hill and the Campaign of 1780 (1919): Daniel Harvey Hill {{PD-1923}} pp. 10-11*

43 *D. H. Hill Papers, NC Archives (1915): [[NC Archives]] {{PD-1923}} D.H. Hill to B Johnson May 18, 1887*

44 *D. H. Hill Papers, NC Archives (1915): [[NC Archives]]//Biography of Daniel Harvey Hill Lieutenant General, CSA (1886): Joseph M. Hill {{PD-1923}} p. 9*

45 *Confederate Veteran Magazine (1917): R. A. Cunningham Vol. XXV {{PD-1923}} p. 366*

46 *D. H. Hill Papers, NC Archives (1915): [[NC Archives]]//Biography of Daniel Harvey Hill Lieutenant General, CSA (1886): Joseph M. Hill {{PD-1923}} pp. 9-10*

47 *Lives of Distinguished North Carolinians (1898) William Joseph Peele {{PD-1923}} p. 526*

48 *Biographical History of North Carolina (1908): Samuel A. Ashe {{PD-1923}} P. 144*

49 *A Guidebook to West Point and Vicinity (1844): J. H. Colton {{PD-1923}} pp. 95-96*

50 *Official Register of the Officers and Cadets (1923) USMA Class of 1839-1842 {{PD-1923}} – June 1839 p. 23; June 1840 p. 14; June 1841 p. 11; June 1842 p. 7*

51 *Official Register of the Officers and Cadets (1923) USMA Class of 1839-1842 {{PD-1923}} – June 1839 p. 23; June 1840 p. 14; June 1841 p. 11; June 1842 p. 7*

52 *D. H. Hill Papers, NC Archives (1915): [[NC Archives]] {{PD-1923}} // Western Democrat (1861)*

53 *Register of Cadet Delinquencies (1842) Daniel H. Hill, Vol. 2; 1838-1842; {{PD-1923}} p. 255*

54 *D. H. Hill Papers, NC Archives (1915): [[NC Archives]]//Biography of Daniel Harvey Hill Lieutenant General, CSA (1886): Joseph M. Hill {{PD-1923}} p. 11*

55 *D. H. Hill Papers, NC Archives (1915): [[NC Archives]]//Biography of Daniel Harvey Hill Lieutenant General, CSA (1886): Joseph M. Hill {{PD-1923}} p. 11*

56 *D. H. Hill Grave Monument, Davidson College Cemetery, Davidson, NC – Inscription*

57 *Christ in the Camp (1887): Reverend J. William Jones {{PD-1923}} P. 277*

58 *Confederate Veteran Magazine (1917): R. A. Cunningham Vol. XXV {{PD-1923}} P. 366*

59 *A Fighter from Way Back (2002): Nathaniel C. Hughes Jr. and Timothy D. Johnson; full text*

60 *D. H. Hill Papers, NC Archives (1915): [[NC Archives]] {{PD-1923}}*

61 *D. H. Hill Papers, NC Archives (1915): [[NC Archives]] {{PD-1923}}*

62 *Biographical Register of the Officers and Graduates of the United States Military Academy (1910): Vol. II; George W. Cullum {{PD-1923}}*

63 *D. H. Hill Papers, NC Archives (1915): [[NC Archives]] {{PD-1923}} - Appointment certificate to second lieutenant in the Fourth Regiment of Artillery, from October 13, 1845, signed February 13, 1846 by Sec. War Marcy and President Polk*

64 *D. H. Hill Papers, NC Archives (1915): [[NC Archives]] {{PD-1923}}*

65 *Returns of Fourth Artillery Regiment (1850) June 1846, M727 Fourth Regiment; Jan. 1841-Dec. 1850 {{PD-1923}}*

66 *Returns of Fourth Artillery Regiment (1850) June 1846, M727 Fourth Regiment; Jan. 1841-Dec. 1850 {{PD-1923}}*

67 *D. H. Hill Papers, NC Archives (1915): [[NC Archives]] {{PD-1923}}*

68 *Complete History of the Late Mexican War (1850): {{PD-1923}} pp. 30-49*

69 *Complete History of the Late Mexican War (1850): {{PD-1923}} pp. 30-49//D. H. Hill Papers, NC Archives (1915): [[NC Archives]] {{PD-1923}}*

70 *D. H. Hill Papers, NC Archives (1915): [[NC Archives]] {{PD-1923}}*

71 *History of the Mexican War (1892): Cadmus Marcellus, Mary Rachel Wilcox editors {{PD-1923}} pp. 358-377*

72 *General Zachary Taylor and the Mexican War (1911): A. C. Quisenberry {{PD-1923}} p. 45*

73 *Complete History of the Late Mexican War (1850): {{PD-1923}} pp. 81-90*

74 *D. H. Hill Papers, NC Archives (1915): [[NC Archives]] {{PD-1923}}*

75 *Complete History of the Late Mexican War (1850): {{PD-1923}} pp. 81-90*

76 *Complete History of the Late Mexican War (1850): {{PD-1923}} pp. 81-90*

77 *D. H. Hill Papers, NC Archives (1915): [[NC Archives]] {{PD-1923}}*

78 *D. H. Hill Papers, NC Archives (1915): [[NC Archives]] {{PD-1923}}*

79 *D. H. Hill Papers, NC Archives (1915): [[NC Archives]] {{PD-1923}}*

80 *Thrilling Incidents of the Wars of the United States (1860): J. K. Neff {{PD-1923}} pp. 593-598*

81 *D. H. Hill Papers, NC Archives (1915): [[NC Archives]] {{PD-1923}}*

82 *History of the Mexican War (1892): Cadmus ; Mary Rachel Wilcox editors {{PD-1923}} pp. 378-406*

83 *Thrilling Incidents of the Wars of the United States (1860): J. K. Neff {{PD-1923}} pp. 593-598*

84 *History of the Mexican War (1892): Cadmus Marcellus, Mary Rachel Wilcox editors {{PD-1923}} pp. 443-*

85 *D. H. Hill Papers, NC Archives (1915): [[NC Archives]] {{PD-1923}}*

86 *Lives of Distinguished North Carolinians (1898) William Joseph Peele {{PD-1923}} p. 526*

87 *South Carolina Legislature (1857): the Honorable James Chesnut Jr., President; December 14th 1857, by order of the Senate with full unanimous concurrence of the State House of Representatives, December 14th 1857, Resolution 25*

88 *Lives of Distinguished North Carolinians (1917) W.J. Peele, NC 1898, p. 526 & Confederate Veteran Magazine (1917): R. A. Cunningham Vol. XXV {{PD-1923}} p. 366*

89 *D. H. Hill Papers, NC Archives (1915): [[NC Archives]] {{PD-1923}}*

90 *D. H. Hill Papers, NC Archives (1915): [[NC Archives]] {{PD-1923}}*

91 *D. H. Hill Papers, NC Archives (1915): [[NC Archives]] {{PD-1923}}*

92 *D. H. Hill Papers, NC Archives (1915): [[NC Archives]] {{PD-1923}}*

93 *D. H. Hill Papers, NC Archives (1915): [[NC Archives]]//Biography of Daniel Harvey Hill Lieutenant General, CSA (1886): Joseph M. Hill {{PD-1923}} p. 10*

94 D. H. Hill Papers, NC Archives (1915): [[NC Archives]]//Biography of Daniel Harvey Hill Lieutenant General, CSA (1886): Joseph M. Hill {{PD-1923}} p. 10

95 D. H. Hill Papers, NC Archives (1915): [[NC Archives]] {{PD-1923}}

96 D. H. Hill Papers, NC Archives (1915): [[NC Archives]] {{PD-1923}}

97 D. H. Hill Papers, NC Archives (1915): [[NC Archives]]//Biography of Daniel Harvey Hill Lieutenant General, CSA (1886): Joseph M. Hill {{PD-1923}} p. 11

98 Biographical History of North Carolina (1908): Samuel A. Ashe {{PD-1923}} P. 138

99 Fishburne, C. D. (1890) North Carolina Division of Archives and History, Raleigh, NC Feb 8, 1890 p. 12

100 The North Carolina Booklet (1916): Vol. XVI; April 1917; No. 4; NC DAR {{PD-1923}} p. 194

101 D. H. Hill Papers, NC Archives (1915): [[NC Archives]] {{PD-1923}}

102 The North Carolina Booklet (1916): Vol. XVI; April 1917; No. 4; NC DAR {{PD-1923}} p. 194

103 The North Carolina Booklet (1916): Vol. XVI; April 1917; No. 4; NC DAR {{PD-1923}} p. 195

104 College Discipline: an inaugural address 28 Feb (1855) D. H. Hill {{PD-1923}} p. 3

105 D. H. Hill Papers, NC Archives (1915): [[NC Archives]]//Biography of Daniel Harvey Hill Lieutenant General, CSA (1886): Joseph M. Hill {{PD-1923}} p. 10

106 D. H. Hill Papers, NC Archives (1915): [[NC Archives]]//Biography of Daniel Harvey Hill Lieutenant General, CSA (1886): Joseph M. Hill {{PD-1923}} pp. 10-11

107 Fishburne, C. D. (1890) North Carolina Division of Archives and History, Raleigh, NC Feb 8, 1890 p. 12

108 College Discipline: an inaugural address 28 Feb (1855) D. H. Hill {{PD-1923}} full text

109 College Discipline: an inaugural address 28 Feb (1855) D. H. Hill {{PD-1923}} p. 6

110 D. H. Hill Papers, NC Archives (1915): [[NC Archives]]//Biography of Daniel Harvey Hill Lieutenant General, CSA (1886): Joseph M. Hill {{PD-1923}} pp. 16-18

111 Charlotte Observer (1961): newspaper article on Davidson College 3 Dec 1961

112 Elements of Algebra (1857): Daniel Harvey Hill {{PD-1923}} full text

113 A Consideration of the Sermon on the Mount (1858): Daniel Harvey Hill (1858) {{PD-1923}} full text

114 The Crucifixion of Christ (1859): Daniel Harvey Hill {{PD-1923}} - full text.

115 D. H. Hill Papers, NC Archives (1915): [[NC Archives]] {{PD-1923}}//The Rebellion Record (1861): Vol. 4; Moore; Everett {{PD-1923}} pp. 48-49

116 The North Carolina Booklet (1916): Vol. XVI; April 1917; No. 4; NC DAR {{PD-1923}} p. 193

117 D. H. Hill Papers, NC Archives (1915): [[NC Archives]] {{PD-1923}}

118 D. H. Hill Papers, NC Archives (1915): [[NC Archives]] {{PD-1923}}

119 Confederate Military History (1899): Clement Anselm Evans Vol. 1 {{PD-1923}} p. 306

120 The North Carolina Booklet (1916): Vol. XVI; April 1917; No. 4; NC DAR {{PD-1923}} P. 200

121 D. H. Hill Papers, NC Archives (1915): [[NC Archives]] {{PD-1923}}

122 D. H. Hill Papers, NC Archives (1915): [[NC Archives]] {{PD-1923}}

123 D. H. Hill Papers, NC Archives (1915): [[NC Archives]] {{PD-1923}}

124 Lives of Distinguished North Carolinians (1898) William Joseph Peele {{PD-1923}} p. 528

125 Under Both Flags - Tales of the Civil War (1896): George M. Vickers {{PD-1923}} p. 314

126 Under Both Flags - Tales of the Civil War (1896): George M. Vickers {{PD-1923}} p. 314

127 *Under Both Flags - Tales of the Civil War (1896): George M. Vickers {{PD-1923}} p. 314*

128 *Under Both Flags - Tales of the Civil War (1896): George M. Vickers {{PD-1923}} p. 314*

129 *Under Both Flags - Tales of the Civil War (1896): George M. Vickers {{PD-1923}} p. 314*

130 *Under Both Flags - Tales of the Civil War (1896): George M. Vickers {{PD-1923}} pp. 314-315. 314*

131 *Under Both Flags - Tales of the Civil War (1896): George M. Vickers {{PD-1923}} p. 315*

132 *Under Both Flags - Tales of the Civil War (1896): George M. Vickers {{PD-1923}} p. 316*

133 *Lives of Distinguished North Carolinians (1898) William Joseph Peele {{PD-1923}} p. 528*

134 *Western Democrat (1861) Charlotte newspaper; Charlotte, NC, WD; (1861) June 29, 1858 {{PD-1923}}*

135 *Western Democrat (1861) Charlotte newspaper; Charlotte, NC, WD; (1861) June 29, 1858 {{PD-1923}}*

136 *Western Democrat (1861) Charlotte newspaper; Charlotte, NC, WD; (1861) August 3, 1858 {{PD-1923}}*

137 *Western Democrat (1861) Charlotte newspaper; Charlotte, NC, WD; (1861) Sep 28, 1858 {{PD-1923}}*

138 *Charlotte Observer (1889): newspaper article {{PD-1923}}*

139 *D. H. Hill Papers, NC Archives (1915): [[NC Archives]] {{PD-1923}}*

140 *Western Democrat (1861) Charlotte newspaper; Charlotte, NC, WD; (1861) Sep 6, 1858 {{PD-1923}}*

141*Catalogue of the Officers and Cadets of the North Carolina Military Institute (1861): Charlotte, N.C. 1st Session. 1859-60 (Charlotte: 1860) {{PD-1923}} pp.5, 8, 15-17*

142 *General James H. Lane Speech delivered at Auburn, Alabama by General Lane; College Archives, Davidson College Library, Davidson, N.C.*

143 *The Rebellion Record (1861): Vol. 8; Moore; Everett {{PD-1923}} // Western Democrat (1861) Charlotte newspaper; Charlotte, NC, WD; (1861) May 21, 1861 {{PD-1923}}*

144 *Lives of Distinguished North Carolinians (1898) William Joseph Peele {{PD-1923}} p. 528*

145 *Address delivered before the Confederate Veterans Association (1898): WC Hartridge {{PD-1923}} p. 45*

146 *The Rebellion Record (1861): Vol. 2; Moore; Everett {{PD-1923}} p. 263*

147 *The Rebellion Record (1861): Vol. 3; Moore; Everett {{PD-1923}} pp. 263-264*

148 *D. H. Hill Papers, NC Archives (1915): [[NC Archives]] {{PD-1923}}*

149 *Stonewall Jackson – The life and military career of T. J. Jackson (1863): Markinfield {{PD-1923}} p. 207*

150*Life and Character of Lieutenant General D. H. Hill (1893): Alphonso C. {{PD-1923}} pp. 8-9*

151 *Southern Historical Society Papers (1885): Vol. XIII & XIV James I. Robertson {{PD-1923}} p. 115*

152 *The Battle of Great Bethel (1864): Frank I. Wilson {{PD-1923}} P. 5*

153 *The Battle of Great Bethel (1864): Frank I. Wilson {{PD-1923}} pp. 5-6*

154 *The Battle of Great Bethel (1864): Frank I. Wilson {{PD-1923}} p. 6*

155 *The Battle of Great Bethel (1864): Frank I. Wilson {{PD-1923}} pp. 6-7*

156 *The Battle of Great Bethel (1864): Frank I. Wilson {{PD-1923}} pp. 7-8*

157 *The Battle of Great Bethel (1864): Frank I. Wilson {{PD-1923}} p. 8*

158 *The Battle of Great Bethel (1864): Frank I. Wilson {{PD-1923}} pp. 8-9*

159 *The Battle of Great Bethel (1864): Frank I. Wilson {{PD-1923}} p. 10*

160 *The Battle of Great Bethel (1864): Frank I. Wilson {{PD-1923}} p. 11*

161 *The Battle of Great Bethel (1864): Frank I. Wilson {{PD-1923}} pp. 11-12*

162 *The Battle of Great Bethel (1864): Frank I. Wilson {{PD-1923}} p. 12*

163 *The Battle of Great Bethel (1864): Frank I. Wilson {{PD-1923}} pp. 12-13*

164 *The Battle of Great Bethel (1864): Frank I. Wilson {{PD-1923}} pp. 13-14*

165 *The Battle of Great Bethel (1864): Frank I. Wilson {{PD-1923}} p. 14*

166 *The Battle of Great Bethel (1864): Frank I. Wilson {{PD-1923}} pp. 14-15*

167 *The Battle of Great Bethel (1864): Frank I. Wilson {{PD-1923}} p. 15*

168 *The Battle of Great Bethel (1864): Frank I. Wilson {{PD-1923}} pp. 15-16*

169 *The Battle of Great Bethel (1864): Frank I. Wilson {{PD-1923}} p. 16*

170 *The Battle of Great Bethel (1864): Frank I. Wilson {{PD-1923}} pp. 16-17*

171 *The Battle of Great Bethel (1864): Frank I. Wilson {{PD-1923}} p. 17*

172 *The Battle of Great Bethel (1864): Frank I. Wilson {{PD-1923}} p. 17*

173 *The Battle of Great Bethel (1864): Frank I. Wilson {{PD-1923}} pp. 17-18*

174 *The Battle of Great Bethel (1864): Frank I. Wilson {{PD-1923}} p. 18*

175 *The Battle of Great Bethel (1864): Frank I. Wilson {{PD-1923}} pp. 18-19*

176 *The Battle of Great Bethel (1864): Frank I. Wilson {{PD-1923}} p. 19*

177 *OFFICIAL RECORDS (OR) of the Union and Confederate Armies (1902): {{PD-1923} Reel 221 - Call Number 1890601.1*

178 *The Rebellion Record (1861): Vol. 1; Moore; Everett {{PD-1923}}//Charleston Mercury (1861); newspaper article 11 May 1861 {{PD-1923}}*

179 *Biography of Daniel Harvey Hill Lieutenant General, CSA (1886): Joseph M. Hill {{PD-1923}} p. 12*

180 *OFFICIAL RECORDS (OR) of the Union and Confederate Armies (1902): {{PD-1923}} Vol. 1-128 et al; Vol. II, Part 1 Serial 1, Chapter IX; p. 914*

181 *Biographical History of North Carolina (1908): Samuel A. Ashe {{PD-1923}} P. 139*

182 *OFFICIAL RECORDS (OR) of the Union and Confederate Armies (1902): {{PD-1923}} Vol. 1-128 et al; Vol. II, Part 1 Serial 1, Chapter IX; p. 913*

183 *Biography of Daniel Harvey Hill Lieutenant General, CSA (1886): Joseph M. Hill {{PD-1923}} p. 12*

184 *Biographical History of North Carolina (1908): Samuel A. Ashe {{PD-1923}} P. 139*

185 *OFFICIAL RECORDS (OR) of the Union and Confederate Armies (1902): {{PD-1923}} Vol. 1-128 et al; Vol.*

186 *Biography of Daniel Harvey Hill Lieutenant General, CSA (1886): Joseph M. Hill {{PD-1923}} p. 12*

187 *Lives of Distinguished North Carolinians (1898) William Joseph Peele {{PD-1923}} p. 531*

188 *OFFICIAL RECORDS (OR) of the Union and Confederate Armies (1902): {{PD-1923}} Vol. 1-128 et al; Vol. II, Part 1 Serial 1, Chapter IX; pp. 913*

189 *Biography of Daniel Harvey Hill Lieutenant General, CSA (1886): Joseph M. Hill {{PD-1923}} p. 12*

190 *Biographical History of North Carolina (1908): Samuel A. Ashe {{PD-1923}} P. 139*

191 *Raleigh Register (1861) Newspaper Article -Battle of Big Bethel {{PD-1923}} 1861-1865--Casualties; Wyatt, Henry Lawson, 1842-1861*

192 *OFFICIAL RECORDS (OR) of the Union and Confederate Armies (1902): {{PD-1923}} Vol. 1-128 et al; Vol. II, Part 1 Serial 1, Chapter IX; pp. 913-914*

193 D. H. Hill Papers, NC Archives (1915): [[NC Archives]]//Biography of Daniel Harvey Hill Lieutenant General, CSA (1886): Joseph M. Hill {{PD-1923}} p. 12

194 Lives of Distinguished North Carolinians (1898) William Joseph Peele {{PD-1923}} p. 531

195 Biographical History of North Carolina (1908): Samuel A. Ashe {{PD-1923}} P. 139

196 Lives of Distinguished North Carolinians (1898) William Joseph Peele {{PD-1923}} p. 532

197 Consolidated index to compiled service records of Confederate Soldiers (1957) US National Archives and Records; CSA {{PD-1923}} Reel 221 - Call Number 1890601.1

198 D. H. Hill Papers, NC Archives (1915): [[NC Archives]] {{PD-1923}}//Biography of Daniel Harvey Hill Lieutenant General, CSA (1886): Joseph M. Hill {{PD-1923}} p. 12

199 Literary and Historical Activities in North Carolina (1900-1905): William Joseph Peele {{PD-1923}} p. 427 - cites newspaper article: Petersburg Express (p. 104, Vol. I, N. C. Regiments 1861-'65)

200 Consolidated index to compiled service records of Confederate Soldiers (1957) US National Archives and Records; CSA {{PD-1923}} Reel 221 - Call Number 1890601.1

201 History of the Civil War in America (1875): Vol. I-IV Comte de Paris {{PD-1923}} pp. 1-4

202 Confederate Military History (1899): Clement Anselm Evans Vol. I {{PD-1923}} PP. 269-273

203 OFFICIAL RECORDS (OR) of the Union and Confederate Armies (1902): {{PD-1923}} SERIES: I VOLUME: XI CAMPAIGN: Peninsular Campaign SERIAL: 014 PAGE: 0677

204 OFFICIAL RECORDS (OR) of the Union and Confederate Armies (1902): {{PD-1923}} SERIES: I VOLUME: XI CAMPAIGN: Peninsular Campaign SERIAL: 014 PAGE: 0675

205 D. H. Hill Papers, NC Archives (1915): [[NC Archives]] {{PD-1923}}//Biography of Daniel Harvey Hill Lieutenant General, CSA (1886): Joseph M. Hill {{PD-1923}} p. 12

206 Consolidated index to compiled service records of Confederate Soldiers (1957) US National Archives and Records; CSA {{PD-1923}} Reel 221 - Call Number 1890601.1

207 Biographical History of North Carolina (1908): Samuel A. Ashe {{PD-1923}} P. 140

208 Irish-American History of the United States (1907): John O'Hanlon {{PD-1923}} p. 411

209 D. H. Hill Papers, NC Archives (1915): [[NC Archives]] {{PD-1923}}//Biography of Daniel Harvey Hill Lieutenant General, CSA (1886): Joseph M. Hill {{PD-1923}} p. 12

210 The North Carolina Booklet (1916): Vol. XVI; April 1917; No. 4; NC DAR {{PD-1923}} p. 144

211 D. H. Hill Papers, NC Archives (1915): [[NC Archives]] {{PD-1923}}//Biography of Daniel Harvey Hill Lieutenant General, CSA (1886): Joseph M. Hill {{PD-1923}} p. 12

212 Consolidated index to compiled service records of Confederate Soldiers (1957) US National Archives and Records; CSA {{PD-1923}} Reel 221 - Call Number 1890601.1

213 OFFICIAL RECORDS (OR) of the Union and Confederate Armies (1902): {{PD-1923}} SERIES: I VOLUME: XI CAMPAIGN: Peninsular Campaign SERIAL: 014 PAGE: 0683

214 D. H. Hill Papers, NC Archives (1915): [[NC Archives]] {{PD-1923}}//Biography of Daniel Harvey Hill Lieutenant General, CSA (1886): Joseph M. Hill {{PD-1923}} p. 12

215 Consolidated index to compiled service records of Confederate Soldiers (1957) US National Archives and Records; CSA {{PD-1923}} Reel 221 - Call Number 1890601.1

216 Lieutenant General Jubal Anderson Early CSA (1912): Jubal A. Early; R. H. Early {{PD-1923}} p. 69

217 Battle of Williamsburg (1880) Richard Maury {{PD-1923}} pp. 4-6

218 OFFICIAL RECORDS (OR) of the Union and Confederate Armies (1902): {{PD-1923}} SERIES: I VOLUME: XI CAMPAIGN: Peninsular Campaign SERIAL: 012 PAGE: 0939

219 Battle of Williamsburg (1880) Richard Maury {{PD-1923}} p. 7

220 *Battle of Williamsburg (1880) Richard Maury {{PD-1923}} p.8*

221 *Battle of Williamsburg (1880) Richard Maury {{PD-1923}} pp. 9-10*

222 *Battle of Williamsburg (1880) Richard Maury {{PD-1923}} pp. 11-12*

223 *Battle of Williamsburg (1880) Richard Maury {{PD-1923}} pp. 13-15*

224 *Battle of Williamsburg (1880) Richard Maury {{PD-1923}} p. 1*

225 *D. H. Hill Papers, NC Archives (1915): [[NC Archives]] {{PD-1923}}//Biography of Daniel Harvey Hill Lieutenant General, CSA (1886): Joseph M. Hill {{PD-1923}} p. 12*

226 *Biographical History of North Carolina (1908): Samuel A. Ashe {{PD-1923}} P. 140*

227 *Lives of Distinguished North Carolinians (1898) William Joseph Peele {{PD-1923}} p. 535*

228 *Battle-Fields of the South (1864): English Combatant {{PD-1923}} Vol. II, p. 1*

229 *Consolidated Index to compiled service records of Confederate Soldiers (1957) US National Archives*

230 *Battle-Fields of the South (1864): English Combatant {{PD-1923}} vol. 2, p. 2*

231 *OFFICIAL RECORDS (OR) of the Union and Confederate Armies (1902): {{PD-1923}} Volume XI | Pages range from 1 to 1077*

232 *OFFICIAL RECORDS (OR) of the Union and Confederate Armies (1902): {{PD-1923}} Volume XI | Pages range from 1 to 1077*

233 *Battle-Fields of the South (1864): English Combatant {{PD-1923}} Vol. 2, p. 2*

234 *OFFICIAL RECORDS (OR) of the Union and Confederate Armies (1902): {{PD-1923}}   SERIES 1, Vol. 11, Part 1 (Peninsular Campaign) pp. 944*

235 *OFFICIAL RECORDS (OR) of the Union and Confederate Armies (1902): {{PD-1923}} SERIES 1, Vol. 11,*

236 *OFFICIAL RECORDS (OR) of the Union and Confederate Armies (1902): {{PD-1923}} Volume XI | P. 943*

237 *Battle-Fields of the South (1864): English Combatant {{PD-1923}} Vol. 2, p. 3*

238 *Battle-Fields of the South (1864): English Combatant {{PD-1923}} Vol. 2, p. 4*

239 *OFFICIAL RECORDS (OR) of the Union and Confederate Armies (1902): {{PD-1923}} SERIES 1, Vol. 11, Part 1 (Peninsular Campaign) pp. 944*

240 *Battle-Fields of the South (1864): English Combatant {{PD-1923}} Vol. 2, p. 4*

241 *The Battle of Bentonville (1905) L. M. Wood; NY, NY, Neale Publishing Co; (1905); not in copyright; {{PD-1923}} pp. 53-62*

242 *OFFICIAL RECORDS (OR) of the Union and Confederate Armies (1902): {{PD-1923}} SERIES 1, Vol. 11, Part 1 (Peninsular Campaign) pp. 943*

243 *Battle-Fields of the South (1864): English Combatant {{PD-1923}} Vol. 2, p. 5*

244 *Battle-Fields of the South (1864): English Combatant {{PD-1923}} Vol. 2, p. 6*

245 *OFFICIAL RECORDS (OR) of the Union and Confederate Armies (1902): {{PD-1923}} SERIES 1, Vol. 11,*

246 *Battle-Fields of the South (1864): English Combatant {{PD-1923}} Vol. 2, p. 6*

247 *Battle-Fields of the South (1864): English Combatant {{PD-1923}} Vol. 2, pp. 7-8*

248 *OFFICIAL RECORDS (OR) of the Union and Confederate Armies (1902): {{PD-1923}} SERIES 1, Vol. 11, Part 1 (Peninsular Campaign) pp. 944*

249 *OFFICIAL RECORDS (OR) of the Union and Confederate Armies (1902): {{PD-1923}} SERIES 1, Vol. 11, Part 1 (Peninsular Campaign) pp. 944*

250 *OFFICIAL RECORDS (OR) of the Union and Confederate Armies (1902): {{PD-1923}} SERIES 1, Vol. 11, Part 1 (Peninsular Campaign) pp. 944-945*

251 Battle-Fields of the South (1864): English Combatant {{PD-1923}} Vol. 2, p. 9

252 OFFICIAL RECORDS (OR) of the Union and Confederate Armies (1902): {{PD-1923}} SERIES 1, Vol. 11, Part 1 (Peninsular Campaign) pp. 946

253 OFFICIAL RECORDS (OR) of the Union and Confederate Armies (1902): {{PD-1923}} SERIES 1, Vol. 11, Part 1 (Peninsular Campaign) pp. 946

54 OFFICIAL RECORDS (OR) of the Union and Confederate Armies (1902): {{PD-1923}} SERIES 1, Vol. 11, Part 1 (Peninsular Campaign) pp. 946

255 Battle-Fields of the South (1864): English Combatant {{PD-1923}} Vol. 2, p. 10

256 Lives of Distinguished North Carolinians (1898) William Joseph Peele {{PD-1923}} p. 526

257 D. H. Hill Papers, NC Archives (1915): [[NC Archives]] {{PD-1923}}//Biography of Daniel Harvey Hill Lieutenant General, CSA (1886): Joseph M. Hill {{PD-1923}} p. 12

258 D. H. Hill Papers, NC Archives (1915): [[NC Archives]] {{PD-1923}}//Biography of Daniel Harvey Hill Lieutenant General, CSA (1886): Joseph M. Hill {{PD-1923}} p. 12

259 Consolidated index to compiled service records of Confederate Soldiers (1957) US National Archives and Records; CSA {{PD-1923}} Reel 221 - Call Number 1890601

260 Confederate War Journal Illustrated (1894): John B. Gordon {{PD-1923}} p. 5

261 Battle-Fields of the South (1864): English Combatant {{PD-1923}} Vol. 2, pp. 119-121

262 From Manassas to Appomattox - Memoirs of the Civil War (1895): Longstreet {{PD-1923}} pp. 112-113

263 General Lee (1894) Fitzhugh Lee; NY, NY, D. Appleton & Co; (1894); not in copyright; {{PD-1923}} Chapter 8 - Copy of General Order 75 dated 24 June 1862

264 OFFICIAL RECORDS (OR) of the Union and Confederate Armies (1902): {{PD-1923}} SERIES: I VOLUME: XI CAMPAIGN: Peninsular Campaign SERIAL: 014 PAGE: 0584

265 The Rebellion Record (1861): Vol. 9; Moore; Everett {{PD-1923}} p. 288

266 OFFICIAL RECORDS (OR) of the Union and Confederate Armies (1902): {{PD-1923}} SERIES 1, Vol. XXII, Part II (Peninsular Campaign) pp. 490

267 OFFICIAL REPORTs -Operations of the Army of Northern Virginia (1864): Robert E. Lee {{PD-1923}} p. 4-5

268 OFFICIAL REPORTs - Operations of the Army of Northern Virginia (1864): Robert E. Lee {{PD-1923}} p. 5

269 OFFICIAL REPORTs-Operations of the Army of Northern Virginia (1864): Robert E. Lee {{PD-1923}} pp. 5-6

270 OFFICIAL REPORTs - Operations of the Army of Northern Virginia (1864): Robert E. Lee {{PD-1923}} p. 5

271 OFFICIAL REPORTs - Operations of the Army of Northern Virginia (1864): Robert E. Lee {{PD-1923}} p. 6

272 Consolidated index to compiled service records of Confederate Soldiers (1957) US National Archives and Records; CSA {{PD-1923}} Reel 221 - Call Number 1890601.1

273 Life and Campaigns of Lieut. Gen. Thomas J. Jackson (1865): Robert L. Dabney {{PD-1923}} p. 6

274 The Rebellion Record (1861): Vol. 9; Moore; Everett {{PD-1923}} document 13 - p. 267

275 OFFICIAL REPORTs - Operations of the Army of Northern Virginia (1864): Robert E. Lee {{PD-1923}} p. 6

276 OFFICIAL REPORTs - Operations of the Army of Northern Virginia (1864):Robert E Lee {{PD-1923}} pp. 6-7

277 Confederate War Journal Illustrated (1894): John B. Gordon {{PD-1923}} p. 5

278 OFFICIAL REPORTs - Operations of the Army of Northern Virginia (1864): Robert E. Lee {{PD-1923}} p. 6

279 Battle-Fields of the South (1864): English Combatant {{PD-1923}} Vol. 2, p. 119

280 OFFICIAL REPORTs - Operations of the Army of Northern Virginia(1864): Robert E Lee {{PD-1923}} pp. 6-7

281 OFFICIAL REPORTs - Operations of the Army of Northern Virginia (1864): Robert E. Lee {{PD-1923}} p. 7

282 OFFICIAL REPORTs - Operations of the Army of Northern Virginia(1864): Robert E Lee {{PD-1923}} pp. 7-8

283 OFFICIAL REPORTs - Operations of the Army of Northern Virginia (1864): Robert E. Lee {{PD-1923}} p. 7

284 OFFICIAL REPORTs - Operations of the Army of Northern Virginia (1864):Robert E Lee {{PD-1923}} pp. 7-8

285 OFFICIAL REPORTs - Operations of the Army of Northern Virginia (1864): Robert E. Lee {{PD-1923}} p. 8

286 Battle-Fields of the South (1864): English Combatant {{PD-1923}} Vol. 2, p. 122//OFFICIAL RECORDS (OR) of the Union and Confederate Armies (1902): {{PD-1923}} SERIES 1, Vol. XXII, Part II (Peninsular Campaign) pp. 490)

287 Battle-Fields of the South (1864): English Combatant {{PD-1923}} Vol. 2, p. 123

288 OFFICIAL REPORTs - Operations of the Army of Northern Virginia (1864): Robert E. Lee {{PD-1923}} p. 8

289 OFFICIAL RECORDS (OR) of the Union and Confederate Armies (1902): {{PD-1923}} SERIES 1, Vol. XXII, Part II (Peninsular Campaign) pp. 490

290 OFFICIAL REPORTs - Operations of the Army of Northern Virginia (1864): Robert E. Lee {{PD-1923}} p. 8

291 Confederate War Journal Illustrated (1894): John B. Gordon {{PD-1923}} pp. 5 & 7

292 OFFICIAL REPORTs - Operations of the Army of Northern Virginia (1864) Robert E Lee {{PD-1923}} pp. 7-8

293 OFFICIAL REPORTs - Operations of the Army of Northern Virginia (1864): Robert E. Lee {{PD-1923}} p. 8

294 OFFICIAL REPORTs - Operations of the Army of Northern Virginia(1864):Robert E. Lee {{PD-1923}} pp. 7-8

295 Battle-Fields of the South (1864): English Combatant {{PD-1923}} Vol. 2, pp. 123-124

296 OFFICIAL RECORDS (OR) of the Union and Confederate Armies (1902): {{PD-1923}} SERIES 1, Vol. XI, Part 2, p. 623

297 OFFICIAL RECORDS (OR) of the Union and Confederate Armies (1902): {{PD-1923}} SERIES 1, Vol. XXII, Part II (Peninsular Campaign) pp. 490-491

298 OFFICIAL REPORTs - Operations of the Army of Northern Virginia (1864): Robert E. Lee {{PD-1923}} p. 8

299 OFFICIAL REPORTs-Operations of the Army of Northern Virginia (1864):Robert E. Lee {{PD-1923}} pp. 8-9

300 OFFICIAL REPORTs - Operations of the Army of Northern Virginia (1864): Robert E. Lee {{PD-1923}} p. 9

301 OFFICIAL REPORTs - Operations of the Army of Northern Virginia (1864): Robert E. Lee {{PD-1923}} p. 9

302 OFFICIAL REPORTs - Operations of the Army of Northern Virginia(1864)Robert E Lee {{PD-1923}} pp. 9-10

303 The Rebellion Record (1861): Vol. 9; Moore; Everett {{PD-1923}} document 13 - p. 269

304 OFFICIAL REPORTs - Operations of the Army of Northern Virginia (1864): Robert E. Lee {{PD-1923}} p. 9

305   Battle-Fields of the South (1864): English Combatant {{PD-1923}} Vol. 2, p. 124

306 The Rebellion Record (1861): Vol. 5; Moore; Everett {{PD-1923}} pp. 250-251

307 OFFICIAL RECORDS (OR) of the Union and Confederate Armies (1902): {{PD-1923}} SERIES 1, Vol. XXII, Part II (Peninsular Campaign) pp. 492-493

308 Battle-Fields of the South (1864): English Combatant {{PD-1923}} Vol. 2, pp. 125-126

309 OFFICIAL RECORDS (OR) of the Union and Confederate Armies (1902): {{PD-1923}} SERIES 1, Vol. XXII, Part II (Peninsular Campaign) pp. 493-494)

310 Consolidated index to compiled service records of Confederate Soldiers (1957) US National Archives and Records; CSA {{PD-1923}} Reel 221 - Call Number 1890601.1

311 Confederate Military History (1899): Clement Anselm Evans Vol. 1 {{PD-1923}} P. 286

312 OFFICIAL RECORDS (OR) of the Union and Confederate Armies (1902): {{PD-1923}} SERIES 1, Vol. XXII, Part II (Peninsular Campaign) pp. 494)//The Rebellion Record (1861): Vol. 5; Moore; Everett {{PD-1923}} pp. 250-251

313 Confederate Military History (1899): J. Hotchkiss Vol. III {{PD-1923}} p. 287

314 The Rebellion Record (1861): Vol. 9; Moore; Everett {{PD-1923}} document 13 - p. 326

315 OFFICIAL RECORDS (OR) of the Union and Confederate Armies (1902): {{PD-1923}} SERIES 1, Vol. XXII, Part II (Peninsular Campaign) pp. 494

316 Confederate Military History (1899): J. Hotchkiss Vol. III {{PD-1923}} pp. 288-289

317 OFFICIAL RECORDS (OR) of the Union and Confederate Armies (1902): {{PD-1923}} SERIES 1, Vol. XXII, Part II (Peninsular Campaign) pp. 494-495

318 Confederate Military History (1899): J. Hotchkiss Vol. III {{PD-1923}} P. 289

319 The Rebellion Record (1861): Vol. 6; Moore; Everett {{PD-1923}} p. 106

320 Confederate Military History (1899): J. Hotchkiss Vol. III {{PD-1923}} P. 290

321 OFFICIAL RECORDS (OR) of the Union and Confederate Armies (1902): {{PD-1923}} SERIES 1, Vol. XXII, Part II (Peninsular Campaign) pp. 495

322 Confederate Military History (1899): J. Hotchkiss Vol. III {{PD-1923}} P. 291

323 Confederate Military History (1899): J. Hotchkiss Vol. III {{PD-1923}} P. 292

324 Biographical History of North Carolina (1908): Samuel A. Ashe {{PD-1923}} P. 141

325 OFFICIAL RECORDS (OR) of the Union and Confederate Armies (1902): {{PD-1923}}   SERIES 1, Vol. XI, Part 2, p. 626.

326 Lives of Distinguished North Carolinians (1898) William Joseph Peele {{PD-1923}} p. 534

327 OFFICIAL REPORTs - Operations of the Army of Northern Virginia (1864): Robert E. Lee {{PD-1923}} p. 10

328 The Rebellion Record (1861): Vol. 5; Moore; Everett {{PD-1923}} p. 254

329 OFFICIAL REPORTs - Operations of the Army of Northern Virginia (1864): Robert E. Lee {{PD-1923}} p. 10

330 OFFICIAL REPORTs-Operations of the Army of Northern Virginia(1864) Robert E Lee{{PD-1923}} pp. 10-11

331 Confederate War Journal Illustrated (1894): John B. Gordon {{PD-1923}} p. 7

332 OFFICIAL REPORTs - Operations of the Army of Northern Virginia (1864): Robert E. Lee {{PD-1923}} p. 10

333 OFFICIAL REPORTs - Operations of the Army of Northern Virginia (1864) Robert E. Lee {{PD-1923}} p. 256

334 OFFICIAL REPORTs - Operations of the Army of Northern Virginia (1864): Robert E. Lee {{PD-1923}} p. 10

335 OFFICIAL REPORTs-Operations of the Army of Northern Virginia(1864):Robert E Lee {{PD-1923}} pp 10-11

336 Consolidated index to compiled service records of Confederate Soldiers (1957) US National Archives and Records; CSA {{PD-1923}} Reel 221 - Call Number 1890601.1

337 OFFICIAL REPORTs - Operations of the Army of Northern Virginia (1864): Robert E. Lee {{PD-1923}} p. 10

338 Confederate War Journal Illustrated (1894): John B. Gordon {{PD-1923}} p. 10

339 OFFICIAL REPORTs - Operations of the Army of Northern Virginia (1864): Robert E. Lee {{PD-1923}} p. 10

340 The Rebellion Record (1861): Vol. 9; Moore; Everett {{PD-1923}} p.271

341 OFFICIAL REPORTs - Operations of the Army of Northern Virginia (1864): Robert E. Lee {{PD-1923}} p. 10

342 OFFICIAL REPORTs - Operations of the Army of Northern Virginia (1864): Robert E. Lee {{PD-1923}} p. 12

343 Battles and Leaders of the Civil War (1887-1888): Vol. 2 R. U. Johnson; C. Buel; {{PD-1923}} p. 386

344 Battles and Leaders of the Civil War (1887-1888): Vol. 2 R. U. Johnson; C. Buel; {{PD-1923}} p. 391

345 OFFICIAL RECORDS (OR) of the Union and Confederate Armies (1902): {{PD-1923}} SERIES 1, Vol. XXII, Part II (Peninsular Campaign) pp. 495

346 Battles and Leaders of the Civil War (1887-1888): Vol. 2 R. U. Johnson; C. Buel; {{PD-1923}} p. 391

347 Confederate War Journal Illustrated (1894): John B. Gordon {{PD-1923}} pp. 10-11

348 The American Conflict: A History of Great Rebellion in the USA (1866): Horace Greely {{PD-1923}} p. 165

349 OFFICIAL RECORDS (OR) of the Union and Confederate Armies (1902): {{PD-1923}} SERIES 1, Vol. XXII, Part II (Peninsular Campaign) pp. 495

350 Consolidated index to compiled service records of Confederate Soldiers (1957) US National Archives and Records; CSA {{PD-1923}} Reel 221 - Call Number 1890601.1

351 OFFICIAL RECORDS (OR) of the Union and Confederate Armies (1902): {{PD-1923}} SERIES 1, Vol. XXII, Part II (Peninsular Campaign) pp. 495-496

352 OFFICIAL REPORTs - Operations of the Army of Northern Virginia (1864): Robert E. Lee {{PD-1923}} pp. 11-12

353 OFFICIAL REPORTs - Operations of the Army of Northern Virginia (1864): Robert E. Lee {{PD-1923}} p. 12

354 Battles and Leaders of the Civil War (1887-1888): Vol. 2 R. U. Johnson; C. Buel; {{PD-1923}} p. 391

355 The Science of War (1908) G. F. R. Henderson {{PD-1923}} p. 442

356 Battles and Leaders of the Civil War (1887-1888): Vol. 2 R. U. Johnson; C. Buel; {{PD-1923}} p. 391

357 OFFICIAL RECORDS (OR) of the Union and Confederate Armies (1902): {{PD-1923}} SERIES 1, Vol. XXII, Part II (Peninsular Campaign) pp. 496

358 OFFICIAL RECORDS (OR) of the Union and Confederate Armies (1902): {{PD-1923}} SERIES: I VOLUME: XI CAMPAIGN: Peninsular Campaign SERIAL: 013 PAGE: 0826

359 History of the Civil War in America (1875): Vol. I-IV Comte de Paris {{PD-1923}} p. 141

360 The Rebellion Record (1861): Vol. 9; Moore; Everett {{PD-1923}} p. 329

361 Lives of Distinguished North Carolinians (1898) William Joseph Peele {{PD-1923}} pp. 540-541

362 Battles and Leaders of the Civil War (1887-1888): Vol. 2 R. U. Johnson; C. Buel; {{PD-1923}} p. 394

363 OFFICIAL REPORTs - Operations of the Army of Northern Virginia (1864): Robert E. Lee {{PD-1923}} pp. 12-13

364 OFFICIAL REPORTs - Operations of the Army of Northern Virginia (1864): Robert E. Lee {{PD-1923}} p. 13

365 OFFICIAL REPORTs - Operations of the Army of Northern Virginia (1864): Robert E. Lee {{PD-1923}} p. 14

366 Battles and Leaders of the Civil War (1887-1888): Vol. 2 R. U. Johnson; C. Buel; {{PD-1923}} p. 394

367 OFFICIAL RECORDS (OR) of the Union and Confederate Armies (1902): {{PD-1923}} SERIES 1, Vol. XI, par. 2, p. 629

368 Battles and Leaders of the Civil War (1887-1888): Vol. 2 R. U. Johnson; C. Buel; {{PD-1923}} p. 394

369 Battles and Leaders of the Civil War (1887-1888): Vol. 2 R. U. Johnson; C. Buel; {{PD-1923}} pp. 394-395

370 D. H. Hill Papers, NC Archives (1915): [[NC Archives]] {{PD-1923}} - Letter from D.H. Hill to Isabella Hill, Family Papers, July 3, 1862

371 D. H. Hill Papers, NC Archives (1915): [[NC Archives]] {{PD-1923}}

372 Reminiscences of the Civil War (1906): General John B. Gordon {{PD-1923}} pp. 67-68

373 Consolidated index to compiled service records of Confederate Soldiers (1957) US National Archives and Records; CSA {{PD-1923}} Reel 221 - Call Number 1890601.1

374 OFFICIAL RECORDS (OR) of the Union and Confederate Armies (1902): {{PD-1923}} SERIES II, VOLUME IV, PART 1, SERIAL 117 pp. 815-816// OFFICIAL RECORDS - (OR) - The War of the Rebellion: A Compilation of the OFFICIAL RECORDSs of the Union and Confederate Armies (1902) SERIES: II VOLUME: IV CAMPAIGN: Prisoners of War SERIAL: 117 PAGE: 0220// OFFICIAL RECORDS - (OR) - The War of the Rebellion: A Compilation of the

OFFICIAL RECORDSs of the Union and Confederate Armies (1902) SERIES: II VOLUME: IV CAMPAIGN: Prisoners of War SERIAL: 117 PAGE: 0210

375 The Rebellion Record (1861): Vol. 9; Moore; Everett {{PD-1923}} pp. 246-247

376 OFFICIAL RECORDS (OR) of the Union and Confederate Armies (1902): {{PD-1923}} SERIES II, VOLUME IV, PART 1, SERIAL 117 pp. 815-816

377 OFFICIAL RECORDS (OR) of the Union and Confederate Armies (1902): {{PD-1923}} SERIES II, VOLUME IX, PART 1, SERIAL 117 page 246-247// The Rebellion Record (1861): Vol. 5; Moore; Everett {{PD-1923}} p. 342

378 OFFICIAL RECORDS (OR) of the Union and Confederate Armies (1902): {{PD-1923}} END OF SERIES II Volume IV Part 1 pages 266-267

379 The Rebellion Record (1861): Base Document; Moore; Everett {{PD-1923}} p. 843//The Rebellion Record (1861): Vol. 5; Moore; Everett {{PD-1923}} p. 342

380 OFFICIAL RECORDS (OR) of the Union and Confederate Armies (1902): {{PD-1923}} END OF SERIES II Volume IV Part 1 pages 266

381 The Rebellion Record (1861): Base Document; Moore; Everett {{PD-1923}} p. 843//The Rebellion Record (1861): Vol. 5; Moore; Everett {{PD-1923}} p. 342

382 OFFICIAL RECORDS (OR) of the Union and Confederate Armies (1902): {{PD-1923}} END OF SERIES II Volume IV Part 1 pages 267

383 The Rebellion Record (1861): Base Document; Moore; Everett {{PD-1923}}p. 843

384 OFFICIAL RECORDS (OR) of the Union and Confederate Armies (1902): {{PD-1923}} END OF SERIES II Volume IV Part 1 pages 267// The Rebellion Record (1861): Vol. 5; Moore; Everett {{PD-1923}} p. 342

385 The Rebellion Record (1861): Base Document; Moore; Everett {{PD-1923}}p. 843

386 OFFICIAL RECORDS (OR) of the Union and Confederate Armies (1902): {{PD-1923}} END OF SERIES II Volume IV Part 1 pages 268

387 The Rebellion Record (1861): Base Document; Moore; Everett {{PD-1923}} p. 843//The Rebellion Record (1861): Vol. 5; Moore; Everett {{PD-1923}} p. 342

388 OFFICIAL RECORDS (OR) of the Union and Confederate Armies (1902): {{PD-1923}} SERIES II, VOLUME IX, PART 1, SERIAL 11; p. 246

389 OFFICIAL RECORDS (OR) of the Union and Confederate Armies (1902): {{PD-1923}} SERIES II, VOLUME IX, PART 1, SERIAL 117 p. 246

390 OFFICIAL RECORDS (OR) of the Union and Confederate Armies (1902): {{PD-1923}} SERIES II, VOLUME IX, PART 1, SERIAL 117 p. 246

391 The Photographic History of the Civil War (1911): Vol. 10; F. T. Miller; R. S. Lanier {{PD-1923}} p. 102

392 OFFICIAL RECORDS (OR) of the Union and Confederate Armies (1902): {{PD-1923}} SERIES: II VOLUME: V CAMPAIGN: Prisoners of War SERIAL: 118 PAGE: 0001

393 OFFICIAL RECORDS (OR) of the Union and Confederate Armies (1902): {{PD-1923}} SERIES: II VOLUME: IV CAMPAIGN: Prisoners of War SERIAL: 117 PAGE: 0830

394 General Lee (1894) Fitzhugh Lee; NY, NY, D. Appleton & Co; (1894); not in copyright; {{PD-1923}} p. 175

395 Consolidated index to compiled service records of Confederate Soldiers (1957) US National Archives and Records; CSA {{PD-1923}} Reel 221 - Call Number 1890601.1

396 OFFICIAL REPORTs - Operations of the Army of Northern Virginia (1864): Robert E. Lee {{PD-1923}} p. 27

397 OFFICIAL REPORTs - Operations of the Army of Northern Virginia (1864): Robert E. Lee {{PD-1923}} pp. 27-28

398 OFFICIAL REPORTs - Operations of the Army of Northern Virginia (1864): Robert E. Lee {{PD-1923}} pp. 27-28

399 OFFICIAL REPORTs - Operations of the Army of Northern Virginia (1864): Robert E. Lee {{PD-1923}} p.

400 The Rebellion Record (1861): Vol. 9; Moore; Everett {{PD-1923}} document 13 - p. 279

401 *OFFICIAL RECORDS (OR) of the Union and Confederate Armies (1902): {{PD-1923}} SERIES: I VOLUME: XIX CAMPAIGN: Antietam SERIAL: 027 PAGE: 0829*

402 *Consolidated index to compiled service records of Confederate Soldiers (1957) US National Archives and Records; CSA {{PD-1923}} Reel 221 - Call Number 1890601.1*

403 *D. H. Hill Papers, NC Archives (1915): [[NC Archives]] {{PD-1923}}*

404 *D. H. Hill Papers, NC Archives (1915): [[NC Archives]] {{PD-1923}}*

405 *OFFICIAL RECORDS (OR) of the Union and Confederate Armies (1902): {{PD-1923}} VOLUME XIX CAMPAIGN: PT.1; pp. 42-43*

406 *Biography of Daniel Harvey Hill Lieutenant General, CSA (1886): Joseph M. Hill {{PD-1923}} p. 16*

407 *OFFICIAL RECORDS (OR) of the Union and Confederate Armies (1902): {{PD-1923}} SERIES 1, Vol. XIX, Part 1, p. 55*

408 *Lives of Distinguished North Carolinians (1898) William Joseph Peele {{PD-1923}} p. 544*

409 *OFFICIAL REPORTs - Operations of the Army of Northern Virginia (1864): Robert E. Lee {{PD-1923}} p. 27*

410 *OFFICIAL REPORTs - Operations of the Army of Northern Virginia (1864): Robert E. Lee {{PD-1923}} p. 32*

411 *OFFICIAL REPORTs - Operations of the Army of Northern Virginia (1864): Robert E. Lee {{PD-1923}} p. 32-33*

412 *Consolidated index to compiled service records of Confederate Soldiers (1957) US National Archives and Records; CSA {{PD-1923}} Reel 221 - Call Number 1890601.1*

413 *OFFICIAL REPORTs - Operations of the Army of Northern Virginia (1864): Robert E. Lee {{PD-1923}} p. 32-33*

414 *OFFICIAL RECORDS (OR) of the Union and Confederate Armies (1902): {{PD-1923}} SERIES: I VOLUME: XIX CAMPAIGN: Antietam SERIAL: 027 PAGE: 0140*

415 *The Rebellion Record (1861): Vol. 9; Moore; Everett {{PD-1923}} document 13 - p. 280*

416 *OFFICIAL REPORTs - Operations of the Army of Northern Virginia (1864): Robert E. Lee {{PD-1923}} p. 28*

417 *OFFICIAL REPORTs - Operations of the Army of Northern Virginia (1864): Robert E. Lee {{PD-1923}} p. 32*

418 *OFFICIAL REPORTs - Operations of the Army of Northern Virginia (1864): Robert E. Lee {{PD-1923}} p. 32-33*

419 *OFFICIAL REPORTs - Operations of the Army of Northern Virginia (1864): Robert E. Lee {{PD-1923}} p. 32*

420 *The Rebellion Record (1861): Vol. 9; Moore; Everett {{PD-1923}} document 13 - p. 282*

421 *OFFICIAL REPORTs - Operations of the Army of Northern Virginia (1864): Robert E. Lee {{PD-1923}} p. 29*

422 *Southern Historical Society Papers (1885): Vol. XIII & XIV James I. Robertson {{PD-1923}} - the Century Magazine (1886) Daniel Harvey Hill; May Issue 1886 New York, Warne & Co.; (1886); p.137*

423 *Battles and Leaders of the Civil War (1887-1888): Vol. 2 R. U. Johnson; C. Buel; {{PD-1923}} pp. 559-560*

424 *OFFICIAL RECORDS (OR) of the Union and Confederate Armies (1902): {{PD-1923}} Vol. 1-128 et al; Vol. 1-128 et al; Vol. XIX, Part I, Serial 27-28, Antietam (Sharpsburg) p. 1019*

425 *OFFICIAL RECORDS (OR) of the Union and Confederate Armies (1902): {{PD-1923}} Vol. 1-128 et al; Vol. 1-128 et al; Vol. XIX, Part I, Serial 27-28, Antietam (Sharpsburg) pp. 42-43*

426 *The Antietam and Fredericksburg (1881): Francis W. Palfrey {{PD-1923}} p. 32*

427 *OFFICIAL RECORDS (OR) of the Union and Confederate Armies (1902): {{PD-1923}} Vol. 1-128 et al; Vol. 1-128 et al; Vol. XIX, Part I, Serial 27-28, Antietam (Sharpsburg) p. 1019*

428 *OFFICIAL RECORDS (OR) of the Union and Confederate Armies (1902): {{PD-1923}} Vol. 1-128 et al; Vol. 1-128 et al; Vol. XIX, Part I, Serial 27-28, Antietam (Sharpsburg) p. 1019*

429 *OFFICIAL RECORDS (OR) of the Union and Confederate Armies (1902): {{PD-1923}} Vol. 1-128 et al; Vol. 1-128 et al; Vol. XIX, Part I, Serial 27-28, Antietam (Sharpsburg) p. 1020*

430 *Lives of Distinguished North Carolinians (1898) William Joseph Peele {{PD-1923}} p. 542*

431 OFFICIAL RECORDS (OR) of the Union and Confederate Armies (1902): {{PD-1923}} Vol. 1-128 et al; Vol. 1-128 et al; Vol. XIX, Part I, Serial 27-28, Antietam (Sharpsburg) p. 1020

432 OFFICIAL RECORDS (OR) of the Union and Confederate Armies (1902): {{PD-1923}}   Vol. 1-128 et al; Vol. 1-128 et al; Vol. XIX, Part I, Serial 27-28, Antietam (Sharpsburg)p. 1020

433 Lives of Distinguished North Carolinians (1898) William Joseph Peele {{PD-1923}} p. 543

434 OFFICIAL RECORDS (OR) of the Union and Confederate Armies (1902): {{PD-1923}}   Vol. 1-128 et al; Vol. 1-128 et al; Vol. XIX, Part I, Serial 27-28, Antietam (Sharpsburg) p. 1020

435 Lives of Distinguished North Carolinians (1898) William Joseph Peele {{PD-1923}} p. 527

436 Lives of Distinguished North Carolinians (1898) William Joseph Peele {{PD-1923}} p. 543

437Life and Character of Lieutenant General D. H. Hill (1893): Alphonso C. {{PD-1923}}

438 OFFICIAL RECORDS (OR) of the Union and Confederate Armies (1902): {{PD-1923}} Vol. 1-128 et al; Vol. 1-128 et al; Vol. XIX, Part I, Serial 27-28, Antietam (Sharpsburg) ; Publisher - Washington Government Printing Office; (1902); p. 1020

439 OFFICIAL RECORDS (OR) of the Union and Confederate Armies (1902): {{PD-1923}} Vol. 1-128 et al; Vol.

440 OFFICIAL RECORDS (OR) of the Union and Confederate Armies (1902): {{PD-1923}}   Vol. 1-128 et al; Vol. 1-128 et al; Vol. XIX, Part I, Serial 27-28, Antietam (Sharpsburg) p. 1020

441OFFICIAL RECORDS (OR) of the Union and Confederate Armies (1902): {{PD-1923}}   Vol. 1-128 et al; Vol. 1-128 et al; Vol. XIX, Part I, Serial 27-28, Antietam (Sharpsburg) p. 1020

442 OFFICIAL RECORDS (OR) of the Union and Confederate Armies (1902): {{PD-1923}}   Vol. 1-128 et al; Vol. XIX, Part I, Serial 27-28, Antietam (Sharpsburg) p. 1020

443 OFFICIAL RECORDS (OR) of the Union and Confederate Armies (1902): {{PD-1923}} Vol. 1-128 et al; Vol. 1-128 et al; Vol. XIX, Part I, Serial 27-28, Antietam (Sharpsburg) p. 1021

444 OFFICIAL RECORDS (OR) of the Union and Confederate Armies (1902): {{PD-1923}}   Vol. 1-128 et al; Vol. 1-128 et al; Vol. XIX, Part I, Serial 27-28, Antietam (Sharpsburg) p. 1021

445 OFFICIAL RECORDS (OR) of the Union and Confederate Armies (1902): {{PD-1923}} Vol. 1-128 et al; Vol. 1-128 et al; Vol. XIX, Part I, Serial 27-28, Antietam (Sharpsburg) p. 1021

446 OFFICIAL RECORDS (OR) of the Union and Confederate Armies (1902): {{PD-1923}} SERIES: I VOLUME: XIX CAMPAIGN: Antietam SERIAL: 027 PAGE: 0839

447 OFFICIAL RECORDS (OR) of the Union and Confederate Armies (1902): {{PD-1923}} SERIES: I VOLUME: XIX CAMPAIGN: Antietam SERIAL: 027 PAGE: 0908

448 OFFICIAL RECORDS (OR) of the Union and Confederate Armies (1902): {{PD-1923}}   Vol. 1-128 et al; Vol. 1-128 et al; Vol. XIX, Part I, Serial 27-28, Antietam (Sharpsburg) p. 1021

449 OFFICIAL RECORDS (OR) of the Union and Confederate Armies (1902): {{PD-1923}}   Vol. 1-128 et al; Vol. 1-128 et al; Vol. XIX, Part I, Serial 27-28, Antietam (Sharpsburg) p. 1021

450 OFFICIAL RECORDS (OR) of the Union and Confederate Armies (1902): {{PD-1923}} Vol. 1-128 et al; Vol. 1-128 et al; Vol. XIX, Part I, Serial 27-28, Antietam (Sharpsburg) p. 1021

451 OFFICIAL RECORDS (OR) of the Union and Confederate Armies (1902): {{PD-1923}} Vol. 1-128 et al; Vol. XIX, Part I, Serial 27-28, Antietam (Sharpsburg) p. 1021

452 Lives of Distinguished North Carolinians (1898) William Joseph Peele {{PD-1923}} p. 543

453 Lives of Distinguished North Carolinians (1898) William Joseph Peele {{PD-1923}} p. 542

454 D. H. Hill Papers, NC Archives (1915): [[NC Archives]] {{PD-1923}}//Biography of Daniel Harvey Hill Lieutenant General, CSA (1886): Joseph M. Hill {{PD-1923}} pp.17-31

455 General George McClellan was reported made this comment to one of his subordinate officers; there is no recording in the OFFICIAL RECORDSs for this famous quote.

456 Memoirs of Robert E. Lee (1886): Armistead Lindsay Long; Marcus Joseph Wright {{PD-1923}} p. 528

457 OFFICIAL REPORTs - Operations of the Army of Northern Virginia (1864): Robert E. Lee {{PD-1923}} p. 32

458 OFFICIAL REPORTs - Operations of the Army of Northern Virginia (1864): Robert E. Lee {{PD-1923}} p. 30

459 OFFICIAL RECORDS (OR) of the Union and Confederate Armies (1902): {{PD-1923}} SERIES: I VOLUME: XIX CAMPAIGN: Antietam SERIAL: 027 PAGE: 0148

460 Consolidated index to compiled service records of Confederate Soldiers (1957) US National Archives and Records; CSA {{PD-1923}} Reel 221 - Call Number 1890601.1

461 The Antietam and Fredericksburg (1881): Francis W. Palfrey {{PD-1923}} pp. 42 and 57

462 The Rebellion Record (1861): Vol. 11; Moore; Everett {{PD-1923}} p. 686

463 OFFICIAL REPORTs - Operations of the Army of Northern Virginia (1864): Robert E. Lee {{PD-1923}} p. 32

464 OFFICIAL REPORTs - Operations of the Army of Northern Virginia (1864): Robert E. Lee {{PD-1923}} pp. 32-33

465 OFFICIAL RECORDS (OR) of the Union and Confederate Armies (1902): {{PD-1923}} Vol. 1-128 et al; Vol. 1-128 et al; Vol. XIX, Part I, Serial 27-28, Antietam (Sharpsburg) p. 1022

466 OFFICIAL REPORTs - Operations of the Army of Northern Virginia (1864): Robert E. Lee {{PD-1923}} p. 32

467 OFFICIAL RECORDS (OR) of the Union and Confederate Armies (1902): {{PD-1923}} Vol. 1-128 et al; Vol. 1-128 et al; Vol. XIX, Part I, Serial 27-28, Antietam (Sharpsburg) p. 1022

468 OFFICIAL RECORDS (OR) of the Union and Confederate Armies (1902): {{PD-1923}} SERIES: I VOLUME: XIX CAMPAIGN: Antietam SERIAL: 027 PAGE: 0967

469 OFFICIAL REPORTs - Operations of the Army of Northern Virginia (1864): Robert E. Lee {{PD-1923}} p. 32

470 OFFICIAL RECORDS (OR) of the Union and Confederate Armies (1902): {{PD-1923}}   Vol. 1-128 et al; Vol. 1-128 et al; Vol. XIX, Part I, Serial 27-28, Antietam (Sharpsburg) p. 1021

471 OFFICIAL REPORTs - Operations of the Army of Northern Virginia (1864): Robert E. Lee {{PD-1923}} p. 32

472 OFFICIAL RECORDS (OR) of the Union and Confederate Armies (1902): {{PD-1923}} SERIES: I VOLUME: XIX CAMPAIGN: Antietam SERIAL: 027 PAGE: 0813

473 OFFICIAL RECORDS (OR) of the Union and Confederate Armies (1902): {{PD-1923}} Vol. 1-128 et al; Vol. 1-128 et al; Vol. XIX, Part I, Serial 27-28, Antietam (Sharpsburg) p. 1021

474 Lives of Distinguished North Carolinians (1898) William Joseph Peele {{PD-1923}} pp. 150-151

475 Reminiscences of the Civil War (1906): General John B. Gordon {{PD-1923}} p. 84

476 Battles and Leaders of the Civil War (1887-1888): Vol. 2 R. U. Johnson; C. Buel; {{PD-1923}} p. 671

477 Battles and Leaders of the Civil War (1887-1888): Vol. 2 R. U. Johnson; C. Buel; {{PD-1923}} pp. 671-672

478 OFFICIAL RECORDS (OR) of the Union and Confederate Armies (1902): {{PD-1923}} Vol. 1-128 et al; Vol. 1-128 et al; Vol. XIX, Part I, Serial 27-28, Antietam (Sharpsburg) p. 1021

479 OFFICIAL RECORDS (OR) of the Union and Confederate Armies (1902): {{PD-1923}} Vol. 1-128 et al; Vol. 1-128 et al; Vol. XIX, Part I, Serial 27-28, Antietam (Sharpsburg) p. 1021

480 OFFICIAL RECORDS (OR) of the Union and Confederate Armies (1902): {{PD-1923}} Vol. 1-128 et al; Vol. 1-128 et al; Vol. XIX, Part I, Serial 27-28, Antietam (Sharpsburg) p. 1021

481 OFFICIAL REPORTs - Operations of the Army of Northern Virginia (1864): Robert E. Lee {{PD-1923}} p. 32

482 OFFICIAL REPORTs - Operations of the Army of Northern Virginia (1864): Robert E. Lee {{PD-1923}} pp. 32-33

483 OFFICIAL REPORTs - Operations of the Army of Northern Virginia (1864): Robert E. Lee {{PD-1923}} p. 32

484 OFFICIAL REPORTs - Operations of the Army of Northern Virginia (1864): Robert E. Lee {{PD-1923}} p. 32-33

485 OFFICIAL REPORTs - Operations of the Army of Northern Virginia (1864): Robert E. Lee {{PD-1923}} p. 33

486 *OFFICIAL RECORDS (OR) of the Union and Confederate Armies (1902): {{PD-1923}} SERIES: I VOLUME: XIX CAMPAIGN: Antietam SERIAL: 027 PAGE: 0149*

487 *OFFICIAL RECORDS (OR) of the Union and Confederate Armies (1902): {{PD-1923}} Vol. 1-128 et al; Vol. XIX, Part I, Serial 27-28, Antietam (Sharpsburg) p. 1022*

488 *Vol. 1-128 et al; Vol. 1-128 et al; Vol. XIX, Part I, Serial 27-28, Antietam (Sharpsburg) p. 1022*

489 *OFFICIAL RECORDS (OR) of the Union and Confederate Armies (1902): {{PD-1923}} Vol. 1-128 et al; Vol. 1-128 et al; Vol. XIX, Part I, Serial 27-28, Antietam (Sharpsburg) p. 1023*

490 *OFFICIAL RECORDS (OR) of the Union and Confederate Armies (1902): {{PD-1923}} Vol. 1-128 et al; Vol. 1-128 et al; Vol. XIX, Part I, Serial 27-28, Antietam (Sharpsburg) p. 1023*

491 *OFFICIAL RECORDS (OR) of the Union and Confederate Armies (1902): {{PD-1923}} Vol. 1-128 et al; Vol. XIX, Part I, Serial 27-28, Antietam (Sharpsburg) p. 1023*

492 *OFFICIAL RECORDS (OR) of the Union and Confederate Armies (1902): {{PD-1923}} Vol. 1-128 et al; Vol. XIX, Part I, Serial 27-28, Antietam (Sharpsburg) p. 1023*

493 *D. H. Hill Papers, NC Archives (1915): [[NC Archives]] {{PD-1923}}//Biography of Daniel Harvey Hill Lieutenant General, CSA (1886): Joseph M. Hill {{PD-1923}} pp.17-31*

494 *OFFICIAL RECORDS (OR) of the Union and Confederate Armies (1902): {{PD-1923}} Vol. 1-128 et al; Vol. XIX, Part I, Serial 27-28, Antietam (Sharpsburg) p. 1023*

495 *OFFICIAL RECORDS (OR) of the Union and Confederate Armies (1902): {{PD-1923}} Vol. 1-128 et al; Vol. XIX, Part I, Serial 27-28, Antietam (Sharpsburg) p. 1023*

496 *OFFICIAL RECORDS (OR) of the Union and Confederate Armies (1902): {{PD-1923}} Vol. 1-128 et al; Vol. XIX, Part I, Serial 27-28, Antietam (Sharpsburg) p. 1023*

497 *OFFICIAL RECORDS (OR) of the Union and Confederate Armies (1902): {{PD-1923}} Vol. 1-128 et al; Vol. XIX, Part I, Serial 27-28, Antietam (Sharpsburg) pp. 1023-1024*

498 *OFFICIAL RECORDS (OR) of the Union and Confederate Armies (1902): {{PD-1923}} Vol. 1-128 et al; Vol. XIX, Part I, Serial 27-28, Antietam (Sharpsburg) p. 1024*

499 *OFFICIAL RECORDS (OR) of the Union and Confederate Armies (1902): {{PD-1923}}Vol. 1-128 et al; Vol. XIX, Part I, Serial 27-28, Antietam (Sharpsburg) p. 1024*

500 *D. H. Hill Papers, NC Archives (1915): [[NC Archives]] {{PD-1923}}//Biography of Daniel Harvey Hill Lieutenant General, CSA (1886): Joseph M. Hill {{PD-1923}} pp.17-31*

501 *OFFICIAL RECORDS (OR) of the Union and Confederate Armies (1902): {{PD-1923}} Vol. 1-128 et al; Vol. XIX, Part I, Serial 27-28, Antietam (Sharpsburg) p. 1024*

502 *OFFICIAL RECORDS (OR) of the Union and Confederate Armies (1902): {{PD-1923}} Vol. 1-128 et al; Vol. XIX, Part I, Serial 27-28, Antietam (Sharpsburg) p. 1024*

503 *OFFICIAL RECORDS (OR) of the Union and Confederate Armies (1902): {{PD-1923}} Vol. 1-128 et al; Vol. XIX, Part I, Serial 27-28, Antietam (Sharpsburg) p. 1024*

504 *OFFICIAL RECORDS (OR) of the Union and Confederate Armies (1902): {{PD-1923}} Vol. 1-128 et al; Vol. XIX, Part I, Serial 27-28, Antietam (Sharpsburg) p. 1024*

505 *OFFICIAL RECORDS (OR) of the Union and Confederate Armies (1902): {{PD-1923}}Vol. 1-128 et al; Vol. XIX, Part I, Serial 27-28, Antietam (Sharpsburg) p. 1024*

506 *OFFICIAL RECORDS (OR) of the Union and Confederate Armies (1902): {{PD-1923}} Vol. 1-128 et al; Vol. XIX, Part I, Serial 27-28, Antietam (Sharpsburg) p. 1024*

507 *OFFICIAL RECORDS (OR) of the Union and Confederate Armies (1902): {{PD-1923}} Vol. 1-128 et al; Vol. XIX, Part I, Serial 27-28, Antietam (Sharpsburg) p. 1025*

508 *OFFICIAL RECORDS (OR) of the Union and Confederate Armies (1902): {{PD-1923}} Vol. 1-128 et al; Vol. XIX, Part I, Serial 27-28, Antietam (Sharpsburg) p. 1025*

509 *OFFICIAL RECORDS (OR) of the Union and Confederate Armies (1902): {{PD-1923}} Vol. 1-128 et al; Vol. XIX, Part I, Serial 27-28, Antietam (Sharpsburg) p. 1025*

510 OFFICIAL RECORDS (OR) of the Union and Confederate Armies (1902): {{PD-1923}} Vol. 1-128 et al; Vol. XIX, Part I, Serial 27-28, Antietam (Sharpsburg) p. 1025

511 OFFICIAL RECORDS (OR) of the Union and Confederate Armies (1902): {{PD-1923}} SERIES: I VOLUME: XIX CAMPAIGN: Antietam SERIAL: 027 PAGE: 0141

512 OFFICIAL REPORTs - Operations of the Army of Northern Virginia (1864): Robert E. Lee {{PD-1923}} p. 34

513 OFFICIAL REPORTs - Operations of the Army of Northern Virginia (1864): Robert E. Lee {{PD-1923}} pp. 34-35

514 OFFICIAL REPORTs - Operations of the Army of Northern Virginia (1864): Robert E. Lee {{PD-1923}} p. 34

515 OFFICIAL REPORTs - Operations of the Army of Northern Virginia (1864): Robert E. Lee {{PD-1923}} pp. 34-35

516 OFFICIAL REPORTs - Operations of the Army of Northern Virginia (1864): Robert E. Lee {{PD-1923}} pp. 33-34

517 OFFICIAL REPORTs - Operations of the Army of Northern Virginia (1864): Robert E. Lee {{PD-1923}} p. 34

518 D. H. Hill Papers, NC Archives (1915): [[NC Archives]] {{PD-1923}}//Biography of Daniel Harvey Hill Lieutenant General, CSA (1886): Joseph M. Hill {{PD-1923}} pp.17-31

519 OFFICIAL RECORDS (OR) of the Union and Confederate Armies (1902): {{PD-1923}} Vol. 1-128 et al; Vol. XIX, Part I, Serial 27-28, Antietam (Sharpsburg) p. 1025

520 OFFICIAL RECORDS (OR) of the Union and Confederate Armies (1902): {{PD-1923}} Vol. 1-128 et al; Vol. XIX, Part I, Serial 27-28, Antietam (Sharpsburg) p. 1025

521 OFFICIAL RECORDS (OR) of the Union and Confederate Armies (1902): {{PD-1923}} Vol. 1-128 et al; Vol. XIX, Part I, Serial 27-28, Antietam (Sharpsburg) pp. 1025-1026

522 OFFICIAL RECORDS (OR) of the Union and Confederate Armies (1902): {{PD-1923}} Vol. 1-128 et al; Vol. XIX, Part I, Serial 27-28, Antietam (Sharpsburg) p. 1025

523 OFFICIAL RECORDS (OR) of the Union and Confederate Armies (1902): {{PD-1923}} Vol. 1-128 et al; Vol. XIX, Part I, Serial 27-28, Antietam (Sharpsburg) p. 1025

524 OFFICIAL RECORDS (OR) of the Union and Confederate Armies (1902): {{PD-1923}} Vol. 1-128 et al; Vol. XIX, Part I, Serial 27-28, Antietam (Sharpsburg) pp. 1026-1027

525 D. H. Hill Papers, NC Archives (1915): [[NC Archives]] {{PD-1923}}//Biography of Daniel Harvey Hill Lieutenant General, CSA (1886): Joseph M. Hill {{PD-1923}} pp.17-31

526 Battles and Leaders of the Civil War (1887-1888) Robert Underwood Johnson, Clarence Clough Buel; Vol. 2; NY -Century Co; (1887); p. 670

527 Southern Historical Society Papers (1885): Vol. XIII & XIV James I. Robertson {{PD-1923}} p. 138

528 Under Both Flags - Tales of the Civil War (1896): George M. Vickers {{PD-1923}} p. 109

529 Under Both Flags - Tales of the Civil War (1896): George M. Vickers {{PD-1923}} pp. 109-110

530 OFFICIAL RECORDS (OR) of the Union and Confederate Armies (1902): {{PD-1923}} SERIES: I VOLUME: XIX CAMPAIGN: Antietam SERIAL: 028 PAGE: 0231

531 Under Both Flags - Tales of the Civil War (1896): George M. Vickers {{PD-1923}} p. 113

532 Under Both Flags - Tales of the Civil War (1896): George M. Vickers {{PD-1923}} pp. 112-113

533 Under Both Flags - Tales of the Civil War (1896): George M. Vickers {{PD-1923}} p. 110

534 Under Both Flags - Tales of the Civil War (1896): George M. Vickers {{PD-1923}} p. 111

535 Under Both Flags - Tales of the Civil War (1896): George M. Vickers {{PD-1923}} pp. 116-117

536 Under Both Flags - Tales of the Civil War (1896): George M. Vickers {{PD-1923}} p. 118

537 Under Both Flags - Tales of the Civil War (1896): George M. Vickers {{PD-1923}} p. 118

538 The Rebellion Record (1861): Vol. 10; Moore; Everett {{PD-1923}} //Consolidated index to compiled service records of Confederate Soldiers (1957) US National Archives and Records; CSA {{PD-1923}} Reel 221 - Call Number 1890601.1

539 Memoirs of the Confederate War for Independence (1867): Heros von Borcke {{PD-1923}} p. 287//

540 OFFICIAL REPORTs - Operations of the Army of Northern Virginia (1864): Robert E. Lee {{PD-1923}} pp. 34-35

541 OFFICIAL REPORTs - Operations of the Army of Northern Virginia (1864): Robert E. Lee {{PD-1923}} p. 36

542 Battles and Leaders of the Civil War (1887-1888): Vol. 2 R. U. Johnson; C. Buel; {{PD-1923}} pp. 559-560

543 OFFICIAL RECORDS (OR) of the Union and Confederate Armies (1902): {{PD-1923}} SERIES: I VOLUME: XIV CAMPAIGN: Secessionville SERIAL: 020 PAGE: 0570

544 Consolidated index to compiled service records of Confederate Soldiers (1957) US National Archives and Records; CSA {{PD-1923}} Reel 221 - Call Number 1890601.1

545 Lives of Distinguished North Carolinians (1898) William Joseph Peele {{PD-1923}} p. 551

546 Makers of North Carolina History (1911): R. D. W. Conner {{PD-1923}} pp. 246-247

547 Makers of North Carolina History (1911): R. D. W. Conner {{PD-1923}} p. 247

548 D. H. Hill Papers, NC Archives (1915): [[NC Archives]] {{PD-1923}}

549 Makers of North Carolina History (1911): R. D. W. Conner {{PD-1923}} pp. 226-227

550 Makers of North Carolina History (1911): R. D. W. Conner {{PD-1923}} p. 227

551 Makers of North Carolina History (1911): R. D. W. Conner {{PD-1923}} pp. 227-228

552 D. H. Hill Papers, NC Archives (1915): [[NC Archives]] {{PD-1923}}

553 Makers of North Carolina History (1911): R. D. W. Conner {{PD-1923}} p. 230

554 Makers of North Carolina History (1911): R. D. W. Conner {{PD-1923}} p. 232

555 Makers of North Carolina History (1911): R. D. W. Conner {{PD-1923}} p. 232-233

556 D. H. Hill Papers, NC Archives (1915): [[NC Archives]] {{PD-1923}}

557 Makers of North Carolina History (1911): R. D. W. Conner {{PD-1923}} p. 230

558 Consolidated index to compiled service records of Confederate Soldiers (1957) US National Archives and Records; CSA {{PD-1923}} Reel 221 - Call Number 1890601.1

559 A Memoir of the Last Year of the War for Independence in the CSA (1867): Jubal A. Early {{PD-1923}} p. 37

560 Life and Character of Lieutenant General D. H. Hill (1893): Alphonso C. {{PD-1923} p. 32

561 The Rebellion Record (1861): Vol. 7; Moore; Everett {{PD-1923}} pp. 31-32

562 Southern Historical Society Papers (1885): Vol. XIII & XIV James I. Robertson {{PD-1923}} p. 148

563 Consolidated index to compiled service records of Confederate Soldiers (1957) US National Archives and Records; CSA {{PD-1923}} Reel 221 - Call Number 1890601.1

564 Lives of Distinguished North Carolinians (1898) William Joseph Peele {{PD-1923}} p. 553

565 Biographical History of North Carolina (1908): Samuel A. Ashe {{PD-1923}} P. 143

566 D. H. Hill Papers, NC Archives (1915): [[NC Archives]]//Biography of Daniel Harvey Hill Lieutenant General, CSA (1886): Joseph M. Hill {{PD-1923}} //Battles and Leaders of the Civil War (1887-1888): Vol. 3 R. U. Johnson; C. Buel; {{PD-1923}} Vol. 3, p. 638

567 D. H. Hill Papers, NC Archives (1915): [[NC Archives]] {{PD-1923}}

568 Battles and Leaders of the Civil War (1887-1888): Vol. 3 R. U. Johnson; C. Buel; {{PD-1923}} p. 638

569 Consolidated index to compiled service records of Confederate Soldiers (1957) US National Archives and Records; CSA {{PD-1923}} Reel 221 - Call Number 1890601.1

570 OFFICIAL RECORDS (OR) of the Union and Confederate Armies (1902): {{PD-1923}} SERIES: I VOLUME: XXX CAMPAIGN: Chickamauga SERIAL: 052 PAGE: 0101

571 Battles and Leaders of the Civil War (1887-1888): Vol. 3 R. U. Johnson; C. Buel; {{PD-1923}} p. 638

572 Lives of Distinguished North Carolinians (1898) William Joseph Peele {{PD-1923}} p. 553

573 OFFICIAL RECORDS (OR) of the Union and Confederate Armies (1902): {{PD-1923}} SERIES: I VOLUME: XXXI CAMPAIGN: Knoxville and Lookout Mountain SERIAL: 054 PAGE: 0216

574 Battles and Leaders of the Civil War (1887-1888): Vol. 3 R. U. Johnson; C. Buel; {{PD-1923}} p. 641

575 Battles and Leaders of the Civil War (1887-1888): Vol. 3 R. U. Johnson; C. Buel; {{PD-1923}} pp. 641-642

576 Battles and Leaders of the Civil War (1887-1888): Vol. 3 R. U. Johnson; C. Buel; {{PD-1923}} pp. 641-642

577 OFFICIAL RECORDS (OR) of the Union and Confederate Armies (1902): {{PD-1923}} SERIES: I VOLUME: XXX CAMPAIGN: Chickamauga SERIAL: 050 PAGE: 0186

578 Battles and Leaders of the Civil War (1887-1888): Vol. 3 R. U. Johnson; C. Buel; {{PD-1923}} p. 642

579 Battles and Leaders of the Civil War (1887-1888): Vol. 3 R. U. Johnson; C. Buel; {{PD-1923}} p. 643

580 Battles and Leaders of the Civil War (1887-1888): Vol. 3 R. U. Johnson; C. Buel; {{PD-1923}} p. 644

581 Battles and Leaders of the Civil War (1887-1888): Vol. 3 R. U. Johnson; C. Buel; {{PD-1923}} pp. 646-647

582 The Land We Love (1866): May-Oct 1866; Daniel Harvey Hill {{PD-1923}} p. 393-403 Lieutenant General D. H. Hill provides his detailed, written account of the entire battle of Chickamauga.

583 Battles and Leaders of the Civil War (1887-1888): Vol. 3 R. U. Johnson; C. Buel; {{PD-1923}} pp. 647-648

584 Lives of Distinguished North Carolinians (1898) William Joseph Peele {{PD-1923}} p. 553

585 D. H. Hill Papers, NC Archives (1915): [[NC Archives]] {{PD-1923}}

586 Battles and Leaders of the Civil War (1887-1888): Vol. 3 R. U. Johnson; C. Buel; {{PD-1923}} p. 640

587 Battles and Leaders of the Civil War (1887-1888): Vol. 3 R. U. Johnson; C. Buel; {{PD-1923}} p. 647

588 D. H. Hill Papers, NC Archives (1915): [[NC Archives]] {{PD-1923}}

589 Biographical History of North Carolina (1908): Samuel A. Ashe {{PD-1923}} pp. 143-144

590 Consolidated index to compiled service records of Confederate Soldiers (1957) US National Archives and Records; CSA {{PD-1923}} Reel 221 - Call Number 1890601.1

591 OFFICIAL RECORDS (OR) of the Union and Confederate Armies (1902): {{PD-1923}} SERIES 1, Vol. XXX, Part II (Chickamauga), pp. 139

592 OFFICIAL RECORDS (OR) of the Union and Confederate Armies (1902): {{PD-1923}} SERIES 1, Vol. XXX, Part II (Chickamauga), pp. 140

593 OFFICIAL RECORDS (OR) of the Union and Confederate Armies (1902): {{PD-1923}} SERIES 1, Vol. XXX, Part II (Chickamauga), pp. 140

594 OFFICIAL RECORDS (OR) of the Union and Confederate Armies (1902): {{PD-1923}} SERIES 1, Vol. XXX, Part II (Chickamauga), pp. 140

595 OFFICIAL RECORDS (OR) of the Union and Confederate Armies (1902): {{PD-1923}} SERIES 1, Vol. XXX, Part II (Chickamauga), pp. 140

596 OFFICIAL RECORDS (OR) of the Union and Confederate Armies (1902): {{PD-1923}} SERIES 1, Vol. XXX, Part II (Chickamauga), pp. 140

597 OFFICIAL RECORDS (OR) of the Union and Confederate Armies (1902): {{PD-1923}} SERIES 1, Vol. XXX, Part II (Chickamauga), pp. 140

598 OFFICIAL RECORDS (OR) of the Union and Confederate Armies (1902): {{PD-1923}} SERIES 1, Vol. XXX, Part II (Chickamauga), pp. 140

599 OFFICIAL RECORDS (OR) of the Union and Confederate Armies (1902): {{PD-1923}} SERIES 1, Vol. XXX, Part II (Chickamauga), pp. 141

600 OFFICIAL RECORDS (OR) of the Union and Confederate Armies (1902): {{PD-1923}} SERIES 1, Vol. XXX, Part II (Chickamauga), pp. 141

601 OFFICIAL RECORDS (OR) of the Union and Confederate Armies (1902): {{PD-1923}} SERIES 1, Vol. XXX, Part II (Chickamauga), pp. 141

602 OFFICIAL RECORDS (OR) of the Union and Confederate Armies (1902): {{PD-1923}} SERIES 1, Vol. XXX, Part II (Chickamauga), pp. 141

603 OFFICIAL RECORDS (OR) of the Union and Confederate Armies (1902): {{PD-1923}} SERIES 1, Vol. XXX, Part II (Chickamauga), pp. 141

604 OFFICIAL RECORDS (OR) of the Union and Confederate Armies (1902): {{PD-1923}} SERIES 1, Vol. XXX, Part II (Chickamauga), pp. 141

605 OFFICIAL RECORDS (OR) of the Union and Confederate Armies (1902): {{PD-1923}} SERIES 1, Vol. XXX, Part II (Chickamauga), pp. 141

606 OFFICIAL RECORDS (OR) of the Union and Confederate Armies (1902): {{PD-1923}} SERIES 1, Vol. XXX, Part II (Chickamauga), pp. 141

607 OFFICIAL RECORDS (OR) of the Union and Confederate Armies (1902): {{PD-1923}} SERIES 1, Vol. XXX, Part II (Chickamauga), pp. 141

608 OFFICIAL RECORDS (OR) of the Union and Confederate Armies (1902): {{PD-1923}} SERIES 1, Vol. XXX, Part II (Chickamauga), pp. 142

609 OFFICIAL RECORDS (OR) of the Union and Confederate Armies (1902): {{PD-1923}} SERIES 1, Vol. XXX, Part II (Chickamauga), pp. 142

610 OFFICIAL RECORDS (OR) of the Union and Confederate Armies (1902): {{PD-1923}} SERIES 1, Vol. XXX, Part II (Chickamauga), pp. 142

611 OFFICIAL RECORDS (OR) of the Union and Confederate Armies (1902): {{PD-1923}} SERIES 1, Vol. XXX, Part II (Chickamauga), pp. 142

612 OFFICIAL RECORDS (OR) of the Union and Confederate Armies (1902): {{PD-1923}} SERIES 1, Vol. XXX, Part II (Chickamauga), pp. 142

613 OFFICIAL RECORDS (OR) of the Union and Confederate Armies (1902): {{PD-1923}} SERIES 1, Vol. XXX, Part II (Chickamauga), pp. 142

614 OFFICIAL RECORDS (OR) of the Union and Confederate Armies (1902): {{PD-1923}} SERIES 1, Vol. XXX, Part II (Chickamauga), pp. 142

615 OFFICIAL RECORDS (OR) of the Union and Confederate Armies (1902): {{PD-1923}} SERIES 1, Vol. XXX, Part II (Chickamauga), pp. 142

616 OFFICIAL RECORDS (OR) of the Union and Confederate Armies (1902): {{PD-1923}} SERIES 1, Vol. XXX, Part II (Chickamauga), pp. 142

617 OFFICIAL RECORDS (OR) of the Union and Confederate Armies (1902): {{PD-1923}} SERIES 1, Vol. XXX, Part II (Chickamauga), pp. 142

618 OFFICIAL RECORDS (OR) of the Union and Confederate Armies (1902): {{PD-1923}} SERIES 1, Vol. XXX, Part II (Chickamauga), pp. 143

619 OFFICIAL RECORDS (OR) of the Union and Confederate Armies (1902): {{PD-1923}} SERIES 1, Vol. XXX, Part II (Chickamauga), pp. 143

620 OFFICIAL RECORDS (OR) of the Union and Confederate Armies (1902): {{PD-1923}} SERIES 1, Vol. XXX, Part II (Chickamauga), pp. 143

621 OFFICIAL RECORDS (OR) of the Union and Confederate Armies (1902): {{PD-1923}} SERIES 1, Vol. XXX, Part II (Chickamauga), pp. 143

622 OFFICIAL RECORDS (OR) of the Union and Confederate Armies (1902): {{PD-1923}} SERIES 1, Vol. XXX, Part II (Chickamauga), pp. 143

623 OFFICIAL RECORDS (OR) of the Union and Confederate Armies (1902): {{PD-1923}} SERIES 1, Vol. XXX, Part II (Chickamauga), pp. 144

624 OFFICIAL RECORDS (OR) of the Union and Confederate Armies (1902): {{PD-1923}} SERIES 1, Vol. XXX, Part II (Chickamauga), pp. 144

625 OFFICIAL RECORDS (OR) of the Union and Confederate Armies (1902): {{PD-1923}} SERIES 1, Vol. XXX, Part II (Chickamauga), pp. 144

626 OFFICIAL RECORDS (OR) of the Union and Confederate Armies (1902): {{PD-1923}} SERIES 1, Vol. XXX, Part II (Chickamauga), pp. 144

627 OFFICIAL RECORDS (OR) of the Union and Confederate Armies (1902): {{PD-1923}} SERIES 1, Vol. XXX, Part II (Chickamauga), pp. 144

628 OFFICIAL RECORDS (OR) of the Union and Confederate Armies (1902): {{PD-1923}} SERIES 1, Vol. XXX, Part II (Chickamauga), pp. 144

629 OFFICIAL RECORDS (OR) of the Union and Confederate Armies (1902): {{PD-1923}} SERIES 1, Vol. XXX, Part II (Chickamauga), pp. 145

630 OFFICIAL RECORDS (OR) of the Union and Confederate Armies (1902): {{PD-1923}} SERIES 1, Vol. XXX, Part II (Chickamauga), pp. 145

631 OFFICIAL RECORDS (OR) of the Union and Confederate Armies (1902): {{PD-1923}} SERIES 1, Vol. XXX, Part II (Chickamauga), pp. 145

632 Lives of Distinguished North Carolinians (1898) William Joseph Peele {{PD-1923}} p. 554

633 Lives of Distinguished North Carolinians (1898) William Joseph Peele {{PD-1923}} pp. 554-555

634 Lives of Distinguished North Carolinians (1898) William Joseph Peele {{PD-1923}} pp. 554-555

635 Lives of Distinguished North Carolinians (1898) William Joseph Peele {{PD-1923}} pp. 554-555

636 D. H. Hill Papers, NC Archives (1915): [[NC Archives]] {{PD-1923}}

637 Biographical History of North Carolina (1908): Samuel A. Ashe {{PD-1923}} p. 142

638 Lives of Distinguished North Carolinians (1898) William Joseph Peele {{PD-1923}} pp. 554-555

639 Battles and Leaders of the Civil War (1887-1888): Vol. 3 R. U. Johnson; C. Buel; {{PD-1923}} p. 642

640 Lives of Distinguished North Carolinians (1898) William Joseph Peele {{PD-1923}} p. 557

641 Biographical History of North Carolina (1908): Samuel A. Ashe {{PD-1923}} pp. 142-143

642 D. H. Hill Papers, NC Archives (1915): [[NC Archives]] {{PD-1923}}

643 Biographical History of North Carolina (1908): Samuel A. Ashe {{PD-1923}} p. 143

644 Lives of Distinguished North Carolinians (1898) William Joseph Peele {{PD-1923}} p. 557

645 D. H. Hill Papers, NC Archives (1915): [[NC Archives]] {{PD-1923}}

646 Consolidated index to compiled service records of Confederate Soldiers (1957) US National Archives and Records; CSA {{PD-1923}} Reel 221 - Call Number 1890601.1

647 D. H. Hill Papers, NC Archives (1915): [[NC Archives]] {{PD-1923}}

648 Histories of Regiments and Battalions - North Carolina (1901) Vol. I-X Walter Clark editor {{PD-1923}} p. 350

649 D. H. Hill Papers, NC Archives (1915): [[NC Archives]] {{PD-1923}}

650 D. H. Hill Papers, NC Archives (1915): [[NC Archives]] {{PD-1923}}

651 Consolidated index to compiled service records of Confederate Soldiers (1957) USNational Archives and Records; CSA {{PD-1923}} Reel 221 - Call Number 1890601.1

652 Lives of Distinguished North Carolinians (1898) William Joseph Peele {{PD-1923}} p. 557

653 *D. H. Hill Papers, NC Archives (1915): [[NC Archives]] {{PD-1923}}// Biography of Daniel Harvey Hill Lieutenant General, CSA (1886): Joseph M. Hill {{PD-1923}} p. 24*

654 *D. H. Hill Papers, NC Archives (1915): [[NC Archives]] {{PD-1923}}// Biography of Daniel Harvey Hill Lieutenant General, CSA (1886): Joseph M. Hill {{PD-1923}} p. 25*

655 *D. H. Hill Papers, NC Archives (1915): [[NC Archives]] {{PD-1923}}// Biography of Daniel Harvey Hill Lieutenant General, CSA (1886): Joseph M. Hill {{PD-1923}} p. 26*

656 *D. H. Hill Papers, NC Archives (1915): [[NC Archives]] {{PD-1923}}// Biography of Daniel Harvey Hill Lieutenant General, CSA (1886): Joseph M. Hill {{PD-1923}} p. 26*

657 *D. H. Hill Papers, NC Archives (1915): [[NC Archives]] {{PD-1923}}// Biography of Daniel Harvey Hill Lieutenant General, CSA (1886): Joseph M. Hill {{PD-1923}} pp. 26-27*

658 *D. H. Hill Papers, NC Archives (1915): [[NC Archives]] {{PD-1923}}// Biography of Daniel Harvey Hill Lieutenant General, CSA (1886): Joseph M. Hill {{PD-1923}} p. 27*

659 *D. H. Hill Papers, NC Archives (1915): [[NC Archives]] {{PD-1923}}// Biography of Daniel Harvey Hill Lieutenant General, CSA (1886): Joseph M. Hill {{PD-1923}} p. 27*

660 *Battles and Leaders of the Civil War (1887-1888): Vol. 4 R. U. Johnson; C. Buel; Vol. 4 {{PD-1923}} p. 263*

661 *Story of the Confederate States (1898): J. T. Derry {{PD-1923}} p. 402*

662 *Story of the Confederate States (1898): J. T. Derry {{PD-1923}} p. 403*

663 *Battles and Leaders of the Civil War (1887-1888): Vol. 4 R. U. Johnson; C. Buel; Vol. 4 {{PD-1923}} pp. 263-277*

664 *Story of the Confederate States (1898): J. T. Derry {{PD-1923}} p. 404*

665 *Battles and Leaders of the Civil War (1887-1888): Vol. 4 R. U. Johnson; C. Buel; Vol. 4 {{PD-1923}} pp. 263-277*

666 *Story of the Confederate States (1898): J. T. Derry {{PD-1923}} p. 404*

667 *Battles and Leaders of the Civil War (1887-1888): Vol. 4 R. U. Johnson; C. Buel; Vol. 4 {{PD-1923}} pp. 263-277*

668 *Story of the Confederate States (1898): J. T. Derry {{PD-1923}} p. 404*

669 *Battles and Leaders of the Civil War (1887-1888): Vol. 4 R. U. Johnson; C. Buel; Vol. 4 {{PD-1923}} pp. 263-277*

670 *Story of the Confederate States (1898): J. T. Derry {{PD-1923}} p. 405*

671 *Story of the Confederate States (1898): J. T. Derry {{PD-1923}} p. 405*

672 *Consolidated index to compiled service records of Confederate Soldiers (1957) US National Archives and Records; CSA {{PD-1923}} Reel 221 - Call Number 1890601.1*

673 *Story of the Confederate States (1898): J. T. Derry {{PD-1923}} p. 406*

674 *Battles and Leaders of the Civil War (1887-1888): Vol. 4 R. U. Johnson; C. Buel; Vol. 4 {{PD-1923}} pp. 263-277*

675 *Battles and Leaders of the Civil War (1887-1888): Vol. 4 R. U. Johnson; C. Buel; Vol. 4 {{PD-1923}} pp. 263-277*

676 *Battles and Leaders of the Civil War (1887-1888): Vol. 4 R. U. Johnson; C. Buel; Vol. 4 {{PD-1923}} pp. 263-277*

677 *Battles and Leaders of the Civil War (1887-1888): Vol. 4 R. U. Johnson; C. Buel; Vol. 4 {{PD-1923}} pp. 263-277*

678 *Battles and Leaders of the Civil War (1887-1888): Vol. 4 R. U. Johnson; C. Buel; Vol. 4 {{PD-1923}} pp. 263-277*

679 *D. H. Hill Papers, NC Archives (1915): [[NC Archives]] {{PD-1923}}*

680 *Battles and Leaders of the Civil War (1887-1888): Vol. 4 R. U. Johnson; C. Buel; Vol. 4 {{PD-1923}} pp. 263-277*

681 *The Land We Love (1867-68): Vol. IV, Nov-Apr 1867-68; Daniel Harvey Hill {{PD-1923}} p. 272 - full article*

682 *The Land We Love (1867-68): Vol. IV, Nov-Apr 1867-68; Daniel Harvey Hill {{PD-1923}} p. 272 – full*

683 *Library of Southern Literature (1907): Vol. XI E. A. Alderman; J. C. Harris, editors {{PD-1923}} pp. 112-113*

684 *Consolidated index to compiled service records of Confederate Soldiers (1957) US National Archives and Records; CSA {{PD-1923}} Reel 221 - Call Number 1890601.1*

685 *D. H. Hill Papers, NC Archives (1915): [[NC Archives]] {{PD-1923}}*

686 *A Fighter from Way Back (2002): Nathaniel C. Hughes Jr. and Timothy D. Johnson - full text*

687 *D. H. Hill Papers, NC Archives (1915): [[NC Archives]] {{PD-1923}}*

688 *The Land We Love (1866): May-Oct 1866; Daniel Harvey Hill {{PD-1923}} full text*

689 *The Land We Love (1867-68): Vol. IV, Nov-Apr 1867-68; Daniel Harvey Hill {{PD-1923}} full text*

690 *D. H. Hill Papers, NC Archives (1915): [[NC Archives]] {{PD-1923}}*

691 *The Land We Love (1867-68): Vol. IV, Nov-Apr 1867-68; Daniel Harvey Hill {{PD-1923}} the Haversack p. 155*

692 *D. H. Hill Papers, NC Archives (1915): [[NC Archives]] {{PD-1923}}*

693 *The Land We Love (1867-68): Vol. IV, Nov-Apr 1867-68; Daniel Harvey Hill {{PD-1923}} p. 272 - full article*

694 *D. H. Hill Papers, NC Archives (1915): [[NC Archives]] {{PD-1923}}//Biography of Daniel Harvey Hill Lieutenant General, CSA (1886): Joseph M. Hill {{PD-1923}} pp. 31-37*

695 *The Southern Home (1870-1881): Daniel Harvey Hill {{PD-1923}} all issues*

696 *D. H. Hill Papers, NC Archives (1915): [[NC Archives]] {{PD-1923}}//Biography of Daniel Harvey Hill Lieutenant General, CSA (1886): Joseph M. Hill {{PD-1923}} pp. 31-37*

697 *D. H. Hill Papers, NC Archives (1915): [[NC Archives]] {{PD-1923}}//Biography of Daniel Harvey Hill Lieutenant General, CSA (1886): Joseph M. Hill {{PD-1923}} pp. 31-37*

698 *Biographical History of North Carolina (1908): Samuel A. Ashe {{PD-1923}} p. 144*

699 *D. H. Hill Papers, NC Archives (1915): [[NC Archives]] {{PD-1923}}//Biography of Daniel Harvey Hill Lieutenant General, CSA (1886): Joseph M. Hill {{PD-1923}} pp. 31-37*

700 *D. H. Hill Papers, NC Archives (1915): [[NC Archives]] {{PD-1923}}//Biography of Daniel Harvey Hill Lieutenant General, CSA (1886): Joseph M. Hill {{PD-1923}} pp. 31-37*

701 *The North Carolina Booklet (1916): Vol. XVI; April 1917; No. 4; NC DAR {{PD-1923}} p. 200*

702 *D. H. Hill Papers, NC Archives (1915): [[NC Archives]] {{PD-1923}}//Biography of Daniel Harvey Hill*

703 *D. H. Hill Papers, NC Archives (1915): [[NC Archives]] {{PD-1923}}//Biography of Daniel Harvey Hill Lieutenant General, CSA (1886): Joseph M. Hill {{PD-1923}} pp. 31-37*

704 *Biographical History of North Carolina (1908): Samuel A. Ashe {{PD-1923}} p. 144*

705 *D. H. Hill Papers, NC Archives (1915): [[NC Archives]] {{PD-1923}}//Biography of Daniel Harvey Hill Lieutenant General, CSA (1886): Joseph M. Hill {{PD-1923}} pp. 31-37*

706 *D. H. Hill Papers, NC Archives (1915): [[NC Archives]] {{PD-1923}}//Biography of Daniel Harvey Hill Lieutenant General, CSA (1886): Joseph M. Hill {{PD-1923}} pp. 31-37*

707 *D. H. Hill Papers, NC Archives (1915): [[NC Archives]] {{PD-1923}}//Biography of Daniel Harvey Hill Lieutenant General, CSA (1886): Joseph M. Hill {{PD-1923}} pp. 31-37*

708 *D. H. Hill Papers, NC Archives (1915): [[NC Archives]] {{PD-1923}}//Biography of Daniel Harvey Hill*

709 *D. H. Hill Papers, NC Archives (1915): [[NC Archives]] {{PD-1923}}//Biography of Daniel Harvey Hill Lieutenant General, CSA (1886): Joseph M. Hill {{PD-1923}} pp. 31-37*

710 *D. H. Hill Papers, NC Archives (1915): [[NC Archives]] {{PD-1923}}//Biography of Daniel Harvey Hill Lieutenant General, CSA (1886): Joseph M. Hill {{PD-1923}} pp. 31-37*

711 *D. H. Hill Papers, NC Archives (1915): [[NC Archives]] {{PD-1923}}//Biography of Daniel Harvey Hill Lieutenant General, CSA (1886): Joseph M. Hill {{PD-1923}} pp. 31-37*

MAP REFERENCES

MAP ONE: *Battle of Big Bethel: Topographical Sketch of The Battle of Bethel, June 10th (1861) Virginia: SN (1861); Handwritten inscription in upper margin: Presented to Mrs. M.E. Taylor with filial respect by her son Wm. B. Taylor. DLC; G3884.H2:2B5S5 1861 .T6; Library of Congress Geography and Map Division Washington, D.C. 20540-4650 USA; not in copyright; {{PD-1923}} digital sponsor Google; g3884h cw1001000 // Military Map Of South Eastern Virginia (1864) Lindenkohl, A.; H. Lindenkohl & Chas. G. Krebs, lith., (1864); Another copy is in the Fillmore map coll. no. 256. DLC - Another copy is in the James A. Garfield papers, Manuscript Division, L.C., series 8, container no. 1. DLC; G3881.S5 1864 .L53; Library of Congress Geography and Map Division Washington, D.C. 20540-4650 not in copyright; {{PD-1923}} digital sponsor Google; g3881s cw0491000*

MAP TWO: Peninsula Campaign: *Birds-Eye View Of The Seat Of War Around Richmond Showing The Battle Of Chickahominy River, 29 June (1862) John Bachmann; New York NY; (1862); Civil War - History; G3884.R5S5 1862 .B23; Library of Congress Geography and Map Division Washington, D.C., USA 20540-4650; not in copyright; {{PD-1923}} digital sponsor Google; g3884r cw0621000*

MAP THREE: *Battle of Yorktown: Yorktown to Williamsburg (1862) Henry L. Abbot; Civil War - History; G3883.Y6S5 1862 .A22; Library of Congress Geography and Map Division Washington, D.C. 20540-4650; g3883y cw0600000// Military Map Of South Eastern Virginia (1864) Lindenkohl, A.; H. Lindenkohl & Chas. G. Krebs, lith., (1864); Civil War - History - Petersburg Region - Petersburg Region (Va.); Another copy is in the Fillmore map coll. no. 256. DLC - Another copy is in the James A. Garfield papers, Manuscript Division, L.C., series 8, container no. 1. DLC; G3881.S5 1864 .L53; Library of Congress Geography and Map Division Washington, D.C. 20540-4650; not in copyright; {{PD-1923}} digital sponsor Google; g3881s cw0491000*

MAP FOUR: *Battle of Williamsburg: Yorktown to Williamsburg (1862) Henry L. Abbot; G3883.Y6S5 1862 .A22; Library of Congress Geography and Map Division Washington, D.C. 20540-4650; g3883y cw0600000// Military Map Of South Eastern Virginia (1864) Lindenkohl, A.; H. Lindenkohl & Chas. G. Krebs, lith., (1864); Another copy is in the Fillmore map coll. no. 256. DLC - Another copy is in the James A. Garfield papers, Manuscript Division, L.C., series 8, container no. 1. DLC; G3881.S5 1864 .L53; Library of Congress Geography and Map Division Washington, D.C. 20540-4650; not in copyright; {{PD-1923}} digital sponsor Google; g3881s cw0491000*

MAP FIVE: *Battle of Seven Pines:l Map Of The Battle Of Seven Pines - Relative Positions At The Beginning Of The Attack, And After Dark On May 31 (1862); Published 1862; G3884.R5 1862; Library of Congress Geography and Map Division Washington, D.C. 20540-4650; not in copyright; {{PD-1923}} digital sponsor Google; g3884r cw0653000//Military Map Of South Eastern Virginia (1862) A. Lindenkohl; H. Lindenkohl & Chas. G. Krebs, lith., [1862]; G3880 1862 .L35; Library of Congress Geography and Map Division Washington, D.C. 20540-4650; not in copyright; {{PD-1923}} digital sponsor Google; g3880 cw0463000*

MAP SIX: *Battle of Seven Days: Military Map Of South Eastern Virginia (1862) A. Lindenkohl; H. Lindenkohl & Chas. G. Krebs, lith., [1862]; G3880 1862 .L35; Library of Congress Geography and Map Division Washington, D.C. 20540-4650; not in copyright; {{PD-1923}} digital sponsor Google; g3880 cw0463000*

MAP SEVEN: *Battle of Mechanicsville: Plan Of the Battle Of Mechanicsville, June 26 (1862) Wells, Jacob; (1885); G3884.M25S5 1862 .W4; Library of Congress Geography and Map Division Washington, D.C. 20540-4650; not in copyright; {{PD-1923}} digital sponsor Google; g3884m cw0584000//Military Map Of South Eastern Virginia (1862) A. Lindenkohl; H. Lindenkohl & Chas. G. Krebs, lith., [1862]; G3880 1862 .L35; Library of Congress Geography and Map Division Washington, D.C. 20540-4650; not in copyright; {{PD-1923}} digital sponsor Google; g3880 cw0463000*

MAP EIGHT: *Battle of Frayser's Farm: Map of the Battle of Frayser's Farm (1885) Charles City Cross Roads or Glendale June 30, (1862); Wells, Jacob; (1885); LC Civil War Maps (2nd ed.), 549 - from Century illustrated monthly magazine, v. 30, July 1885. p. 470; G3882.W44S5 1885 .W4; Library of Congress Geography and Map Division Washington, D.C. 20540-4650; not in copyright; {{PD-1923}} digital sponsor Google; g3882w cw0549000 http://hdl.loc.gov/ loc.gmd/ g3882w.cw0549000// Military Map Of South Eastern Virginia (1862) A. Lindenkohl; H. Lindenkohl & Chas. G. Krebs, lith., [1862]; G3880 1862 .L35; Library of Congress Geography and Map Division Washington, D.C. 20540-4650; not in copyright; {{PD-1923}} digital sponsor Google; g3880 cw0463000*

MAP NINE: *Battle of Gaines' Mill: Map Of The Battle Field Of Gaines's Mill - the Topography from the Official Map June 27, (1862) Wells, Jacob; (1885); G3884.O45S5 1862 .W4; Library of Congress Geography and Map Division Washington, D.C. 20540-4650; not in copyright; {{PD-1923}} digital sponsor Google; g3884o cw0558000//Military Map Of South Eastern Virginia (1862) A. Lindenkohl; H. Lindenkohl & Chas. G. Krebs, lith., [1862]; G3880 1862 .L35; Library of Congress Geography and Map Division Washington, D.C. 20540-4650; not in copyright; {{PD-1923}} digital sponsor Google; g3880 cw0463000*

MAP TEN: *Battle of Savage Station: Plan of the Battle at Savage's Station June 29, (1862) Wells, Jacob; (1885); - LC Civil War Maps (2nd ed.), 650 - from Century illustrated monthly magazine, v. 30, July 1885. p. 460; G3882.S3S5 1862 .W4; Library of Congress Geography and Map Division Washington, D.C. 20540-4650; not in* copyright; {{PD-1923}} *digital sponsor Google; g3882s cw0650000//Military Map Of South Eastern Virginia (1862) A. Lindenkohl; H. Lindenkohl & Chas. G. Krebs, lith., [1862]; G3880 1862 .L35; Library of Congress Geography and Map Division Washington, D.C. 20540-4650; not in copyright; {{PD-1923}} digital sponsor Google; g3880 cw0463000*

MAP ELEVEN: *Battle of Malvern Hill: Map of the Battle of Malvern Hill July 1, (1862) Wells, Jacob; (1885); LC Civil War Maps (2nd ed.), 560; from Century illustrated monthly magazine, v. 30, Aug. 1885. p. 617; G3882.M28S5 1862 .W4; Library of Congress Geography and Map Division Washington, D.C. 20540-4650; not in copyright; {{PD-1923}} digital sponsor Google; g3882m cw0560000//Military Map Of South Eastern Virginia (1862) A. Lindenkohl; H. Lindenkohl & Chas. G. Krebs, lith., [1862]; G3880 1862 .L35; Library of Congress Geography and Map Division Washington, D.C. 20540-4650; not in copyright; {{PD-1923}} digital sponsor Google; g3880 cw0463000*

MAP TWELVE: *Maryland Campaign: Panorama Of The Seat Of War. Birds-Eye View Of Virginia, Maryland, Delaware, And The District Of Columbia (1861) John Bachmann; New York NY; John Bachmann - Publisher; Baltimore MD; Jas. S. Waters – Distributor; (1861); Civil War - History; G3791.S5 1861 .B3 MLC//Library of Congress Geography and Map Division Washington, D.C. 20540-4650 USA; not in copyright; {{PD-1923}} digital sponsor Google; g3791s cw1044000.*

MAP THIRTEEN: *Battle of Harper's Ferry: Harper's Ferry   (1863) N. Michler; N.Y., Photolith by the N.Y. Lithographing, Engraving & Printing Co., Julius Bien, Supt. (1867); LC Civil War Maps (2nd ed.), 697.5; G3894.H25 1867 .M5; Library of Congress Geography and Map Division Washington, D.C. 20540-4650; not in copyright; {{PD-1923}} digital sponsor Google; g3894h cw0697500//Sifton, Praed's New Map of Virginia and Maryland to illustrate the Campaigns of 1861 to 1864 – (1912) Sifton, Praed & Company, Ltd; London, Sifton, Praed & Co., Ltd., "The Map House", (1912); LC Civil War Maps (2nd ed.), 499.5; G3880 1864 .S5; Library of Congress Geography and Map Division Washington, D.C. 20540-4650; not in copyright; {{PD-1923}} digital sponsor Google; g3880 cw0499500*

MAP FOURTEEN: *Battle of South Mountain: Battle Field Map Showing Field of Operations of The Armies Of The Potomac And James (1892) J. C. Van Hook; Washington (1892); LC Civil War Maps (2nd ed.), 520.5; Another copy is in the Jeremiah T. Lockwood papers, Manuscript Division, L.C.; G3881.S5 1892 .V3; Library of Congress Geography and Map Division Washington, D.C. 20540-4650; not in copyright; {{PD-1923}} digital sponsor Google; g3881s cw0520500//Sifton, Praed's New Map of Virginia and Maryland to illustrate the Campaigns of 1861 to 1864 – (1912) Sifton, Praed & Company, Ltd; London, Sifton, Praed & Co., Ltd., "The Map House", (1912); LC Civil War Maps (2nd ed.), 499.5; G3880 1864 .S5; Library of Congress Geography and Map Division Washington, D.C. 20540-4650; not in copyright; {{PD-1923}} digital sponsor Google; g3880 cw0499500*

MAP FIFTEEN: *Battle of Sharpsburg: Map of The Battlefield of Antietam (1862) William H. Willcox; Philadelphia PA., Lith. of P. S. Duval & Son, (1862); LC Civil War Maps (2nd ed.), 252; G3844.S43S5 1862 .W55; Library of Congress Geography and Map Division Washington, D.C. 20540-4650; not in copyright; {{PD-1923}} digital sponsor Google; g3844s cw0252000//Sifton, Praed's New Map of Virginia and Maryland to illustrate the Campaigns of 1861 to 1864 – (1912) Sifton, Praed & Company, Ltd; London, Sifton, Praed & Co., Ltd., "The Map House", (1912); LC Civil War Maps (2nd ed.), 499.5; G3880 1864 .S5; Library of Congress Geography and Map Division Washington, D.C. 20540-4650; not in copyright; {{PD-1923}} digital sponsor Google; g3880 cw0499500*

MAP SIXTEEN: *Battle of Chickamauga: Chickamauga Battlefield - accompanies the Battle of Chickamauga (1895) Joseph C. Mcelroy; Cincinnati, OH, the Henderson-Achert-Krebs Lith. Co., (1895);; LC Civil War Maps (2nd ed.), 156; G3922.C52S5 1895 .M32; Library of Congress Geography and Map Division Washington, D.C. 20540-4650; not in copyright; {{PD-1923}} digital sponsor Google; g3922c cw0156000//Map of Chickamauga & Chattanooga National Park (1895) Nashville, Chattanooga and St. Louis Railway; Nashville, Nashville, Chattanooga & St. Louis Ry., (1895; LC Civil War Maps (2nd ed.), 157.6; Copyright, 1895 by Nashville, Chattanooga & St. Louis Railway; G3922.C5 1895 .N3; Library of Congress Geography and Map Division Washington, D.C. 20540-4650; not in copyright; {{PD-1923}} digital sponsor Google; g3922c cw0157600*

MAP SEVENTEEN: *Battle of Bentonville: Battle of Bentonville, March 19, (1865) author unknown; np; (1865); G3904.B56S5 1865 .B3; Library of Congress Geography and Map Division Washington, D.C. 20540-4650; not in copyright; {{PD-1923}} digital sponsor Google; g3904b cw030900a//North Carolina - with adjacent parts of Virginia and South Carolina (1865) A. Lindenkohl; U.S. Coast Survey, A. D. Bache, Supdt., (1865);; LC Civil War Maps (2nd ed.), 305a.6; G3900 1865 .L52; Library of Congress Geography and Map Division Washington, D.C. 20540-4650; not in copyright; {{PD-1923}} digital sponsor Google; g3900 cw0305a60*

FAMOUS QUOTE REFERENCES

1 "Hill's presence was always sufficient to give full assurance that we were in the right place and we had only to fight to win" *Histories of the Several Regiments and Battalions from North Carolina (1861-1865)* Vol. I-X; Goldsboro, NC, Walter Clark ed; Raleigh E. M. Uzzel; (1901); not in copyright; {{PD-1923}} digital sponsor Google; University of Michigan; civil war documents; Americana; www archive org; copy of text in D R Hill Family Library MARCXML

2 "was a man of considerable capacity and always seemed to go from choice into the most dangerous place he could find on the field" General James Longstreet; *From Manassas to Appomattox: Memoirs of the Civil War in America (1895) James Longstreet;* Philadelphia, PA, J. B. Lippincott & Co; (1908); not in copyright; {{PD-1923}} digital sponsor Google; Harvard University; civil war documents; Americana; www archive org; copy of text in D R Hill Family Library MARCXML

3 "Do you know that in Mexico the young officers called you the bravest man in the army?" *Joseph E. Johnston; Lives of Distinguished North Carolinians (1898) William Joseph Peele; Raleigh, NC, The North Carolina Publishing Society; (1897); not in copyright; {{PD-1923}} digital sponsor Google; Harvard University; civil war documents; Americana; www archive org; copy of text in D R Hill Family Library MARCXML*

4 "Intemperance or dissipation in any form was for him the unpardonable sin. D. H. Hill was a man of literary attainments, an assiduous student of Holy Scripture, and as a teacher of mathematics unsurpassed among American teachers." Henry Elliott Shepherd; *Library of Southern Literature (1907) Edwin Anderson Alderman, Joel Chandler Harris, ed.; Atlanta, GA; The Martin & Hoyt Co.; (1907); Vol. XI; not in copyright; {{PD-1923}} digital sponsor Google; University of Virginia Library; civil war documents; Americana; www archive org; copy of text in D R Hill Family Library MARCXML*

5 "shooters before tooters" Henry Elliott Shepherd; *Library of Southern Literature (1907) Edwin Anderson Alderman, Joel Chandler Harris, ed.; Atlanta, GA; The Martin & Hoyt Co.; (1907); Vol. XI; not in copyright; {{PD-1923}} digital sponsor Google; University of Virginia Library; civil war documents; Americana; www archive org; copy of text in D R Hill Family Library MARCXML*

6 "never a more plucker or determined fighter." General James Longstreet; *From Manassas to Appomattox: Memoirs of the Civil War in America (1895) James Longstreet;* Philadelphia, PA, J. B. Lippincott & Co; (1908); not in copyright; {{PD-1923}} digital sponsor Google; Harvard University; civil war documents; Americana; www archive org; copy of text in D R Hill Family Library MARCXML

7 "in action & under fire he commands the admiration & respect of everyone" James N. *Edmondston, May 1863; OFFICIAL RECORD - (OR) - A Compilation of the Official Records - Union and Confederate Armies (1902) US War Department; Scott, Davis, Perry, Kirkley, Ainsworth, Fred C. Ainsworth & Joseph W. Kirkley – ed; (1902) PART2; Publisher - Washington Government Printing Office; not in copyright; {{PD-1923}} digital sponsor Google; University of Virginia; civil war* documents; Americana; www archive org; copy of text in D R Hill Family Library MARCXML

8 "The annals of war have not set before us a more heroic or dauntless soul. He excelled in the characteristics of invincible tenacity, absolute unconsciousness of fear, courage never to submit or yield, no one has risen above him, not even in the annals of the Army of Northern Virginia." Henry Elliott Shepherd; *Life of Robert Edward Lee (1906) Henry Elliot Shepherd; New York and Washington, The Neale Publishing Company; (1906); not in copyright; {{PD-1923}} digital sponsor Google; New York Public Library; civil war documents; Americana; www archive org; copy of text in D R Hill Family Library MARCXML*

9 It would be great presumption in me to criticize any movement directed by General Johnston, in whose skill and generalship I have always entertained implicit confidence, and I should not now venture to express an opinion as to the propriety" Joseph E. Johnston; *Battles and Leaders of the Civil War (1887-1888) Robert Underwood Johnson, Clarence Clough Buel; Vol. 4; NY -Century Co; (1887); not in copyright; {{PD-1923}} digital sponsor Google; Internet Archive; Boston Public Library; civil war documents; Americana; www archive org; copy of text in D R Hill Family Library; {{PD-1923}} MARCXML.*

10 "Qualities of leadership which inspired the utmost confidence and loyalty in his soldiers and made him the idol of the Carolinas" *James W. Ratchford;* Some Reminiscences of Persons and Incidents of the Civil War (1909) James W. Ratchford; unk; (1909); not in copyright; {{PD-1923}} digital sponsor Google; Internet Archive; Boston Public Library; civil war documents; Americana; www archive org; copy of text in D R Hill Family Library; {{PD-1923}} MARCXML.

11 "He was the very "Ironsides" of the South – Cromwell in some of his essential characteristics coming again in the person and genius of D. H. Hill." Henry Elliott Shepherd; *Life of Robert Edward Lee (1906) Henry Elliot Shepherd; New York and Washington, The Neale Publishing Company; (1906); not in copyright; {{PD-1923}} digital sponsor Google; New York Public Library; civil war documents; Americana; www archive org; copy of text in D R Hill Family Library MARCXML*

12 "His absolute unconsciousness of danger was enough to thrill the ordinary brain with a sort of vertigo as it revealed itself in the most phenomenal situations or supreme crises." Henry Elliott Shepherd; *Life of Robert Edward Lee (1906) Henry Elliot Shepherd; New York and Washington, The Neale Publishing Company; (1906); not in copyright; {{PD-1923}} digital sponsor Google; New York Public Library; civil war documents; Americana; www archive org; copy of text in D R Hill Family Library MARCXML*

13 "Upon one occasion, his horse being shot under him, as he was in the act of writing an order, holding the paper in his hand, steed and rider sank to the earth and without the relaxation of a muscle or a movement of the head, he finished the order, handed it to a courier, as calm and unconcerned as if reviewing the battalion of cadets in the grounds of the Institute at Charlotte." *Henry Elliot Shepherd; New York and Washington, The Neale Publishing Company; (1906); not in copyright; {{PD-1923}} digital sponsor Google; New York Public Library; civil war documents; Americana; www archive org; copy of text in D R Hill Family Library MARCXML*

14 "Fancy a man in whom the grim determination of a veteran warrior is united to a gentle tenderness of manner . . . . affix a pair of eyes that possess the most indisputably honest and kindly expression; animate him with a mind clear, deep and comprehensive, and imbued with a humor as rich as it is deep and effective; infuse man and mind with a soul which in its lofty views compels subordinates of the material to the spiritual, and holds a supreme trust in the wisdom and goodness of the Almighty – is zealous in the discharge of duty, and looks with scorn on all that is mean and sinful. Add to all these a carriage that is indomitable, and a love of truth and honor which is sublime, and you have the earthly embodiment of D. H. Hill." The Honorable A. C. Avery; *Lives of Distinguished North Carolinians (1898) William Joseph Peele; Raleigh, NC, The North Carolina Publishing Society; (1897); not in copyright; {{PD-1923}} digital sponsor Google; Harvard University; civil war documents; Americana; www archive org; copy of text in D R Hill Family Library MARCXML*

15 "Had done as much hard fighting as any other general and had also displayed great ability in holding his men to their work by supervision and example." E. P. Alexander; Military Memoirs of a Confederate (1907); NY NY Charles Scribner's Sons; (1907); *not in copyright; {{PD-1923}} digital sponsor Google; New York Public Library; civil war documents; Americana; www archive org; copy of text in D R Hill Family Library MARCXML*

16 "High and well deserved reputation as a hard fighter...seemed to go from choice into the most dangerous place he could find on the field." John Haskell; Military Memoirs of a Confederate (1907); NY NY Charles Scribner's Sons; (1907); *not in copyright; {{PD-1923}} digital sponsor Google; New York Public Library; civil war documents; Americana; www archive org; copy of text in D R Hill Family Library MARCXML*

17 "Stonewall Jackson repeatedly declared in my hearing that there was not...a man in the Southern Army, superior in military genius to D.H. Hill." *James W. Ratchford; Some* Reminiscences of Persons and Incidents of the Civil War (1909) James W. Ratchford; unk; (1909); not in copyright; {{PD-1923}} digital sponsor Google; Internet Archive; Boston Public Library; civil war documents; Americana; www archive org; copy of text in D R Hill Family Library; {{PD-1923}} MARCXML.

18 "....a capable, well read soldier, and positively about the bravest man ever seen. He seemed not to know peril and was utterly indifferent to bullets and shell...." General G. Moxley Sorrell; *Recollections of a Confederate Staff Officer (1905) G. Moxley Sorrell; NY, NY; The Neale Publishing Co; (1905); not in copyright; {{PD-1923}} digital sponsor Google; Lenox and Tilden Foundations; Michigan University Library; civil war documents; Americana; www archive org; copy of text in D R Hill Family Library; {{PD-1923}}* 19

"Like Jackson he was, too, a born fighter – as aggressive, pugnacious and tenacious as s bull-dog, or as any soldier in the service, and he had a sort of monomania on the subject of personal courage." Stiles, Robert. Four Years Under Marse Robert (1910) Robert Stiles; NY, NY, The Neale Publishing Co; (1909); *not in copyright; {{PD-1923}} digital sponsor Google; Princeton University Library; civil war documents; Americana; www archive org; copy of text in D R Hill Family Library; {{PD-1923}}*

20 "The officers and men under your command will be treated as prisoners of war, but you will be castrated." D. H. Hill; The War Between the Union and the Confederacy (1905) William C. Oates; NY, NY, The Neale Publishing Co.; (1905); *not in copyright; {{PD-1923}} digital sponsor Google; University of Minnesota Library; civil war documents; Americana; www archive org; copy of text in D R Hill Family Library; {{PD-1923}}*

21 In a portrayal of the character of Daniel Harvey Hill his all-prevailing moral courage first reveals itself with its correlated traits: absolute loyalty to truth, frankness, ingenuousness, an incapacity to play the hypocrite, effacement of self, and insensibility to fear. In this rarest of human virtues he was preeminent; his ethical creed might be concisely embodied in the language of a poet. "

22 "Because right is right, to follow right were wisdom in the scorn of consequences" Henry E. Shepherd, *Confederate Veteran Magazine (1917) R. A. Cunningham – Founder; Nashville, TN; (1917); not in copyright; {{PD-1923}} digital sponsor Google; Duke University; civil war documents; Americana; www archive org; copy of text in D R Hill Family Library MARCXML*

23 "Fast riding in the wrong direction is not military, but is sometimes healthy." D. H. Hill; *Battles and Leaders of the Civil War (1887-1888) Robert Underwood Johnson, Clarence Clough Buel; Vol. 2; NY -Century Co; (1887); not in copyright; {{PD-1923}} digital sponsor Google; Boston Public Library; civil war documents; Americana; www archive org; copy of text in D R Hill Family Library;   MARCXML.*

24 "He was a skill-full officer, intelligent and keen eyed, stern to rebuke violation of orders and lack of discipline-a determined fighter-as the boys expressed it, "A fighter from way back"; William Smith, 14th NC Infantry; The Anson Guards: History of Company "C" 14th Regiment North Carolina Volunteers, Army of Northern Virginia," Maj. W.A. Smith, Charlotte, NC, Stone Publishing Company; (1914;) *not in copyright; {{PD-1923}} digital sponsor Google;; civil war documents; Americana; www archive org; copy of text in D R Hill Family Library;   MARCXML.*

25 "In my official reports. . . . I criticized the management of General Lee at Malvern Hill and South Mountain. He was then alive, my commander, and in the full tide of success. He is dead now and failed in his efforts. What I could and did do, when in the meridian of his power, I cannot do now." D. H. Hill; Letter, D.H. Hill, dated Jan 28, 1885 to Editor of Century, Century Collection; *not in copyright; {{PD-1923}} digital sponsor Google; New York Public Library; civil war documents; Americana; www archive org; copy of text in D R Hill Family Library;* MARCXML.

26 "D. H. Hill impressed me as a zealous, unselfish patriot and great soldier, who knew not fear and shrank from no duty. His Christian faith was unbounded. He could always be found at the most dangerous place in the line, doing what he could to encourage and also protect the men." Charles G. Elliott; *Southern Historical Society Papers (1885) James I. Robertson, Southern Historical Society; Vol. XIII & XIV; Richmond, VA (1885); not in copyright; {{PD-1923}} digital sponsor MSN; University of Toronto; Roberts; civil war documents; Americana; www archive org; copy of text in D R Hill Family Library MARCXML*

27 "There was never a better soldier, or a man better qualified to judge of the merits of one. The clash of battle was not a confusing din to him, but an exciting scene that awakened his spirit and his genius." *Histories of the Several Regiments and Battalions from North Carolina (1861-1865) Vol. I-X; Goldsboro, NC, Walter Clark ed; Raleigh E. M. Uzzel; (1901); not in copyright; {{PD-1923}} digital sponsor Google; University of Michigan; civil war documents; Americana; www archive org; copy of text in D R Hill Family Library MARCXML*

28 "No tribute can do justice to the unknown and unrecorded dead. Most of them exiles from home and family; men who had endured every hardship, trial, and privation for so long a period, but to find at last nameless graves, uncheered by the world's applause and uninfluenced by the hope of distinction, they sacrificed ease, comfort, happiness, life itself, upon the altar of their country." D.H.Hill; *OFFICIAL RECORD - (OR) - A Compilation of the Official Records - Union and Confederate Armies (1902) US War Department; Scott, Davis, Perry, Kirkley, Ainsworth, Fred C. Ainsworth & Joseph W. Kirkley – ed; Publisher - Washington Government Printing Office; (1902); SERIES: I VOLUME: XXX CAMPAIGN: Chickamauga SERIAL: 050; not in copyright; {{PD-1923}} digital sponsor Google; University of Virginia; civil war documents; Americana; copy of text in D R Hill Family Library www archive org; MARCXML*

29 "In a portrayal of the character of Daniel Harvey Hill his all-prevailing moral courage first reveals itself with its correlated traits; absolute loyalty to truth, frankness, ingenuousness, an incapacity to play the hypocrite, effacement of self, and insensibility to fear. In this rarest of human virtues he was preeminent; his ethical creed might be concisely embodied in the language of a poet." Henry Elliott Shepherd; *Library of Southern Literature (1907) Edwin Anderson Alderman, Joel Chandler Harris, ed.; Atlanta, GA; The Martin & Hoyt Co.; (1907); Vol. XI; not in copyright; {{PD-1923}} digital sponsor Google; University of Virginia Library; civil war documents; Americana; www archive org; copy of text in D R Hill Family Library MARCXML*

30 "Qualities of leadership which inspired the utmost confidence and loyalty in his soldiers and made him the idol of the Carolinas." *James W. Ratchford;* Some Reminiscences of Persons and Incidents of the Civil War (1909) James W. Ratchford; unk; (1909); *not in copyright; {{PD-1923}} digital sponsor Google; Internet Archive; Boston Public Library; civil war documents; Americana; www archive org; copy of text in D R Hill Family Library; {{PD-1923}} MARCXML.*

ILLUSTRATION REFERENCES

1 Library of Congress Prints and Photographs Division Washington, D.C. 20540 USA LC-USZC4-12532 // 3g12532//not in copyright; {{PD-1923}}; copy in D R Hill Family Library;

2 Library of Congress Prints and Photographs Division Washington, D.C. 20540 USA LC-HS503-1219 // 2011630674 //not in copyright; {{PD-1923}}; copy in D R Hill Family Library;

3 Library of Congress Prints and Photographs Division Washington, D.C. 20540 USA LC-HS503-1219 // 2011630674//not in copyright; {{PD-1923}}; copy in D R Hill Family Library;

4 Library of Congress Prints and Photographs Division Washington, D.C. 20540 USA LC-USZ62-52439 // 2006681376//not in copyright; {{PD-1923}}; copy in D R Hill Family Library;

5 Library of Congress Prints and Photographs Division Washington, D.C. 20540 USA- LC-DIG-PGA-02604//2001701801//not in copyright; {{PD-1923}}; copy in D R Hill Family Library;

6 Library of Congress Prints and Photographs Division Washington, D.C. 20540 USA- LC-USZC4-1751//CPH-3g01751//not in copyright; {{PD-1923}}; copy in D R Hill Family Library;

7 Library of Congress Prints and Photographs Division Washington, D.C. 20540 USA-LC-DIG-PGA-01880//CPH-3b52972//not in copyright; {{PD-1923}}; copy in D R Hill Family Library;

8 Library of Congress Prints and Photographs Division Washington, D.C. 20540 USA-LC-DIG-PGA-01886//CPH-3b52015//not in copyright; {{PD-1923}}; copy in D R Hill Family Library;

9 Library of Congress Prints and Photographs Division Washington, D.C. 20540 USA LC-USZC2-3769//CPH-3f03769//not in copyright; {{PD-1923}}; copy in D R Hill Family Library;

10 Library of Congress Prints and Photographs Division Washington, D.C. 20540 USA LC-USZ62-3579//CPH-3a07065//not in copyright; {{PD-1923}}; copy in D R Hill Family Library;

11 Library of Congress Prints and Photographs Division Washington, D.C. 20540 USA LC-DIG-PGA-00615//CPH-3a08648//not in copyright; {{PD-1923}}; copy in D R Hill Family Library;

12 Library of Congress Prints and Photographs Division Washington, D.C. 20540 USA LC-USZC4-1033//PGA-00358//not in copyright; {{PD-1923}}; copy in D R Hill Family Library;

13 Library of Congress Prints and Photographs Division Washington, D.C. 20540 USA LC-USZ62-1263//CPH-3a05091//not in copyright; {{PD-1923}}; copy in D R Hill Family Library;

14 Library of Congress Prints and Photographs Division Washington, D.C. 20540 USA LC-USZC4-4186//CPH-3g04186//not in copyright; {{PD-1923}}; copy in D R Hill Family Library;

15 Library of Congress Prints and Photographs Division Washington, D.C. 20540 USA LC-USZC2-2991//CPH-3g01738//not in copyright; {{PD-1923}}; copy in D R Hill Family Library;

16 Courtesy of Library of Congress Prints and Photographs Division Washington, D.C. 20540 USA LC-USZ62-7630//CPH//not in copyright; {{PD-1923}}; copy in D R Hill Family Library;3a10273

17 Library of Congress Prints and Photographs Division Washington, D.C. 20540 USA LC-USZC4-2086//CPH-3g02086//not in copyright; {{PD-1923}}; copy in D R Hill Family Library;

18 Library of Congress Prints and Photographs Division Washington, D.C. 20540 USA LC-USZC4-3365//CPH-3g03365//not in copyright; {{PD-1923}}; copy in D R Hill Family Library;

19 Library of Congress Prints and Photographs Division Washington, D.C. 20540 USA LC-USZC4-6126//CPH-3g06126//not in copyright; {{PD-1923}}; copy in D R Hill Family Library;

20 Library of Congress Prints and Photographs Division Washington, D.C. 20540 USA LC-DIG-PGA-04033//CPH-3b52684//not in copyright; {{PD-1923}}; copy in D R Hill Family Library;

21 Library of Congress Prints and Photographs Division Washington, D.C. 20540 USA LC-DIG-PGA-03266//CPH-3a04473//not in copyright; {{PD-1923}}; copy in D R Hill Family Library;

22 *Library of Congress Prints and Photographs Division Washington, D.C. 20540 USA LC-DIG-PGA-02746//CPH-3a10010//not in copyright; {{PD-1923}}; copy in D R Hill Family Library;*

23 *Library of Congress Prints and Photographs Division Washington, D.C. 20540 USA LC-DIG-PGA-02608//CPH-3g03036//not in copyright; {{PD-1923}}; copy in D R Hill Family Library;*

24 *Library of Congress Prints and Photographs Division Washington, D.C. 20540 USA LC-DIG-PGA-01843//PGA-01843/not in copyright; {{PD-1923}}; copy in D R Hill Family Library;*

25 *Library of Congress Prints and Photographs Division Washington, D.C. 20540 USA LC-USZC4-1618//CPH-3b53120//not in copyright; {{PD-1923}}; copy in D R Hill Family Library;*

26 *Library of Congress Prints and Photographs Division Washington, D.C. 20540 USA LC-DIG-PGA-01839//91721203//not in copyright; {{PD-1923}}; copy in D R Hill Family Library;*

27 *Library of Congress Prints and Photographs Division Washington, D.C. 20540 USA LC-USZC4-1642//90709071//not in copyright; {{PD-1923}}; copy in D R Hill Family Library;*

28 *Library of Congress Prints and Photographs Division Washington, D.C. 20540 USA LC-USZ62-469//98501341//not in copyright; {{PD-1923}}; copy in D R Hill Family Library;*

29 *Library of Congress Prints and Photographs Division Washington, D.C. 20540 USA LC-DIG-PGA-04030//2003663826//not in copyright; {{PD-1923}}; copy in D R Hill Family Library;*

30 *Library of Congress Prints and Photographs Division Washington, D.C. 20540 USA LC-DIG-PGA-04038//90712278//not in copyright; {{PD-1923}}; copy in D R Hill Family Library;*

31 *Library of Congress Prints and Photographs Division Washington, D.C. 20540 USA LC-DIG-PGA-01881//2003656852//not in copyright; {{PD-1923}}; copy in D R Hill Family Library;*

32 *Library of Congress Prints and Photographs Division Washington, D.C. 20540 USA LC-DIG-PGA-04031//2003663827//not in copyright; {{PD-1923}}; digital sponsor Google; copy in D R Hill Family Library;*

33 *Library of Congress Prints and Photographs Division Washington, D.C. 20540 USA LC-DIG-PGA-01849//91482118//not in copyright; {{PD-1923}}; copy in D R Hill Family Library;*

34 *Library of Congress Prints and Photographs Division Washington, D.C. 20540 USA LC-DIG-PGA-00539//96502868//not in copyright; {{PD-1923}}; copy in D R Hill Family Library;*

35 *Library of Congress Prints and Photographs Division Washington, D.C. 20540 USA LC-DIG-PGA-01850//91482215//not in copyright; {{PD-1923}}; copy in D R Hill Family Library;*

36 *Library of Congress Prints and Photographs Division Washington, D.C. 20540 USA LC-DIG-PGA-04037//92500191//not in copyright; {{PD-1923}}; copy in D R Hill Family Library;*

37 *Library of Congress Prints and Photographs Division Washington, D.C. 20540 USA LC-USZC4-6127//98513713//not in copyright; {{PD-1923}}; copy in D R Hill Family Library;*

38 *Library of Congress Prints and Photographs Division Washington, D.C. 20540 USA LC-USZC2-657//90709065//not in copyright; {{PD-1923}}; copy in D R Hill Family Library;*

39 *Library of Congress Prints and Photographs Division Washington, D.C. 20540 USA LC-DIG-PGA-04034//2003663829//not in copyright; {{PD-1923}}; copy in D R Hill Family Library;*

40 *Library of Congress Prints and Photographs Division Washington, D.C. 20540 USA LC-DIG-PGA-04032//93510295//not in copyright; {{PD-1923}}; digital sponsor Google; copy in D R Hill Family Library;//not in copyright; {{PD-1923}}; copy in D R Hill Family Library;*

41 *Library of Congress Prints and Photographs Division Washington, D.C. 20540 USA LC-DIG-PGA-01844//91482103//not in copyright; {{PD-1923}}; copy in D R Hill Family Library;*

42 *Library of Congress Prints and Photographs Division Washington, D.C. 20540 USA LC-DIG-PGA-01845//91482116//not in copyright; {{PD-1923}}; copy in D R Hill Family Library;*

43 *Library of Congress Prints and Photographs Division Washington, D.C. 20540 USA LC-DIG-PGA-01846//91482113//not in copyright; {{PD-1923}}; copy in D R Hill Family Library;*

44 *Library of Congress Prints and Photographs Division Washington, D.C. 20540 USA LC-USZ61-65//CPH-3a01863//not in copyright; {{PD-1923}}; copy in D R Hill Family Library;*

45 *Library of Congress Prints and Photographs Division Washington, D.C. 20540 USA LC-USZ62-8300//2001701357//not in copyright; {{PD-1923}}; copy in D R Hill Family Library;*

46 *Library of Congress Prints and Photographs Division Washington, D.C. 20540 USA LC-USZ62-8299//2001701356//not in copyright; {{PD-1923}}; copy in D R Hill Family Library;*

47 *Library of Congress Prints and Photographs Division Washington, D.C. 20540 USA LC-USZC4-2135//92515475//not in copyright; {{PD-1923}}; copy in D R Hill Family Library;*

48 *Library of Congress Prints and Photographs Division Washington, D.C. 20540 USA POS-TH-1900.R42//1994001365/PP//not in copyright; {{PD-1923}}; copy in D R Hill Family Library;*

49 *Library of Congress Prints and Photographs Division Washington, D.C. 20540 USA LC-DIG-PGA-00791//002699687//not in copyright; {{PD-1923}}; copy in D R Hill Family Library;*

50 *A West Point Cadet (1908) Capt. Paul B. Malone; Publishing Co.; (1908); p. 185//not in copyright; {{PD-1923}}; copy in D R Hill Family Library;*

51 *A West Point Cadet (1908) Capt. Paul B. Malone; Philadelphia, PA, the Penn Publishing Co.; (1908); p. 279//not in copyright; {{PD-1923}}; copy in D R Hill Family Library;*

52 *History of the University of Arkansas (1910) J. H. Reynolds and D. Y. Thomas; Fayetteville, AR, University of Arkansas; (1910); p. 298//not in copyright; {{PD-1923}}; digital sponsor Google; copy in D R Hill Family Library;*

53 *History of the University of Arkansas (1910) J. H. Reynolds and D. Y. Thomas; Fayetteville, AR, University of Arkansas; (1910); p. 128//not in copyright; {{PD-1923}}; digital sponsor Google; copy in D R Hill Family Library;*

54 *History of the University of Arkansas (1910) J. H. Reynolds and D. Y. Thomas; Fayetteville, AR, University of Arkansas; (1910); p. 128//not in copyright; {{PD-1923}}; digital sponsor Google; copy in D R Hill Family Library;*

55 *ALL CIVIL WAR GENERALS: Library of Congress Prints and Photographs Division Washington, D.C. 20540 USA LCUSZ628347-3c35819u//State Library of North Carolina: Confederate Portrait Album: Civil War, 1861-1865 (1890); North Carolina State Archives; 973.79A5118c; digital collection-Civil War; OCLC1855570//Confederate Military History (1899); Clement Anselm Evans; Vol I; Atlanta GA - Confederate Publishing Co; (1899); Appendix I//Civil War Confederate Portrait Album (1890) Thomas D. Osborne; loc; unk, American Chicle Co.; (1890); pp. 7-18//Confederate War Journal Illustrated (1894) John B. Gordon; (1894); Vol. 1, No. 1; New York & Lexington, KY; (1894)//Southern Historical Society Papers (1885) James I. Robertson, Southern Historical Society; Vol. XIII & XIV; Richmond, VA (1885)//Confederate Veteran Magazine (1917) R. A. Cunningham – Founder; Nashville, TN; (1917)//Battles and Leaders of the Civil War (1887-1888) Robert Underwood Johnson, Clarence Clough Buel; Vol. 1-4; NY -Century Co; (1887)//The Photographic History of the Civil War (1911) Francis Trevelyan Miller, Robert Sampson Lanier; Vol. 10; NY – The Review of Reviews Co.; (1911)//Pictorial History of the Civil War in the United States of America (1866) Benson John Lossing; PA – G. W. Childs; (1866)//The Civil War Through the Camera (1912) Henry William Elson; NY – McKinlay, Stone & Mackenzie; (1912)//not in copyright; {{PD-1923}}; digital sponsor Google; copy in D R Hill Family Library;*

56 *ALL MEXICAN WAR GENERALS: Library of Congress Prints and Photographs Division Washington, D.C. 20540 USALC-USZC4-6127-3a31080u//Complete History of the Late Mexican War (1850) New York, F. J. Dow & Co; (1850)//History of the Mexican War (1892) Cadmus Marcellus, Mary Rachel Wilcox ed; (1982)//Pictorial History of Mexico and the Mexican War (1862); John Frost, William H. Croome; (1862)//The Pictorial Field-Book of the Revolution (1851); Benson John Lossing; Vol. 1; NY – Harper & Bros; (1851)//Thrilling Incidents of the Wars of the United States (1860) Jacob K. Neff; NY – R. Sears; (1860)//not in copyright; {{PD-1923}}; digital sponsor Google; copy in D R Hill Family Library;*

57 *REVOLUTIONARY WAR GENERAL Thomas Sumter: Library of Congress Prints and Photographs Division Washington, D.C. 20540 USA LC-USZ62-136504_3c36504u//not in copyright; {{PD-1923}}; digital sponsor Google; copy in D R Hill Family Library;*

58 *SPECIAL ORDER 191 General Robert E. Lee's Special Order (1862) General Thomas J. Jackson; Correspondence, CSA, Stonewall Jackson; Frederick County, MD; hand-written dispatch given to General D. H. Hill, donated to North Carolina State Archives by Hill Family – PAGES 1 and 2; not in copyright; {{PD-1923}}; Call No. V.C.6; Digital Collection Treasures; civil war documents; digital.ncdcr.gov*

59 *Library of Congress Prints and Photographs Division Washington, D.C. 20540 USA LC-3g02958u//not in copyright; {{PD-1923}}; digital sponsor Google; copy in D R Hill Family Library;*

BIOGRAPHICAL REFERENCES

A Consideration of the Sermon on the Mount (1858) Daniel Harvey Hill (1858); W. S. & A. Martien; not in copyright; {{PD-1923}} digital sponsor Google; University of Michigan; Americana; www archive org; copy of text in D R Hill Family Library MARCXML

A Consideration of the Sermon on the Mount (1858) Daniel Harvey Hill; Philadelphia PA, William S. & Alfred Martien; (1859); not in copyright; {{PD-1923}} digital sponsor Google; University of Michigan; civil war documents; Americana; www archive org; copy of text in D R Hill Family Library MARCXML

A Fighter from Way Back (2002) Nathaniel C. Hughes Jr. and Timothy D. Johnson; Kent, OH, Kent State University Press; (2002); not available in digital form; copy of text in D R Hill Family Library;

A Guide Book To West Point and Vicinity (1844); NY, NY, J. H. Colton; (1844); not in copyright; {{PD-1923}} digital sponsor Google; Harvard; civil war documents; Americana; www archive org; copy of text in D R Hill Family Library MARCXML

A Memoir of the Last Year of the War for Independence in the Confederate States of America (1867): Jubal A. Early; Lynchburg, VA; Charles W. Button; (1867); not in copyright; {{PD-1923}} digital sponsor Google; University of Harvard; civil war documents; Americana; www archive org; copy of text in D R Hill Family Library; {{PD-1923}}

A Memoir of the Last Year of the War for Independence, in the Confederate States of America (1867) Jubal Anderson Early; Blelock & co; (1867); not in copyright; {{PD-1923}} digital sponsor Google; University of Michigan; civil war documents; Americana; www archive org; copy of text in D R Hill Family Library; {{PD-1923}}; p. 37

Address Delivered before the Confederate Veterans Association (1898) Walter C. Hartridge; Savannah, GA, George H. Nichols; (1898); not in copyright; {{PD-1923}} digital sponsor Google; Cambridge University of New York; civil war documents; Americana; www archive org; copy of text in D R Hill Family Library; {{PD-1923}};

Battle-Fields of the South (1864) English Combatant; New York, J. Bradburn; (1864); not in copyright; {{PD-1923}} digital sponsor MSN; University of California Libraries; civil war documents; Americana; www archive org; copy of text in D R Hill Family Library MARCXML

Battles and Leaders of the Civil War (1887-1888) Robert Underwood Johnson, Clarence Clough Buel; Vol. 2; NY - Century Co; (1887); not in copyright; {{PD-1923}} digital sponsor Google; Boston Public Library; civil war documents; Americana; www archive org; copy of text in D R Hill Family Library; MARCXML.

Battles and Leaders of the Civil War (1887-1888) Robert Underwood Johnson, Clarence Clough Buel; Vol. 3; NY - Century Co; (1887); not in copyright; {{PD-1923}} digital sponsor Google; Boston Public Library; civil war documents; Americana; www archive org; copy of text in D R Hill Family Library; MARCXML.

Battles and Leaders of the Civil War (1887-1888) Robert Underwood Johnson, Clarence Clough Buel; Vol. 4; NY - Century Co; (1887); not in copyright; {{PD-1923}} digital sponsor Google; Internet Archive; Boston Public Library; civil war documents; Americana; www archive org; copy of text in D R Hill Family Library; {{PD-1923}} MARCXML.

Battle of Williamsburg (1880) Richard Maury; Richmond, VA, Johns & Goolsby, Steam Printers; (1880); not in copyright; {{PD-1923}} digital sponsor Google; Library of Congress; civil war documents; Americana; www archive org; copy of text in D R Hill Family Library; MARCXML.

Biographical History of North Carolina (1908) Samuel A. Ashe; Greensboro, NC, Charles L. Van Noppen; (1908); not in copyright; {{PD-1923}} digital sponsor Google; New York Public Library; civil war documents; Americana; www archive org; copy of text in D R Hill Family Library; {{PD-1923}}

Biographical Register of the Officers and Graduates of the United States Military Academy (1910): George W. Cullum; Saginaw, MI, Seemann & Peters; not in copyright; {{PD-1923}} digital sponsor Google; Harvard College Library; civil war documents; Americana; www archive org; copy of text in D R Hill Family Library; {{PD-1923}} MARCXML.

Biography of Daniel Harvey Hill Lieutenant General, Confederate States of America (1886); Joseph M. Hill; Lexington, AR, Official Publication of the Arkansas History Commission; (1886); Library: Main Library; Shelf Location: NC Room; Call #: NC SP. COLL. #368; not in copyright; {{PD-1923}} Rare Books, North Carolina Room, New Hanover Library, Wilmington, NC; civil war documents; Americana; www archive org; copy of text in D R Hill Family Library MARCXML

Camp-Fire Sketches and Battle-Field Echoes (1886) W. C. King and W. P. Derby; Springfield, MA, King, Richardson & Co; (1886); not in copyright; {{PD-1923}} digital sponsor Google; University of Michigan; civil war documents; Americana; www archive org; copy of text in D R Hill Family Library MARCXML USED FOR MULTIPLE ILLUSTRATIONS BUT NOT FOR TEXT REFERENCE.

Catalogue of the Officers and Cadets of the North Carolina Military Institute (1861): NC General Assembly; Raleigh, NC, State Printing Office; (1861); not in copyright; not in copyright; {{PD-1923}} Rare Books, North Carolina State Archives; Charlotte, N.C. 1st Session. 1859-60 (Charlotte: 1860); civil war documents; {{PD-1923}}

Charleston Mercury (1861); newspaper article 11 May 1861 {{PD-1923}}

Charlotte Observer (1961): newspaper article on Davidson College 3 Dec 1961 {{PD-1923}} accessible through the public domain under archive records of the State of North Carolina digital records.

Christ in the Camp (1887) Reverend J. William Jones, D. D; Richmond, VA, B. F. Johnson & Co; (1888) not in copyright; {{PD-1923}} digital sponsor Brigham Young University; Harold B. Lee Library; call number ABG5787; civil war documents; Americana; www archive org; copy of text in D R Hill Family Library MARCXML

Civil War Confederate Portrait Album (1890) Thomas D. Osborne; loc; unknown, American Chronicle Co.; (1890); not in copyright; {{PD-1923}}; State Library of North Carolina; call number 973.79A5118c; digital sponsor; State Library of North Carolina; Civil War Collection; 1855570 USED FOR MULTIPLE ILLUSTRATIONS BUT NOT FOR TEXT REFERENCE.

College Discipline: an inaugural address 28 Feb (1855) D. H. Hill; Salisbury, NC, the Watchman Office; (1855); not in copyright; {{PD-1923}}; digital sponsor Lyrasis Members and Sloan Foundation; Presbyterian College, call number JSC37819H551C; civil war documents; Americana; www archive org; copy of text in D R Hill Family Library MARCXML

Col. William Hill and the Campaign of 1780 (1919) Daniel Harvey Hill; Raleigh, NC, n.p.; (1919); not in copyright; {{PD-1923}} digital sponsor Google; Heritage Library of North Carolina; civil war documents; Americana; www archive org; copy of text in D R Hill Family Library MARCXML

Col. William Hill's Memoirs of the Revolution (1921) William Hill – author, Alexander Samuel Salley Jr. ed; (1921); Columbia, SC -Historical Commission of South Carolina; not in copyright; {{PD-1923}} digital sponsor Lyrasis Members and Sloan Foundation; Presbyterian College, James H. Thomason Library; civil war documents; Americana; www archive org; copy of text in D R Hill Family Library MARCXML

Complete History of the Late Mexican War (1850) New York, F. J. Dow & Co; (1850); not in copyright; {{PD-1923}} digital sponsor MSN; University of California Libraries; civil war documents; Americana; www archive org; copy of text in D R Hill Family Library MARCXML

Confederate Military History (1899) Clement Anselm Evans. Vol. I; Atlanta GA - Confederate Publishing Co; (1899); not in copyright; {{PD-1923}} digital sponsor MSN; University of California Libraries; civil war documents; Americana; www archive org; copy of text in D R Hill Family Library MARCXML

Confederate Military History (1899): J. Hotchkiss Vol. III {{PD-1923}}; Atlanta GA - Confederate Publishing Co; (1899); not in copyright; {{PD-1923}} digital sponsor MSN; University of Michigan; civil war documents; Americana; www archive org; copy of text in D R Hill Family Library MARCXML

Confederate Veteran Magazine (1917) R. A. Cunningham – Founder; Nashville, TN; Vol. XXV. Confederated Southern Memorial Association (U.S.); Sons of Confederate Veterans; United Confederate Veterans; United Daughters of the Confederacy; not in copyright; {{PD-1923}} digital sponsor Google; Duke University Libraries; civil war documents; Americana; www archive org; copy of text in D R Hill Family Library MARCXML

Confederate Veteran Magazine (1917) R. A. Cunningham – Founder; Nashville, TN; (1917); not in copyright; {{PD-1923}} digital sponsor Google; Duke University; civil war documents; Americana; www archive org; copy of text in D R Hill Family Library MARCXML

Confederate War Journal Illustrated (1894) John B. Gordon; (1894); Vol. 1, No. 1; New York & Lexington, KY; (1894); not in copyright; {{PD-1923}} digital sponsor Google; Princeton University; civil war documents; Americana; www archive org; copy of text in D R Hill Family Library MARCXML

Consolidated index to compiled service records of Confederate Soldiers (1957) United States National Archives and Records Service – Wilcox-Wilkierson; Washington D.C.; Confederate States of America; Army; Reel 221 - Call Number 1890601.1; digital sponsor: Internet Archive; Allen County Public Library Genealogy Center; collection volunteer units confederate; Hill-Mecklenburg: microfilm; Americana; MARCXML

D. H. Hill Grave Monument, Davidson College Cemetery, Davidson, NC – Inscription

D. H. Hill Papers #2035-z, Southern Historical Collection (1940), The Wilson Library, University of North Carolina at Chapel Hill; Received from Charles W. Dabney prior to 1940; from Pauline Hill in 1951; from John R. Peacock in 1953.

D. H. Hill Papers #2035-z, Southern Historical Collection (1940), The Wilson Library, University of North Carolina at Chapel Hill; Received from Charles W. Dabney prior to 1940; from Pauline Hill in 1951; from John R. Peacock in 1953// D. H. Hill Papers, North Carolina State Archives (1915) Joseph Hill to D. H. Hill, Jr; March , 1915; Jackson-Arnold Collection, Russell-Arnold Archives, Presbyterian College, Charlotte, NC; (1915)// Biography of Daniel Harvey Hill Lieutenant General, Confederate States of America (1886); Joseph M. Hill; Lexington, AR, Official Publication of the Arkansas History Commission; (1886); Library: Main Library; Shelf Location: NC Room; Call #: NC SP. COLL. #368; not in copyright; {{PD-1923}} Rare Books, North Carolina Room, New Hanover Library, Wilmington, NC; civil war documents; Americana; www archive org; copy of text in D R Hill Family Library MARCXML

D. H. Hill Papers, North Carolina State Archives (1915) Joseph Hill to D. H. Hill, Jr; March , 1915; Jackson-Arnold Collection, Russell-Arnold Archives, Presbyterian College, Charlotte, NC; (1915)

Elements of Algebra (1857) Daniel Harvey Hill; J. B. Lippincott (1857); not in copyright; {{PD-1923}} digital sponsor Google; Harvard University; civil war documents; Americana; www archive org; copy of text in D R Hill Family Library MARCXML

Fishburne, C. D. (1890) North Carolina Division of Archives and History, Raleigh, NC February 8, 1890 p. 12 D. H. Hill Papers, North Carolina State Archives (1915) Joseph Hill to D. H. Hill, Jr; March , 1915; Jackson-Arnold Collection, Russell-Arnold Archives, Presbyterian College, Charlotte, NC; (1915)

From Manassas to Appomattox: Memoirs of the Civil War in America   (1895) James Longstreet; Philadelphia, PA, J. B. Lippincott & Co; (1908); not in copyright; {{PD-1923}} digital sponsor Google; Harvard University; civil war documents; Americana; www archive org; copy of text in D R Hill Family Library MARCXML

General James H. Lane Speech delivered at Auburn, Alabama by General Lane. College Archives: Davidson College Library, Davidson, N.C.

General Lee (1894) Fitzhugh Lee; NY, NY, D. Appleton & Co; (1894); not in copyright; {{PD-1923}} digital sponsor Google; Harvard University;   civil war documents; Americana; www archive org; copy of text in D R Hill Family Library MARCXML

General Zachary Taylor and the Mexican War (1911) Anderson C. Quisenberry; Frankfort, KY, Frankfort Printing Co.; (1911); not in copyright; {{PD-1923}} digital sponsor Google; Kentucky Historical Society; Americana; civil war documents; www archive org; copy of text in D R Hill Family Library; {{PD-1923}} MARCXML

Histories of the Several Regiments and Battalions from North Carolina (1861-1865) Vol. I-X; Goldsboro, NC, Walter Clark ed;   Raleigh E. M. Uzzel;   (1901); not in copyright; {{PD-1923}} digital sponsor Google; University of Michigan; civil war documents; Americana; www archive org; copy of text in D R Hill Family Library   MARCXML

History of South Carolina (1920) Yates Snowden; Chicago, IL, the Lewis Publishing Co.; (1920); not in copyright; {{PD-1923}} digital sponsor Google; Harvard College Library; civil war documents; Americana; www archive org; copy of text in D R Hill Family Library; {{PD-1923}}

History of the Civil War in America (1875) Vol. I-IV; Louis-Philippe-Albert d'Orleans Paris, comte de; Philadelphia, PA, Porter & Coates;   (1875);   not in copyright; {{PD-1923}}   digital sponsor LYRASIS Members and Sloan Foundation; University of Pittsburgh Library System; civil war documents; Americana; www archive org; copy of text in D R Hill Family Library MARCXML

History of the Mexican War (1892) Cadmus Marcellus, Mary Rachel Wilcox ed; (1982); Washington, DC – Church News Publishing Co.; not in copyright; {{PD-1923}} digital sponsor Google; University of Michigan; Americana; www archive org; copy of text in D R Hill Family Library; {{PD-1923}} MARCXML

History of the Presbyterian Church of Bethel (1938); Rev. R. A. Webb; Clover, SC Privately Printed: Bethel Presbyterian Church; (1938); JSC 285.175743 W383H; digital sponsor Lyrasis Members and Sloan Foundation; Library of Presbyterian College; www archive org; copy of text in D R Hill Family Library;

History of the University of Arkansas (1910) J. H. Reynolds and D. Y. Thomas; Fayetteville, AR, University of Arkansas; (1910); not in copyright; {{PD-1923}} digital sponsor Google; University of Arkansas Library; civil war documents; Americana; www archive org; copy of text in D R Hill Family Library; {{PD-1923}}

Holy Bible (1843) C. I. Scofield, D. D.; New York, Oxford University Press; (1843); D.R. Hill Family Bible; not in copyright; {{PD-1923}} no digital copy available; copy of text in D R Hill Family Library; {{PD-1923}}

Irish-American History of the United States (1907)   John O'Hanlon; New York, P. Murphy;   (1907); not in copyright; {{PD-1923}} digital sponsor Google; University of Michigan; civil war documents; Americana; www archive org; copy of text in D R Hill Family Library   MARCXML

King's Mountain and its Heroes: History of the Battle of King's Mountain (1881) Lyman Copeland Draper, Anthony Allaire; Cincinnati, OH, Peter G. Thompson; (1881); not in copyright; {{PD-1923}} digital sponsor Google; Harvard University; civil war documents; Americana; www archive org; copy of text in D R Hill Family Library MARCXML

Library of Southern Literature (1907) Edwin Anderson Alderman, Joel Chandler Harris, ed.; Atlanta, GA; The Martin & Hoyt Co.; (1907); Vol. XI; not in copyright; {{PD-1923}} digital sponsor Google; University of Virginia Library; civil war documents; Americana; www archive org; copy of text in D R Hill Family Library MARCXML

Lieutenant General Jubal Anderson Early, C.S.A.: Autobiographical Sketch and Narrative of the War Between the States (1912) Jubal Anderson Early, Ruth Hairston Early; Philadelphia PA, J. B. Lippincott & Co; (1912); not in copyright; {{PD-1923}} digital sponsor University of North Carolina at Chapel Hill; call no. b3199993; civil war documents; Americana; www archive org; copy of text in D R Hill Family Library MARCXML

Life and Campaigns of Lieut. Gen. Thomas J. Jackson (1865) Robert Lewis Dabney; Greensboro, NC, Sterling, Campbell and Albright; (1866); not in copyright; {{PD-1923}} digital sponsor Duke University Libraries; Conf Pam 12mo #324; civil war documents; Americana; www archive org; copy of text in D R Hill Family Library MARCXML

Life and Character of Lieutenant General D. H. Hill (1895) Honorable Alphonso C. Avery; Raleigh, NC, Edwards & Broughton; (1895); memorial address delivered May 10th 1893; Associate Justice of the NC Supreme Court; ; Memorial Address; not in copyright; {{PD-1923}}; digital sponsor Google; copy of text in D R Hill Family Library

Life of Robert Edward Lee (1906) Henry Elliot Shepherd; New York and Washington, The Neale Publishing Company; (1906); not in copyright; {{PD-1923}} digital sponsor Google; New York Public Library; civil war documents; Americana; www archive org; copy of text in D R Hill Family Library MARCXML

Literary and Historical Activities in North Carolina (1900-1905) William Joseph Peele; Raleigh, NC, E. M. Uzzell & Co; (1907); not in copyright; {{PD-1923}} digital sponsor MSN; New York Public Library; civil war documents; Americana; www archive org; copy of text in D R Hill Family Library MARCXML

Lives of Distinguished North Carolinians (1898) William Joseph Peele; Raleigh, NC, The North Carolina Publishing Society; (1897); not in copyright; {{PD-1923}} digital sponsor Google; Harvard University; civil war documents; Americana; www archive org; copy of text in D R Hill Family Library MARCXML

Makers of North Carolina History (1911) R. D. W. Conner; (1911); Raleigh, NC, The Thompson Publishing Company; not in copyright; {{PD-1923}} digital sponsor Google; Alderman Library; Americana; www archive org; copy of text in D R Hill Family Library MARCXML

Memoirs of Robert E. Lee (1886) Armistead Lindsay Long, Marcus Joseph Wright; London, Sampson Low, Marston, Searle, and Rivington; New York, NY, J. M. Stoddart & Co.; (1886); not in copyright; {{PD-1923}} digital sponsor Google; Harvard University; civil war documents; Americana; www archive org; copy of text in D R Hill Family Library; {{PD-1923}}; p. 528

Memoirs of the Confederate War for Independence (1867) Heros von Borcke; Philadelphia, PA, J. B. Lippincott); (1867); not in copyright; {{PD-1923}} digital sponsor Google; Harvard University; civil war documents; Americana; www archive org; copy of text in D R Hill Family Library MARCXML

OFFICIAL RECORD - (OR) - A Compilation of the Official Records - Union and Confederate Armies (1902) US War Department; Scott, Davis, Perry, Kirkley, Ainsworth, Fred C. Ainsworth & Joseph W. Kirkley – ed; (1902) Vol. 1-128 et al; Vol. I; Publisher - Washington Government Printing Office; not in copyright; {{PD-1923}} digital sponsor Google; University of Virginia; civil war documents; Americana; www archive org; copy of text in D R Hill Family Library MARCXML

OFFICIAL RECORD - (OR) - A Compilation of the Official Records - Union and Confederate Armies (1902) US War Department; Scott, Davis, Perry, Kirkley, Ainsworth, Fred C. Ainsworth & Joseph W. Kirkley – ed; (1902)Vol. 1-128 et al; Vol. II, Manassas; Publisher - Washington Government Printing Office; not in copyright; {{PD-1923}} digital sponsor Google; University of Virginia; civil war documents; Americana; copy of text in D R Hill Family Library www archive org; MARCXML

OFFICIAL RECORD - (OR) - A Compilation of the Official Records - Union and Confederate Armies (1902) US War Department; Scott, Davis, Perry, Kirkley, Ainsworth, Fred C. Ainsworth & Joseph W. Kirkley – ed; Publisher - Washington Government Printing Office; (1902); SERIES: I VOLUME: XIX CAMPAIGN: Antietam SERIAL: 027; not in copyright; {{PD-1923}} digital sponsor Google; University of Virginia; civil war documents; Americana; copy of text in D R Hill Family Library www archive org; MARCXML

OFFICIAL RECORD - (OR) - A Compilation of the Official Records - Union and Confederate Armies (1902) US War Department; Scott, Davis, Perry, Kirkley, Ainsworth, Fred C. Ainsworth & Joseph W. Kirkley – ed; Publisher - Washington Government Printing Office; (1902); SERIES: I VOLUME: XI CAMPAIGN: Peninsular Campaign SERIAL: 014; not in copyright; {{PD-1923}} digital sponsor Google; University of Virginia; civil war documents; Americana; copy of text in D R Hill Family Library www archive org; MARCXML

OFFICIAL RECORD - (OR) - A Compilation of the Official Records - Union and Confederate Armies (1902) US War Department; Scott, Davis, Perry, Kirkley, Ainsworth, Fred C. Ainsworth & Joseph W. Kirkley – ed; Publisher - Washington Government Printing Office; (1902); SERIES: II VOLUME: V CAMPAIGN: Prisoners of War SERIAL: 118; not in copyright; {{PD-1923}} digital sponsor Google; University of Virginia; civil war documents; Americana; copy of text in D R Hill Family Library www archive org; MARCXML

OFFICIAL RECORD - (OR) - A Compilation of the Official Records - Union and Confederate Armies (1902) US War Department; Scott, Davis, Perry, Kirkley, Ainsworth, Fred C. Ainsworth & Joseph W. Kirkley – ed; Publisher - Washington Government Printing Office; (1902); SERIES: II VOLUME: IV CAMPAIGN: Prisoners of War SERIAL: 117; not in copyright; {{PD-1923}} digital sponsor Google; University of Virginia; civil war documents; Americana; copy of text in D R Hill Family Library www archive org; MARCXML

OFFICIAL RECORD - (OR) - A Compilation of the Official Records - Union and Confederate Armies (1902) US War Department; Scott, Davis, Perry, Kirkley, Ainsworth, Fred C. Ainsworth & Joseph W. Kirkley – ed; Publisher - Washington Government Printing Office; (1902); SERIES: I VOLUME: XXXI CAMPAIGN: Knoxville and Lookout Mountain SERIAL: 054; not in copyright; {{PD-1923}} digital sponsor Google; University of Virginia; civil war documents; Americana; copy of text in D R Hill Family Library www archive org; MARCXML

OFFICIAL RECORD - (OR) - A Compilation of the Official Records - Union and Confederate Armies (1902) US War Department; Scott, Davis, Perry, Kirkley, Ainsworth, Fred C. Ainsworth & Joseph W. Kirkley – ed; Publisher - Washington Government Printing Office; (1902); SERIES: I VOLUME: XXX CAMPAIGN: Chickamauga SERIAL: 052; not in copyright; {{PD-1923}} digital sponsor Google; University of Virginia; civil war documents; Americana; copy of text in D R Hill Family Library www archive org; MARCXML

OFFICIAL RECORD - (OR) - A Compilation of the Official Records - Union and Confederate Armies (1902) US War Department; Scott, Davis, Perry, Kirkley, Ainsworth, Fred C. Ainsworth & Joseph W. Kirkley – ed; Publisher - Washington Government Printing Office; (1902); SERIES: I VOLUME: XXX CAMPAIGN: Chickamauga SERIAL: 050; not in copyright; {{PD-1923}} digital sponsor Google; University of Virginia; civil war documents; Americana; copy of text in D R Hill Family Library www archive org; MARCXML

OFFICIAL RECORD - (OR) - A Compilation of the Official Records - Union and Confederate Armies (1902) US War Department; Scott, Davis, Perry, Kirkley, Ainsworth, Fred C. Ainsworth & Joseph W. Kirkley – ed; Publisher - Washington Government Printing Office; (1902); SERIES: I VOLUME: XIX CAMPAIGN: Antietam SERIAL: 028; not in copyright; {{PD-1923}} digital sponsor Google; University of Virginia; civil war documents; Americana; copy of text in D R Hill Family Library www archive org; MARCXML

OFFICIAL RECORD - (OR) - A Compilation of the Official Records - Union and Confederate Armies (1902) US War Department; Scott, Davis, Perry, Kirkley, Ainsworth, Fred C. Ainsworth & Joseph W. Kirkley – ed; Publisher - Washington Government Printing Office; (1902); SERIES: I VOLUME: XIX CAMPAIGN: Antietam SERIAL: 027; not in copyright; {{PD-1923}} digital sponsor Google; University of Virginia; civil war documents; Americana; copy of text in D R Hill Family Library www archive org; MARCXML

OFFICIAL RECORD - (OR) - A Compilation of the Official Records - Union and Confederate Armies (1902) US War Department; Scott, Davis, Perry, Kirkley, Ainsworth, Fred C. Ainsworth & Joseph W. Kirkley – ed; Publisher - Washington Government Printing Office; (1902); SERIES: I VOLUME: XIV CAMPAIGN: Secessionville SERIAL: 020; not in copyright; {{PD-1923}} digital sponsor Google; University of Virginia; civil war documents; Americana; www archive org; copy of text in D R Hill Family Library MARCXML

OFFICIAL RECORD - (OR) - A Compilation of the Official Records - Union and Confederate Armies (1902) US War Department; Scott, Davis, Perry, Kirkley, Ainsworth, Fred C. Ainsworth & Joseph W. Kirkley – ed; Publisher - Washington Government Printing Office; (1902); SERIES: I VOLUME: XI CAMPAIGN: Peninsular Campaign SERIAL: 014; not in copyright; {{PD-1923}} digital sponsor Google; University of Virginia; civil war documents; Americana; www archive org; copy of text in D R Hill Family Library MARCXML

OFFICIAL RECORD - (OR) - A Compilation of the Official Records - Union and Confederate Armies (1902) US War Department; Scott, Davis, Perry, Kirkley, Ainsworth, Fred C. Ainsworth & Joseph W. Kirkley – ed; Publisher - Washington Government Printing Office; (1902); SERIES: I VOLUME: XI CAMPAIGN: Peninsular Campaign SERIAL: 013; not in copyright; {{PD-1923}} digital sponsor Google; University of Virginia; civil war documents; Americana; www archive org; copy of text in D R Hill Family Library MARCXML

OFFICIAL RECORD - (OR) - A Compilation of the Official Records - Union and Confederate Armies (1902) US War Department; Scott, Davis, Perry, Kirkley, Ainsworth, Fred C. Ainsworth & Joseph W. Kirkley – ed; Publisher - Washington Government Printing Office; (1902); SERIES: I VOLUME: XI CAMPAIGN: Peninsular Campaign SERIAL: 012; not in copyright; {{PD-1923}} digital sponsor Google; University of Virginia; civil war documents; Americana; www archive org; copy of text in D R Hill Family Library MARCXML

OFFICIAL RECORD - (OR) - A Compilation of the Official Records - Union and Confederate Armies (1902) US War Department; Scott, Davis, Perry, Kirkley, Ainsworth, Fred C. Ainsworth & Joseph W. Kirkley – ed; (1902)Vol. 1-128 et al; Vol. 1-128 et al; Vol. XIX, Part I, Serial 27-28, Antietam (Sharpsburg) ; Publisher - Washington Government

Printing Office; not in copyright; {{PD-1923}} *digital sponsor Google; University of Virginia; civil war documents; Americana; www archive org; copy of text in D R Hill Family Library MARCXML*

Official Register of the Officers and Cadets of the U. S. Military Academy, West Point; 1839-1842

Pictorial History of Mexico and the Mexican War (1862); John Frost, William H. Croome; (1862); Philadelphia PA – Cushings & Bailey; not in copyright; {{PD-1923}} digital sponsor Sloan Foundation; Library of Congress; Americana; www archive org; copy of text in D R Hill Family Library; {{PD-1923}} MARCXML USED FOR MULTIPLE ILLUSTRATIONS BUT NOT FOR TEXT REFERENCE.

Pictorial History of the Civil War in the United States of America (1866) Benson John Lossing; PA – G. W. Childs; (1866); not in copyright; {{PD-1923}} digital sponsor Google; Harvard University: civil war documents; Americana; www archive org; copy of text in D R Hill Family Library; {{PD-1923}}   MARCXML USED FOR MULTIPLE ILLUSTRATIONS BUT NOT FOR TEXT REFERENCE.

Raleigh Register (1861) Newspaper Article -Battle of Big Bethel {{PD-1923}} 1861-1865–Casualties; Wyatt, Henry Lawson, 1842-1861

Raleigh Register (1861) Newspaper Article, North Carolina History – Civil War, 1861-1865; North Carolina--History- -Civil War, 1861-1865–Sources; United States--History–Civil War, 1861-1865; Confederate States of America; Army. North Carolina Infantry Regiment, 1st (1861 May-Nov.); Battle of Big Bethel - Casualties; Wyatt, Henry Lawson, 1842-1861; not in copyright; copy of newspaper article in D R Hill Family Library; {{PD-1923}};

 Register of Cadet Delinquencies (1842): Records of the U. S. Military Academy; accessioned records group 0404; Records of the. Department of Tactics, Administrative Records-{{PD-1923}}
West Point, NY; Vol. 2; 1838-1842;   Hill, D. H. p. 255

Reminiscences of the Civil War, General John B. Gordon; NY, NY, Charles Scribner's Sons; (1906); not in copyright; {{PD-1923}} digital sponsor Google; Lenox and Tilden Foundations; New York Public Library; call no. 735576; civil war documents; Americana; www archive org; copy of text in D R Hill Family Library; {{PD-1923}}; pp. 67-68

Reports of the Operations of the Army of Northern Virginia (1864) Robert Edward Lee, Confederate States of America, Army of Northern Virginia; Richmond, VA, R. M. Smith Printing; (1864); not in copyright; {{PD-1923}} digital sponsor Duke University Libraries; civil war documents; Americana; www archive org; copy of text in D R Hill Family Library MARCXML

Southern Historical Society Papers (1885) James I. Robertson, Southern Historical Society; Vol. XIII & XIV; Richmond, VA (1885); not in copyright; {{PD-1923}} digital sponsor MSN; University of Toronto; Robarts; civil war documents; Americana; www archive org; copy of text in D R Hill Family Library   MARCXML

Stonewall Jackson – The life and military career of Thomas Jonathan Jackson, Lieutenant General in the Confederate Army (1863); Addey Markinfield; New York, Charles T. Evans; (1863); not in copyright; {{PD-1923}} digital sponsor Google; New York Public Library;; civil war documents; Americana; www archive org; copy of text in D R Hill Family Library; {{PD-1923}}; p.207

Story of the Confederate States (1898) Joseph T. Derry; Richmond, VA, B. F. Johnson Publishing Company; (1898); not in copyright; {{PD-1923}}   digital sponsor Google; Columbia University; civil war documents;   Americana; www archive org; copy of text in D R Hill Family Library MARCXML

The American Conflict: A History of Great Rebellion in the United States of America (1860-1865) Horace Greely; Hartford, CT, O. D. Case & Co; (1866); not in copyright; {{PD-1923}}   digital sponsor Google; University of Michigan;   civil war documents;   Americana;   www archive org; copy of text in D R Hill Family Library MARCXML

The American Generals (1855) John Frost; Columbus, Ohio, William and Thomas Miller; (1855) not in copyright; {{PD-1923}} digital sponsor Google; New York Public Library; Americana; www archive org; copy of text in D R Hill Family Library MARCXML

The Annals of the War Written by Leading Participants North and South   (1879)   Alexander K. McClure; Philadelphia, PA, The Times Publishing Co; (1879); not in copyright; {{PD-1923}} digital sponsor MSN; University of California Libraries;   civil war documents;   Americana;   www archive org; copy of text in D R Hill Family Library MARCXML

The Antietam and Fredericksburg (1881) Francis Winthrop Palfrey; New York, C. Scribner's Sons; (1881); not in copyright; {{PD-1923}} digital sponsor LYRASIS members and Sloan Foundation; State Library of North Carolina – Government & Heritage Library; civil war documents; Americana;   www archive org; copy of text in D R Hill Family Library MARCXML

The Battle of Bentonville (1905) L. M. Wood; NY, NY, Neale Publishing Co; (1905); not in copyright; {{PD-1923}} digital sponsor Google; unknown library; civil war documents: www archives org; copy of text in D R Hill Family Library {{PD-1923}} pp. 53-62

The Battle of Bethel Church (1861) North Carolina Convention (1861-1862); Raleigh, NC, Syme & Hall; (1861); not in copyright; {{PD-1923}} digital sponsor Duke University Libraries; Duke University Libraries; call number : conf pamphlet #498; Americana; civil war documents: www archives org; copy of text in D R Hill Family Library {{PD-1923}}; MARCXML pp. 1-8

The Battle of Bethel Church (1861) North Carolina Convention (1861-1862); Raleigh, NC, Syme & Hall; (1861); not in copyright; digital sponsor Duke University Libraries; Duke University Libraries; Call number : conf pamphlet #498; Americana; MARCXML pp. 1-8

The Battle of Great Bethel (1864) Frank I. Wilson; Confederate Congress – 1864; District of Pamlico, NC (1864); not in copyright; {{PD-1923}} digital sponsor Duke University Libraries; civil war documents; Americana; www archive org; copy of text in D R Hill Family Library MARCXML

The Century Illustrated Monthly Magazine (1871) Daniel Harvey Hill; NY, Scribner; (1871); not in copyright; {{PD-1923}} digital sponsor MSN; Robarts – University of Toronto; civil war documents; Americana; www archive org; copy of text in D R Hill Family Library; {{PD-1923}}; MARCXML P.137

The Civil War Through the Camera (1912) Henry William Elson; NY – McKinlay, Stone & Mackenzie; (1912); not in copyright; {{PD-1923}} digital sponsor MSN; University of California Libraries; civil war documents; www archive org; copy of text in D R Hill Family Library; {{PD-1923}} MARCXML USED FOR MULTIPLE ILLUSTRATIONS BUT NOT FOR TEXT REFERENCE.

The Congregationalist (1873) Robert W. Dale and James G. Rogers ; London, Hodder and Stoughton; (1873); not in copyright; {{PD-1923}} digital sponsor Google; University of Michigan; copy of text in D R Hill Family Library; {{PD-1923}}; pp. 43-52 - the Exclusion Crisis

The Crucifixion of Christ (1859) Daniel Harvey Hill; Philadelphia PA, William S. & Alfred Martien; (1859); not in copyright; {{PD-1923}} digital sponsor Google; Harvard University; civil war documents; Americana; www archive org; copy of text in D R Hill Family Library   MARCXML

The Granite State Monthly (1918) Otis G. Hammond; Concord, NH, Granite Monthly Company; (1918); not in copyright; {{PD-1923}} digital sponsor Google; University of Michigan; civil war documents; Americana; www archive org; copy of text in D R Hill Family Library MARCXML

The History of Mecklenburg County from 1740 to 1900 (1902) J. B. Alexander; Charlotte, NC, Observer Printing House; (1902); not in copyright; {{PD-1923}} digital sponsor Google; Mecklenburg County Public Library; copy of text in D R Hill Family Library; {{PD-1923}}

The Land We Love   (1866) Daniel Harvey Hill (1899); Vol. I May-Oct 1866; Charlotte, NC – Jas. P. Irwin & D. H. Hill; (1866); not in copyright; {{PD-1923}} digital sponsor Google; Harvard University; civil war documents; Americana; www archive org; copy of text in D R Hill Family Library MARCXML

The Land We Love (1867-68) Daniel Harvey Hill (1899); Vol. IV, Nov-Apr 1867-68; Charlotte, NC – Jas. P. Irwin & D. H. Hill; (1868); not in copyright; {{PD-1923}} digital sponsor Google; Harvard University; civil war documents; Americana; www archive org; copy of text in D R Hill Family Library   MARCXML

The Land We Love (1868) Daniel Harvey Hill (1899); Vol. V – May-Oct 1968; Charlotte, NC – Jas. P. Irwin & D. H. Hill; (1868); not in copyright; {{PD-1923}} digital sponsor Google; Harvard University; civil war documents; Americana; www archive org; copy of text in D R Hill Family Library MARCXML

The North Carolina Booklet (1916) North Carolina Society Daughters of the Revolution; Raleigh, NC; NCSDR; (1916); Vol. XVI; April 1917; No. 4; not in copyright; {{PD-1923}} digital sponsor Google; Harvard College Library; civil war documents; Americana; www archive org; copy of text in D R Hill Family Library MARCXML

The Photographic History of the Civil War (1911) Francis Trevelyan Miller, Robert Sampson Lanier; Vol. 10; NY – The Review of Reviews Co.; (1911); not in copyright; {{PD-1923}} digital sponsor University of Illinois Urbana-Champaign; civil war documents; Americana; www archive org; copy of text in D R Hill Family Library; MARCXML. USED FOR MULTIPLE ILLUSTRATIONS BUT NOT FOR TEXT REFERENCE.

The Pictorial Field-Book of the Revolution (1851); Benson John Lossing; Vol. 1; NY – Harper & Bros; (1851); not in copyright; {{PD-1923}} digital sponsor Google; University of Michigan; Americana; www archive org; copy of text in D R Hill Family Library; {{PD-1923}} MARCXML   USED FOR MULTIPLE ILLUSTRATIONS BUT NOT FOR TEXT REFERENCE.

The Rebellion Record (1861) Frank Moore, Edward Everett; (1863); Vol. 1; NY – G. P. Putnam; (I) Diary of events; (II) Documents; (III); Poetry; not in copyright; {{PD-1923}} digital sponsor Google; unknown library; Americana; www archive org; copy of text in D R Hill Family Library MARCXML

The Rebellion Record (1861) Frank Moore, Edward Everett; (1863); Vol. 10; NY – G. P. Putnam; (II) Documents; not in copyright; {{PD-1923}} digital sponsor Google; unknown library; Americana; www archive org; copy of text in D R Hill Family Library   MARCXML

The Rebellion Record (1861) Frank Moore, Edward Everett; (1863); Vol. 11; NY – G. P. Putnam; (II) Documents; not in copyright; {{PD-1923}} digital sponsor Google; unknown library; civil war documents; Americana; www archive org; copy of text in D R Hill Family Library   MARCXML

The Rebellion Record (1861) Frank Moore, Edward Everett; (1863); Vol. 2; NY – G. P. Putnam; (I) Diary of events; (II) Documents; (III); Poetry; not in copyright; {{PD-1923}} digital sponsor Google; unknown library; Americana; www archive org; copy of text in D R Hill Family Library MARCXML

The Rebellion Record (1861) Frank Moore, Edward Everett; (1863); Vol. 3; NY – G. P. Putnam; (I) Diary of events; (II) Documents; (III); Poetry; not in copyright; {{PD-1923}} digital sponsor Google; unknown library; Americana; www archive org; copy of text in D R Hill Family Library MARCXML

The Rebellion Record (1861) Frank Moore, Edward Everett; (1863); Vol. 4; NY – G. P. Putnam; (I) Diary of events; (II) Documents; (III); Poetry; not in copyright; {{PD-1923}} digital sponsor Google; unknown library; Americana; www archive org; copy of text in D R Hill Family Library MARCXML

The Rebellion Record (1861) Frank Moore, Edward Everett; (1863); Vol. 5; NY – G. P. Putnam; (I) Diary of events; (II) Documents; (III); Poetry; not in copyright; {{PD-1923}} digital sponsor Google; unknown library; Americana; www archive org; copy of text in D R Hill Family Library   MARCXML

The Rebellion Record (1861) Frank Moore, Edward Everett; (1863); Vol. 6; NY – G. P. Putnam; (I) Diary of events; (II) Documents; (III); Poetry; not in copyright; {{PD-1923}} digital sponsor Google; unknown library; Americana; www archive org; copy of text in D R Hill Family Library   MARCXML

The Rebellion Record (1861) Frank Moore, Edward Everett; (1863); Vol. 7; NY – G. P. Putnam; (I) Diary of events; (II) Documents; (III); Poetry; not in copyright; {{PD-1923}} digital sponsor Google; unknown library; Americana; www archive org; copy of text in D R Hill Family Library   MARCXML

The Rebellion Record (1861) Frank Moore, Edward Everett; (1863); Vol. 8; NY – G. P. Putnam; (I) Diary of events; (II) Documents; (III); Poetry; not in copyright; {{PD-1923}} digital sponsor Google; unknown library; Americana; www archive org; copy of text in D R Hill Family Library   MARCXML

The Rebellion Record (1861) Frank Moore, Edward Everett; (1863); Vol. 9; NY – G. P. Putnam; (II) Documents; (III); Poetry; not in copyright; {{PD-1923}} digital sponsor Google; unknown library; Americana; www archive org; copy of text in D R Hill Family Library   MARCXML

The Science of War (1908) G. F. R. Henderson; New York, NY, Longmans Green and Co; (1908); not in copyright; {{PD-1923}} digital sponsor Google; Stanford University Libraries; Americana; civil war documents; www archive org; copy of text in D R Hill Family Library; {{PD-1923}} MARCXML

The Southern Home (1870-1881) Daniel Harvey Hill; Charlotte, NC, D. H. Hill & James Irvin; (1870-1881); not in copyright; {{PD-1923}} (1870-1881); 1871: Jan 3; Jan 17; Mar 14; Mar 28; Sep 19; 1871: Oct 3; 1872: Mar 11; Mar 25; Apr 15; May 13; Jun 24; Jul 8; Oct 1; Oct 28; Nov 25; 1872: Dec 16; 1876: Apr 3; 1876: Apr 17; May 8; May 22; Jun 5; Jun 19; Jul 3; Jul 31; Aug 8; Aug 14; Sep 25; Oct 9; Oct 23; Nov 6; Dec 4; Dec 18; Dec 25; 1877: Jan 15; May 7; May 21; Jun 4; Jun 6; Jun 18; Jul 2; Charlotte Mecklenburg Public Library.

Thrilling Incidents of the Wars of the United States (1860) Jacob K. Neff; NY – R. Sears; (1860); not in copyright; {{PD-1923}} digital sponsor Google; New York Public Library; New York Public Library; Americana; civil war documents; www archive org; copy of text in D R Hill Family Library; {{PD-1923}} MARCXML   USED FOR MULTIPLE ILLUSTRATIONS BUT NOT FOR TEXT REFERENCE.

Under Both Flags - Tales of the Civil War as told by the Veterans (1896) George Morley Vickers; Palo Alto, CA, Veteran Publishing Co; (1896); not in copyright; {{PD-1923}} unknown library; digital sponsor Google; civil war documents; Americana; www archive org; copy of text in D R Hill Family Library MARCXML

Western Democrat (1861) Charlotte newspaper; Charlotte, NC, WD; (1861); editions dated 29, 1858; August 3, 1858; September 28, 1858; not in copyright; {{PD-1923}}; North Carolina State Archives, Raleigh, NC; {{PD-1923}} MARCXML

OTHER TITLES BY THIS AUTHOR:

Made in the USA
San Bernardino, CA
30 January 2020

63813406R00193